Class, Community and the Labour Movement: Wales and Canada 1850-1930

South Wales miners emigrating to Canada, 1923
1st on right—Dai Dan Evans of Ystradgynlais, later General Secretary of the National Union of Mineworkers (South Wales Area) 1958-63.
(Courtesy of Dr Hywel Francis, South Wales Miners' Library).

CLASS, COMMUNITY AND THE LABOUR MOVEMENT: WALES AND CANADA, 1850-1930

EDITED BY

Deian R. Hopkin

and

Gregory S. Kealey

with an introduction by

David Montgomery

LLAFUR / CCLH

1989

First published in 1989 by Llafur/CCLH

British ISBN 0 9514580 0 0
Canadian ISBN 0 9692060 6 2

Set in Times Garamond on Lasercomp at Oxford University Computer Service

Printed and bound in Wales by Cambrian News (Printers) Ltd.

CONDITIONS OF SALE

Contents

Contributors

ROBERT BABCOCK. Professor of History at the University of Maine at Orono, USA

CRAIG HERON. Associate Professor of History, York University, Toronto, Ontario.

DEIAN R.HOPKIN. Senior Lecturer in History, University College of Wales, Aberstwyth

DOT JONES. Research Officer, Department of Economics, University College of Wales, Aberystwyth

MERFYN JONES. Senior Lecturer in Modern History, Department of Continuing Education, University of Liverpool.

GREGORY S.KEALEY. Professor of History, Memorial University of Newfoundland, St John's, Newfoundland.

LINDA KEALEY. Associate Professor of History, Memorial University of Newfoundland, St John's, Newfoundland.

VARPU LINDSTROM-BEST. Assistant Professor of History, Atkinson College, York University, Toronto, Ontario.

DAVID MONTGOMERY. Farnam Professor of History, Yale University, New Haven, USA

BRUNO RAMIREZ. Professor of History, Université de Montréal, Québec.

ALLEN SEAGER. Associate Professor of History, Simon Fraser University, Burnaby, British Columbia.

CHRISTOPHER TURNER. Assistant Registrar, Welsh College of Medicine, University of Wales.

JOHN WILLIAMS. Professor of Economic History, University College of Wales, Aberystwyth

Maps

Note: The placenames indicated in the maps are those which occur most frequently in the text.

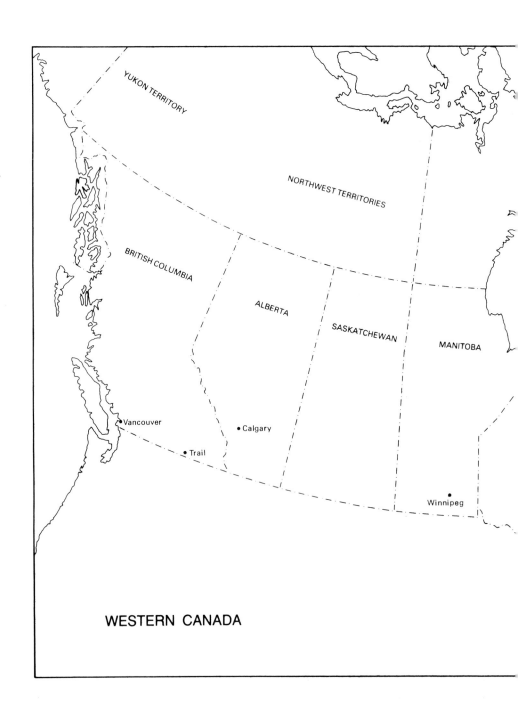

YUKON TERRITORY

NORTHWEST TERRITORIES

BRITISH COLUMBIA

ALBERTA

SASKATCHEWAN

MANITOBA

• Vancouver

• Calgary

• Trail

• Winnipeg

WESTERN CANADA

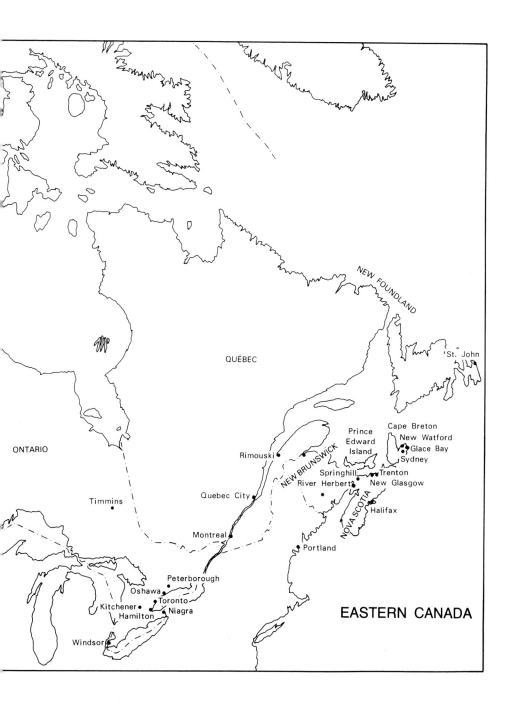

ONTARIO

QUÉBEC

NEW FOUNDLAND

St. John

Cape Breton
New Watford
Prince
Edward
Island
Glace Bay
Sydney

Rimouski
NEW BRUNSWICK
Springhill
Trenton
River Herbert
New Glasgow

Timmins
Quebec City
NOVA SCOTIA
Halifax

Montreal
Portland

Peterborough
Oshawa
Kitchener
Toronto
Hamilton
Niagra
Windsor

EASTERN CANADA

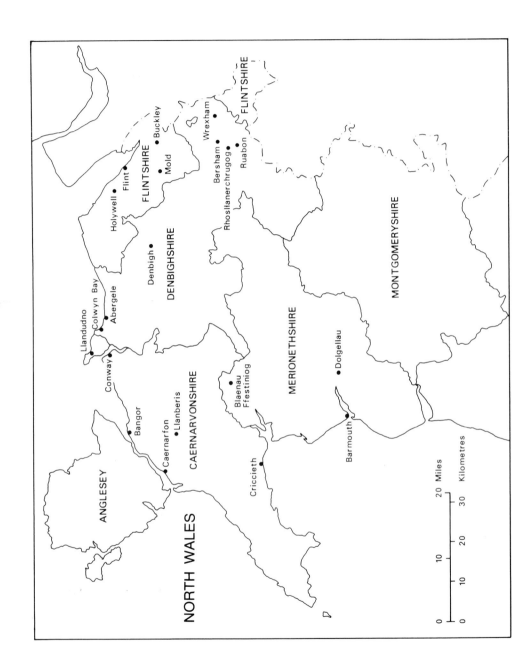

NORTH WALES

ANGLESEY

CAERNARVONSHIRE

Bangor
Caernarfon
Llanberis
Llandudno
Colwyn Bay
Abergele
Conway
Criccieth

Blaenau
Ffestiniog

MERIONETHSHIRE

Barmouth

Dolgellau

DENBIGHSHIRE

Denbigh

Holywell
Flint

FLINTSHIRE

Mold
Buckley

Bersham
Rhosllanerchrugog
Ruabon

Wrexham

FLINTSHIRE

MONTGOMERYSHIRE

0   10   20   Miles
0   10   20   30   Kilometres

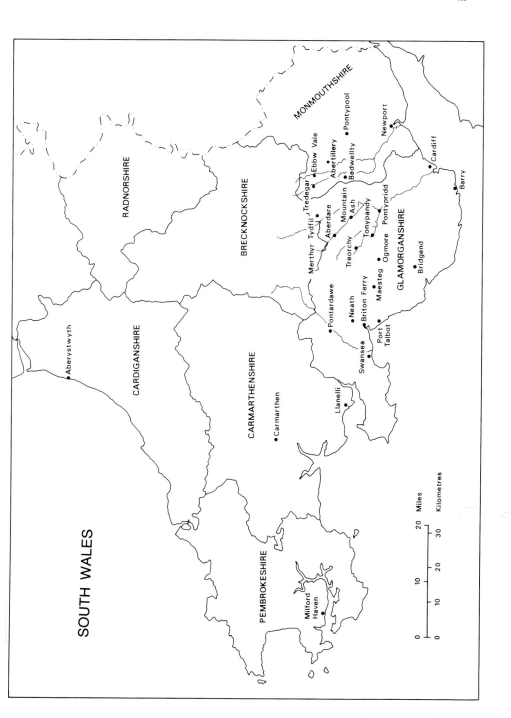

SOUTH WALES

Preface

In April 1987 an unusual conference took place in the beautiful setting of Gregynog Hall near Newtown in Mid-Wales. A group of Welsh and Canadian historians met to discuss the comparative industrial histories of their two countries and to attempt to establish a basis for further study. The choice of countries was the unusual aspect; after all, Canada and Wales differ somewhat in size and location. And yet, there were obvious starting points for the comparison; the issue of bilingualism, the proximity of both countries to larger, expansionary neighbours, and the internal contrasts between intense industrialisation and rurality. Both countries moreover have seen a resurgence in Labour historiography in recent years. Coincidentally, both the Committee for Canadian History and the Society for Welsh Labour History were formed in the same year, 1971, and it was appropriate that 15 years on, the two societies should meet in conference. This volume is the result.

Most of the papers given at the Gregynog conference are included in this book, together with introduction by David Montgomery based on his splendid end-of-conference summary. Some valuable contributions are missing: Ian McKay's comprehensive account of the Nova Scotia miners, Bryan Palmer's stimulating exploration of workers' communities in Ontario, Gerry Friesen's trenchant account of the activities and impact of R. B. Russell, the Scottish immigrants who played such a central part in the working class struggles of Winnipeg; from the Welsh side, Dai Smith's characteristically challenging analysis of Anglo-Welsh culture, Paul O'Leary's highly original account of the political role of the Irish in Wales and finally Hywel Francis's fascinating accounts of the contacts between Welsh and Canadian mining leaders, of which his father was so central a figure. All of these are expected to appear elsewhere in due course and will no doubt be enjoyed as much as they were at the conference itself.

The papers that are included deal with a range of factors reflecting both the special interests of the historians themselves and the common issues with which all of us are concerned. Naturally, there are gaps and omissions and it may well be concluded that there were more explorations than explanations. Yet, some important methodological issues were confronted, not least the capacity of the historian to recapture the experience of workers and their organisations. In this respect the disparities of size or geography between Wales and Canada were less important than the quality of source material, the techniques of the historian and the nature of historical synthesis. The conference revealed some interesting differences in the historical practice of the two countries, the scope and range and scope of their respective labour historiographies.

What, of course, cannot be conveyed in a volume such as this is the quality of the debate and discussion which accompanied the papers, both at the time and in informal gatherings afterwards, or the character of the relationship which quickly developed between the Canadian and Welsh contingents, as well as the other historians who were present, some from as far afield as Australia. Links between Wales and Canada have, in any case, been growing in recent years, largely as the result of the activities and publications of the Canadian Studies in Wales Group, who acted as the intermediaries for the Gregynog conference.

The editors, who also organised the conference itself, wish to thank a number of organisations and individuals. The treasurer of CSWG, Denis Balsom was an inspiration in the planning and resourcing of the conference. We are indebted, moreover, to the CSWG itself for direct and generous financial support. For their part, the Canadian participants received valued support from the Social and Humanities Research Council of Canada and from their own institutions. We are also grateful to the Canadian High Commission, and especially to Michael Hellyer and the Academic Relations section, for their usual generosity and encouragement. Thanks are also due to Marc Boucher of Quebec House, London.

Special thanks are due to Dr Peter Denley of Westfield College for his expertise and industry in preparing the manuscript for laser production and to Oxford University Computing Service for their promptness and efficiency. Finally, the committees of the two societies are to be congratulated for showing confidence in this project, the first joint production. We hope they will approve of the product.

Introduction

David Montgomery

During the decades that closed the nineteenth century and opened the twentieth, wrote David Landes, the industrial revolution caught its 'second wind'.[1] Rapid economic growth and changing structures of economic activity wove the more heavily populated portions of the world into networks of interdependence, while magnifying the global power of the few industrialized countries and the contrast between the life styles of their inhabitants and those of the rest of humanity.

The epoch lends itself well to comparative history. Dependency theory in its various guises has served to illuminate common patterns of economic development within the formidable cultural and political diversity of the colonial and semi-colonial world. The question of whether industrialization's 'second wind' also produced a convergence not only of economic activities, but also of urban cultures and popular movements across national boundaries within its heartland has produced some of the most rewarding historical reflection of recent years.[2]

The essays in this collection contribute to the effort to situate local and regional experiences within an international context by investigating the activities of working men and women in Canada and Wales at the turn of the century. None of the authors have adopted national characteristics as a point of departure; indeed, Robert Babcock explicitly challenges the style of historical analysis that is based on the comparison of national cultures and institutions. Rather than posing the antiquity and compactness of Wales against the youth and vast expanses of Canada, the contributors to this volume have focused their attention on processes and settings found within the two countries during the Second Industrial Revolution, which turn out to be sometimes instructively similar and sometimes provocatively different. The two national settings shared some important common features, to be sure: coal miners played major roles in the development of both countries' trade unions, the headquarters of major Canadian unions and practically all Welsh unions were located in neighbouring countries which also over-shadowed each nation's economic life, and both peoples were governed by the British parliamentary monarchy. By studying patterns of economic change, migration, community development, and industrial conflict, however, the participants in this colloquium have suggested questions of international significance about the remaking of the working class during these decades, which research into the Welsh and Canadian experiences can help us answer.

The surveys of the Welsh and Canadian economies provide by John Williams and Craig Heron draw the reader's attention immediately to the dramatic rise in the numbers and importance of coal miners after 1890, and also to the global decline suffered by their industry in the 1920s. In marked contrast to the technological leaps which characterized the manufacturing sector itself during the Second Industrial Revolution, its voracious appetite for coal drew ever greater numbers of men underground and encouraged the development of huge mining companies, but did little to change the labour-intensive ways in which miners hewed and loaded coal in either Wales or Canada. Consequently, the most productive mining regions attracted newcomers from afar. In the mines of Nanaimo, British Columbia, Alan Seager reveals, less than two percent of the miners of 1891 had been born in the province. Although the collieries of northern and western Wales had drawn most of their miners from the surrounding countryside, as had those of Nova Scotia, the soaring output of steam coal in Glamorgan County, where 70 percent of Wales' population growth was to be found, was made possible not only by a southward drift of the Welsh population, but also by a great influx of people from England, Ireland, and Spain.

The communities created by migrants to the mine fields are explored by Christopher Turner, Dot Jones, and Varpu Lindstrom-Best, as well as by Seager and Heron. They reveal the importance of related industries, like steel and tin plate production, and especially of shipping, in shaping a region's job structure (export of coal by water, for example, generated a different occupational pattern from that based on railroad shipment). Because miners were paid in money, their neighbourhoods supported an abundance of shopkeepers. The encounter between the hopes which had brought men and women to the pit towns and the anxieties generated by life in those towns provided fertile soil for religious revivals, as well as political mobilization and trade unions.

As Dot Jones reveals in her remarkable comparison of women's lives in rural Cardiganshire and in the Rhondda Valley, the migration of as many as one-fourth of Cardiganshire's farm women to mining areas caused even more wrenching changes for them than it did for men. Women's work in both settings held the key to family survival, but it was hidden by census categories. Moreover, early marriage, frequent child-bearing, squalid surroundings, and endless rounds of household toil made young wives of miners in the Rhondda Valley die at a greater rate than their husbands, who spent their days amid noxious gasses, roof-falls, and maverick explosions.

Large as coal mining looms in these essays, however, it does not crowd out other topics. On the contrary, the presentations of Merfyn Jones and Robert Babcock, as well as those of Williams, Seager, and Heron, put the growth of mining in context by revealing how industrialization's 'second wind' redefined economic regions and relations among them. The north coast of Wales lay within the economic orbit of Liverpool and Manchester, even though the line which marked the border with England was also a boundary in culture and popular politics. Canada's maritime provinces were deindustrialized and partially depopulated, as manufacturing became concentrated in Montreal and southern Ontario. The country's growing export of farm produce favoured Portland, Maine, as its winter outlet, drawing workers to that seaport in the United States and away from its Canadian rival, St. John, New Brunswick. Production of coal, metallic ores, and timber, as well as grain, fed directly into international markets from both countries, while Canada's factories then supplied an emerging national market. Economically dominant and dependent regions thus emerged within the nation-states whose industry gave them mastery over the rest of the world.

These developments produced complex patterns of migration. Bruno Ramirez examines those of Quebec, where farm families from congested rural regions colonized interior woodlands at the urging of the Catholic Church and lumber companies, while others moved south to industrial New England, and immigrants from Europe (especially Italy) took up the unskilled tasks of Montreal. Though the clergy struggled to preserve French-Canadian culture on the land, industrial towns offered the Quebecois wider possibilities to experiment with a new life and much quicker rewards for hard work than did the wilderness. With urbanization, however, also came dramatic and often painful changes in the relationships between wives and husbands.

The photo-montage of Canadian mining towns is part of wider work by Varpu Lindstrom-Best on the role of women in creating new communities of Finnish immigrants. Although the large proportion of women among Finnish immigrants indicated a propensity to settle permanently in the new country, the mining and lumbering towns they inhabited were remote from other population centers and prone to destruction by fire, as well as to extreme fluctuations in the demand for male labor and very limited wage-earning prospects for women. Keeping boarders, selling drink, prostitution, and housekeeping for the mine managers provided women's only prospects for earning money, but Finnish women carved out a prominent role for themselves in the towns' socialist and communist politics.

It is the Welsh studies that devote the closest attention to workers' religious lives. Christopher Turner notes not only the vigourous response of residents of south Wales' mining towns to Christian revivals, but also the magnetic pull of working-class life on religious teachings and practice. Although prominent activists of the 1898 coal strike left the Nonconformist churches, which had opposed the strike, the militants were able to attract large numbers of miners to the Independent Labour Party only by couching socialist teachings in rhetoric borrowed from the Gospels. Conversely, in the aftermath of the 1904 revivals many preachers began to advocate social, as well as personal reform. Orthodox Nonconformists coupled their resistance to socialism with appeals to Welsh nationalism.

The social basis of this religious and political controversy is analyzed by Merfyn Jones, who notes that Wales' leading businessmen had become great landowners with aristocratic life-styles during the nineteenth century, and that rural struggles over tithes, enclosures, and sales of royal lands had accompanied the strikes of miners, quarrymen, and other workers. The radical Liberals of north Wales had harnessed such popular protests to their own campaign against the Tory Establishment, while maintaining a discrete distance from the illegality of those protests. Jones' description of the radical-Liberal political discourse of the 1880s is remarkably similar to Turner's depiction of the rhetoric of the ILP in south Wales twenty years later: both identified the popular enemy with landlords and usury.

The remaking of the working class during the Second Industrial Revolution had a major impact on national politics in both Canada and Wales. The final set of questions posed by these essays revolves around an evaluation of that influence. Seager finds considerable variety in political movements between one mining region of western Canada and another. In general, he argues, miners carried far more weight in local than in dominion politics. Linda Kealey examines women activists, and especially the Women's Labour League during 1919, in several parts of Canada and underscores the local character and impact of their mobilizations. Women defined their endeavours more in terms of family and community needs than of national organizations, brought unions to telephone, clerical, sales, and restaurant workers, distributed birth control information, and vigourously pursued demands through minimum wage boards.

Both Gregory Kealey and Deian Hopkin scrutinize national strike statistics in order to test the argument that a contagious upsurge in industrial disputes on the eve of World War I explains evident changes in workers' political behaviour. Hopkin points out that the strike activity of 1891–1913 was located primarily in the Glamorgan coal fields, where it lasted for decades rather than years and peaked well before the famous period of 1911–1913. The mushrooming coal towns dominated by big-anti-union companies produced twenty years of continuous strike activity, while most outbursts of social violence were located elsewhere. Although south Wales shifted its loyalty from Liberals to Labour during these decades, the contours of its industrial conflict did not exhibit a rise of labour militancy to crisis proportions on the eve of the Great War.

Kealey's data are more comprehensive than the British statistics, and they suggest to him a pattern of strikes in Canada rather different from what Hopkin had found in Wales. Canadian strike statistics for the period between 1891 and 1930 display three prominent strike waves: 1899–1903, 1911–13, and 1917–20. Miners were leading actors at all times, and workers in transportation played a prominent role in the first strike wave, but the immediate prewar years also saw metal workers, building tradesmen, labourers, and others engaged in industrial disputes of unprecedented size and frequency. The postwar strikes were the most widespread of all, both geographically and occupationally, with employees of the public sector conspicuously joining the militant ranks. Consequently, Kealey endorses James Cronin's conception of a Great Unrest evident among workers throughout the industrialized world on the eve of the war and resumed toward its end -- a thesis on which Hopkin's evidence casts doubt.[3]

The two authors agree, however, that strike statistics are used most profitably when they are disaggregated. Strikes in both countries were created by particular groups of workers in specific localities. Workers in some industries who had remained quiescent while miners, building workers, and others struck often, entered the fray at particular moments to impart a wave-like appearance to Canadian strikes. Sympathetic stoppages, contagious examples, and the influence of national or international unions often linked such local actions to each other. None of these phenomena, however, were peculiar to Canada either before or after the war, nor was the persistent prominence of coal miners uniquely Welsh. The specificity with which both authors identify the determinants of strike activity makes a comparison of their findings especially fruitful.

International scholarly collaboration of the type evident in these essays helps historians discover regional and global patterns within working-class activity, which is best studied at the community level. The interlocking economic changes of the Second Industrial Revolution and the personal and family projects which inspired people to migrate in quest of wages fashioned common meanings for human experience out of the endeavours of millions of men and women who never met each other and who spoke in many different tongues.

Notes

1 David S. Landes, *The Unbound Prometheus: Technological Change and Industrial Development in Western Europe from 1750 to the Present* (Cambridge: Cambridge University Press), 231–358.

2 See James E. Cronin and Carment Sirianni, eds., *Work, Community, and Power: The Experience of Labour in Europe and America, 1900–1925* (Philadelphia: Temple University Press, 1983); Peter N. Stearns, *Lives of Labor: Work in a Maturing Industrial Society* (New York: Holmes and Meier, 1975); Ira Katznelson and Aristide R. Zolberg; *Working-Class Formation: Nineteenth-Century Patterns in Western Europe and the United States* (Princeton: Princeton University Press,

1986); Dick Geary, *European Labour Protest, 1848–1939* (London: Croom Helm, 1981). For a bibliography of dependency theory debate, with special reference to Latin America, see Steve J. Stern, "Feudalism, Capitalism, and the World-System in the Perspective of Latin America and the Caribbean", *American Historical Review*, 93 (October, 1988), 829–872.

3 James E. Cronin, "Labor Insurgency and Class Formation: Comparative Perspectives on the Crisis of 1917–1920 in Europe", in Cronin and Sirianni, 20–48.

I

The Rise and Decline of the Welsh Economy, 1890-1930

John Williams

The course taken by the Welsh economy in the half century preceding 1930 is simple and straightforward: it is one of rise and fall. But the direct statement, whilst accurate enough, disguises the nature of both the growth and the decline. The scale of each was of dramatic proportions. Indeed, the tragedy embodied classical elements in that the seeds of the collapse were contained in the forces, including even traces of hubris, which fuelled the soaring rise. The purpose of the present paper is to sketch the scale and nature of these movements, and to comment upon some of their characteristics which are of particular relevance to labour historians.

The tables serve to summarise the nature of the Welsh experience. Effectively they show a rapid increase in nearly all the critical indicators up to the first world war; a more varied experience during the war itself and into the immediate post-war years; and a sharp decline for the rest of the 1920s and beyond. Population together with output and employment in the main industries rose sharply and then fell away. The figures can be left to speak for themselves but in some significant respects they speak too softly and justify some amplification. In particular their message becomes almost deafening when attention is concentrated on their locational and structural aspects.

The population increase before 1914, for example, is quite substantial. But it was very unevenly spread. Six of the (then) thirteen counties actually experienced an absolute decline in population: these constituted the rural heartland of, especially, mid-Wales. There were small gains in three of the northern counties (Caernarvonshire, Denbeigh and Flint) mostly associated with the North Wales coalfield. But overwhelmingly the population trend was dominated by the few counties (Glamorgan, Monmouth and — to a lesser extent — Carmarthen) which were most directly affected by developments in the coalfield of South Wales. Indeed, of the total population increase for Wales of nearly 850, 000 between 1881 and 1911, 610,000 (or 70 per cent) was accounted for by the single county of Glamorgan. Whether such a widely spread and heterogeneous geographical experience can be usefully described as the pre-1914 expansion of the economy of Wales must be open to some doubt.

The imbalance largely reflects a similar skewness in the industrial structure. Indeed the broad occupational groups used in the census seem in some respects hardly to be appropriate to describe the Welsh economic structure — except in a negative sense. In Wales the numbers falling into most of these occupational groups were insignificant. In 1911 ten of the 22 occupational groups each accounted for less than 1 per cent of the total occupied male population.[1] This was a persistent feature of the nineteenth century Welsh economy; with minor variations the same occupational groups had been similarly insignificant at the time of the first comprehensive and comparable occupational census in 1851.[2] At the other end of the scale nearly all the (233,000) growth in the male occupied population could be accounted for by just six groups. And even within this leading half dozen growing sectors there was a huge imbalance: five of them (Transport; Metals, machines; Food, tobacco etc.; Building; and Commercial) accounted between them for just under half (105,000) the increase, the other half (112,000) was entirely accounted for by the single sector of Mines and Quarries. As a result, by 1911 out of the entire male occupied population in Wales one in every three (31·6 per cent) was a miner or quarryman. Few industrial *countries* can have had so markedly concentrated an occupational structure. But if we add to those in Mining the slowly dwindling numbers engaged in Agriculture, an even more remarkable fact emerges: in what is generally considered to be one of the most industrialised sectors of the most industrialised pre-1914 nation (Britain) almost half (43·5 per cent) of the occupied male population was engaged in primary production.

The dominant sector in the Welsh economy was clearly that of Mines and Quarries, but as the nineteenth century progressed Mines and Quarries came increasingly to mean coal. By 1911 the number employed in lead mining was tiny whilst those in the slate industry numbered less than twenty thousand (Table 5). The increasing dominance of coal, and especially of South Wales coal, is thus the final point to be emphasized in this brief survey of the Welsh economy in the generation before the first world war. It is a dominance which can be economically and effectively established and demonstrated.

By 1911 30 per cent of the occupied males were in the one industry of coal-mining: an extraordinary percentage when it is recalled that most Welsh counties contained no coal deposits. In the 30 years before 1914, unemployment in the industry grew from about 80,000 to 242,000 (Table 3). And of this increase of 162,000 nearly all (157,000) took place in the South Wales coalfield. In a little over a decade at the beginning of the twentieth century the South Wales coal industry absorbed an *additional* 100,000 miners.[3] At a more impressionistic level the thrusting, restless activity can be conveyed by two brief illustrations, one direct and one indirect. In 1891 in the immediate hinterland of Cardiff alone it was reported that at the present time the new Clydach pit was being developed (and it is rumoured that another was to be sunk); Naval Colliery Co. is going to sink a new pit; Lewis Merthyr Co. to do the same; Tylor and Co. now well on with new Cefn-nant-ddu colliery; Mardy Co. had started new shaft; Dowlais Co. is sinking two new shafts; Universal Colliery Co. to sink new pits north of Pontypridd. In Rhymney Valley, Llanbraddach Co. had found fresh coal; Rhymney Co. is sinking two new shafts at Pengam; Powell Duffryn Co. contemplated sinking in the same area. Universal Co. had started two pits at the top of Aber valley, a new pit is being sunk at Llanhilleth; Ebbw Vale Co. is sinking at Cwm and at Abertillery.

The indirect effects, especially in the provision of the transportation infrastructure, were equally dramatic. By 1890 South Wales already possessed what was certainly one of the most densely-developed rail networks of the entire world. Even so, the years before 1914 saw a few minor extensions — another 32 miles for the Barry Railway, 23 miles for the Cardiff Railway, 17 miles for the Rhondda and Swansea Bay line, and 21 additional miles for the Port Talbot Railway. But the real post-1890 outburst took the form of the provision of extra port facilities. Between 1890 and 1910 more investment was made to build more dock accommodation than ever before.

The Barry No. 2 Dock covering 34 acres was opened in 1898. At Cardiff the Queen Alexandra Dock was opened in 1907 at a cost of £1·3 million. Its 52 acres increased the Bute Docks system by almost one-third. At Newport a dock extension of 20 acres was opened in 1893 whilst the South Dock extension of 48 acres was finally completed in 1914. At Port Talbot a new dock was opened in 1898, the same year as a 28 acre extension to the Prince of Wales dock in Swansea. A decade later, in 1909, the King's Dock of 70 acres was also opened in Swansea . . . [5]

Much of this extra dock accommodation was soon to be rendered redundant. That should not, however, be allowed to disguise the essential message arising from the energetic activity of the quarter-century following 1890: it proclaimed not only that the economy was expanding very rapidly but that contemporaries were confident that the still-growing coal industry justified capital expenditure on the infrastructure on a scale which anticipated a much greater future demand. The boosters were wrong, as they usually are sooner or later, but it would be equally mistaken to use hindsight simply to write all this off as hysteria. At the very end of this period a shrewd, sober and knowledgeable judge of the industry — Professor Stanley Jevons — was still calling for additional dock accommodation for Cardiff: 'The South Wales coalfield is now producing at the rate of nearly 60 million tons per annum, and the rate of production is pretty sure to increase within 30 or 40 years to about 100 million tons per annum.'[6]

In the event, 1913 turned out to be the peak year for coal output (56·8m. tons) in South Wales. It is impossible to know whether this would have still been the case if the first world war had not broken out in August, 1914 but it is unlikely that a downturn could have been long delayed. It is tolerably certain that the needs of war, after a great deal of initial disruption, soon called for as much output as a reduced and (because of an early patriotic exodus of skilled colliers) less efficient workforce could produce from mines which were not getting enough capital for their effective maintenance. War thus — eventually — sustained output: the post-war boom with high prices greatly stimulated output. But the wartime capital neglect, and the post-war profit incentive brought into production thinner seams and pits which had previously been closed down as too small or inefficient. Employment thus peaked in 1920 at 271,516 (over 38,000 more than in 1913) but the 1920 output at 45·3m. tons was 11·5m. tons *less* than that of 1913.

The post-war boom died at the end of 1920. The ensuing decline of the Welsh economy can again be summarised in the broad statistical indicators (Tables 1 — 6). But again these under-state what was happening: the Welsh fall, like the Welsh rise, is not fully captured in these figures. Thus the fact of an absolute decline in population (from 2·656m. in 1921 to 2·593m. in 1931) is itself significant, especially when contrasted with the still-rising U.K. trend (from 44·07 on to 46·07m.). But it obscures three facts: that Wales had suffered a dramatic reversal from having an above-average rate of population growth before 1914; that the fall was unevenly distributed — the Rhondda lost 13 per cent of its population in the decade before 1931; and the overall loss of population under-states the extent to which people were moving out of the country, and particularly from the southern coalfield. In the decade before 1931, for example the actual loss of population from the four counties containing coalfield was 70,000. But the region had long had, and continued to have, an exceptionally high birth rate. There would thus have been a continued substantial natural rate of increase by 1931 if this had not been offset by out-migration. It was estimated that 242,000 left the coalfield during the 1920s.[7]

The decline, moreover, was not spread over the entire decade so that, when it came, it was sharper than the overall figures might suggest. In the immediate post-war boom the price of coal for export had risen exceptionally strongly. That demand came to an end in late 1920 and, together with the coincident shift of government policy to deflationary measures, hit South Wales badly. But after the disruption of the national three month coal dispute of 1921, support was lent for the view that the downturn would soon be over by the return to high levels of output and exports in 1922. 1923 was still better (because the French invasion of the Ruhr disrupted a major competitor) and the generally good trading conditions of 1924 sustained a high level of activity. In 1923 output at 54·3m. tons was almost back to its 1913 peak (56·8m. tons), and coal exports from South Wales in 1923 were actually slightly higher (30.0m tons) than in 1913 (29·8m. tons).[8] Unemployment in coalmining in South Wales was in 1923 and 1924 — as it had been before 1914 — well below the

U.K. average. With national figures already above 10 per cent an overwhelmingly coal district like the Rhondda registered less than 2 per cent in 1923 and was still only 7 per cent by the end of 1924, and — partly reflecting the dominance of coal — the average for Wales in each of these years was below 10 per cent (6·4 and 8·6 respectively).[9]

When the bubble burst the pace and scale of the fall were devastating. Most of the reasons for the collapse of the Welsh coal economy were secular but their malign effects were hugely aggravated by a series of short-run, *ad hoc*, influences: the war; the feverish post-war boom; the invasion of the Ruhr; and, above all, by Britain's return to the gold standard in 1925 at an over-valued pound which hit directly at exporting areas like Wales. Before the war 70 per cent of the commercially disposable coal of South Wales was exported as cargo or bunkers. Compared with just two years earlier in 1923 the output of the southern coalfield had fallen by 10m. tons by 1925, fluctuated around that level (44–48m. tons) until the end of the decade before plummeting by a further 10m. tons (to 34·9m. tons) in 1932. In the decade from 1923 to 1932 the number employed in the industry fell by over 100,000. Neither output nor employment recovered in the years of the British economic recovery of the 1930s. Moreover, despite the steady fall (through migration, natural wastage etc.) in the total number of insured miners, both the number and the percentage of miners unemployed increased to over 80,000 and 42 per cent in 1932.

The experience of the South Wales coal industry was the most dramatic, but it was echoed in the other major industrial sectors of Wales (Tables 4 — 5). But the more important feature was the fewness of these other major industrial sectors. The Welsh economy remained throughout these years one which was narrowly based to a quite extraordinary degree. The 1921 occupational census showed that 43 per cent of the occupied male population were engaged in just 2 (out of 26) occupational groups: Mining and quarrying; and Metal manufacturing and engineering. If those engaged in transportation (largely dependent on these two industries and the fourth largest sector after Agriculture) are added over one-half the male occupied population is accounted for. The precariousness of such an economic structure was greatly compounded by the fact that each of these sectors was heavily reliant on its ability to export. The South Wales coal industry still exported about two-thirds of its (dwindling) output in the early 1930s; Welsh steel production was overwhelmingly destined for local tinplate and sheetworks which in the early 1930s still exported two-thirds of their output; and in the late 1920s over 80 per cent of the more than 800,000 tons of galvanised sheets were sent abroad.[11]

Explanations are more elusive than description and cannot be managed in the same preemptory way. They are thus not here attempted. Instead some general comments are offered on a few selective aspects of the developments in the Welsh economy which have been briefly depicted. One of the most significant is the effect and influence of technical change.

The customary story was that there was before 1914 a long-run decline in the level of labour productivity in coal mining stemming largely from the natural operation of diminishing returns in an extractive industry. The charge was that this secular trend was not countered by the adoption of technical innovation, and the responsibility for this was variously attached to entrepreneurial failure or labour resistance to the new methods of work. It was considered that this was sufficiently demonstrated by the fact that in 1913 only just over one per cent of output in South Wales was mechanically cut, a much lower proportion than in other coalfields.[12]

More recently this has been challenged on two main grounds. It is questioned whether there was the long-run decline in productivity before 1914 (Figure 1). Instead by 1914 there seems simply to have been a return to the levels of the early 1870s; the aberration seems rather to have been the very high productivity levels of 1880–88; and the fall from these levels were concentrated in two brief bursts from 1888–90 and after 1908 each of which could be explained by *ad hoc* factors. More specifically, the geological conditions in South Wales were unsuitable to the cutting machines which were then available. The machines required smooth and continuous working conditions if they were to be economically viable, but the seams of the coalfield were notoriously unstable. Indeed, the over-riding geological characteristic of the coalfield was that it was much more disturbed and much less stable than other coalfields. Thus the seams tended to dip quite sharply; they were heavily faulted; and the floor and the roof showed high propensities to buckle and to fall, to 'work' or move. One result of this was to make the actual process of cutting the coal a less urgent problem. Welsh colliers customarily ended their shift by under-cutting the seam, confident that by the next morning much of the overhanging coal would have been brought down by the pressure operating from the roof. Improved, more robust and adaptable, machinery together with some changes in the economics of the industry, led to a more widespread adoption of mechanical mining methods in the inter-war years though the same factors still meant that South Wales tended for good reasons to lag behind other coalfields. But for the period up to 1914 the significance is rather that alleged labour intransigence over the adoption of machinery was never a very live issue. And, more generally, it meant that the vast expansion in output could only be achieved by an equivalent increase in the labour force.

The more important technical change was probably taking place not on the production (supply)side but on the side of consumption (demand). It took the best part of the nineteenth century for steam to oust sail as the main source of propulsion for ocean shipping. In Scotland the *Charlotte Dundas* had operated on steam as early as 1802 whilst in 1833 the Canadian *Royal William* had crossed from Nova Scotia to Portsmouth using steam as an auxiliary to sail. But as late as 1870 the still-growing number of sailing vessels of the U.K. merchant fleet constituted four times the tonnage of the steam fleet (4·6 against 1·1m. tons). Thereafter the change-over was rapid:

by 1890 the steam fleet (5m. tons) was approaching double the tonnage of sail (2·9m. tons): by 1910 it was nine times as great (10·4 against 1·2m. tons). In the crucial four decades from c. 1870 South Wales, with its huge supplies of coal especially suited for steam-raising and with the added boon for naval vessels and passenger liners of being (relatively) smokeless, was a prime beneficiary of this process. It provided the major driving force behind the dramatic increase in output which more than trebled between the late 1870s and the first world war. That conflict was, with the possible exception of the Russo-Japanese war of 1904–5, to be the only one in which a significant war at sea was mainly fought with coal-fired ships. And unfortunately for Wales the pace of the downswing was much more rapid than the upswing had been. The Admiralty only initiated sea trials using oil at the beginning of the twentieth century but twenty years later had ceased commissioning coal-fired vessels of war. The prestigious Admiralty demand for Welsh coal had plummeted from 1·75m. tons in the last peacetime year of 1913 to one-fifth of this level in 1925 when it was still falling. In 1913, about 90 per cent of shipping generally was coal-driven: by the end of our period this had fallen to about one-half. Still more ominously, less than one-third of new shipping in 1930 was designed to use coal; oil fired boilers and internal combustion engines which had been fitted to an insignificant proportion of the world's tonnage in 1913 had within two decades already become the norm.[13]

In part this was simply one of a series of factors making for a decline in the demand for Welsh coal in the 1920s. It was, in this respect, reinforced for example by the developments being made in fuel economy. More efficient domestic appliances were supplemented by the use of powdered fuel and small coals in factories and in steel works. There was also the more particular factor of the return to the gold standard which exerted an especially baleful influence on an overwhelmingly exporting district like South Wales. And the more general influences of the exhaustion of some of the more accessible coal reserves, and the development of new (and often subsidized) sources of competition in countries like Poland and Germany. But what needs to be emphasized is that the significance of the decline in the use of coal for steam-raising, especially for shipping, extended far beyond the simple loss of a market.

Before 1913 Welsh coal always commanded a price premium. This was generally regarded as a reflection of the higher quality of Welsh coal and hence looked upon as a permanent source of prosperity for the region. And in part, of course, it did reflect the peculiar qualities of Welsh steam coal. But the higher price also reflected the greater cost of producing Welsh coal. Even before, and apart from, the retarding effects on the introduction of coal-cutting machinery, the exceptionally difficult geological conditions made the coalfield a relatively high-cost producer. During the boom years some of the implications of this fact eluded those on all sides of the industry whose pride in the high quality of the coal led them to believe that it ensured that it would stay in high demand. Causation and causal directions in history are always tricky. None the less, when taken in conjunction with the high cost characteristics, it can be asserted with some confidence that in the Welsh coal industry the causation ran (and still runs) the other way. The nineteenth century saw the emergence of new demands for coal — especially for steam raising, and especially for steam ships — for which Welsh coal happened to be well suited. The smokeless and steam raising qualities of Welsh coal were sufficiently marked to ensure a surging demand for it despite the fact that it necessarily cost more to produce. The higher costs were inescapable. Once the special demand for Welsh coal declined much of the industry was doomed: its higher quality would not then be able to offset the greater cost of getting it. On this reading, therefore, the connection between cost, price, demand and quality pointed not to the security given to the Welsh coal industry by the high quality of its product, but to the precariousness which came from its high cost of production.

The point has been presented here with an exaggerated starkness. The justification stems from a conviction that it is not possible to comprehend the shifts in the Welsh economy over this period without an appreciation of the basic economics of the dominant industry. It is a useful background which helps to illuminate such other characteristics of the industry as the especial vehemence with which the Welsh coalowners attempted in the inter-war years to reduce these costs by cutting wages. The high cost disadvantage in a competitive industry could only be overcome if, as in the 1950s, there was a general acute fuel shortage or if there was a particular demand for the particular qualities of the product. The latter aspect was demonstrated in the 1920s by the experience of the anthracite industry. For most of the nineteenth century the anthracite coalfield of West Wales had experienced very slow growth. The seams here were generally even more faulty and costly to work so sale was confined to a few specialised uses — like horticulture and brewing — where its exceptional purity was important enough to command a high price. Towards the end of the century a new wider demand opened with the spread of coal-burning closed stoves on the continent. Output rose from 1·2m. tons in 1890 to 4·0m. tons by 1910. After the war, this demand continued so that, hugely against the general trend, output rose to 5·6m. tons in 1930 and over-rode even the handicap of an over-valued pound after 1925 by continuing to export nearly 70 per cent of total output. (In the early 1930s, and especially after the Ottowa agreements, Canada became a major market taking over 1m. tons a year).

More pertinent to the purposes and interests of labour historians is another feature which flows directly from the economic structure of Wales and the way it developed over this period. Both before 1914 and during the 1920s there was a natural prominence, perhaps even dominance, of essentially labour questions. This was natural because of two broad features of the economy which have already been mentioned: the occupational structure and the pace and scale of the rise and fall of the economy. The occupational structure was throughout overwhelmingly geared towards manual workers. It was also heavily concentrated in industries which were strongly labour-intensive: coal, slate, lead, tinplate, railways, docks. Given these features a period which saw sharp changes in the economy was bound to create labour difficulties and tensions.

Other essays will pick up more specific aspects of these influences. The more immediate purpose is to offer a few broad comments on the implications of the Welsh economic structure for labour historians, and once again this can be most economically effected by concentrating on the coal industry. Something has already been said to counter the common charge of technological backwardness, especially before 1914. But even if it can be demonstrated that diminishing returns were just about kept at bay, and even if the apparently slow adoption of coal-cutting machines can be plausibly rationalised, some basic facts still remain. There was no sustained increase in productivity. There was no significant break-through in the fundamental process of coal-getting itself: the actual cutting of the coal was unmechanized, obtained by human muscle assisted only by a few primitive tools (mostly mandrils and shovels) and a little gunpowder. There was a huge increase in output between 1890 and 1914. The unavoidable consequence of all this was that more and more colliers were required to produce the coal, and the resultant influx of labour impinged upon all aspects of its social development.

Simply to ask where these extra bodies came from, is already to raise a number of crucial and contentious issues. At one level the answers are straightforward enough. A population increase of this sort can only come from natural increase or by migration, and the census figures — unsatisfactory as they are in many respects — clearly show that both these influences were at work. It can thus be observed that, strongly against the national trend, a high birth rate was maintained in the colliery districts up to 1914. We have the fact, but the explanation eludes us. Some commentators point to the operation of social factors: the enclosed nature of mining communities retarding the spread of outside influences, or the lack of alternative leisure facilities. Others stress economic factors: the absence of employment opportunities for women or, still more directly, the strong demand inducing the workforce to (more than) reproduce itself. But there are weighty objections to each of these approaches. Similarly, the fact of substantial net immigration into the coalfield in the two decades before the first world war is not in doubt. Where they came from, and why, are much more problematic. The Brinley Thomas thesis that emigrants from rural Wales were absorbed into the industrial south, with its accompanying implications for Welsh language and culture has more recently been challenged by Dudley Baines.[14] Even if it were possible, the aim here is not to resolve the issue but merely to point out that the answer is relevant to a wide range of social and industrial issues.

Amongst these would be the progress of labour organisations. In the case of the United States it is often asserted that much of the slow growth of trade union organisation through the nineteenth century can be attributed to the particular problems of unionising a rapidly growing, significantly immigrant workforce from different cultural backgrounds. It is not intended to press a false analogy between Wales and the United States. But it is pertinent to point out that against this background, there seems to be a perversity in the Welsh experience: in the period before the major human flood-tide trade unions in Wales were seen to be weak; it is in the, apparently, unfavourable conditions of the early twentieth century that the first secure foundations are laid. Right into the 1890s informed observers like the Webbs were dismissive of miners' unions in Wales: by 1914 — after Tonypandy, after the leading part played in the national strike for a minimum, after *The Miners' Next Step* — such a stance was inconceivable.

The rapid expansion of an economy whose structure emphasized labour-intensive sectors thus raises major puzzles for labour historians. These have been illustrated: they could be multiplied by looking at such features as the provision of social capital or political affiliations. The more important point is that when the decline comes in the inter-war years it necessarily makes for a similar dominance of labour problems. The industrial structure is still much the same (indeed, that is a large part of the problem), and the industries are still labour-intensive. The process was reversed, but the issues were not simply reversible. Thus immigration gave way to emigration, but it was certainly not a straightforward case of the arrivals of the 1900s returning from whence they came. Similarly trade unions under attack and in retreat were faced with a quite different set of problems. Hywel Francis and David Smith have, for example, brilliantly told how "The Fed" partly met this challenge by becoming, in significant respects, the universal providers for the community.[15] There were more subtle changes. Before 1914 franchise changes had secured the election of many workers as Poor Law Guardians, but this had not led to any significant loosening of the application of the Poor Law. Outdoor relief for adult males continued to be stringently withheld. Miners acted mostly as ratepayers since there was very little unemployment for them at this time. In the 1920s, as mass unemployment becomes a common experience, there are persistent attempts to bend or break the regulations.[16]

The Welsh economy, especially before 1914, has recently been portrayed by some writers as occupying a central role in the development of an Atlantic Economy which is seen as a major manifestation of late nineteenth and early twentieth century capitalism. Wales played a vibrant part because its world-wide network of exports led to investment and migration which in some cases — the Dowlais influence on Bilbao in Spain and the Swansea and North Wales dominance of Chile — was significant for a whole economy.[17] Others portrayed Wales as merely constituting part of

England's internal colonisation and being thus persistently and consciously exploited.[18] But perhaps these dramatic scenarios, in their quite different ways, exaggerate our significance. Wales may be best depicted as an integral but peripheral part of a general United Kingdom economy. The problem would then be simply that for a crucial period the Welsh role in that economy was so obviously best suited to primary production that no sizeable, stable manufacturing was established. It is more dubious whether this crucial omission can be attributed to the malevolence, or even the unconcern, of capitalist hyenas in London or New York, or just to Welsh donkeys in Cardiff and Caernarvon.

The Tables are taken from, or calculated from
J. Williams, *Digest of Welsh Historical Statistics*, 2 vols., Cardiff, Welsh Office, 1985.

Notes

1 Defence; Fishing; Precious metals, jewels, watches, instruments and games; Chemicals, oil, grease, soap and resin; Skins, leather, hair and feathers; Gas, water, electricity, sanitary work; Wood, furniture, fittings, decoration; Brick, cement, pottery and glass; Paper, print, books, stationary; Textile fabrics.
2 L. J. Williams and T. Boyns, "Occupations in Wales, 1851–1971". *Bulletin of Economic Research*, 29, 1977.
3 In 1899 the coal industry in South Wales employed 132,682 men: by 1913 this reached 233,134. *Welsh Historical Statistics*, I, 300.
4 *South Wales Daily News*, 1 July 1891, quoted in J. Williams, "The Climacteric of the 1890s" in Baber and Williams (eds.), *Modern South Wales*, Cardiff, U. of Wales Press, 200.
5 Baber and Williams (eds.), *op.cit.*, 203.
6 H. S. Jevons, *The British Coal Trade* (1915), 109,111.
7 *Second Industrial Survey of South Wales* (Cardiff, 1937), I, p. 16.
8 When bunker fuel and the coal equivalent of coke and patent fuel exported are added the 1913 exports were 36·8m. tons compared to 35·8m. tons in 1923.
9 *Second Industrial Survey*, *op.cit.*, 426, and *Welsh Historical Statistics*, I, 142.
10 In the mid-1930s 15 of the 18 steelworks in South Wales were mostly engaged in supplying for tinplate manufacture. *Ibid.*, 90.
11 *Ibid.*, 103,108.
12 A. J. Taylor, "Labour Productivity and Technological Innovation in the British Coal Industry, 1850–1914", *Economic History Review*, XIV (August 1961); Rhodri Walters, "Labour Productivity in the South Wales Steam Coal Industry, 1870–1914", *Economic History Review*, XXVIII (May 1975); Trevor Boyns, *Labour Productivity in the British Coal Industry, 1874–1913*. Univ. of Wales, Ph.D. thesis, 1982. There is a brief discussion in J. Williams, "Climacteric of the 1890s", *op.cit.*, 197–200.
13 Board of Trade, *First Industrial Survey of South Wales*, (London, H.M.S.O., 1932), 26; *Second Industrial Survey of South Wales* (Cardiff, 1937), I, 48; H. Marquand, *South Wales Needs a Plan* (London, 1936), 28–9.

14 B. Thomas, *The Welsh Economy* (Cardiff, 1962), (especially Chapter I, "Wales and the Welsh Economy', and for a more recent re-statement, B. Thomas, 'The Industrial Revolution and the Welsh Economy" in C. Baber and J. Williams, *op.cit.*, pp.6–21; D. Baines, *Migration in a Mature Country* (Cambridge, 1985), Ch. 10.

15 H. Francis and D. Smith, *The Fed* (London, 1980).

16 D. M. Lloyd, 'Some Aspects of the Poor Law in South Wales, 1870–1930', (Unpublished M.Sc. (Econ) thesis, Univ. of Wales, 1978).

17 See, e.g., G. A. Williams, *When Was Wales?* (Harmondsworth, 1985), Ch. 10.

18 M. Hechter, *Internal Colonialism* (London, 1975).

Table 1. Population. Wales and Selected Counties, 1881-1931. (000s)

Year	Wales			Glamorgan			Caerns.			Cards.		
	M	F	T	M	F	T	M	F	T	M	F	T
1881	786	785	1,572	263	249	511	59	61	119	32	39	70
1891	892	879	1,771	360	327	687	56	61	117	27	35	63
1901	1,011	1,001	2,013	444	416	860	60	65	126	27	34	61
1911	1,232	1,189	2,421	582	539	1,121	59	66	125	27	33	60
1921	1,330	1,326	2,656	638	615	1,252	60	71	131	28	33	61
1931	1,294	1,300	2,593	617	609	1,226	57	64	121	25	30	55
1939[1]	1,228	1,259	2,487	—	—	1,158	—	—	119	—	—	52

[1] Mid-year estimate

Table 2. Occupations. Wales, 1881-1931. (000s)

Year	Mines & Quarries		Agric.		Metal Manuf. & Engineering		Transport & Communic.		Total	
	M	F	M	F	M	F	M	F	M	F
1881	102	1	100	11	56	4	37	—	490	155
1891	145	1	99	9	62	5	52	—	576	192
1901	189	—	92	12	68	2	70	1	656	180
1911	256	—	96	20	91	3	85	1	809	216
1921	278	—	95	11	99	5	87	3	880	213
1931	235	—	93	9	81	2	95	3	873	206

Table 3. Iron, Steel and Tinplate

Average of:	No. of Works	Iron and Steel								Tinplate	
		South Wales Furnaces		Production		No. of Works	North Wales			No. of mills	Output
		Built	In blast	Pig Iron	Steel Ingots		Built	In blast	Pig Iron	Working	(00s of boxes)
1879-81	28	142	63	824	416	4	10	6	41	241[3]	5,236
1911-13	9	32	12	787	1,807[1]	2	3	3	76[2]	534	16,574
1930-32	6	20	3	392	1,375	n.a.			n.a.	403	15,194

[1] 1913 figure   [2] 1909-11 to keep comparable basis.   [3] Ave. 1878-80

Table 4. Coal

Year Average of:	Output (000s tons)	of which Anthracite	South Wales Shipments Foreign & Coastal	No. Employed	North Wales Output (000s tons)	No. Employed
1879-81	20,406	906[1]	9,330	69,515	2,442	10,175
1911-13	52,383	4,359	37,098	226,519	3,400	15,690
1930-32	39,022	5,435	24,811	159,024	3,104	13,813

[1] 1888

Table 5. Lead[1] and Slate, Wales

Year Average of:	No. of Mines	Lead Output (tons)	No. Employed	Slate Output (000s tons)	No. Employed
1879-81	98	20,118	6,363	443[4]	14,019[5]
1911-13	26	7,042	1,867	312	18,764
1930-32	,,	192[2]	[3]	201	18,435[6]

[1] Covers lead, zinc and copper.   [2] From 1933 there was revival from Flints. Ave. 1934-6, 18,837.
[3] 1925-6 (last years available) less than 500.   [4] 1882-4 Earliest available.
[5] Figs. deficient before 1895 Quarries Act made them compulsory.   [6] 1924-6 Last years available.

Table 6. Unemployment. Wales, number and per cent. Males, Annual Averages, 1923-32.

Year	Number	Per cent.	Year	Number	Per cent.
1923	34,209	6.4[1]	1928	127,030	24.4
1924	49,995	8.6[1]	1929	105,294	19.2
1925	96,557	16.5[1]	1930	142,758	27.5
1926	104,011	18.0[1]	1931	177,146	34.3
1927	117,108	20.9	1932	207,292	39.1

[1] Ave. percentage only available for all unemployed (males, females and juveniles). This figure normally a little over 1 per cent below figure for males only.

2

Comparing Canada with the United States

Labour and Industrial Capitalist Development in the North Atlantic Region, 1880–1920

Robert Babcock

I. The Comparative Approach

I think it was the philosopher Morris Cohen who once said that the absolutely unique is indescribable. The scholar must find similarities among the objects within his gaze if he is to measure the differences. Most often such comparisons are implicit, as when an historian refers to the American Revolution or to the Canadian Rebellions of 1837: the words 'revolution' and 'rebellion' are categories of events implying fundamental similarities in scope or process, while at the same time they are broad enough to permit the introduction of unique features stemming from the particular time or locale. Years ago I published a study of the origins of the North American trade- union movement that implied both similarities and differences between Canada and the United States. I argued then that similar economic conditions facilitated the extension of the American trade-union movement northward into Canada. But differences in Canadian society and culture generated some notable tensions. While my recognition of important similarities and differences between Canada and the United States helped to explain the tensions that I had found, my method had not been designed to weigh these factors precisely. Instead I was intent upon showing that Gompers and the AFL were American imperialists of the same order as their contemporaries in business and government who were extending America's 'informal' empire into the Caribbean basin.[1]

It did not seem necessary at that time to measure these differences, because several North American social scientists had already posited widely accepted descriptions of the two distinct 'national' cultures straddling the 49th parallel. According to Louis Hartz, S. M. Lipset and others, Canadians were the product of an evolutionary rather than a revolutionary heritage, and consequently they were more deferential, less individualistic, and more elitist than Americans. Not only did their Tory heritage account for these presumed 'national' values, but it also made impossible reciprocal left-wing political tendencies which 'explained' the persistence of a democratic socialist tradition in Canada long after it had withered in the United States.[2] These theories represented pioneering attempts to make explicit comparisons between the two nations, but they have never been tested by extensive historical research and nowadays they seem more than a little teleological.

In recent years the idea of national value-differences has come under indirect attack from neo-Marxists who stress the basic imperatives of industrial capitalist development occurring anywhere. The social relations of capitalist production rather than nationality, they assert, dictate the basic trans-national character of class structure and class interaction despite local variations in either the timing or pace of economic change. In studies of social formation and class conflict in Canadian or American communities, these scholars have developed their arguments without making explicit comparisons across regional or national boundaries.[3] Hence their assumptions about the similarity of patterns of capitalist development in Canada or the United States remain (like those of Lipset) untested for the most part by a cross-border study designed to filter out what was continental in scope from what was local or national. The one effort thus far, by Carlos Schwantes, generally fails to disentangle some crucial determinants, perhaps because of the sheer scope and diversity of the regions he attempted to compare. Schwantes ultimately falls back on a Hartzian typology to explain the differences between American 'individualism' in Washington and Oregon and the 'collectivist touch' that he observes in British Columbia.[4]

Comparative historical approaches may be dated from at least the late Twenties when Marc Bloch called for explicit comparisons across time and space as well as between neighbouring societies within the same temporal frame.[5] But comparative history only blossomed after World War II when social scientists launched comparative studies of the underlying processes of economic and political development in Third World societies. Comparisons by historians of slave societies in the southern United States with those in the Caribbean and Latin America revealed with startling precision how a particular mixture of economic, social, and demographic features accounted for the major elements of the slave economy in Virginia, Cuba, or Brazil.[6] More recently, students of cities are examining the urban process in a comparative framework in order to make more precise statements about the key variables in city-building. Yet the most recent comparative study of Canadian and American urban centers still relies upon Lipset's value-difference hypothesis to bolster its argument.[7]

It is time to examine critically such postulates rather than to assume their *a priori* validity. This paper presents a portion of the findings from an ongoing, large-scale project comparing the impact of industrial capitalist development on a Canadian and an American city at the turn of the century. Portland, Maine, and Saint John, New Brunswick, shared enough geographic, demographic, economic and social features between 1880 and 1920 to make the urban context an invariant frame of reference for comparison. In other words, they fit Bloch's Type II paradigm: they were cities that

are at once neighbouring and contemporary, exercising a constant mutual influence, exposed throughout their development to the action of the same broad causes just because they are close and contemporaneous, and owing their existence in part at least to a common origin. . . Because Type II is more capable of rigourous classification, and more critical about the objects it compares, it may hope to reach conclusions of fact that are less hypothetical and more precise.[8]

It seems particularly appropriate to compare the industrial capitalist development of Portland and Saint John, particularly their economic structures and the character of their class relations, during the critical transition from mercantile and competitive capitalism to Monopoly Capital. Sharing the same ambitions in 1880, both cities' boosters saw little reason why their urban economies could not displace those of the larger cities of Boston and Montreal. At that time many manufactured goods from smaller cities were sold throughout North America and even overseas, and the growth of smaller centers into metropolitan giants appeared to be a matter of local initiative. But at the turn of the century, heavily capitalized and vertically-integrated industries based on new or improved technologies sprang up in many industrial sectors. Both nationally and internationally, these giant firms ruthlessly competed against the older and smaller factories, often driving them out or taking them over in an effort to exert greater control over product markets. By the end of the First World War it was clear to citizens of both Portland and Saint John that Monopoly Capital had augmented cities like Boston and Montreal at the expense of their own towns. By then both Portland and Saint John had been relegated to satellite status; their economics had been forced to adapt to and remain satisfied primarily with local and regional markets. In this changing context, their entrepreneurial elites sought to articulate new development strategies to maximize their opportunities and minimize or overturn their satellite roles. As we shall see, Canada's winter port trade played an important part in the struggles of both Portland and Saint John to prosper by maintaining or extending their dominance over the Canadian hinterland.[9]

In this paper I will compare the geographic settings, demographic changes, economic structures and the development strategies of local elites in these two urban centers during the transitional period to Monopoly Capitalism from 1880 to 1920. While the specific demographic and aggregate economic date vary somewhat, I argue that the character of class relationships did not significantly differ because of similarities in the workplace environment. The labour force in these two cities remained much alike in age, occupation, and gender distributions, and workers responded to the transition to Monopoly capitalism in similar fashion. Although the evidence on the full range of responses of Portland and Saint John workers is incomplete at this stage, the portion presented here suggests comparable levels of class mobilization rather than the presence in Saint John of a less militant and more deferential group of workers, as Lipset's thesis would posit for Canada's pre-eminently Loyalist city. In both cities, workers mobilized politically as well, with structural differences between the two municipal political systems accounting for the differences more persuasively than any reference to amorphous 'national' values.

I. Geographic Settings

Portland is located on a small peninsula jutting into the waters of Casco Bay and includes several islands within a few miles of the mainland. On the southerly side it is divided from the shore by an arm of the Atlantic which constitutes the inner harbour, an area of 627 acres. Two hills of under 200 feet at either end of the peninsula cradle a city bisected by the principal thoroughfare running the city's entire length from east to west. Both the Fore River which empties into Portland Harbour and the cove separating the north side of the peninsula from the mainland are shallow tidal areas virtually un-navigable to ocean-going vessels without extensive dredging. The twenty-foot tides are sufficient to keep both the inner and outer harbours ice free in winter.

The 450-mile long St. John River, the largest stream in the North Atlantic region, gives Saint John a somewhat different geographical character. Unlike Portland's Fore River, the broad and deep St. John serves as a boulevard into the interior. The river's waters empty into the harbour through a narrow channel marked by 100-foot high cliffs of limestone. The waters rush over and around several rocky islets and through this narrow pass with great force at low tide. But at flood tide the current moves upstream, overflowing ('reversing') the falls and briefly permitting navigation between river and harbour. At first the city's inhabitants perched on a rocky peninsula jutting into the harbour and separating the river on the west from Courtenay Bay on the east. Later settlements across the river and harbour, originally organized into the separate community of Carleton, were eventually incorporated into Saint John. In 1889 the adjacent (North End) river town of Portland, New Brunswick, was also annexed.

Both cities had developed as lumber ports in the early 19th century.[10] Square timber and deals from the vast reaches drained by the St.

John River found their way into burgeoning English markets, transforming the Fundy city into one of the chief timber ports on the Atlantic. Much of Portland's timber was exported to the booming seaboard American cities. Substantial quantities of lumber, barrels, shooks, and staves were shipped to the West Indies as well. Saint John merchants established hegemony over the river valley and Fundy shore of New Brunswick and western Nova Scotia. Their counterparts in Portland controlled the terms of trade in northern New Hampshire and Vermont as well as in southern Maine and along the Downeast shore. For both ports, the advent of the railway offered simultaneous dangers and opportunities. On the one hand, rival urban centres — whether Boston or Montreal or Halifax — threatened to tap their hinterlands and confine their economic expansion. On the other, in an age when bulk transport was significantly cheaper by water than by land, both cities fully expected to convert their proximity to northern European ports into a permanent trade advantage over larger cities to the south and west. Both viewed a rail link to Montreal as a means to tap the continental hinterland of British North America for their own commercial benefit. Each city could claim and advantage in their rivalry for Canada's winter trade. Portland was closer to Montreal by rail, but Saint John lay nearly a day's less travel by sea to Liverpool.[11]

The accompanying maps suggest the major geographical features of both cities between 1880/81 and 1920/21. Portland's waterfront area experienced minimal change. In contrast, Saint John's waterfront sprawled from the lower cove section of the peninsula (Intercolonial Wharf) to the West side, where new winter port facilities were constructed after the completion of the CPR 'Short Line' rail link to Montreal in 1889.[12] Geographical obstacles limited suburbanization to the periphery of the city proper and channeled it across the river to Fairville and the West End. Both the bridge across the Reversing Falls and the harbour ferry became increasingly important bonds linking the two major portions of New Brunswick's largest urban community.

II. Demographic changes

The population of the cities and their hinterlands is particularly revealing of both their comparative situation in 1880/81 and the changes wrought over the succeeding decades. (Table 1) Initially, Saint John was the largest city. Its immediate and extended hinterlands, however, were substantially smaller than Portland's, and it appears to have achieved a maximum state of 'metropolitanization' over this territory by 1881. Saint John's proportion of New Brunswick's population actually declined thereafter, but Portland's share of Maine's population nearly doubled. By the turn of the century the Maine city's population was nearly 20 per cent greater than Saint John's, and the gap in size slowly widened.

Let us examine next the immigrant proportion of these urban populations. In 1880/81, about the one-fifth of the population of both cities (Table 2) was foreign-born. In Portland the proportion remained about the same throughout this period. However, by 1921 it had been halved in Saint John. Of all the ethnic groups, the Irish-born made up the largest single number of European immigrants in both cities. During the transition to Monopoly Capital, their proportion of the total foreign-born population dropped precipitously, and more steeply in Saint John than in Portland. While the percentage of Russian-born (mostly Jews) was nearly the same for both cities by 1920/21, Portland attracted many more Scandinavians. The number of English/Welsh- born in Saint John remained steady at about 1,100 for thirty years before increasing during the war decade. By 1921 they comprised a third of all the foreign-born in the Fundy port. The number of Scots-born also remained steady, with Saint John attracting about 40 per cent more than Portland. During the war Saint John's Asian population rose sharply. Finally, for most of the period from 1900/01 to 1920/21, we should note that about a fifth of the foreign-born in Saint John were Americans. In contrast, the Canadian-born accounted for a whopping 37 to 45 per cent of the foreign-born in Portland, and by 1920/21 the Maine city had 5 and 1/2 times as many Canadian-born as Saint John had American-born. Such figures clearly reflect a stream in the well- known current of outmigrants flowing from the Maritime Provinces to the "Boston States" at the turn of the century.

What else do these demographic facts suggest? In some respects, at least, they reinforce the notion that Saint John had already peaked as an urban centre at the start of this period. Its overall population actually declined during the last two decades of the 19th century, and its proportion of primary (county) and secondary (provincial) hinterland population remained essentially unchanged. In sharp contrast, Portlanders experienced considerable urban expansion, especially during the 1890s. Portland's proportions of both its immediate and extended hinterlands grew significantly, reflecting in part the more rapid growth of both the state of Maine and of Cumberland county. The Irish-born held the largest share of the European-born population in both cities. But Portland attracted many more foreign-born immigrants overall, including a substantial number of Maritimers in general and undoubtedly some Saint John natives as well. Population data, in short, suggests a more 'successful' assertion of metropolitan functions in Portland than in Saint John during the transition to Monopoly Capital. The precise character of a few of those elements will be analyzed in the next section.

III. Economic Structures

In 1880/81 both Portland and Saint John were manufacturing and transportation centers, distribution points and entrepots. Neither enjoyed any status as a political or cultural centre. They looked alike; in both, a wholesale trading and manufacturing complex formed the economic core, encompassing many stores, factories, warehouses and workshops. After an initial spurt in the 1880s, both suffered a reduction in their capacity to fabricate goods for national or international markets, and they appeared to become increasingly tributary to Boston and Montreal interests. Because Portland's hinterland was more populous and pockmarked with diverse one-industry towns specializing in wood pulp, shoes and textiles, its population surpassed Saint John's as we have seen. Not surprisingly, Portland's largest factories produced consumer goods such as shirts, hats, and shoes as well as metal products. In contrast, Saint John's largest factories, with the notable exception of the cotton mills, concentrated on metalworking and wood products. Both cities processed and marketed seafood, grain, cattle, and hides. Portland canned corn and fish; Saint John sawed huge quantities of shooks, lath, shingles, and deals.[13]

In this section we will compare the distribution of workers among larger factories and examine the amount of capital per worker invested in each industry in the context of each city's development strategies. These comparisons enables us to estimate the relative degree of worker alienation caused by factory size and by skill dilution resulting from the introduction of improved machinery. Alienated, class-conscious workers can be expected to join their own trade-union organizations, declare strikes, and often vote for candidates clearly identified with their own class interest. According to Lipset, we should expect to find less of this behaviour in Saint John than in Portland.

In 1880 Portland's four industries employing 100 or more hands provided jobs for 700 people who represented 19 per cent of the workforce (Table 3).[14] Thirteen factories employing 40–99 hands provided jobs for 901 people representing 24 per cent of the workforce. Finally, 12 Portland factories employing 30–39 hands provided employment for 393 people representing 11 per cent of the city's workers. The largest factory in the Maine city was the Portland Company, founded in 1846 to provide rolling stock for the city's railway to Montreal. Its 285 male employees turned out locomotives, railway cars, steam engines, and a variety of casting and machine work. Two factories employed over 100 hands in food processing: Burnham & Morrill canned fish and vegetables, while the Maine Beet Sugar Company tried to satisfy everyone's sweet tooth. Shaw and Goding employed 150 hands in a shoe trade that serviced the northern New England market. Finally, we should note parenthetically that Portland also contained at least two canning companies that employed hundreds, perhaps even thousands, on a seasonal basis.

Saint John actually contained more large factories than Portland did at this time. The twelve factories employing 100 or more hands provided jobs for 1,610 people who represented 24 per cent (or five per cent more than

Portland's) for this category. The 24 firms employing 40–99 hands hired
1,464 people, the exact same proportion (24 per cent) for this category in
Portland. The 16 firms engaging 30–39 employees provided jobs for 519
hands representing 7 per cent of the city's workforce (4 per cent less than
Portland's). Five of Saint John's dozen large factories we saw, planing, or
molding mills which operated seasonally. The largest foundry, J. Harris
and Company, employed 300 men to turn out rails and rolling stock for the
region's railways. The New Brunswick Cotton mill's 1089 women or girls
and 43 men specialized in flannelette yarn for use in Upper Canada. Two
construction firms, a men's clothing factory, a shipyard, and a stone mill
rounded out the group of larger enterprises in the Fundy port at this time.

During the transition to Monopoly Capitalism, each city sought to
enlarge its hinterland. In the 1880s Portland still handled most of Canada's
winter port trade, but the effects on the city's economy appeared uneven at
best, in part because control was in the hands of external corporate and
political leaders.[15] An improvement in the volume of trade in the early
1880s was followed by a sharp decline toward the end of the century. The
downturn resulted from depression conditions and from Portland's
inadequate terminal; the grain elevator, for instance, could load only one
ship per week. The slow decline of the South American timber market and
the sudden decision by West Indies planters to market their sugar in cloth
bags rather than wooden boxes added to the port's problems. The Maine
city's port facilities became increasingly antiquated.

Perhaps because the city of Portland was still paying interest and
principal on nearly a million dollars in bonds for now bankrupt railways to
the west, business elites relied upon the private rather than the public sector
to make harbour improvements. Nevertheless the Grand Trunk Railway
spent a mere $40,000 in 1886 to rebuild its wharf, and the Maine Central
Railroad financed hardly any harbour improvements at all. Washington
continued to dredge Portland harbour, but there was no additional aid
from the city, state, or federal governments for wharves, sheds, additional
grain elevators, or a dry-dock, despite recognition in some quarters that the
port was inadequate in all these areas.

Then the Canadian wheat boom began at the turn of the century.
Portland freight sheds seemed ready to burst with merchandise. Railway
cars clogged Grand Trunk sidings and timekeepers rushed around the
wharves night and day, trying to keep track of crews of longshoremen. A
record fifty-four steamers departed from Portland in 1897. Under the
aggressive leadership of the Grand Trunk's new manager, the railway
began a major new investment of over $2 million in its Portland facilities.
Two huge new grain elevators with a combined capacity exceeding two
million bushels soon dominated the Maine city's skyline, enabling three
ships to be loaded simultaneously. The Army Corps of Engineers was
persuaded to dredge the harbour to a depth of 30 feet at low tide. Working
through a lobbying agency, Portland board of trade officials badgered the

government to station a ship nearby to destroy derelict vessels. Although they failed to persuade the navy to establish a base or construct a dry-dock at Portland, they pressed successfully for greater fortification of the harbour. Within four years, well over a million dollars was spent by the war department to construct or improve Portland's coast defence fortifications against a possible attempt by British forces to use the Grand Trunk to ferry troops and supplies into the Canadian interior. The thousand-odd artillerymen seconded to these installations aided the local economy; their batteries provided Portlanders with one of the most heavily fortified harbours in the nation. These new forts, along with a new lightship, a new revenue cutter, and a new immigration quarantine station, also testified to the political clout of Main congressmen as well as to current military strategy. But these piecemeal gifts failed to blend into a coordinated program of port expansion and development, and civic and business leaders ultimately adopted a new strategy based on tourism.

In the latter part of the 19th century, steamers plying the waters between Boston, New York City, and Portland began to deposit thousands of visitors in hotels and cottages on the shores of Casco Bay. By the turn of the century, this stream had grown into a torrent of 200,000 tourists who spent somewhere between $10 million and $50 million in Maine. Portland officials began to look at their city with a tourist's eye. Why did tourism rather than the winter port trade capture the imagination of Portland's civic and business leaders? Tourist dollars seemed to be more evenly distributed throughout the business community. It was well nigh impossible, merchants declared, 'to name a branch of trade that has not been directly or indirectly benefited by our ever-increasing summer tourist business', which was believed to be worth a million dollars a year to Portland. While this amounted to just two-thirds of the estimated annual winter port earnings, tourism was believed to have a more positive effect on property values. Moreover, it was easy for civic leaders to quantify the beneficial effects of this wonderful new 'industry', and consequently they were able to generate public support for it. The tourist industry also prompted Portland businessmen to cultivate their northern New England market rather than the more elusive Canadian hinterland. Later, light manufacturing joined tourism, retailing, and the convention business as additional elements in Portland's new development strategy. Far better than the grimy factories employing numerous immigrants from southeastern Europe that had sprouted up on the Portland waterfront, the new strategy meshed with middle-class Portlanders' image of their town as one filled with clean, tree-lined avenues, fresh air, beautiful vistas, and pleasant shopping areas uncultured by the 'rabble' from Europe.

Neither public officials nor private businessmen in Saint John shared such disdain for port-related enterprise. They joined together in the 1880s to make the New Brunswick port the ocean terminal of Canada's great new Canadian Pacific Railway. At the end of the decade a 482-mile 'short line' track was completed from Montreal across northern Maine to the New Brunswick port. The arrival of CPR trains in Saint John completed the first stage of that city's campaign to displace Portland as Canada's winter port. The second stage began when local officials invested public funds in waterfront development, aided by a provision in Saint John's royal charter granting ownership and control of the harbour to the city. By 1904 Saint John had invested approximately $900,000 in dredging, wharves, warehouses, and related facilities. At a time when British and Canadian imperialists were calling for the economic and strategic integration of the Empire, two of the board of trade's officers capitalized on talk about a subsidized 'Fast Atlantic' steamship service between England and its senior dominion. When the initial contract fell through, they persuaded a small steamship company that had participated in the Portland service to make Ottawa a reduced request. A subsidy was agreed upon and regular trips between Liverpool and Saint John began during the winter of 1895/96, generating more optimism among all the classes in Saint John than had been felt for years.

Saint John businessmen henceforth received crucial assistance from a succession of Grit and Tory cabinet members who regularly advocated Saint John's winter port development strategy in federal cabinet meetings. As a result, the goals of both private businessmen and politicians were generally better harmonized and achieved in Saint John than in Portland. During the first two decades of the twentieth century, the Canadian federal government invested nearly $14 million in harbour improvement. Port-related business stimulated a flow of capital into Saint John's construction, metals, and provisioning industries. It also spawned new enterprise such as shipbuilding and repairing, and sugar-refining. In short, the New Brunswick city had used its harbour to reach beyond its own constricting hinterland and enhance some of its metropolitan functions. But this strategy was not without its costs for both business elites and workers. Henceforth the port-related activities were to be controlled from Montreal and Ottawa rather than by local interests. Civic leaders and businessmen countered by mobilizing the community across class lines on behalf of the city, port, and region. In short, Portland avoided a substantial increase in the penetration of monopoly capital by opting instead for a wide range of service industries. Largely because of its close proximity to these major American centers, the city attracted and redistributed surplus value generated for monopoly capitalists in places like Boston, New York, and Philadelphia. Saint John, however, did not have the tourism/retailing option and instead fell into the tight embrace of Montreal corporate interests. Saint John's winter port development firmly enmeshed the city in the creation of surplus value for Canada's huge privately- owned transportation system, the Canadian Pacific Railway.

The results of these two development strategies can be seen in the changing economies of the two cities.[16] By 1913/14, Portland had become an important regional centre for the manufacture of wearing apparel distributed throughout the region's booming mill towns. Three shoe factories employed a total of nearly 600 people; a hat firm provided jobs for over 200, and three women's wear concerns employed a total of 400. In metals, the Portland Company remained the largest firm in the city, employing 400 men to service the equipment needs of the burgeoning pulp and paper industry, while T. Loughlin produced a wide variety of marine hardware for both commercial and pleasure craft. Firms manufacturing window screens (for tourist cottages), wooden boxes, canned goods, and sewer pipe rounded out the list of Portland's largest employers on the eve of the First World War.

Lumber products still dominated Saint John's roster of large factories. Six mills operated seasonally along the banks of the St. John River, while a pulp mill and box factory drew upon the same timber resource. Six large firms produced metal goods ranging from engines and boilers to sheet iron and wire nails. The largest single employer, a direct product of the city's new winter port strategy, was the Atlantic Sugar Refinery with 450 hands and controlled by Montreal interests. Other large firms specialized in cotton yarns and sheeting, brushes, biscuits, and coffee and tea.

The shift in the winter port trade from Portland to Saint John exerted a significant impact on overall capitalization and productivity. Initially, Portland's entrepreneurs had invested about twice as much capital in their businesses as Saint John's, but by 1910/11 Saint John had caught up with Portland (Table 4). By 1919, despite the Fundy City's significantly smaller size, entrepreneurs had invested over $26 million there in comparison to Portland's $22 million. The dollar value of the products of these factories and workshops reveals a similar trend. At the turn of the century, Portland produced goods worth almost twice as much as Saint John. But only two decades later, the dollar value of the New Brunswick city's goods exceeded Portland's by 25 per cent.

Changes in the method of counting manufacturing establishments make it more difficult to compare these figures. But by 1910/11 both countries had adopted the same criteria. Comparing the 1910/11 and 1919 date, it is evident that the smaller New Brunswick city had matched its Maine rival in the number of workshops, while the number of employees in Portland exceeded Saint John's by 13 per cent. Hence we can conclude that Saint John probably had a larger number of small shops than Portland did. By the end of World War I, the proportion of the workforce employed in large factories had more than doubled in both. As Table 5 shows, in Portland it grew from 19 per cent of the labour force in firms of 100 + hands (1880) to 44 per cent by 1913/14; in Saint John it grew even more from 24 per cent of firms of 100 + hands (1878) to 58 per cent by 1914. By this time 14 per cent more Saint John workers toiled in factories of 100 + hands as compared with Portland's workforce. Recall that this gap had widened from 5 per cent in 1880. Far from lagging behind Portland's industrial capitalist expansion, as the textbooks in Canadian economic history would imply, this data indicates that the structure of development in Saint John, stimulated doubtless by the expansion of port-related activities, matched or exceeded Portland's. On this data alone, one would expect to find the same (or even slightly greater) rates of working-class mobilization in Saint John as in Portland during the transition to Monopoly Capital, rather than the lesser rates posited by the Lipset hypothesis.

Rates of capital invested per worker offer another measure with which to explore the intensification of the labour process resulting from the introduction of new machinery. Data obtained from the censuses reveals the extent of capitalization across industrial sectors in both cities. Unfortunately, comparative data is not available at this time for either 1880/81 or 1920/21. Table 6 reveals that Portland's investment per worker exceeded Saint John's in 24 industries representing a broad spectrum of sectors. In some cases, as in boots and shoes, the amounts are relatively close and suggest comparable levels of technology used in the labour process. In other cases, though, as in foundries in 1910/11, the amount of capital per worker in the Maine city was more than double that invested in the Fundy port. The same Table reveals those six industries where investment levels were at comparable levels and also shows data from 9 industries where Saint John entrepreneurs had invested more capital per worker than their Portland counterparts.

Since nearly all of the available census data is limited to the decade of the 1890s, no generalizations can be offered yet for the full period from 1880 to 1920. But from what has already been said about the relative disparity in urban populations as well as in aggregate production and capitalization levels, we can see that investment per capita figures tend to reinforce the overall pattern already elucidated. In that decade Portland elites invested 30 to 50 per cent more capital overall than their counterparts in the Fundy port. Nevertheless, aggregate Saint John investment, as we have seen in Table 4, caught up with Portland's in 1910/11 and substantially exceeded it by 1919. Much of this was probably associated with winter port development after the turn of the century. Finally, we must remember that this table ignores industries unique to each city.

We can correct for that distortion by listing the top 10 industries among *all* those listed in the census data for each city. Thus, the industries such as the cotton mills in Saint John or the canning factories in Portland are included in Table 7. By ranking these industries according to the amount of capital per worker from highest to lowest values, we can make a crude estimate of the relative intensity of capital in various sectors. Some, such as flour mills and patent medicines, were capital- intensive by nature and remained high on the list in both cities throughout the transition to Monopoly Capital. Tables 6 and 7 also help us to identify the leading industrial sectors in each city during a particular decade. Overall, Portland's largest, most capital-intensive, and presumably profitable industries could be found in foundries, food processing, men's and ladies' clothing, boots and shoes, furniture, and cooperage among others. Saint John specialized in cotton, railway rolling stock (at least until the departure of the Harris Company to Amherst, N.S. in 1891), metal working and printing and publishing. Both cities shared a substantial number of industries in common. More importantly, despite variations in some industrial sectors, both cities appear to have experienced quite similar *patterns* of economic change during the transition to Monopoly Capital, thanks to such common features as geographical location, the winter port trade, and an urban satellite status.

IV. Social Formation of the Working Classes

No one will be surprised to learn that the workforce in both cities during the transition to Monopoly Capital was overwhelmingly male. But Table 8 reveals some interesting variations. First of all, Saint John counted nearly half-again as many children under the age of 16 years at the workplace in 1880 as Portland enumerators did. Thereafter the percentage of youngsters fell precipitously in both cities before it disappeared altogether. The figures from Portland suggest that children took the place of male workers; in Saint John, they more likely supplanted women at the workplace. Finally, in Portland the percentage of women workers rose 5 per cent between 1880 and 1920, whereas in Saint John the proportion of females in the labour force actually declined between 1891 and 1921.

Data from the census on occupations for 1910/11 and 1920/21 in Table 9 reveal those industrial sectors where women found employment in larger or smaller numbers. In both Portland and Saint John, the percentage of women employed in manufacturing declined. Opportunities in clerical (trade) positions increased by nearly the same proportion in the two cities. The proportion of women in the professions increased in Saint John but remained the same in Maine's largest city; the trend was reversed in the traditional female work associated with domestic service. Finally, opportunities in transportation doubled for Saint John women but increased only marginally in Portland. As a whole the proportions of male and female workers remained unchanged in Portland, whereas the percentage of women workers in Saint John went up by just one point. Perhaps the most important observation to make concerns the nearly identical proportions of women workers in manufacturing during the last decade of this period. At the aggregate level, then, it appears unlikely that gender divisions within the industrial workforce mediated sharply contrasting working-class responses during the last decade of the transition to Monopoly Capital.

The data on the distribution of occupations according to sectors reinforces a number of points made earlier in this paper. Manufacturing declined marginally in Portland between 1910/11 and 1920/21 but fell more sharply in Saint John, suggesting the relatively greater syphoning effects of Montreal over Boston. Portland's strategy of promoting regional trade probably accounts for the significantly larger share of occupations in the clerical sector. Whereas professional and public service occupations increased 3 percentage points in Saint John during this period, they unaccountably fell by one point in Portland. The proportions engaged in domestic service fell in both cities. Finally, in the absence of major increases in manufacturing or transportation sectors, it seems likely that large amounts of the capital investment noted earlier for Saint John in Table 4 went directly into fixed plant costs (i.e., dry-dock, sugar refinery) rather than into more labour-intensive industries.

V. Mobilization of Workers

As we have already seen, by 1880 both cities had already experienced significant industrial capitalist development. A substantial proportion of the labour force in Portland and Saint John was employed in large factories of 100 or more hands that used steam or water-powered machinery. As a result, several of the more highly skilled workers in particular had already organized into trade unions, some purely local groups and others affiliated with international unions headquartered in the United States. In this section we shall compare the mobilization of workers in Portland and Saint John, first at the workplace and then at the ballot box. If the working class of Saint John behaved according to the 'national values' hypothesis of Lipset, we should find significantly lower levels of economic and political mobilization among the presumably more deferential Saint John workers than among their counterparts in Portland.

I am still assembling data on the trade union, strike, and political activity of workers in Portland and Saint John between 1880 and 1920, and at this stage only a fraction can be presented in a comparative format. Hence this section offers impressionistic evidence derived from work still in progress on both cities, supplemented by a few tables presenting comparative data.

First, Portland. The oldest trade union, the longshoremen's protective association, was founded in 1880, and shortly thereafter locals of the printers, cigarmakers, and a few other national crafts appeared.[17] During the 1880s the Maine city was one of the top ten centers of activity by the Knights of Labour. Four assemblies in Portland focused their largely successful political efforts on getting the state legislature to enact a child labour law and establish a bureau of labour. Many women and children worked at this time in Portland shoe and match factories. While there seem to have been no large strikes, smaller ones occurred among cigarmakers, boilermakers and construction workers. Both depression conditions and stiffening employer resistance made the Nineties more difficult for Portland workers. The master builders organized an exchange in 1890 and defeated a plasterer's strike. Stonemasons organized in 1894. Lasters struck at one of the shoe factories but lost their struggle.

In contrast, workers in Saint John seemed somewhat better organized in the late 19th century. Powerful organizations of ship-labourers and millmen had flourished in mid-century before falling on hard times in the Depression-ridden 1870s.[18] By the Eighties, as Table 10 reveals, at least 14 labour organizations had been established, dominating labour markets through their craft exclusivity as well as by means of a head tax levied by the city government on non-resident labour. Most of these organizations were purely local.[19] The city's workers were virtually untouched by the Knights of Labour or any other outside influence, which may be one reason why they were pronounced nearly 'dead' by a visiting labour leader from Toronto in 1889. Responding perhaps to John Armstrong's criticism, Saint John workers demonstrated strong cross-craft solidarity only a year later in successfully pushing for the 9-hour day. On the eve of the Depression of 1893, Forsey counts 13 locals in the Fundy port, with four of them affiliated to international trade unions. Essentially, these organizations represented only those workers in the building trades or on the waterfront, which is probably why the city's trade council collapsed after a brief spell.

The turn of the century ushered in a wave of trade-union organization in both cities. For Saint John, it signaled the end of the city's relative isolation from continental pulls. The AFL's Canadian organizer visited the city in 1901, linking many more of Saint John's workers to external labour markets at the same time that the Montreal Shipping Federation was exerting control over the new winter port facilities.[20] Table 11 compares the distribution of trade union locals in Portland and Saint John by industrial sectors between 1902 and 1919. By the conclusion of the turn-of-the-century organization drives, both cities claimed roughly the same number of locals distributed in a parallel manner throughout their urban economies. Construction and railway running trades led the way with metal workers close behind. These gains had been won through many hard-fought struggles by moulders, printers, longshoremen and several other trades in both cities. Economic downturns in 1907–1909 and in 1912–1914 reverberated more sharply through Saint John's staples-dependent economy.

Conditions stabilized for workingmen's organizations during the early war years as a surge of 'new union' activity burst forth in both cities. Inflation and postwar economic dislocation provoked a rash of strikes. Millmen in Saint John, laundry workers and fish handlers in Portland, and public service workers in both communities, among many others, organized into nationally or internationally affiliated locals. However, postwar economic and social dislocation appear to have generated a much sharper revolt in Saint John than in Portland, judging by the number of trade union locals formed in 1919. Even so, a year later the American Federation of Labour's Portland organizer boasted that his district was about 95 per cent organized. It will be interesting to compare both the number of striker-days in both cities during this period as well as to determine the proportion of strikes that were waged for purely economic reasons as opposed to those involving control over the workplace. It is here, most likely, that Lipset's hypothesis will face the crucial test.

In both Portland and Saint John, workers mobilized politically after the turn of the century.[21] In the New Brunswick port, however, working-class representation at the municipal level was made all but impossible by city-wide voting on candidates from working-class wards. In 1904, the longshoremen and their supporters managed to elect one of their number to a single term on the city council. In sharp contrast, Table 12 shows that recently mobilized Portland workers, particularly those living in the most heavily industrialized first and second wards, chose 'class' representatives on a regular basis after 1900. Meanwhile, frustrated Saint John workers, unable to elect one of their own on a city-wide ticket, finally organized a municipal labour party to contest office in 1912 and 1914 in failed efforts to elect one of their own to city council. After the war they put up labour candidates for both provincial and federal office. The best explanation for this divergence lies not in the supposition that Canadian workers shared a national bias in favour of independent labour candidates, as Lipset argues, but rather in the structural differences between the two electoral systems.

This project is an exercise in comparative urban and labour history. It seeks first of all to compare the impact of industrial capitalism on the economic structures of two metropolitan centers, one American and the other Canadian, whose fates were intertwined. As we have seen both Portland and Saint John aspired to become major mercantile and manufacturing centers by exploiting their proximity to North Atlantic trade routes. Each in turn sought to escape the limits imposed by its own immediate hinterland through the establishment of a rail connection with Montreal in order to tap a vaster area of continental scope during the four or five months when the Gulf of St. Lawrence was frozen.

While neither city was successful in escaping from its satellite status in relation to the dominant metropolitan centers of Boston and Montreal, the economies of both experienced significant change during the transition to Monopoly Capital. Portland shifted emphasis from port-related activities to merchandising consumer goods and promoting tourism. Saint John plumbed for the winter port trade formerly controlled by Portland and attracted substantial new public and private investment in port-related activities. The census data between 1880 and 1921 analyzed in this paper suggests important structural similarities lying beneath surface variations. From the viewpoint of the workers, perhaps most important was the fact that neither city spawned large firms employing many hundreds or thousands of workers; instead, both cities increased the proportion of their labour forces working in factories of 100 to 500 hands. Age and gender divisions as well as the distribution of occupations in the two cities suggest quite similar socio-economic processes at work in Portland and Saint John.

The second purpose of this project is to discover whether the responses of Canadian workers in Saint John, New Brunswick, to industrial capitalism were mediated or not by so-called national values as defined by the sociologist S. M. Lipset and others. Although 'the jury' is still deliberating on this question, the scattered evidence presented in the last section of this paper undermines Lipset's contentions. In both their economic and political mobilization, workers in Portland and Saint John seem to have responded in basically similar ways. The differences are better explained by examining local conditions or structural features of the economic and political systems rather than by reference to all-pervasive national values.

Notes

I am indebted to my colleague, Professor Jacques Ferland, for helpful comments on an earlier draft of this essay.

1 Robert H. Babcock, *Gompers in Canada: A Study in American Continentalism Before the First World War* (1974).

2 Hartz *et al.*, *The Founding of New Societies* (1964); Gad Horowitz, *Canadian Labor in Politics* (1968); Lipset, *The First New Nation* (1963); "Revolution and Counter-Revolution — the United States and Canada", in T. R. Ford, ed., *The Revolutionary Theme in Contemporary America (1965)*; "Canada and the United States: The Cultural Dimension", in C. F. Doran and J. H. Sigler, eds., *Canada and the United States* (1985), 109–160. For a text that relies heavily upon these ideas, see K. McNaught, *The Pelican History of Canada, Revised Edition* (1982).

3 For example, G. F. Kealey, *Toronto Workers Respond to Industrial Capitalism 1867–1892* (1980); B. D. Palmer, *A Culture in Conflict: Skilled Workers and Industrial Capitalism in Hamilton, Ontario, 1860–1914* (1979); A Dawley, *Class and Community: The Industrial Revolution in Lynn* (1976).

4 Carlos Schwantes, *Radical Heritage: Labor, Socialism, and Reform in Washington and British Columbia, 1885–1917* (1979)

5 Bloch, "Toward a Comparative History of European Societies", (1928) in F. C. Lane and J. C. Riemersina, eds., *Enterprise and Secular Change* (1953), 494–521.

6 For examples, see C. Degler, *Neither Black nor White: Slavery and Race Relations in Brazil and the United States* (1971); H. Klein, *Slavery in the Americas: A Comparative Study of Virginia and Cuba* (1967).

7 M. A. Goldberg and J. Mercer, *The Myth of the American City: Continentalism Challenged* (1986).

8 Bloch, *op.cit.*

9   For background see R. Babcock, "Economic Development in Portland (Me.) and Saint John (N.B.) During the Age of Iron and Steam, 1850–1914", *American Review of Canadian Studies* IX (Spring, 1979), 3–37; "The Rise and Fall of Portland's Waterfront, 1850–1920, " Maine Historical Society *Quarterly* XI (Fall, 1982), 63–93.

10 The best history of Saint John from its founding to the Confederation period is the recent study by T. W. Acheson, *Saint John: The Making of a Colonial Urban Community* (1985). For Portland, there is the outdated and less useful volume by A. Moulton, *Portland by the Sea* (1926).

11 Besides Babcock, "Economic Development", cited above, see also Laura E. Poor, *The First International Railway: Life and Writings of John Alfred Poor* (1892) on the major promoter of a shorter route to Europe.

12 M. E. Angus, "The Politics of the 'Short Line'", unpublished MA thesis, University of New Brunswick, 1958.

13 See E. Elwell, *The Successful Business Houses of Portland* (1875); *Saint John and Its Business* (1875).

14 (Portland) U.S. Census, 1880; (Saint John) "Report of Edward Willis on Manufacturing Industries of Certain Sections of the Maritime Provinces", Canada, House of Commons, *Sessional Papers* (1885), No.37.

15 The next five paragraphs are condensed from R.Babcock, "Private vs. Public Enterprise: A Comparison of Two Atlantic Seaboard Cities, 1850–1925", in G. Stelter and A. Artibise, eds., *Power and Place: Canadian Urban Development in the North American Context* (1986), 51–81.

16 (Portland) State of Maine, *Second Biennial Report of Dept. of Labor and Industry, 1913–14* (Waterville, 1915); (Saint John) *Saint John New Brunswick Canada, Canada's Winter Shipping Port* (Saint John, 1914).

17 For background see C. A. Scontras, *Two Decades of Organized Labor and Labor Politics in Maine 1880–1900* (1969).

18 See R. Rice, "The History of Organized Labor in Saint John, N.B., 1813–1898", unpublished MA thesis, University of New Brunswick, 1968.

19 E. Forsey, *Trade Unions in Canada 1812–1902* (1982), 298–303.

20 Babcock, *Gompers in Canada*, 46.

21 This is discussed in greater detail in Babcock, "Labor, Socialism, and Reform Politics in Portland (Me.) and Saint John (N.B.), 1895–1914", unpublished paper presented at the Canadian Historical Association meetings, June 1980.

Table 1. A Comparison of the populations of Portland and Saint John and their hinterlands, 1880-1920.

	1880-81	1890-91	1900-01	1910-11	1920-21
PORTLAND	33,810	36,425	50,145	58,571	69,272
SAINT JOHN	41,353	39,179	40,711	42,511	47,166
CUMBERLAND COUNTY	75,723	90,949	100,689	112,014	124,376
SAINT JOHN COUNTY	52,966	49,574	51,759	53,572	60,486
Proportion of City Population in County: percent					
PORTLAND	44.6	40.0	49.8	52.3	55.7
SAINT JOHN	78.1	79.0	78.7	79.4	78.0
MAINE	648,936	661,086	694,466	742,371	768,014
NEW BRUNSWICK	321,233	321,263	331,120	351,889	387,876
Proportion of City Population in state/ province: per cent					
PORTLAND	5.2	5.5	7.2	7.9	9.0
SAINT JOHN	12.9	12.9	12.3	12.1	12.2

Source: U.S. and Canadian Census data

Table 2. Comparison of foreign-born population in Portland and Saint John, with percentages of the total foreign-born 1880/81-1920/21.

	1880/81 pop.	%age	1890/91 pop.	%age	1900/01 pop.	%age	1910/11 pop.	%age	1920/21 pop.	%age
Portland Canadian-born	4748	45	2923	37	4376	42	4529	37	5029	38
Saint John American-born	717	9	384	11	1026	18	785	18	967	20
Portland English/Welsh born	907	9	554	7	612	6	679	6	276	2
Saint John English/Welsh born	1186	16	747	22	1103	19	1155	27	1592	33
Portland Scots-born	255	5	190	2	223	2	222	2	253	2
Saint John Scots-born	654	9	335	10	478	8	433	10	455	9
Portland Scandinav-born	351	3	507	7	873	8	932	8	957	7
Saint John Scandinav-born	34	—	14	—	78	1	62	1	89	2
Portland German-born	142	1	132	2	205	2	189	2	127	1
Saint John German-born	59	1	40	1	52	1	59	1	17	0.4
Portland Russian-born							1333	11	1103	8
Saint John Russian-born					180	3	330	8	349	7
Portland Asian-born	8	—	22	—	30	—	38	—	43	—
Saint John Asian-born			3	—	42	1	45	1	181	4
Portland Irish-born	3941	57	3140	40	3273	31	2952	24	2425	18
Saint John Irish-born	4922	64	1755	51	2233	38	776	18	429	9
PORTLAND FOREIGN-BORN	6902	20	7825	22	10435	21	12151	21	13346	19
SAINT JOHN FOREIGN-BORN	7666	19	3452	9	5803	11	4303	10	4836	10

Source: U.S. and Canadian censuses

Table 3. Size of firms in Portland and Saint John, 1876-1880

PORTLAND £ factories	£ employees & %age	cohorts	SAINT JOHN £ employees & %age	£ factories
—	—	400+	—	—
—	—	300+	300 (4%)	1
1	285 (8%)	200+	—	—
2	415 (11%)	100+	1310 (20%)	11
4	425 (11%)	70+	724 (11%)	9
9	476 (13%)	40+	740 (11%)	15
12	393 (11%)	30+	519 (8%)	16
28	1994 (54%)	totals	3593 (54%)	52
	3714	workforce	6689	

Table 4.   A comparison of capital invested, values of products, number of establishments, and people employed in Portland and Saint John, 1880-1919.

	1880-81	1890-91	1900-01	1910-11	1919
Capital Invested:					
PORTLAND	$4,243,225	6,887,557	6,991,251	9,597,000	22,194,281
SAINT JOHN	$2,143,064	4,838,766	5,252,797	9,242,338	26,129,347
Value of Products:					
PORTLAND	$9,832,931	11,371,487	11,440,201	11,950,000	29,168,000
SAINT JOHN	$4,336,733	8,131,790	6,712,769	10,081,667	40,253,494
Number of Establishments:					
PORTLAND	302	662	639	271*	308*
SAINT JOHN	204	773	187*	177*	307*
Number of Employees:					
PORTLAND	7,129	5,338	5,699	5,891	6,710
SAINT JOHN	2,690	5,888	4,688	5,270	5,855

Table 5.   Size of firms in Portland and Saint John, 1913-14.

	PORTLAND			SAINT JOHN	
£ factories	£ employees & %age	cohorts	£ employees & %age	£ factories
1	400	400+	1300 (20%)	3
—	—	300+	300 (5%)	1
5	1141 (20%)	200+	675 (10%)	3
7	978 (17%)	100+	1515 (23%)	12
8	648 (11%)	70+	606 (9%)	8
15	764 (13%)	40+	1483 (23%)	21
3	93 (2%)	30+	337 (5%)	11
	4024 (71%)	totals	6216 (96%)	

Table 6a. Industries where Portland's investment per worker exceeded Saint John's with dates and amounts

sector	industry	census date	amount of investment per worrker	
			PORTLAND	SAINT JOHN
food & tobacco				
	flour mills	1890/91	$4000	$1600
		1900/01	5767	1817
		1910/11	4769	1519
	tobacco	1890/91	678	234
leather				
	harness, saddlery	1890/91	497	246
		1900/01	1129	328
	boots, shoes	1890/91	477	358
metals				
	blacksmithing	1890/91	467	358
	foundries	1890/91	2437	732
		1900/01	1867	1026
		1910/11	3344	1402
	tinware	1890/91	678	66
clothing				
	men's	1890/91	1138	126
		1900/01	718	432
	women's	1910/11	763	281
	dressmaking	1890/91	263	77
woodworking				
	carriages	1890/91	656	438
		1900/01	1446	981
		1910/11	1877	1500
	cooperage	1890/91	2795	387
	cabinetry	1890/91	815	724
		1900/01	3159	600
	planed lumber	1890/91	1677	479
		1900/01	1897	1059
		1910/11	2565	870
	coffins	1890/91	1795	320
	trunks	1890/91	1122	499
construction				
	carpenters	1890/91	691	208
	brick, tile	1900/01	769	600
	plumbing	1890/91	824	424
marine				
	shipbuilding	1890/91	1023	148
other				
	chemicals	1890/91	1056	576
	patent medicines	1890/91	3001	1001
	photography	1890/91	526	363
	awnings	1890/91	440	54

SOURCE: calculated from U.S., Canadian censuses

Table 6b. Industries where Saint John's investment per worker exceeded Portland's, with
dates and amounts

sector	industry	census date	amount of investment per worker	
			PORTLAND	SAINT JOHN
food & tobacco				
	tobacco	1900/01	$ 363	$ 481
	fish canning	1900/01	735	1731
printing & publishing				
	printing	1900/01	1234	1422
		1810/11	1189	1390
clothing				
	hats, millinery	1900/01	941	1054
construction				
	painters	1890/91	453	1012
other				
	dentistry	1890/91	318	3450
	dyeing	1900/01	955	1208
	soap, candles	1890/91	1410	2393
	watchmakers	1890/91	274	806

SOURCE: calculated from U.S., Canadian censuses

Table 6c. Industries where Portland's and Saint John's investment of capital per worker is
comparable, with dates and amounts

sector	industry	census date	amount of investment per worker	
			PORTLAND	SAINT JOHN
food & tobacco				
	bakeries	1900/01	$1103	$ 1200*
printing & publishing				
	printing	1890/91	856	885
metals				
	tinware	1890/91	678	667
woodworking				
	cabinets	1890/91	815	724
construction				
	brick, tile	1890/91	230	215
	plumbing	1900/01	876	830**

* = includes confectionary
** = includes tinsmithing
            SOURCE: calculated from U.S., Canadian censuses

Table 7. Rank Order of Capital Invested per Worker, Portland and Saint John, 1880, 1890/91, 1900/01, 1910/11, 1920

(Ten Leading Industries Only)

1880

Portland industry	amount
drugs	$2862
flour mills	2467
slaughtering	2239
leather	1802
planed lumber	1441
men's clothing	1323
tinware	1320
foundries	1252
coffins	1091
coffee, spice	1089

1890/91

Portland industry	amount	Saint John industry	amount
flour mills	$4000	elec. light	$7520
oil, lube	3945	paint works	5000
patent med.	3001	dentistry	3450
cooperage	2795	soap, candles	2393
foundries	2437	rope, twine	2226
clay products	2330	flour mills	1600
coffins	1795	leather	1459
planed lumber	1677	cotton mills	1358
monuments	1578	boatbuilding	1349
soap, candles	1410	brass found.	1134

1900-01

Portland industry	amount	Saint John industry	amount
flour mills	$5767	slaughtering	$2204
oil, lube	4228	flour mills	1817
cabinets	3159	fish canning	1731
elec. const.	2438	lime	1435
fruits, vegs	2235	printing	1422
planed lumber	1897	dyeing	1208
foundries	1867	bakeries	1200
flavoring ext	1671	planed lumber	1059
locks, guns	1553	hats, millin.	1054
carriages	1446	foundries	1026

1910/11

Portland industry	amount	Saint John industry	amount
flour mills	$4769	wood pulp	$4788
fruits, vegs	3564	iron, steel	2943
foundries	3344	slaughtering	2872
patent med.	3226	fish canning	2238
planed lumber	2565	bakeries	1987
confectionery	2245	flour mills	1519
tinware	1887	carriages	1500
carriages	1877	log prod.	1498
bricks, tile	1778	foundries	1402
marble	1566	printing	1390

1920

Portland industry	amount
flour mills	$30,496
flavoring ext.	7771
fish canning	4976
awnings, tents	4453
foundries	4234
printing/pub	3924
confectionery	3893
malt liquors	3381
planed lumber	3376
mineral waters	3300

SOURCE: compiled from U.S., Canadian censuses

Table 8. Workforce—Age and Gender Divisions in Portland and Saint John, 1880/81-1920/21 (percentages)

census year	Portland male	female	children	Saint John male	female	children
	68%	22%	10%	74%	12%	14%
1880/81	79	21	n/a	64	28	8
1890/91	75	24	0.5	77	23	n/a
1900/01	73	27	n/a	77	23	n/a
1910/11	73	27	n/a	76	24	n/a
1920/21						

SOURCE: U.S., Canadian census data

Table 9. Distribution of Occupations in Portland and Saint John, 1910-11

sector	Portland males	%age	females	%age	total	%age	Saint John female	%age	male	%age	total	%age
agriculture	467	98	9	2	476	2	6	2	282	98	288	2
mining	14	100	—	—	14	—	—	—	74	100	74	—
manufacturing	6663	82	1441	18	8104	31	1130	18	5216	82	6346	38
transportation	2888	96	109	4	2997	12	82	4	2024	96	2106	13
trade, clerical	5587	76	1775	24	7362	29	733	18	3276	82	4009	24
public service	1203	99	6	0.5	1209	5	24	3	714	97	738	4
professional	914	50	912	50	1826	7	479	51	456	49	935	6
domestic svce	1029	27	2787	73	3816	15	1335	67	664	33	2019	12
TOTALS	18,765		7,039		25,804		3,809		12,706		16,515	

DISTRIBUTION OF OCCUPATIONS IN PORTLAND AND SAINT JOHN, 1920-21

sector	Portland males	%age	females	%age	total	%age	Saint John female	%age	male	%age	total	%age
agriculture	481	98	9	2	490	2	1	—	270	100	271	1
mining	8	39	1	11	9	—	—	—	22	100	22	—
manufacturing	7841	85	1348	15	9189	30	821	16	4265	84	5086	28
transportation	4162	95	216	5	4377	14	229	18	2506	82	2735	15
trade, clerical	6355	69	2882	31	9237	30	1162	26	3272	74	4434	25
public service	999	99	11	1	1010	3	50	5	946	95	996	7
professional	1178	50	1197	50	2375	8	694	57	525	43	1219	10
domestic svce	1086	30	2516	70	3602	12	1192	6	602	34	1794	6
unspecified							131	12	935	88	1066	
TOTALS	12,110		8179		30,289		4292		13,709		18,001	

SOURCE: U.S., Canadian census data

Table 10. Trade Union Locals in Saint John, 1881-1902

1881*	1883*	1887	1888	1889	1890
carpenters	boilermakers	barbers organized	stonecutters	cartmen	carpenters
bakers	bakers		scowmen	painters	millmen organized
cabinetmakers	cartmen			shiplaborers	plumbers organized
caulkers	cabinetmakers			tailors	shiplaborers-2
boilermakers	carpenters			tinsmiths	
painters	caulkers				
sailmakers	masons & plasterers				
shipcarpenters	moulders				
shiplaborers	painters				
	shiplaborers				
	shipcarpenters				
	sailmakers				
	tinsmiths				
	tailors				

1892*	1894	1895	1900*	1902*
bricklayers†	bricklayers†	caulkers	bricklayers†	masons & plasterers
carpenters †	carpenters†	cartmen	caulkers	bricklayers†
cartmen	carriageworkers	bricklayers	printers†	carpenters†
moulders†	cartmen	moulders	shiplaborers-2	cigarmakers†
painters	millmen	printers†	shoe clerks	molders†
printers 85†	moulders 277†	shiplaborers-2		freightlandlers†
millmen	shiplaborers-2	stenographers		painters†
shipcarpenters	printers†			shingle weavers†
shiplaborers-2				shiplaborers
stonecutters				teamsters†
Shipwrights				woodworkers
tinsmiths				

* = complete roster
† = local of an international union

SOURCE: Forsey, *Trade Unions in Canada*, 298-303

Table 11. Trade Union Locals in Portland and Saint John, 1902-1919.

sector	1902 P	1902 SJ	1903 P	1903 SJ	1904 P	1904 SJ	1905 P	1905 SJ	1906 P	1906 SJ	1907 P	1907 SJ	1908 P	1908 SJ	1909 P	1909 SJ	1910 P	1910 SJ
food/tobacco	2	1	2	2	2	2	2	2	2	1	1	1	1	1	1	1	—	1
leather	1	—	—	—	2	—	2	1	2	—	1	—	1	—	1	1	1	—
metals	2	2	2	6	2	4	4	4	5	3	5	4	4	4	2	3	1	3
clothing	—	—	—	1	—	1	—	1	—	4	—	4	—	4	—	3	—	—
woodworking	—	1	1	2	1	3	—	4	—	—	—	—	—	—	—	—	4	5
construction	5	3	5	4	6	5	5	5	5	3	5	3	5	3	6	3	7	5
marine	2	1	2	—	3	2	3	3	3	2	3	2	3	2	3	2	2	2
printing	2	1	2	2	2	2	2	2	2	2	2	2	2	2	2	2	2	2
transport	9	7	8	7	8	9	8	8	7	8	7	8	8	8	6	6	12	7
electrical	—	—	—	—	1	1	—	1	—	—	1	—	1	—	1	1	—	1
other	2	2	4	—	8	3	4	—	5	4	5	5	5	4	5	6	10	6
city cntls	1	1	1	—	1	1	1	1	1	1	1	1	1	1	1	1	1	1
TOTALS	26	19	27	24	36	33	31	32	32	28	31	30	31	29	28	29	38	32

sector	1911 P	1911 SJ	1912 P	1912 SJ	1913 P	1913 SJ	1914 P	1914 SJ	1915 P	1915 SJ	1916 P	1916 SJ	1917 P	1917 SJ	1918 P	1918 SJ	1919 P	1919 SJ
food/tobacco	—	—	—	1	—	1	—	—	—	—	—	1	—	1	—	—	—	1
leather	—	—	—	—	1	—	—	1	—	1	—	—	—	—	—	—	—	—
metals	2	—	1	1	—	3	2	—	1	2	2	2	2	1	2	1	2	2
clothing	—	—	—	—	—	—	—	—	—	—	—	—	—	—	—	1	—	—
woodworking	1	2	1	—	1	1	1	4	1	—	1	—	1	—	1	—	1	—
construction	7	5	7	5	6	5	7	9	7	7	9	4	7	4	6	5	6	6
marine	4	2	4	2	4	7	4	9	5	7	5	4	2	5	3	5	3	3
printing	2	2	2	2	2	2	2	2	2	2	2	2	2	2	2	2	3	2
transport	7	9	9	9	9	9	8	10	9	11	6	9	8	9	6	9	6	12
electrical	—	—	—	—	—	—	—	—	—	1	—	1	—	1	—	—	—	—
other	11	2	10	2	10	3	10	—	10	5	9	4	8	4	11	3	12	5
city cntls	1	1	1	1	1	1	1	1	1	1	1	1	1	—	1	1	1	1
TOTALS	35	23	35	23	34	32	35	36	36	34	35	28	29	27	32	27	34	31

SOURCE: (US) Maine bureau of Industrial and Labour Statistics; Portland City Directories
(CDN) Labor Gazette

Table 12. Portland workers elected to positions on the Board of Aldermen or City Council, 1807-1921.
(By Wards)

1897	1898	1899	1900	1901	1902	1903	1904	1905	1906	1907
none	none	none	1-painter	1-painter	2-driver	3-heeler	3-heeler	2-wheelwright	2-wheelwright	2-wheelwright
				2-driver	3-heeler	2-driver		3-custodian	3-custodian	2-laborer
				3-heeler	3-molder					
				3-molder	4-telegraph operator					
				4-telegraph operator	9-compositor					
				9-compositor						

1908	1909	1910	1911	1912	1913	1914	1915
2-laborer	2-ry engineer	2-ry engineer	2-ry engineer	2-boilermaker	2-machinist	1-pressman	1-sailmaker
4-chauffer		4-chauffer	4-chauffer	2-plasterer	4-barber	2-machinist	1-truck driver
		5-painter	4-barber	4-barber	4-feeder	2-molder	1-pressman
			4-printer	8-machinist	9-barber	4-meter reader	2-molder
			9-chauffer	9-conductor		6-machinist	7-carpenter
						9-blacksmith	9-barber
							9-blacksmith

1916	1917	1918	1919	1921
1-pressman	1-pressman	1-pressman	1-plasterer	1-plasterer
1-truck driver	1-truck driver	1-plasterer	3-mason	2-truckman
2-molder	2-mason	2-mason	3-trunkmaker	4-car oiler
5-electrician	3-carpenter	4-laborer	9-helper	
3-blacksmith			5-machinist	
5-electrician			9-shipworker	
9-barber				
9-blacksmith				

SOURCE: Portland City Directories

3

The Second Industrial Revolution in Canada, 1890–1930

Craig Heron

In August 1889 a group of English businessmen on a tour of North America missed their train to New York at Niagara Falls. Someone evidently suggested to them that if they were bored with the wonders of the Niagara gorge, they could venture 40 miles back into Canada to visit the bustling factory centre of Hamilton, Ontario, where a summer carnival was in progress. These gentlemen did so, and were so impressed with the city that they stayed several weeks (a decision, I should hasten to add, that would make little sense to most Canadians a century later). They later wrote to the Hamilton Board of Trade recommending more publicity for what the locals liked to call "The Birmingham of Canada." The city fathers followed that advice and three years later produced a large, glossy, well-illustrated publication praising the city's industrial accomplishments for the benefit of the many travellers expected to visit the 1893 Chicago World's Fair.[1] Hamilton was one of the largest of several factory towns that had grown up since 1850 in central and eastern Canada during Canada's First Industrial Revolution, and that lavishly illustrated, boosterist booklet opens a window on the state of industrial development in such communities by the 1890s. Flipping through this publication, the late-twentieth-century reader would be struck not only by the charming elegance of the late Victorian factory architecture, but also by the astonishing variety of products turned out (beer, pork, glass, furniture, cutlery, carriages and wagons, lamps, woodenware, sundry leather goods, vinegar, coffins, pianos and organs, drugs, shoe polish, and countless other goods), by the generally small size of the factories (few had more than 200 employees), and by the prominence of local ownership and control. These were all key features in the first half century of Canadian industrialization. Before considering what was to follow in the next half century in industrial centres like Hamilton, we should pause to assess how far Canada had already leaped into the industrial capitalist age by the early 1890s.

In the first place, the opportunities available to the pioneering industrialists had been almost entirely in the home market. In fact, they had agitated successfully to have a high tariff wall erected around the manufacturing sector in 1879 in a conscious policy of import substitution.² Their strategy for industrial growth had been first and foremost to supply consumer goods to a large agrarian hinterland, which they hoped would continue to expand as the new Prairie region of western Canada was opened up with a new transcontinental railway and new immigration. The federal Conservative government had packaged this industrial development strategy in 1879 as the so-called 'National Policy'. Yet a decade later the difficulties of settling the West and creating the crucial consumer market were still preventing the fulfillment of that dream of an prosperous, integrated east-west economy.

As the Hamilton booklet revealed, with the important exception of the railways, the driving force behind most of this industrial development had been the individual entrepreneur, his family, and his short-term partners, all strongly rooted in a single town or city. Wealthier capitalists were controlling more of the country's trade and finance from the metropolitan centres of Montreal, Toronto, Halifax, and Saint John, but there were also still plenty of local merchants and bankers who often helped to promote industrial development in their own communities during these years. As a result of this pattern of entrepreneurship, industrialization before 1890 had been widely dispersed throughout the Maritime and central Canadian provinces (though in Quebec there was more concentration around Montreal), serving regional markets of rural and urban consumers and the expanding transportation sector. Aside from a few textile towns, there was relatively little specialization in the urban development of this first phase of industrialization.³

Another pattern dimly evident in the Hamilton booklet was in the modes of production found in Canadian factory life by 1890. Steam power had certainly transformed many industries, but, as in Britain, with the exception of the textile industry, the new technology that it ran was in most cases none too complex. Many industries had moved only a few steps away from handicraft production, and manual labour, both skilled and unskilled, was still heavily in demand. Workshops were still more common than full-fledged factories in most Canadian manufacturing industries.⁴ The vigour of organized craftsmen in the new craft unions of the late nineteenth century is therefore not surprising.⁵

Of course, manufacturing was by no means the only, or even the most important, sector in the late-nineteenth-century Canadian economy. It was still a relatively small island in quite a large sea of economic activity directed towards extracting natural resources for foreign markets. In the new industrial age before 1890, Canada's resource industries had changed considerably. Commercial agriculture had expanded in central Canada through the efforts of thousands of independent farm families, who still comprised by far the largest group of gainfully employed Canadians.⁶ Lumbering had replaced timber production as the major forest industry, in response to the rapidly growing demand in urban markets, especially in the United States.[7] Coal mining had developed into a significant industry at each end of the country, in Nova Scotia and British Columbia, to fuel North America's new steam-powered industries.[8] Oil was gushing out of many wells in southwestern Ontario. And the same new industrial demands had prompted isolated, largely unsuccessful efforts to mine iron, copper, and other minerals buried in the more rugged stretches of the Canadian landscape north of most areas of settlement.[9] But it is significant that aside from farming (and perhaps coal mining), little of this resource development was linked directly to the National Policy project that shaped manufacturing development. The forest and mining industries existed as a parallel stream of industrial development, most often physically isolated from the factory communities and attuned much more to highly unstable international markets for their products. The patterns of entrepreneurial ownership and limited technological development were nonetheless quite similar to those in manufacturing.

Finally, it is worth emphasizing that, as in most other settler dominions of the British Empire, [10] industrialists had recruited a work force for all this new activity not from an aboriginal population, but from the ranks of new British and American immigrants and the sons and daughters of the settled farming population. Class relations had therefore developed a pattern more similar to those in Britain, Europe, and the United States than to those found in most of the Third World.

At the moment when those English visitors passed through the "Birmingham of Canada, " then, Canada's industrial economy was relatively small-scale, decentralized, technologically simple, and divided into two quite different spheres — the National Policy economy of agriculture and manufacturing and the resource economy for export — which operated in quite different contexts.

The next half century would see profound changes in the Canadian industrial experience, although some features remained constant. In particular, the general structure of the economy did not change its essentially dualistic shape. The National Policy strategy of manufacturing and agriculture finally became a working proposition as the Prairie West began to fill up with settlers after the turn of the century. These new farmers were sending out bumper crops of wheat by World War I.[11] That economic framework would, of course, collapse completely in the Great Depression of the 1930s, when the bottom fell out of the wheat market. During these same years, natural resources continued to be extracted from the land and shipped out in an unprocessed or merely semi-processed form to foreign markets, especially in the United States.

Yet, within that general framework, the modes of capital accumulation were radically transformed in what amounted to a Second Industrial Revolution. The essential features of this transformation are certainly quite familiar to participants in a conference of this sort; so I will simply summarize quite briefly those that emerged in Canada. I am more interested in introducing some qualifications to the received wisdom about these changes and in pointing out the ways in which Canada departed from the familiar patterns of industrial development in the age of monopoly capitalism.

Nothing figures more prominently in that early-twentieth-century transformation than the emergence of the large corporation as the driving force of the industrial capitalist economy in Canada. The concentration of ownership and production that came to highlight Canadian economic activity took two forms. The first was the familiar American pattern of the large-scale merger; the second was the creation of brand new corporate megaprojects, often made possible by healthy injections of British and American capital. The railways had already consolidated into two giants by the 1880s, one of which, along with some bankrupt newcomers, would fall into the hands of the federal state by 1920.[12] The economic power of the privately owned Canadian Pacific Railway was truly awe-inspiring: by 1923 the corporation's diverse investments accounted for 21 per cent of the aggregate assets of the country's 100 largest corporations.[13] Corporate amalgamations in other sectors took place more slowly than in American industry in the same period. But after a minor flurry at the turn of the century, full-fledged merger mania broke out in the half decade before the war and again in the late 1920s (prompting in 1910 the only state measure in Canada to attempt to regulate the creation of what the Americans called 'trusts' — an ineffectual piece of legislation that was seldom invoked).[14] By the 1920s Canadian banks and other financial institutions had been reduced to a mere handful of extremely powerful corporate competitors.[15] Similarly a few electrical utilities empires held control of the new hydro-electric generating and transmission facilities and the urban street railways (until campaigns for public ownership succeeded in breaking the hold of some of these corporations).[16] At the same time, the resource industries, especially those extracting coal and forest products, saw some of the most remarkable concentrations of capital in the first three decades of this century (by the 1920s, for example, one corporation controlled all the coal, iron, and steel production in eastern Canada.)[17] And in manufacturing, large new corporations dominated several product markets, a tendency reinforced by the arrival of scores of branch plants of giant American manufacturing corporations.[18] These American firms were eager to overcome the Canadian tariff barriers, and by the turn of the century they were being welcomed by the civic leaders of manufacturing centres throughout central Canada (like the Birmingham of Canada).[19] As in the other industrial countries that these multinational corporations were penetrating in the same period, American ownership was concentrated for the most part in newer, technologically more sophisticated manufacturing industries, and overall remained an important but distinctly minority phenomenon in Canadian industrial life before World War II.

All of this corporate concentration of both domestic and American manufacturers brought about remarkable oligopolistic control of many markets by the early 1930s: one firm produced 90 per cent of Canada's cement; 83–90 per cent of tobacco production, canning, and meatpacking was controlled by two corporations in each case; three firms in each market controlled between 79 and 100 per cent of the output of automobiles, cotton, copper, and electrical equipment; three-quarters of the country's agricultural implements and rubber footwear were produced by four corporations in each industry; five turned out two-thirds of the rubber tires; five controlled 90 per cent of pulp and paper output; and five had the entire sugar-processing industry sewn up.[20] By 1930 control of Canadian industry had become as highly concentrated as almost any other major industrial country — a pattern that has held ever since.

Presiding over this new corporate economy was a tightly knit new national capitalist class based in Montreal and Toronto, with overlapping directorships controlling the major banks, railways, and utilities, and with investments in several of the major resource and manufacturing corporations.[21] These men were principally responsible for pulling together a new, more integrated national economy. In place of the decentralized, locally controlled industrial development of the late nineteenth century, Canada's haute bourgeoisie used their new corporate structures to consolidate production in larger centres, most often in central Canada. The Maritime provinces in eastern Canada were the big losers in this process. Many of their entrepreneurs entered the mergers and allowed the regions' plants to be closed down in preference to those in central Canada. Other Maritime businessmen simply conceded defeat to their central Canadian competitors. By the 1920s the Maritimes' economy had come to depend much more on resource extraction, and on supplying labour to other parts of industrialized North America.[22] The Prairie West and, for the most part, British Columbia also found their development restricted to extracting and shipping out resources that were at most only semi-processed — products such as canned fish, lumber, or nickel matte.[23] The chief beneficiaries of this process of industrial centralization were southern Ontario towns and cities and the Montreal metropolitan area. The geographic concentration was reinforced by the decisions of almost all the American branch plants in manufacturing to locate in central Canada. Within that region, moreover, the many industrially diverse manufacturing towns gave way to a smaller number of more specialized communities whose fortunes revolved increasingly around a single major industry — clothing in Montreal and Toronto, steel and metal fabrication in Hamilton, automobiles in Windsor and Oshawa, rubber goods in Kitchener, electrical parts in Peterborough, and so on. Within the new manufacturing centres, the use of space also changed. The new factories often went up in new industrial suburbs, and much of the older downtown manufacturing went into long-term decline. Similarly, older working-class neighbourhoods were overshadowed by large new residential areas, which often lacked the former easy proximity to the workplace (hence the growing networks of street railways). Working-class community life consequently had to be rebuilt in many cases.[24]

The great changes in industrial structure were not simply spacial. The new capitalists and their new corporations also created brand new industries. By the early 1900s Canada was becoming for the first time a major manufacturer of steel, electrical parts, chemicals, and numerous other producer goods, as well as new consumer products like automobiles, ready-made clothing, and processed food.[25] The dense forests of the uninhabited Canadian hinterland also allowed for the development of a brand new pulp and paper industry, which was turning out one of Canada's leading export commodities by the end of the 1920s.[26] The rugged northern regions of New Brunswick, Quebec, and Ontario and the interior of British Columbia also became dotted with large new hardrock mining operations to extract minerals hitherto ignored or undervalued — nickel, zinc, lead, copper, gold, silver, asbestos, and so on.[27] Several new centres of mineral processing grew up in these regions — Bathurst, Sudbury, and Trail, for example.

Overall, it would be difficult to exaggerate the proportions of these changes sweeping through the Canadian economy in the early 1900s. Such major economic growth required new construction project on an unprecedented scale — not merely the rapid expansion of urban residential, commercial, and industrial buildings, but also great extensions of the transportation networks, including two new railway lines across the West. In the years before World War I, Canada was caught up in the breathless exhilaration of a remarkable boomtime.

How, then, would Canadian workers have experienced these great changes of the Second Industrial Revolution? Many of them would have had to travel out to large new industrial suburbs on the outskirts of the industrial centres to look for work, rather than to the more central, downtown areas where nineteenth-century factories and workshops had been located. There they would often have found much larger plants built according to new principles, generally only one storey high and sprawling over acres of land to permit the easier flow of goods through production processes. They might also have encountered a more authoritarian demeanor on the new factory buildings, surrounded as they often were by high fences and guarded by company police.[26] The most striking changes, however, would have been evident on the job itself.

By the turn of the century, many Canadian industrialist were feeling the quickening pulse of potential profits, but frequently felt constrained by the existing methods of production in their mines and mills. In particular, they were troubled by the high cost, frequent scarcity, and obstreperousness of the many skilled workers they still needed, and by the unreliability and occasional rebelliousness of unskilled labour.[29] As in the United States, worker resistance and labour scarcity played the major roles in pushing many Canadian industrialists towards a new organization of production for their new plants. Employers looked to new industrial recruits, new technology, and new methods of managing labour.

After 1900, the Canadian federal government aggressively and successfully promoted large-scale immigration form the United States, Britain, and Europe to fill up the farmlands of the Prairie West. Many of these newcomers were available in the early years of their settlement to work for wages on a seasonal basis. But employers managed to pry open the immigration doors even wider to let in full-time skilled industrial labour, principally form England and Scotland, and increasing numbers of short-time migrants from southern and eastern Europe, most of whom did not plan to stay in Canada and who could be put to work at the hardest, most unpleasant, least skilled work for much cheaper wages. This new work force of highly mobile migrant labourers from peasant backgrounds in Europe was replenished regularly through the networks of ethnic intermediaries who organized the international commerce in migration, connected workers with jobs in Canada as well as the United States, and provided room and board during their stay in Canada. The railways, mine owners, and other western-Canadian employers also reached out to China, Japan, and India for labour, as they had been doing since the late nineteenth century, but a racist backlash from workers in British Columbia forced the federal government to curb the flow of new Asian immigration after 1908. Through their new industrial recruitment policies, Canadian industrialists thus gave the Canadian working class a new ethnic colouring (in Canada we like to use the pretentious word 'mosaic').[30]

Recruitment patterns were not all that was changing, however. Canadian employers in this period also put their workers to work on a lot of new machinery. This new wave of mechanization was both part of an accelerated process of diluting craft skill and, in contrast to much of British industry, a major effort to replace unskilled labourers -- massive, electric travelling cranes, small-gauge electric trains, conveyor belts, assembly lines, and, by the end of the period, fork-lift trucks run by gasoline-fuelled combustion engines.[31] Cheap electricity was the key new ingredient that made it so much easier to replace human muscle with machinery. One of the most striking consequences was the rapidly shrinking demand for children in the work force, who had been so important in the First Industrial Revolution. Some Canadian employers also began to turn to university-trained engineers and scientists to help solve specific production problems, improve quality control, and generally introduce more predictability into running an industrial enterprise. These men were injected into the terrain of the craftsmen, who had previously handled many of these concerns independently with more empiricism than formal theory. The Canadian state did its bit to nudge these developments along with relatively modest new technical training programmes in high schools and universities, as well as launching in 1916 what was to become the National Research Council (the same year that Britain, the United States, and several Commonwealth countries did the same).[32]

Canadian employers also turned to new managerial methods for controlling their workers, following closely the developments in the United States towards more centralised, authoritarian management.[33] The decentralized production systems that had left most shop-floor decision-making with craftsmen, subcontractors, or foremen were disrupted at the turn of the century by the new cost-accounting procedures of so-called 'systematic management'. Before World War I, there were some isolated but highly publicized Canadian experiments with the most sophisticated new managerial systems developed by Frederick Winslow Taylor and his disciples and imitators, and by the 1920s many more firms were buying into these new schemes for centralized planning and scheduling. In general, a more professionalized management, backed by a growing staff of female clerical labour, was taking hold.[34]

So the Second Industrial Revolution in Canada brought together a much more diverse work force in much larger, more mechanized workplace, in more centralized locations, under the control of much more powerful corporate employers. In the process, the occupational structure in that work force had moved away from the late-nineteenth-century pattern of owner, craftsmen, and labourers. Now the blue-collar jobs made up a hierarchy of subtler gradations, shading upward from the more limited numbers of labourers, through a great mass of semi-skilled machine-operators, to smaller numbers of skilled production workers and tradesmen. The expanded managerial function had also created a more differentiated white-collar hierarchy, from foremen through the growing army of clerical workers to top managers. The great gulf between blue and white collar workers that was such a hallmark of twentieth-century working-class formation in Canada as elsewhere had begun to open up. Women now had an expanded role in the waged economy, as their numbers grew in manufacturing, service, and clerical work.[35]

To the well-tuned ear, this may all sound a lot like the story that was unfolding in the United States at the same time — especially the importance of corporate concentration, mass-population methods, and ethnic and gendered recomposition of the work force. In fact, if our British visitors had been able to return forty years after their first visit, they would have found Hamilton's city fathers referring not to the Birmingham of Canada, but to the Pittsburgh of the North. The transformation does seem closer to the American pattern than to the British or European. But let me hasten to suggest some major qualifications both to the general pattern and to the specific Canadian experience.

In the first place, there has been a tendency in North American historiography and social theory to see all this technological and managerial innovation as spelling the end of skill within industry.[36] That perspective seems to me to be overly hasty and poorly documented (it has been resisted much more vigourously in Britain[37]). In all the technological change that characterized these years, there was relatively little full-fledged automation (the new automatic looms in the cotton plants were among the few major exceptions.[38]). In almost all cases, workers were required to activate the new machinery and often to guide its movements. In order to get the maximum production out of this new equipment, employers thus came to rely on the experience, responsibility, and competence of the thousands of new semi-skilled workers, who certainly lacked the occupational qualifications of craftsmen, but were more valuable than labourers.

They also still needed a considerable number of skilled workers, both for maintaining and setting up the machinery and, in many cases, for carrying out some lingering or newly created skilled tasks in the mainstream of the production process — blast-furnace keepers, open-hearth melters, and rollers in the steel industry, paper makers in the pulp and paper industry, tire-builders and pit-men in the rubber tire industry, and so on.[39] The new machines eliminated labouring jobs, reduced the size of the skilled labour force needed for a large output, and narrowed the range of skills in the workplace. But they did not allow employers to create a new work force of interchangeable parts that could be easily and painlessly replaced at the whim of management. Without this understanding of the ambiguous, unintended consequences of mechanization and managerial innovation in the Second Industrial Revolution in Canada and the United States, two developments are inexplicable: first, the corporations tries hard to hold on to their experienced work forces, especially through welfare programmes that tried to tie workers to their employers;[40] and, second, a new wave of industrial unionism was able to take off in the 1930s and 1940s. How could workers who no longer had any leverage on the job fight back so successfully? The answer, in part, must be that all their skills and their value to their employers had not been eliminated.

Since the new corporate employers were not able to find a final technological solution to 'the labour problem' in this period, they had to put more emphasis on new managerial methods for manipulating the labour power of their workers. We would be quite wrong, however, if we concluded that the managerial solution in Canadian (or American) workplaces lay simply in the hands of white-collared efficiency experts with their stop watches, any more than it did with new machinery. Beyond their general cost-accounting functions, these men had too limited an impact on Canadian factories and were generally useless in the country's extensive resource industries.[41] Far more important in solidifying managerial control over this new work world were versions of the more old-fashioned methods of the carrot and the stick. The stick came down hard on Canadian workers in the early twentieth century. The authoritarianism was absolute and probably more potent in the hands of large corporations than it had been with local entrepreneurs. It became a cornerstone of corporate management in Canada in the early twentieth century to have no truck nor trade with unions of any kind. That meant spying on, firing, and blacklisting any union activists. It meant stonewalling any unions that somehow managed to organize any of the help of imported strikebreakers, professional strikebreaking firms, and federal troops, all which were used much more frequently in Canada in the early 1900s than ever before.[42] It also meant leaving considerable power in the hands of front-line supervisors — the foremen and superintendents. Besides weeding out trouble-makers these shop-floor despots were encouraged to use a kind of regular bullying and harassment of workers to get maximum production that became known as the 'drive method'. In many cases, they also retained effective control over hiring, firing, and promotion, despite the development of centralized employment offices. Favouritism and other abuses were rampant under these circumstances.[43] Much recent writing on the development of North American management in the early twentieth century has overemphasized how much the development of more centralized, professionalized management clipped the wings of these lower-level company officials. In contrast, historians of the North American labour upsurge of the 1930s and 1940s have discovered that a central demand of the new industrial unionism was curtailing the arbitrary power of the foremen and superintendents with new grievance and seniority systems.[44] Before that point, Canadian and American employers still relied on the fear that this blunt, rough-edged supervision engendered to keep their workers in line.

At the same time, however, workers who kept their heads down and their noses clean were encouraged to expect that their corporate employers could meet some of their important material needs. New wage-incentive schemes like the premium bonus and so on promised increased income if workers produced more. Workers could also expect some limited job security and social mobility up a firm's internal job ladders, since the more skilled jobs in the new workplaces tended to be filled from inside the company. Similarly, the new welfare programmes appeared in a few plants before the war and then right across the industrial landscape during the crisis of post-war labour militancy and radicalism. These schemes often appealed to workers' concerns about economic security with such measures as pension plans, life insurance, and occasionally even profit-sharing.[45]

In the final analysis, however, it is the element of fear and insecurity that must remain at the centre of any understanding of early-twentieth-century managerial practices in Canada. The newer features of corporate labour policies — the bureaucracy of 'systematic' or 'scientific' management and the gentler touch of welfarism — had their role, but in the day-to-day administration of the workplace, it was the older methods and incentives that seemed to insure the fullest utilization of workers' labour power. Canadian employers in this Second Industrial Revolution offered their workers a trade-off based on personal self-interest: in return for complete obedience and passive acceptance of corporate control, the workers got the promise of higher earnings and the possibility of economic security. As a system of workplace discipline and control, it relied most heavily on instilling fear of unemployment and poverty to keep workers' minds fixed on meeting their material needs in this way and to curb any resistance. Unfortunately for Canadian industrialists, many workers found the price of this trade-off too high. Serious working-class resistance to these corporate labour policies consequently did arise, in both individual and collective forms.[46]

We also have to qualify the impact of the Second Industrial Revolution by considering distinctively Canadian developments. First, the markets for Canadian industrial products had a quite different impact on the country's industrial life from that in the United States. Canadian manufacturers had a much smaller market to rely upon than their American counterparts. They were often hampered in developing the specialized, high-volume mass-production systems that were the hallmark of American industry in the period. Arguably, many more pockets of labour-intensive methods, both skilled and unskilled, survived in the Canadian economy (although there has still been too little careful investigation of these holdouts to be able to say much about them). Certainly, for some industries (like the steel industry), market problems could be crippling, [47] but commentators in the business press saw limited markets as a significant factor for most Canadian manufacturers at some point or other. The resource-extractive industries faced a different problem. Their markets were mostly external and therefore often highly unstable. In fact, the mercurial international market for wheat became the fatal flaw in the National Policy strategy of industrialization. There was consequently a good deal of fragility and instability in the new Canadian economy of the early twentieth century that could both generate plenty of unemployment for workers and narrow some of the options for technological and managerial innovation.

Second, the emergence of the American-style corporation in so many sectors should not blind us to the continuing importance of small-scale employers, especially in manufacturing. In 1930 only a quarter of the employees in Canadian manufacturing were found in factories with more than 500 workers, and more than half worked in plants of less than 200.[48] The larger operations undoubtedly accounted for a much larger percentage of output, and there were variations between sectors. But for the Canadian working class as a whole, the smaller plant remained a common experience.

Third, Canada's Second Industrial Revolution started later and was more compressed than the parallel American process, which had a ten-to-twenty-year head start. It was probably not much before 1905 (in some cases, not until after the 1907–9 depression) that the new patterns of industrial life began to become evident on a large scale in Canada. Before that point, industrial enterprises, especially in manufacturing, still tended to be smaller and less thoroughly transformed. In 1901 and 1911 Canada's census-takers found that water wheels still provided a third of the power supplied to industrial enterprises in the country (the comparable figure for the United States in 1901 was only 15 per cent).[49] Manufacturing metropolises on the scale of Pittsburgh, Cleveland, Milwaukee, or Detroit were slower to emerge. Managerial experimentation consequently came later on the whole, and the importance of applied scientific research for industry generally remained underdeveloped until the 1920s.[50] Moreover, as the Canadian corporations struggled to catch up, they relied heavily on imported American managerial personnel. A British commentator who visited Canada in 1901 found Americans and to a lesser extent British men in charge of the new corporate concerns and saw no identifiable, indigenous managerial class in Canada.[51] By World War I, workers were occasionally heard complaining about the 'Yankee methods' of running an enterprise that their American-born supervisors were imposing.[52] Canadian managers certainly emerged over time, but many of them had learned their trade at the feet of the American experts. The recruitment of new ethnic groups was also later, not really taking on significant proportions until the early 1900, in contrast to the increased use of such labour in the United States, which dated from the 1880s. This late start in industrial development arguably made a big difference to class relations by World War I, since the social and occupational recomposition of the working class was more recent and perhaps more partial, and Canadian workers had far less experience under their collective belt at working and living together and articulating collective concerns within this new industrial regime. (Certainly that was true in the case I know best, the steel industry, where the second-generation immigrant population that investigators discovered was so important in the US steel strike in 1919 was virtually non-existent in Canada[53]).

Fourth, the ethnic recomposition of the working class was less far reaching in most of industrialized Canada than in the United States. The new immigration form Europe did not hit all industries or communities evenly. Outside the coal-mining and steelmaking areas of Cape Breton, the Maritimes were largely bypassed by the newcomers. In central Canada several cities had small European ghettoes where these newcomers gathered in their tightly-packed boarding houses, but not on the scale of many American cities in the same period, such as New York, Pittsburgh, or Chicago. It was in Western Canadian towns and cities where the new immigration made its greatest impact, particularly in the resource industries. Across the country, the non-British foreign-born amounted to only 11 per cent of the population by 1930. In fact, relative to the United States, it was the many British immigrants, most of whom headed for the cities rather than becoming farmers, who made the biggest numerical difference to the Canadian working class in this period.

Fifth, expanding the reserve army of labour in this way was a mixed blessing for Canadian employers. The typical Canadian worker of the early twentieth century was not putting down roots very quickly. There was a tremendous amount of transience across the continent in search of new job prospects. If the work was unpleasant, if production slowed down, or if the spirit of adventure simply heated the blood of this footloose work force, they moved on to the other jobs in other communities. By World War I employers were complaining loudly about this massive refusal to settle down, which had by then been labelled 'labour turnover.'[54] It is impossible to fully understand Canadian working-class life or industrial development in the period before 1920 without recognizing how many workers were flooding into the country in a short time and how many were regularly on the move. (Of course, union organizers would find this work force as difficult to hold onto as employers did.)

Sixth, we need to bear in mind the continuing great importance of the resource industries in Canada, where considerable numbers of workers could be found. In those sectors, the technological and managerial thrust of the Second Industrial Revolution remained much more blunted. We should not let the huge new factories in the largest manufacturing centres dominate our vision of Canadian industry or of the Canadian working-class experience. Mining methods remained for the most part only partially mechanized down to the 1920s, and the still craftsman-like world of the independent collier made mining towns regular flash points of industrial conflict.[55] Logging was touched even less by changes in the labour process. British Columbia logging operations introduced the so-called 'steam donkey' into four hauling logs out of the woods. but, otherwise, felling and transporting logs was still a seasonal operation and still relied on the kinds of simple saws and axes and human and animal muscle-power that had prevailed since well back in the nineteenth century.[56]

Perhaps even more important was the fact that much of the logging work force disappeared at the end of each season. These workers returned each year to their family farms, many of them marginal, where they were simply re-absorbed into agrarian life.[57] Other industries also used this kind of seasonal and part-time labour, especially in the Maritimes and Quebec.[58] No estimate has yet been attempted of Canadian workers who moved back and forth between these worlds of wage-earning and independent commodity production, but their numbers seem to have been substantial. Certainly the pool of such labour was large, since the rural population in Canada was still a majority until the 1920s. When placed alongside the large numbers of European peasant-labourers who migrated to Canada on short-term sojourns, this part-time, rurally based element in the Canadian work force could provide part of the explanation for the instability and lack of working-class cohesiveness in Canada during these years.[59] The process of using the agricultural sector of small-scale producers to absorb the unemployed and underemployed is also a large part of the explanation for the extremely limited role of the Canadian state in providing social welfare.[60]

So our British visitors would probably have been quite amazed at the changes that they would have encountered if they had been able to return 40 years after their first sojourn in Hamilton, Ontario. But I hope that they would have been astute enough to note both the eye-catching differences and the partial, incomplete qualities of many of the changes. Canadian capitalists had taken an enormous leap of faith in the early twentieth century when they set out to reshape their methods of capital accumulation by consolidating their resources, expanding into brand new industrial ventures, and creating new production systems. By 1930 they had brought Canada into the big league of industrial nations. But they had had to struggle with serious obstacles. Some were built into the fragile structure of the whole economy. Others results from the incompleteness and unevenness of the innovations in production processes. Still others were the result of human resistance to this transition to monopoly-capitalist industry. The new industrialists had to confront the anger and resentment of small businessmen and of the great mass of Canadian farmers, whose political interventions before and after the war actually posed the greatest threat to the world of Canadian corporate capitalism.[61] But industrialists also had to pull apart the working-class world that had grown up by the end of the nineteenth century and put together a new one. In that process they had to overcome some severe resistance from entrenched workers, especially craftsmen, but also to assemble and marshal effectively a new seasoned, disciplined work force. In the quarter-century before 1920, that proved a difficult process. During those years, the Canadian economy was on a boom-and-bust roller coaster on such an unprecedented scale that there was always an unsettled, tentative quality to industrial life. It was not really until the 1920s that the surging and flowing of humanity across the continent began to subside and many more workers began to settle down in industrial communities. In fact, it was really only in that decade that the great leap of capitalist faith that had brought a Second Industrial Revolution was finally consolidated and legitimized. From that point on, there was no turning back.

Notes

1 *Hamilton: The Birmingham of Canada* (Hamilton 1892).
2 Glen Williams, *Not for Export: Towards a Political Economy of Canada's Arrested Industrialization* (Toronto 1983).
3 Paul Craven and Tom Traves, "Canadian Railways as Manufacturers, 1850–1880", *Canadian Historical Association, Historical Papers*, 1983,254–81; H.

C. Pentland, *Labour and Capital in Canada, 1650–1860* (Toronto 1981), 130–75; John McCallum, *Unequal Beginnings: Agriculture and Economic Development in Quebec and Ontario until 1870* (Toronto 1980); Gregory S. Kealey, *Toronto Workers Respond to Industrial Capitalism, 1867–1892* (Toronto 1980), 3–34; T. W. Acheson, "The Social Origins of Canadian Industrialism: A Study in the Structure of Entrepreneurship" (Ph.D. Thesis, University of Toronto 1971); Gerald Tulchinsky, *The River Barons: Montreal Businessmen and the Growth of Industry and Transportation, 1837–53* (Toronto 1977); L. D. McCann, "The Mercantile-Industrial Transition of the Metal Towns of Pictou County, 1860–1931", *Acadiensis*, 10 (1981), 29–64; Robert Babcock, "Economic Development in Portland (Me.) and Saint John (N.B.) during the Age of Iron and Steam, 1860–1914", *American Review of Canadian Studies*, 9 (1979), 1–37; Ian McKay, "Capital and Labour in the Halifax Baking and Confectionary Industry in the Last Half of the Nineteenth Century", *Labour/Le Travailleur*, 3 (1978), 63–108; Douglas McCalla, "An Introduction to the Nineteenth-Century Business World", in Tom Traves, ed., *Essays in Canadian Business History* (Toronto 1984), 13–23; Williams, *Not For Export*.

4 Greg Kealey, ed., *Canada Investigates Industrialism: The Royal Commission on the Relations of Labour and Capital, 1889 (Abridged)* (Toronto 1973).

5 Eugene Forsey, *Trade Unions in Canada, 1812–1902* (Toronto 1982); Bryan D. Palmer, *Working-Class Experience: The Rise and Reconstitution of Canadian Labour, 1800–1980* (Toronto 1983), 60–135.

6 David Gagan, *Hopeful Travellers: Families, Land, and Social Change in Mid-Victorian Peel County, Canada West* (Toronto 1981); R. L. Jones, *History of Agriculture in Ontario, 1613–1880* (Toronto 1946); and "The Agricultural Development of Lower Canada, 1850–1867", *Agricultural History*, 19 (1945), 212–24; D. A. Lawr, "The Development of Ontario Farming, 1870–1914; Patterns of Growth and Change", *Ontario History*, 44 (1972); 239–51; Marvin McGinnis, "The Changing Structure of Canadian Agriculture, 1867–1897." *Canadian Journal of Economics*, 1982; Vernon Fowke, *The National Policy and the Wheat Economy* (Toronto 1957).

7 A. R. M. Lower, *Great Britain's Woodyard: British American and the Timber Trade, 1763–1867* (Montreal 1973); and *The North American Assault on the Canadian Forest: A History of the Lumber Trade Between Canada and the United States* (Toronto 1938).

8 C. O. Macdonald, *The Coal and Iron Industries of Nova Scotia* (Halifax 1909); Del Muise, "The Making of an Industrial Community: Cape Breton Coal Towns, 1867–1900", in Don Macgillivray and Brian Tennyson, (eds.), *Cape Breton Historical Essays* (Sydney 1980), 76–94; Martin Robin, *The Rush for Spoils: The Company Province, 1871–1933* (Toronto 1972).

9 Dianne Newell, *Technology on the Frontier: Mining in Old Ontario* (Vancouver 1986).

10 Philip Ehrensaft and Warwick Armstrong, "The Formation of Dominion Capitalism: Economic Truncation and Class Structure", in Allan Moscovitch and Glenn Drover (eds.), *Inequality: Essays on the Political Economy of Social Welfare* (Toronto 1981), 99–155.

11 Fowke, *National Policy and Wheat Economy*; John Herd Thompson, *The Harvests of War: The Prairie West, 1914–1918* (Toronto 1978).

12 W. T. Eastbrook and Hugh G. J. Aitken, *Canadian Economic History* (Toronto 1965), 409–44.

13 Canada, Royal Commission on Corporate Concentration, *Report* (Hull 1978), 1.

14 Michael Bliss, *A Living Profit: Studies in the Social History of Canadian Business, 1883–1911* (Toronto 1974), 33–54; Abraham Ernest Epp, "Co-operation Among Capitalists: The Canadian Merger Movement, 1909–1913" (Ph.D. Thesis, Johns Hopkins University 1973); J. C. Weldon, "Consolidations in Canadian Industry, 1900–1948", in L. A. Skeotch, ed., *Restrictive Trade Practices in Canada* (Toronto 1966); Tom Traves, *The State and Enterprise: Canadian Manufacturers and the Federal Government, 1917–1931* (Toronto 1979), 73–100; Michael Bliss, "Another Anti-Trust Tradition: Canadian Anti-Combines Policy, 1889–1910", in Glenn Porter and Robert Cuff, ed., *Enterprise and National Development: Essays in Canadian Business History and Economic History* (Toronto 1973), 39–50.

15 E. P. Neufeld, *The Financial System of Canada: Its Growth and Development* (Toronto 1972).

16 Christopher Armstrong and H. V. Nelles, *Monopoly's Moment* (Philadelphia 1986).

17 David Frank, "The Cape Breton Coal Industry and the Rise and Fail of the British Empire Steel Corporation", *Acadiensis*, 7 (autumn 1977), 3–34.

18 Mira Wilkins, *The Emergence of Multinational Enterprise: American Business Abroad from the Colonial Period to 1914* (Cambridge, Mass. 1970); Herbert Marshall et al., *Canadian-American Industry: A Study in International Investment* (Toronto 1976); Michael Bliss, "Canadianizing American Business; The Roots of the Branch Plant", in Ian Lumsden, ed., *Close the 49th Parallel etc.: The Americanization of Canada* (Toronto 1970), 27–42; Stephen Scheinberg, "Invitation to Empire: Tariffs and American Economic Expansion in Canada", in Porter and Cuff, *Enterprise and National Development*, 80–100.

19 W. Craig Heron, "Working-Class Hamilton, 1895–1930" (Ph.D. Thesis, Dalhousie University 1981), 1–44.

20 Traves, *State and Enterprise*, 85.

21 Acheson, "Social Origins"; Giles Piédalue, "Les groupes financiers au Canada, 1900–1930; étude préliminaire", *Revue d'histoire de l'Amérique française*, 30 (1976), 3–34; Wallace Clement, *The Canadian Corporate Elite: An Analysis of Economic Power* (Toronto 1975), 71–87; Michael Bliss, *A Canadian Millionaire: The Life and Business Times of Sir Joseph Flavelle, Bart., 1858–1939* (Toronto 1978); H. V. Nelles, *The Politics of Development: Forest, Mines and Hydro-Electric Power in Ontario, 1849–1941* (Toronto 1974); Tom Naylor, *The History of Canadian Business, 1867–1914* (2 vols., Toronto 1975).

22 S. A. Saunders, *The Economic History of the Maritimes Provinces* (Ottawa 1939); T. W. Acheson, "The Maritimes and "Empire Canada"", in D. J. Bercuson, ed., *Canada and the Burden of Unity* (Toronto 1977), 87–114.

23 R. E. Caves and R. H. Holton, "An Outline of the Economic History of British Columbia, 1881–1951", in J. Friesen and H.K. Ralston, eds, *Historical Essays on British Columbia* (Toronto 1976), 152–66; Philip Resnick, "The Political Economy of British Columbia: A Marxist Perspective", in Paul Knox and Philip Resnick (eds.), *Essays in B.C. Political Economy* (Vancouver 1974), 3–12; Patricia Marchak, *Green Gold: The Forest Industry in British Columbia* (Vancouver

1983); Allen Seager, "Working Lives: Introduction", in The Working Lives Collective, *Working Lives: Vancouver, 1886–1986* (Vancouver 1985), 9–23.

24 John C. Weaver, *Hamilton: An Illustrated History* (Toronto 1982), 79–127; J. M. S. Careless, *Toronto to 1918: An Illustrated History* (Toronto 1984), 149–99; Michael J. Piva, *The Condition of the Working Class in Toronto — 1900–1921* (Ottawa 1979); Paul-Andre Linteau, *The Promoters' City: Building the Industrial Town of Maisonneuve* (Toronto 1985).

25 W. J. A. Donald, *The Canadian Iron and Steel Industry: A Study in the Economic History of a Protected Industry* (Boston 1915); William Kilbourn, *The Elements Combined: A History of the Steel Company of Canada* (Toronto 1960); Duncan McDowall, *Steel at the Sault: Francis H. Clergue, Sir James Dunn, and the Algoma Steel Corporation, 1901–1956* (Toronto 1984); Frank, "British Empire Steel Corporation"; Traves, *State and Enterprise*; O. J. McDiarmid, "Some Aspects of the Canadian Automobile Industry", *Canadian Journal of Economics and Political Science*, 6 (1940), 258–74; Gerald Tulchinsky, "Aspects of the Clothing Manufacturing Industry in Canada, 1850s to 1914" (paper presented to the Canadian Business History Conference, Trent University, 1984); Bliss, *Canadian Millionaire*.

26 Nathan Reich, *The Pulp and Paper Industry in Canada* (Toronto 1929); J. W. Shipley, *Pulp and Paper-Making in Canada* (Toronto 1929); James Hiller, "The Origins of the Pulp and Paper Industry in Newfoundland", *Acadiensis*, 11 (Spring 1982), 42–68; Carl Wiegman, *Trees to News* (Toronto 1953); Paul-Andre Linteau, Rene Durocher et Jean-Claude Robert, *Histoire de Quebec contemporain* (Quebec 1979), 360–63; James P. Hull, "Science and the Canadian Pulp and Paper Industry, 1903–1933" (Ph.D. Thesis, York University 1985).

27 D. M. Leboudais, *Metals and Men: The Story of Canadian Mining* (Toronto 1957); Nelles, *Politics of Development*; Linteau et al., *Histoire de Quebec contemporain*, 364–68.

28 Craig Heron, *Working in Steel: The Early Years in Canada, 1883–1935* (Toronto 1988).

29 Craig Heron and Bryan D. Palmer, "Through the Prism of the Strike: Industrial Conflict in Southern Ontario, 1901–1914", *Canadian Historical Review*, 58 (1977), 423–58; Ian McKay, "Strikes in the Maritimes, 1901–1914", in P. A. Buckner and David Frank (eds.), *Atlantic Canada After Confederation* (Fredericton 1985), 216–59.

30 Donald Avery, *"Dangerous Foreigners": European Immigrant Workers and Labour Radicalism in Canada, 1896–1932* (Toronto 1979); W. Peter Ward, *White Canada Forever: Popular Attitudes and Public Policy Toward Orientals in British Columbia* (Montreal 1978).

31 Wayne Roberts, "Toronto Metal Workers and the Second Industrial Revolution, 1889–1914", *Labour/Le Travailleur*, 6 (Autumn 1980), 49–72; Craig Heron, "The Crisis of the Craftsman: Hamilton's Metal Workers in the Early Twentieth Century", *ibid.*, 7–48; and *Working in Steel*, Chapter 2; and "Working-Class Hamilton", 213–36; Stephen Meyer III, *The Five Dollar Day: Labor Management and Social Control in the Ford Motor Company, 1908–1921* (Albany 1981), 9–66.

32 Hull, "Science and the Canadian Pulp and Paper Industry"; Robert Miles Stamp, "The Campaign for Technical Education in Ontario, 1876–1914" (Ph.D. Thesis, University of Toronto 1970); Donald MacLeod, "Practicality

Ascendant: The Origins and Establishment of Technical Education in Nova Scotia", *Acadiensis*, 15 (Spring 1986), 53–92; David Noble, *America By Design: Science, Technology, Technology, and the Rise of Corporate Capitalism* (New York 1977).

33 Joseph A. Littler, "Systematic Management: The Search for Order and Integration", *Business History Review*, 35 (1961), 461–76; Bryan D. Palmer, "Class, Conception, and Conflict: The Thrust for Efficiency, Managerial Views of Labour, and the Working Class Rebellion", *Review of Radical Political Economics*, 7 (1975), 31–49; Daniel Nelson, *Managers and Workers: Origins of the New Factory System in the United States, 1880–1920* (Madison 1975); Alfred D. Chandler, Jr., *The Visible Hand: The Managerial Revolution in American Business* (Cambridge, Mass. 1977).

34 Graham S. Lower, "The Rise of Modern Management in Canada", *Canadian Dimension*, December 1979, 32–38; and "Mechanization, Feminization, and Managerial Control in the early Twentieth-Century Canadian Office", in Craig Heron and Robert Storey (eds.), *On the Job: Confronting the Labour Process in Canada* (Kingston and Montreal 1986), 177–210; Paul Craven, *"An Impartial Umpire": Industrial Relations and the Canadian State, 1900–1911* (Toronto 1980); Heron and Palmer, "Through the Prism of the Strike", 430–34;

35 Wayne Roberts, *Honest Womanhood: Feminism, Femininity, and Class Consciousness Among Toronto Working Women, 1893–1914* (Toronto 1976); Janice Acton et al., eds., *Women at Work: Ontario, 1893–1930* (Toronto 1974); Veronica Strong-Boag, "The Girl of the New Day: Canadian Working Women of the 1920s", *Labour/Le Travailleur*, 4. (1979), 131–64; Graham S. Lowe, "Class, Job, and Gender in the Canadian Office", *ibid.*, 10 (Autumn 1982), 11–38; Mercedes Steedman, "Skill and Gender in the Canadian Clothing Industry, 1890–1940", in Heron and Storey, *On the Job*, 152–76.

36 Particularly in Harry Braverman, *Labor and Monopoly Capital: The Degradation of Work in the Twentieth Century* (New York 1974).

37 See Charles More, *Skill and the English Working Class, 1870–1914* (London 1980); Stephen Wood, ed., *The Degration of Work?: Skill, Deskilling and the Labour Process* (London 1982); Craig R. Littler, *The Development of the Labour Process in Capitalist Societies* (London 1982).

38 Gail Cuthbert-Brandt, "The Transformation of Women's Work in the Quebec Cotton Industry, 1920–1950", in Bryan D. Palmer, ed., *The Question of Class Struggle: Essays in Canadian Working-Class History* (Toronto 1986), 115–34.

39 Heron, *Working in Steel*, Chapter 2; William E. Greening, *Paper Makers in Canada: A History of the Paper Makers' Union in Canada* (Cornwall 1952); Craig Heron et al., *All That Our Hands Have Done: A Pictorial History of the Hamilton Workers* (Oakville 1981), 40–41.

40 Stuart D. Brandes, *American Welfare Capitalism, 1880–1940* (Chicago 1976); Sanford M. Jacoby, *Employing Bureaucracy: Managers, Unions, and the Transformation of Work in American Industry, 1900–1945* (New York 1985).

41 Ian Radforth, "Logging Pulpwood in Northern Ontario", in Heron and Storey, *On the Job*, 250–51; David Frank, "Contested Terrain: Workers' Control in Cape Breton Coal Mines in the 1920s", *ibid.*, 104–6.

42 Palmer, *Working-Class Experience*, 136–84.

43 Heron, *Working in Steel*, Chapter 3.

44 Robert Henry Storey, "Workers, Unions, and Steel: The Shaping of the

Hamilton Working Class, 1935–1948" (Ph.D. Thesis, University of Toronto 1981); David Frank and Don Macgillivray (eds.), *George MacEachern: An Autobiography — The Story of a Cape Breton Labour Radical* (Sydney 1987); Mike Solski and John Smaller, *Mine Mill: The History of the International Union of Mine, Mill and Smelter Workers in Canada Since 1895* (Ottawa 1984).

45 Heron, "Working-Class Hamilton", 99–101; and *Working in Steel*, Chapter 3; D. James Naylor, "The New Democracy" (Ph.D. Thesis, York University 1988); William H. Lazonick, "Technological Change and the Control of Work: The Development of Capital-Labour Relations in US Mass Production Industries", in Howard F. Gospel and Craig R. Littler, (eds.), *Managerial Strategies and Industrial Relations: An Historical and Comparative Study* (London 1983), 111–36.

46 Palmer, *Working-Class Experience*, 136–84.

47 McDowall, *Steel at the Sault*; Frank, "British Empire Steel Corporation."

48 M. C. Urquhart and K. A. H. Buckley (eds.), *Historical Statistics of Canada* (Toronto 1965).

49 Canada, *Census*, 1901, Vol.3, xix-xxi; 1911, Vol.3,138–39.

50 Hull, "Science and the Canadian Pulp and Paper Industry."

51 James Stephen Jeans, *Canada's Resources and Possibilities, With Special Reference to the Iron and Allied Industries, and the Increase of Trade with the Mother Country* (London 1904), 206.

52 Heron, *Working in Steel*, Chapter 4.

53 Interchurch World Movement, Commission of Inquiry, *Report on the Steel Strike of 1919* (New York 1920), 129,135.

54 Edmund Bradwin, *The Bunkhouse Man* (Toronto 1972); Ross McCormack, "Wobblies and Blanketstiffs: The Constituency of the IWW in Western Canada", in W. J. C. Cherwinski and G. S. Kealey, (eds.), *Lectures in Canadian Labour and Working-lass History* (St. John's, 1985), 101–14; Heron, *Working in Steel*, Chapter 4.

55 Frank, "Contested Terrain."

56 Radforth, "Logging Pulpwood"; Myrtle Bergren, *Tough Timber: The Loggers of British Columbia — Their Story* (Toronto 1967).

57 Radforth, "Logging Pulpwood."

58 See, for example, L. Anders Sandberg, "The Deindustrialization of Pictou County, Nova Scotia — Capital, Labour, and the Process of Regional Decline, 1881–1921" (Ph.D. Thesis, McGill University 1985), 162.

59 James Sacouman, "Semi-Proletarianization and Rural Underdevelopment in the Maritimes", *Canadian Review of Sociology and Anthropology*, 17 (1980), 232–45; Leo Johnson, "Precapitalist Economic Formations and the Capitalist Labour Market in Canada, 1911–71", in James E. Curtis and Williams G. Scott (eds.), *Social Stratification: Canada* (Scarborough 1979), 89–104.

60 James Struthers, *No Fault of Their Own: Unemployment and the Canadian Welfare State, 1914–1941* (Toronto 1983).

61 Nelles, *Politics of Development*, 215–306; Ernest R. Forbes, *The Maritime Rights Movement, 1919–1927: A Study in Canadian Regionalism* (Montreal 1979); Louis Aubrey Wood, *A History of Farmers' Movement in Canada* (Toronto 1975).

4

Conflicts of Faith? Religion and Labour in Wales 1890–1914

Christopher B. Turner

A number of historians, writing from differing standpoints, have concluded that Nonconformity has played an important part in founding and fashioning the British labour movement. Denominational writers have claimed, for example, that the labour movement owes more to Methodism than to Marx.[1] The problem at source is to establish how valuable if at all was the contribution not only of individuals but also of religious ideology to labour development. Other historians have detailed the way in which the struggle to achieve the socialist ideal became a religion in itself. It utilised Biblical phrases, such as the "Social Gospel" and the "Ten Commandments of Socialism", in its addresses to working people and adopted an evangelical flavour to its missionary activity. The process of becoming a socialist was regarded as a "conversion", involving as it did the same process of individual regeneration which was a feature of all religious revivals.[2]

Much contemporary opinion, however, could see only a conflict between the imported materialist socialism as preached by Robert Blatchford on the one hand and the Welsh brand of inspirational and 'other worldly' nonconformity as practised in Wales throughout the 19th century. Occasional attempts were made to fuse the Christian with the socialist ideal but were these in any way significant? Eric Hobsbawm has concluded from a wide-ranging European survey that modern working class movements are almost exclusively anti-religious and even the British movement was "standard socialism, elaborated by secular thinkers and translated into the familiar biblical terminology".[3] Within a Welsh context the fundamental question to resolve is how a distinctly Nonconformist nation became, in time, a stronghold of the Labour Party. There were of course many factors which contributed to this political change, nor was the change achieved overnight, but the religious dimension deserves closer attention that it has perhaps received in the past.

By the beginning of the 20th century there were relatively few signs that the influence of Welsh nonconformity was waning. In 1911 the Royal Commission on the Church and other Religious Bodies in Wales concluded, "that the people of Wales show a marked tendency to avail themselves of the provision made by the Churches of all denominations for their spiritual welfare."[4] It hardly needed a Royal Commission to announce that fact but the statistical evidence is nevertheless illuminating. Only in industrial Glamorgan and Monmouthshire did the total population outnumber the seats provided by the denominations and the Church of England. Forty per cent of the population aged three and over in Wales were considered to be communicants or members of their respective denominations. This figure becomes even more impressive when it is noted that a feature of Welsh nonconformity was the popularity of the Sunday School, whose primary function was to act as a training place for the creation of full members. Nor should we ignore the attachment to the chapels of a large number of adherents or "gwrandawyr". These were people who were not full members but who came simply to hear the sermons and of course to enjoy the congregational singing of hymns.[5] Membership totals therefore reveal only one element of the strength and vitality of chapel congregations at the turn of the century.

As far as the nonconformists were concerned it was their numerical superiority over the Established Church which proved the strength of their case for disestablishment. But other problems did exercise the minds of the nonconformist hierarchy at the end of the century. One such problem emerged from the large scale immigration of non-Welsh people, particularly into the industrial areas of South Wales. The Royal Commission continually pointed to this situation and asked why the churches were conspicuously failing to attract such people. Religious leaders, as a response, had evolved new 'direct action' approaches. One example was the Calvinistic Methodist Forward Movement which was founded in 1891 under the guidance of Rev. John Pugh.[6] As a first stage and in order to announce the movement's arrival Pugh erected large tents in all the large towns of Wales. As well as tent- preaching Pugh also conducted house to house visitations and temperance marches. He also engaged a number of charismatic preachers to deliver simple but telling sermons. One of these was the Rev. Seth Joshua, a reclaimed drunkard, who was convinced that the masses desperately wanted to hear the Gospel:

The people are crying out for it. There is no grip in anything else. The people are sick and tired of the present day attempts to dress up the Gospel in new clothes. A new tribe of theological tailors have wearied the people by forcing the Gospel to become a quick change artist.[7]

Joshua was here referring to the emergence of a modern approach to theology which was another development to worry denominational leaders. By the 1890's even the traditionalist Welsh theological colleges were subject to wider European influences, which included the rationalist philosophers. A congregational minister, the Rev. David Adams, was one who attempted to apply the scientific principles of evolution to spiritual values. He submitted a paper to the National Eisteddfod entitled "The Fall, the Incarnation and the Resurrection in the light of Evolution".[8] Critics, who were certainly in the majority, were shocked by the implications of Adam's theology, especially in the way it appeared to challenge the divine authority of the Bible. Yet however we define the nature and extent of the religious problem in Wales at the end of the 19th century it is certain that any "crisis of faith" which might have existed was not caused by the undermining of religious belief by socialist philosophy.

The infiltration of socialist ideas, especially those developed by Keir Hardie and the Independent Labour Party, began in earnest only on the occasion of the acrimonious coal strike of 1898. Previously there had been some ILP activity in South Wales starting in 1894, and a few branches of the Social Democratic Federation had also been established but without much permanency.[9] In the early 1890's several attempts were made to form Labour Churches on the John Trevor model. The Liberal newspaper *The South Wales Daily News* expressed some hope for the Labour Church in Wales because it was seen as a movement of vitality and a genuine attempt to combine the forces of social and religious improvement.[10] The leader of the transiently successful Labour Church at Cardiff was S. G. Hobson who saw his Church as a necessity because, "unfortunately the old established churches are altogether too far committed to an endorsement of the worst aspects of latter day industrialism". His aim was the creation of the "Christian brotherhood" in which would be applied economic as well as moral principles. Branches of the Labour Church were established at Cardiff, Swansea and Aberdare but they were short-lived and, although several new branches were formed in 1907, they seemingly failed to capture the imagination of the Welsh people.[12] As Hobson admitted in his autobiography, *Pilgrim to the Left* (1936), the Labour Church for him was merely a half-way house on the road to a socialism which ultimately regarded religion as peripheral if not completely unnecessary.[13]

The background to the coal strike of 1898 was the miners' determination to replace the sliding scale method of payment with a minimum wage rate. In the face of extreme suffering nonconformist ministers did not hesitate to organise relief committees, to man soup-kitchens and to collect distress funds from charitable organisations. Their public pronouncements, however, were carefully worded not to give offence to the coalowners. The Cardiff Free Churches Council, for example, resolved only that both sides in the dispute should be reconciled:

We believe if this were done confidence and harmony would be restored between employers and employed, and we are assured that the side that makes the first move towards this end would not thereby prejudice or endanger the justice of the cause.[14]

The exposition of this "harmony of interest" ideal was entirely to be expected since similar statements had been applied to labour disputes for thirty years. The difference was that in 1898 a rival ideology was at work in the coalfield in the form of Keir Hardie and the ILP. The moral impact of Hardie's personality and message was crucial. He very quickly comprehended the religious basis on which the Welsh outlook was founded, "The meetings which I addressed, " he said, "revealed how eagerly the people will drink in the teachings of socialism, when placed before them in a language which they can understand".[15]

He was appalled by the many examples of Christian hypocrisy in the face of prolonged human suffering. How, he asked, could men like the coalowner Richard Cory take an active part in evangelistic work like the Forward Movement yet be unmoved by the human misery directly before them? Hardie rebutted Cory's counter charge that all socialists were atheists and declared of the Welsh workman that

Like all true Celts they are socialists by instinct, and the deep religious feeling which strikes even the most casual observer as a prominent trait in their character makes them specially susceptible to socialist teaching.[18]

Hardie's message and relief work certainly impressed the colliers. The ILP organiser for South Wales, Willie Wright, reported that 31 branches existed by 1899 and,

Branches though not always active, have succeeded in banding intelligent young men together, many of them once the hope of the various chapels, who have lost faith in the old political parties and the old industrial methods of fighting labour questions, of the practical work done or not done — by the chapels in which they have been reared. . . The effect upon the churches is no less noticeable. The writer has been dubbed a Black Angel, a Foreigner, a Firebrand and an Atheist — several young men have been called before the 'Church Council' to give account of themselves for the part they have in the matter. Vestries have been refused despite the fact that applicants were diligent Church workers for some years past.[17]

The local press noted several examples of excommunication of socialists but some also made their own conscious decision to leave the chapels. The Aberdare miners' leader David Morgan, "Dai o'r Nant", had been imprisoned during the strike for his part in a demonstration. He returned home a local hero but the significance of this event lay in the fact that Morgan was also a prominent deacon at Calfaria Baptist Chapel, generally regarded as a citadel of Dissent in South Wales. A meeting of his fellow deacons resolved *not* to pass a vote of sympathy with Morgan on his imprisonment. He subsequently left the chapel and urged all local ministers not to meddle in labour problems but to concentrate on that which they were ordained to do.[18] Others clearly followed the example. Figures for the East Glamorgan Congregational Association showed that the "adherents" group fell by 35% between 1897 and 1898.[19] Nor did the figures recover — at least we must assume this to be the case since the Association omitted this particular statistic from their reports after 1900. There were also falls in the membership totals of the main denominations but the falls were not exceptionally large and while the situation must have worried the denominations it was far from critical.

The ILP built on this successful initiative. In the next few years socialist societies, most of them indistinguishable from ILP branches, appeared in the towns and valley communities. Judging by the debates and discussions which were held within these societies religion was far from being a dead issue. The Aberdare Socialist Society, originally established in 1895 but formally affiliated to the ILP in 1902, was a good example. The Society consisted of men such as C. B. Stanton, the fiery miners' leader but grew under the organisational skill of the schoolteacher, W. W. Price. From the outset the Society wished to make it clear that not all socialists were unbelievers. It was true that discussions on theology were not allowed but lectures concentrating on the social teachings of Christ were to be encouraged.[20] Addressing the Society in 1902 Bruce Glasier, who toured south Wales extensively at this time, asked,

When would the Church come back to the teachings of Christ and endeavour to abolish such wicked environments and lighten the burdens of labour by assisting the socialists to sweep away the curse of landlordism and usury and establish a 'Kingdom of Peace on Earth'?[21]

The Aberdare society also established a Socialist Sunday School at which children were instructed in the socialist Ten Commandments. A number of local ministers addressed the Society including the Rev. D. Rees of Pentre, Rhondda and the Rev. George Neighbour, Mountain Ash, who gave a paper on "Labour's Hope". Another visiting speaker, Enid Stacey, delivered a paper on "Should Christians be Socialists?" and decided that true socialism was true religion in action.[22]

In the years after 1898 there does not appear to have been a *concerted* nonconformist effort against socialist principles in general or Keir Hardie and the ILP in particular. It was probably perceived that as yet the threat was not real enough. In any case by 1904 Welsh nonconformity had something much more fundamental and challenging with which to concern itself, a religious revival. Not since 1859 had Wales experienced such a large scale revival, although in the first half of the 19th century these so called "showers of blessing" had been commonplace.

The origins of the revival were to be found in a series of nondenominational "holiness" meetings in Cardiganshire. The meetings were organised primarily so that ministers and ministerial students could find greater spiritual awareness within themselves. The emphasis therefore was not on the conversion of the unbeliever and certainly not on the merits of a more progressive theology but the intention was to bring "the Children of God into life more abundant". The meetings brought together a number of people who were involved in direct missionary activity. These included the Baptist, the Rev. W. S. Jones who had first hand experience of the American, "Torrey-Alexander" revival. Others were Seth Joshua of the

Forward Movement and Gipsy Smith of the Free Church Council.[23] More important as a catalyst though was that in 1903 the Calvinistic Methodists of South Cardiganshire, under the direction of two local ministers, the Revs. Joseph Jenkins and John Thickens, desired to experience again the awakening of 1859. They set out to recapture that feeling of spiritual anxiety which they believed to be a pre-requisite of a genuine revival. The revival was soon under way and seemed particularly potent among the younger Church members and ministerial students.[24] One of these students, Evan Roberts, was the instrument by which this revival of the already converted became the revival of the occasional adherents and even those who had completely forsaken their religious affiliations. The spread of the revival in the last three months of 1904 was unparalleled.[25] At first Evan Roberts took the revival to his home town of Loughor, between Swansea and Llanelli, and from there he and his co-revivalists moved quickly eastward into the valleys and coastal towns of the South before moving north in 1905. By the end of 1904 it was estimated that 34,000 conversions had taken place — a final figure of more than 100,000 conversions was also quoted. Despite the close, almost indecent, attention of the *Western Mail* and other newspapers one of the chief characteristics of revival services was their spontaneity. The services were of necessity unplanned because Roberts constantly claimed to be awaiting holy inspiration for his actions.[26] A number of ministers complained about the emotional excesses and the way in which their ministerial guidance was ignored as young people completely took over the meetings. Indeed, £60 worth of damage was caused to Roberts's own chapel at Moriah, Loughor.

Roberts though was no preacher or theologian. His addresses were short and concentrated mainly on God's love. He promised ultimate salvation if only the people would make a full and public profession of repentance. As a result many communities witnessed scenes of unbridled emotion, public houses closed through lack of custom and rugby football teams burnt their jerseys in a unique ritual.[27] In many ways of course the revival was a reaction to the oppressive social conditions which then existed. It brought colour into a dull and harsh existence. Religiously, it demonstrated the power of inspirational faith as opposed to the dogma of a more rationalist theology. But what did the revival offer the labour movement? Contemporary opinion suggested a variety of sometimes conflicting theories. Bruce Glasier in the *Labour Leader* asked for the revival to be understood in context, "Welsh religion is, as we all know, a gloomy, narrow and unaesthetic religion. But so alas! are the present day conditions of Welsh industrial life generally".[28] He saw revivals as "infections of social enthusiasm" in which he acknowledged there were excesses but he believed that this was better for people than living their lives in "cold and soul-less apathy". Glasier called for the "glory of brotherhood" to be established out of the revival. He hoped that the power of the revival, "could be evoked at this hour against the appalling bondage of capitalism, or the grasp of monopoly, or the terror of wage servitude, and the fear of masters". Another correspondent to the *Labour Leader*, "Cymro", noted that one lesson of the revival was that enthusiasm was essential to any missionary movement and that Welshmen were particularly well placed to generate such eagerness. He described religious enthusiasm as a "spiritualising force and a driving power which would be invaluable to Socialism in its approaching struggle with capitalism and class privilege". Interestingly, "Cymro" also acknowledged the efforts of nonconformist ministers who themselves had emerged from the working classes but he regretted that their circumscribed environment had made the Bible their one and only subject for study.[29]

A number of active trade unionists reflected on the revival in later years. Many of them were critical of the naked emotionalism and transitory aspects of the awakening. They viewed it as a diversionary tactic to direct attention away from unionism and socialism.[30] The miners' leader "Mabon", on the other hand, held out great hope for the regenerative impulse but even he as a moderate "Lib-Lab" MP was anxious that the awakening should not interfere with their efforts to improve union organisation. For Mabon the revival was to herald what he termed a period of progressive Christianity.[31] One Dowlais collier, interviewed at the time by the French social investigator J. Rogues de Fursac, was adamant that socialism had lost nothing by the revival. His analysis was that since the religious movement had been essentially popular and democratic it had necessarily strengthened unity and brotherhood, both watchwords of socialism.[32] There was certainly nothing in the revival message itself which could have contributed in a positive way to any progressive impulse. Evan Roberts was a mystic and a fundamentalist and not a preacher of the social Gospel. The revival, however, did cause some ministers and ordinary members alike to reconsider their faith in a new light. What is more important is that the revival was closely followed by the intrusion into Wales of a short-lived but nonetheless influential social philosophy. This was the New Theology whose foremost exponent was the Rev. R. J. Campbell, minister of the Congregational City Temple in London. In essence, New Theology represented the fusion of modern liberal theology with a developed social conscience. It particularly stressed the Immanence or omniprescence of God rather than His intangible transcendance. Campbell also challenged the doctrine of original sin, believing that the existence of evil was simply the result of the immaturity of society and not part of a Divine plan. He also denied the special divinity of Christ and the theory of the Virgin birth. The literal truth of the Bible was rejected as untenable in the light of scientific reasoning.[33] Many theologians attacked Campbell's ideas as vague and superficial. Indeed, he was later to modify them on his way out of Congregationalism and into the Church of England. But for a number of years his message found a receptive audience in Wales especially, it seemed, where the New Theology stressed the *practical* application of Christian principles in the modern world. Campbell described his philosophy as "the religious articulation of the social movement". In discussing the thorny question of the "atonement" his advice was "Go with Keir Hardie to the House of Commons and listen to his pleading for justice to his order, and you see the atonement".[34] He was in fact a close friend of Keir Hardie and stood with and in place of the Labour leader on a number of engagements. In 1907–8 Campbell toured South Wales lecturing and preaching, often to ILP branches, in towns and villages as far west as Carmarthen.

When Campbell lectured at Pentre in Rhondda in 1908 on "Christianity and the Kingdom of God" he was greeted by a large audience. The local press also noted the hasty organisation of a less well attended counter-demonstration and the holding of so-called "traditional" services in nearby chapels. In his lecture Campbell stated that, "The Kingdom of God was the brotherhood of man in the future". But, he warned, it would be ridiculous to describe Jesus as a socialist in the ordinary sense of the word. He had no economic theory but he did subscribe to that economic system which meant the helping of one another rather than the hampering of each other.[35] Campbell had been invited to the Rhondda by the Treorchy Progressive Theology League. The League was one of a number formed in the valleys in 1907, mainly through the efforts of a progressive missionary to South Wales, the Rev. T. Rhondda Williams. Williams was a Welshman but at that time a Congregational minister at Bradford. He wrote a great deal in English and occasionally in Welsh on progressive theology and the New Theology, and was especially productive in relating these to the problems of modern society.

In 1904 Williams wrote a pamphlet entitled *The true Revival versus Torreysim* in which he attacked the American revivalist's complete faith in Biblical infallibility. He believed that Torrey's mission undermined the progressive movement. But in his book *Does Science Destroy Religion?* he defended Christianity against the rationalist theories of Haeckel and Robert Blatchford. He called for more sympathy for labour aspirations and less Forward Movements, Christian Endeavour Societies, sensational revivals and Free Church Federations. His other works included *The Evangel of the New Theology* and *The Social Gospel* and both encapsulated his belief that Christianity must adapt itself to the needs of modern society. Williams was a committed socialist, though in his addresses to ILP meetings in South Wales he consistently preached the evolutionary socialism and "no class war" theories which some advanced socialists could not accept.[36]

On a number of occasions Williams was refused the use of a chapel for his "heretical" meetings. The Progressive Theology Leagues, especially in the Rhondda, were forced to resort to Unitarian meeting places. For many nonconformists this simply placed the progressivists in the Unitarian camp. This was confirmed when a number of progressive ministers, including Rhondda Williams, were known to have been trained at the

Carmarthen Presbyterian College, where Unitarian principles were said to have been espoused since the early 1890's.[37] The Rev. James Nicholas, Baptist minister at Moriah, Tonypandy was another trained at Carmarthen. His efforts on behalf of progressive theology were aided by Rev. James Lewis of Pentre English Congregational Church who was local organiser of the Treorchy Progressive Theology League.[38] In Merthyr the Rev. John Morgan Jones of Hope Presbyterian Church was an assiduous worker in the cause of New Theology. In 1910 he published a series of sermons entitled *Religion and Socialism*, which included his sermon on "Was Jesus a Socialist?"[39] Both James Nicholas and John Morgan Jones, however, were uncertain as to their socialist affiliations. Nicholas could not declare himself a convert to socialism, though he had great sympathy for its ideals.[40] He was convinced though that Christianity needed the Labour Party and the Labour Party needed Christianity and it was for this reason that he supported Keir Hardie in the 1910 election.[41] It was understandable that there should be degrees of affiliation to the progressive movement but it was significant that what was in essence a theological issue was being debated widely, and in open session, at many ILP meetings as well as in sympathetic chapels.

In the Aberdare Valley one minister stood out openly as an avowed socialist. He was the Rev. George Neighbour of Nazareth Baptist Chapel, Mountain Ash. In 1907 he addressed the Rhondda miners at Tonypandy on the question, "Is Socialism anti-Christian?" He wanted to convince them that socialism was not anti-Christian, irreligious, unethical or immoral. He claimed to be fighting alone among the ministers of the Aberdare Valley but in spite of constant opposition he was a convinced and ardent socialist.[42] His message emphasised "universal brotherhood" and for Neighbour the highest aims of life consisted of the sacrifice of the individual for the benefit of the society. His socialism ultimately brought him into conflict not only with other nonconformist ministers but also with his own deacons. The deacons asked him to sign an agreement saying he would not preach socialism from the pulpit. He refused and in October 1907 he left the chapel and with a majority of its members formed what was known as the "Brotherhood Church". This Church was still in existence two years later and this was despite the fact that it had been refused coal at a reduced rate by Nixon's colliery. It was the privilege of all local chapels to receive cheap coal but the other chapels in the area prevailed upon Messrs Nixon not to recognise the Brotherhood Church as a true Christian church and the company not surprisingly obliged.[43]

The western valleys of the coalfield, where English immigration was much less and a specifically Welsh language culture still existed, were also subjected to the combined thrust of ILP propaganda and New Theology. For example, R. J. Campbell and Rhondda Williams visited Ystalyfera in the Swansea Valley and also the Amman Valley. Their work was supplemented by the so-called "social crusade" of the American brother evangelists the Revs. Ben and Stitt Wilson who toured the area in 1908 with the full support for the ILP.[44]

The Wilsons used simple Bible terminology in their demand for social justice and at Ystalyfera Stitt addressed the gathered on the less than obvious subject of "Moses — the first Labour Leader". But we must not imagine that Campbell and the Wilsons were solely responsible for labour progress in these areas. The Welsh poet and theologian John "Gwili" Jenkins was primarily responsible for setting the New Theology and its social message in a Welsh context.[45] Amongst his other views he echoed Campbell's theory of the Immanence of God and he greatly offended his own Baptist denomination when he stated that not all the Old Testament was divinely inspired. One of his most important and influential works was *Y Ddwy Deyrnas* (The Two Kingdoms) in which he stated the need to reconcile the spiritual with the material world. For the Labour movement to succeed it must have a theological basis in Christianity. Gwili was convinced that the primary objective of true Christianity was to promote social change to hasten the creation of a new social order. To him it was a far less important objective of Christianity that it should prepare the individual for life after death.

Nor did Gwili confine himself to the western valleys. In 1910 he accepted an invitation to preach at Seion Welsh Baptist Chapel at Cwmaman, Aberdare. His text was, "Seek ye first the Kingdom of God and His righteousness" and he evidently shocked the large congregation by using the pulpit to make a bitter attack on landlords who he said had appropriated the land which was given to the people.[44] It was also significant that his sermon was given in the week of the 1910 election in Keir Hardie's constituency. During the course of his sermon Gwili openly advocated the giving of *one* vote in favour of Keir Hardie even though the Merthyr/Aberdare constituency was a two member seat.

It was at election times that a surprisingly large number of nonconformist ministers seemed prepared to support ILP candidates. Despite George Neighbour's protestations that he was the only socialist preacher in Aberdare it is known that the Rev. Ernest Tidman, also a Baptist, supported Keir Hardie in 1906.[47] By 1910 other Aberdare ministers, who were said to be progressive in theological terms, judged Keir Hardie to be an admirable candidate. These included the Rev. D. Silyn Evans of Siloa, Congregational Chapel and the Rev. J. M. Jones a Calvinistic Methodist minister.[48]

In the Gower election of 1906 the support of the Rev. Gomer Lewis, of Capel Gomer Baptist Chapel, for the successful Labour candidate was believed to have been crucial. In a famous election address Lewis stated that "He felt a desire to leave the ministry and become an agitator, to devote himself to the work of uplifting the toilers".[49] Speaking at the Calvinistic Methodist assembly in Caernarfon in 1908 a member of the denominational hierarchy, the Rev. Dr. J. Cynddylan Jones, shocked his audience by stating that he had voted labour for a number of years although it has to be said that the Labour men of his acquaintance were those of the Lib-Lab grouping such as Mabon and William Brace.[50] Nevertheless, it is important to recognise that some sections of the nonconformist ministry were advocating a move away from Liberalism, even progressive Liberalism, to a support for independent Labour candidates.

Undoubtedly the most colourful Labour supporter among the nonconformist ministry was the Rev. T. E. Nicholas (Nicholas y Glais) of Seion Congregational Chapel, Glais. In 1911 he became the editor of the Welsh section of the Labour newspaper the *Merthyr Pioneer*. He was imprisoned for his pacifist views during the war and in 1920 he became a founder member of the Communist Party of Great Britain.[51] In that sense Nicholas was an exception but this need not necessarily lessen his influence on his congregation or his ministerial brethren in the critical period up to 1914.

In North Wales the steady if unspectacular growth of ILP influence after 1904, following the end of the three year Penrhyn lock-out, owed much to the Rev. R. Silyn Roberts of Bethel Calvinistic Methodist Chapel, Tanygrisiau (1905–12). Roberts worked mainly with the slate quarrymen for whom he published in 1908 a pamphlet entitled *Y Blaid Lafur Annibynol: Ei hanes a'i hamcan* (The Independent Labour Party: its history and purpose). In this he expounded in intelligible terms the inherent Christianity which pervaded the gradualist approach to the achievement of the socialist ideal.[52] The labour movement in North Wales inevitably displayed a distinctly Welsh flavour in its development. At the annual demonstration of the North Wales Quarrymen's Union at Blaenau Ffestiniog one speaker regarded it as the duty of Welsh workmen to see how they could adapt their aspirations to those of the socialists in England without sacrificing their particular Welsh interests. At the same demonstration Silyn Roberts advocated nothing less than the nationalisation of land, mountains and the means of transmission of merchandise.[53]

The blending of socialist and nationalist aspirations received its best expression in a significant, if abortive, meeting at Carmarthen in 1911. A group of Labour sympathisers came together to discuss the formation of a specifically Welsh Labour Party. The aim was to work within the ILP framework for the standard programme of social improvement but this was to be allied to the just demands for a national identity for Wales. In effect, the meeting was an attempt to fuse the movement in the quarrying areas of the North with that of the western part of the South Wales coalfield, the anthracite area. The common factor apart from their socialist beliefs being that both areas enjoyed an almost exclusively Welsh language culture. Delegates at the meeting included Silyn Roberts, Nicholas y Glais, Gwili Jenkins and a Baptist minister, Herbert Morgan. The group also included the academic T. Hudson Williams who had been responsible for the Welsh translation of John Clifford's Fabian tract entitled *Socialism and the Teaching of Christ.*

Keir Hardie noted the nationalist demands of the Welsh and in his election addresses he was always ready to declare himself a Welsh home ruler. In 1912 he published *The Red Dragon and the Red Flag* in which he outlined, not always convincingly, the common aims of socialism and Welsh national aspirations, though he was opposed to the formation of a Welsh Labour Party, "The national party I have in view is this — the people of Wales fighting to recover the land of Wales, the working people of Wales acquiring the mines, furnaces, railways, and the public works generally."[55]

The period 1906–12 was one in which a number of nonconformist ministers, whilst not overtly advocating socialism, were preaching a progressive Gospel in which social change and not charitable work was seen as fundamental. In North Wales the Rev. J. Puleston Jones, a Calvinistic Methodist minister from Pwllheli, was adopting a policy of social evangelism towards his congregations. He claimed to be inspired both by the religious revival and by new developments in theology. He wanted theology to be related to the problems of this life. Much of his preaching emphasised the practical aspects of Bible teaching, especially the lessons of the Epistle of St. James.[56] At Merthyr the Rev. Rowland Jones of Tabernacle Baptist Church withstood immense criticism for preaching to the ILP national conference which was held in the town in 1912. He and his deacons were particularly vilified for actually inviting the conference into the chapel.[57] In the same year the Rev. David Pughe, who claimed to be a Fabian socialist, led a "Brotherhood" campaign in Merthyr on behalf of the Wesleyan Methodists. He pointed out to his listeners that he wanted his form of socialism to reflect true Christian values, and the campaign was apparently well-received.[58] One of the most significant results of the progressive movement within Nonconformity was the creation in 1911 of the Welsh School of Social Service. The idea was originally promoted among English Congregationalists but the Welsh version was devised on specifically non-denominational lines. Two of the leading figures were Baptists, the Rev. Gwilym Davies, a notable peace campaigner and the Rev. Herbert Morgan, minister of a leading Baptist chapel in London. Morgan was the defeated Labour candidate in his home town of Neath in 1918. The School was probably more representative of Progressive Liberalism but at the inaugural meeting the Rev. T. Richards of Newport pleaded with the churches to devote their efforts to solving the social problem in all its manifestations. His reasoning was based on the political reality that their congregations were made up of a large number of socialist and ILP members as well as Liberals and Conservatives.[59] Herbert Morgan at the next meeting in 1912 called for social justice and not charity as a remedy for poverty. For example, he wanted the drink problem to be properly diagnosed — it was caused by bad housing conditions, by uncongenial surroundings, and by depressing conditions of employment and not by the degeneracy of the individual.[60] This outlook can be profitably compared with those views which brought into being the Forward Movement in the 1890's. Its architects firmly believed that the masses ". . . have been sent here in order that we should Christianize them and cleanse them from their pernicious habits".[61]

Orthodox Liberal Nonconformity, which remained the majority view by far, regarded both New Theology and socialism with equal horror. Typical of the invective was that New Theology was an import from England, and as such the very last place it should be heard was in the chapels of the Welsh Calvinistic Methodists. The Mid-Rhondda Free Church Council attacked New Theology as being appropriate to heathen London where Campbell had claimed that only one-fifth of the city's inhabitants attended any church. But in Wales, they argued, Old Theology had proved gloriously triumphant and therefore what need had they for any watering down process.[62] Speaking at the opening of the John Pugh Memorial Hall at Porth in 1908, as part of the Forward Movement's campaign, Alderman T. H. Howell,

Marvelled that men holding the views of the New Theologians were allowed to preach in the Chapels in Wales — the land of Sunday Schools and Bible-readers . . ..the men who held these views had a perfect right to expound them in proper places, but it was a 'desecration and a violation of holy things' for them to teach these views in the pulpits of Welsh chapels'.[64]

The nonconformist criticism of socialism was equally unintellectual. There were constant references to the charge that socialists "spat in the face of Christ", while the Rev. W. E. Harries of Beulah Baptist Chapel, Aberdare said that Keir Hardie was an atheist and anyway he did not want a Scotsman to represent a Welsh borough.[64] One ILP councillor in Aberdare claimed that he knew of a preacher in the town who preached on the premise that the immediate need was *not* better houses for the people but better people for the houses.[65]

An aggressive critic of socialism and New Theology was the Calvinistic Methodist minister, the Rev. W. F. Phillips, who was defeated by the Labour candidate in the Gower election in 1910. Possibly, a critical factor in his defeat was the revelation in *Llais Llafur* (Voice of Labour) that Phillips had been for a few months a member of the Newport branch of the ILP. Phillips published numerous articles in Welsh and English on the theme *Is Socialism Anti-Christian in its tendency?*. For Phillips the question was largely rhetorical. He readily concurred with the emphasis on social questions but he was critical of the "class war" implication of socialist speakers. The literary monthly *Y Geninen* 1907–12, recorded in some detail the essence of the debate between Old and New Theology, and also the related discussions on Christianity and Socialism. Opponents of the progressivists seized on the abolition of private property and division of wealth as being entirely anti-Christian. One sympathetic writer in *Y Geninen* declared that it was not so much the ministers who were opposed to Labour but the "sêt-fawr", the deacons, who were largely self-made men, capitalists and Liberal voters. It was they who decided that the Liberal candidate could have the loan of the chapel, but the Labour Party could not use the chapel because the trust deeds prohibited its use for political purposes. The implication was that the deacons looked upon the Liberal Party as a religious denomination, an adjunct to their faith, but upon the Labour Party as a purely political section. The same writer believed that energetic young men who once attended chapel were leaving to take up the ILP as their religion.[67]

There are a number of examples among the miners' leaders of those who had claimed a religious affiliation in early life but who saw an irreconcilable dichotomy between the Christianity of orthodox nonconformity and the socialist ideal. For example, A. J. Cook as a young man was a Baptist lay preacher, but he became disillusioned by the failure of the Churches to translate revival enthusiasm into a programme for socialist improvement.[68] Frank Hodges was another leader who left the Primitive Methodist Church to take a greater interest in unionism and the ILP.[69] It would also be possible to point to the policy document of the syndicalists, *The Miners' Next Step* as containing no religious references not even to oppose it. But how typical were Cook, Hodges or Noah Ablett, the best known author of *The Miners Next Step*? In general, they were of English extraction, educated at Ruskin or the Central Labour College, and rather detached from the spirit of Welsh nonconformity which still pervaded many communities on the coalfield.

There is therefore another side to the attempted reconciliation between religion and socialism in the pre-war years. For James Griffiths, at that time leader of the anthracite miners, the revival and the New Theology were essential elements in the creation of a new social outlook based upon the moral certainties of Christianity. Griffiths, brought up as a Welsh Congregationalist, recalled in later years that two events gave his socialism a solid Christian foundation and allowed him to translate his ideology in a tangible and comprehensible way. Firstly, he remembered hearing R. J. Campbell at Ystalyfera in May 1908. This was followed by a visit to the Miners' Hall at Gwauncaegurwen to listen to Keir Hardie. We should not be surprised that Griffiths was of the opinion that Keir Hardie's type of socialism made a stronger appeal to his religious idealism than the rival Social Democratic Federation with its rigid Marxism and anti-religious bias.[70] The incipient labour movement must have been aided to some extent in the industrial Welsh communities by the genuine attempt to combine religion and socialism in a practical way. Gwili's development of the New Theology gave an intellectual as much as a theological basis to the Welsh labour movement. Possibly Wales rather lacked the ideological framework which the Fabians provided in England, but some Welsh religious leaders could provide a comprehensible ideology based on recognisable Christian precepts. Even Fabian discussions, where they did take place in Wales, were almost exclusively religious in nature as, for example, at the Bala Theological College in the 1890's. Rhondda Williams and Gwili provided some Welsh working people with a single faith in which they could incorporate their religious and social values. This might also partly explain the exceptional increase in ILP branches in South Wales, from 29 in 1906 to 85 in 1908. The areas of greatest ILP growth were the Rhondda and the anthracite region, precisely those areas where New Theology had received its most attentive and enthusiastic audiences.[71]

Moreover, we should not ignore the popular dimension of nonconformity, for it was that dimension which had secured its centrality in 19th century Welsh society. The revival of 1904 had shown that Welsh nonconformity still had a dynamic element within it and that ordinary people, however intermittently, wished to retain the right to contribute in some way to the conduct of religious life. Similarly, when orthodox ministers criticised the New Theology working men wrote to the local press asking for more information and requesting that chapels be made available for discussion of this important topic. It was colliers who made up the bulk of the membership of the eight branches of the League of Progressive Theology and Social Service to be established in the Rhondda. One New Theology lecturer visiting the Rhondda in 1908 was heartened by the numbers of young colliers joining the League. He noted that the religious revival had swept through the Rhondda but now there were signs of a more lasting revival in which the message was not so much individual ecstasy as social service to others.[72]

In November 1908, 17 followers of the New Theology were expelled from Bethlehem Welsh Congregational Church in the mining village of Abercwmboi, Aberdare. Whilst many local ministers supported the action of the minister and deacons, local people were incensed that the voice of ordinary chapel members was not being heard. The expelled members again set up a "Brotherhood Church" with the support of the omnipresent Rhondda Williams who regretted the split but concluded that, "the truth cannot be quenched and the Progressive Movement must and will go on". Williams also maintained with some foresight that the best course of action for the churches was, "to remain neutral regarding political parties, and let the members and officers and ministers have perfect liberty to join any party they like. He begged of religious people to let their ministers exercise this liberty. If they did not then they would certainly alienate the workmen of the country."[73]

In analysing the achievement of the movement which attempted to provide the religious underpinning of the developing social and political movement, it is relatively easy to accept the traditional view of most labour historians that the quasi-religious phase which the Welsh labour movement experienced in the years 1906–14 was merely a half way house or stepping off point to complete religious alienation.[74] For some this was certainly the case but in those Welsh communities where the chapel was and remained a way of life, a historical reality, the religious basis of ILP propaganda, and the support given to it by a significant section of the nonconformist ministry, made it acceptable as a working faith. Far from hindering socialism it provided an intelligible framework and a moral basis, by reference to which many people were able to justify their socialist views. It allowed the situation to occur, as Rhondda Williams had hoped, whereby it was entirely possible, indeed desirable, for a man to be a socialist and a member of the nonconformist chapel. Nonconformity did not collapse overnight and nor did the labour movement. The war was to affect both in fundamental ways but in the period before 1914 this particular brand of Welsh Christian socialism was just successful enough to attract the next generation of labour activists from within chapel congregations and this to the detriment of the Liberal party.

Whatever latter day observers may think of the moderate approach of the ILP in Wales before 1914 it is doubtful whether sufficient numbers of unexceptional Welsh workers would have joined ILP branches in this formative period had not the socialist creed been based on a solid Christian and moral foundation and not simply a socialism couched in occasional Biblical language.

Notes

1 A good introduction to the problem in its Welsh context is C. Gwyther, "Sidelights on Religion and Politics in the Rhondda Valley, 1906–26", *Llafur*, 3, i (1980) 30–43; see also C. R. Williams, "The Welsh Religious Revival, 1904–5", *British Journal of Sociology*, 3 (1952), 242–259.

2 S. Yeo, "A New Life: The Religion of Socialism in Britain 1893–1896," *History Workshop*, 4 (1977), 5–56.

3 E. J. Hobsbawm, "Religion and the Rise of Socialism", in his *Worlds of Labour* (London, 1984), 33.

4 *Report Evidence and Indexes of the Royal Commission appointed to inquire into the Church and other Religious Bodies in Wales*, 1910, xiv, 19.

5 *Ibid.* 19 and 25.

6 For the early history of the Forward Movement see Rev. Howell Williams, *The Romance of the Forward Movement of the Presbyterian Church of Wales* (Denbigh, 1946), 34–40.

7 T. Mardy Rees, *Frank and Seth Joshua, The Renowned Evangelists* (Wrexham, 1926), 114.

8 See The Rev. W. Evans, *An Outline of the History of Welsh Theology* (London, 1900), 261 and *The Treasury*, XV (1927), 137–40.

9 See *Labour Leader*, 26 May 1894 and 30 June 1894.

10 *South Wales Daily News*, (hereafter SWDN), 9 November 1891. See also *Labour Leader*, 16 June 1894.

11 S. G. Hobson, *The Possibilities of the Labour Church* (Cardiff, 1893), 4.

12 *SWDN*, 6 July 1907.

13 S.G. Hobson, *Pilgrim to the Left* (London, 1936).

14 *SWDN*, 20 August 1898.

15 Quoted in Emrys Hughes, *Keir Hardie* (London, 1956), 90.

16 *Labour Leader*, 9 July 1898.

17 *Ibid.*, 11 February 1899.

18 The incident is recounted in *Aberdare Times*, 13 August 1898 and 15 February 1898. See also *Labour Leader*, 10 September 1898 and *Aberdare Times*, 28 May 1898 for other examples of chapel desertions.

19 *Adroddiadau Cyfundeb Dwyreiniol Morgannwg, 1898–1900*, cited in E. T. Davies, *Religion in the Industrial Revolution in South Wales* (Cardiff, 1965), 155 6.

20 The establishment and growth of the society is documented in its minute books; see Glamorgan Record Office (hereafter GRO), Aberdare Socialist Society Minute Books, 1895–1908, D/DX/J 2–5.

21 *Aberdare Leader*, 26 August 19092.

22 *Aberdare Leader*, 19 July 1902; GRO, Aberdare Socialist Society Minute Books, D/DX hj 2 16–17.

23 See W.T. Stead, *The Revival in the West* (London, 1905), 24–5.

24 The local origins of the revival have been analysed by David Jenkins in *The Agricultural Community in South West Wales at the turn of the twentieth century* (Cardiff, 1971), 219–28.

25 See D. M. Phillips, *Evan Roberts, The Great Welsh Revivalist and his Work* (London, 1906), 211–12; and D. Matthews, *I saw the Welsh Revival* (Chicago, 1951), especially 49–50.

26 The course of events is detailed in "Awstin", *The Religious Revival in Wales, 1904–5*, (Cardiff, 1905). This was a special reprint in six volumes of articles which had originally appeared in the *Western Mail*.

27 "Awstin", *The Religious Revival in Wales*, 2, 22. For a retrospective summary of the revival see *SWDN*, 7,8, 9 February 1906.

28 *Labour Leader*, 6 January 1905.

29 *Ibid.*, 10 February 1905.

30 See transcripts of recorded interviews in the South Wales Miners' Library, 13/1–3 Ernest Lewis (Blaenavon), 77/11 John Jones (Caerau) and 12/5 Abel Morgan (Ynysybwl).

31 *Rhondda Leader*, 6 May 1905.

32 J. Rogues de Fursac, *Un Movement Mystique Contemporain: Le Reveil Religieux du Pays de Galles 1904–5* (Paris, 1907), 89–90.

33 See Rev. R.J. Campbell, *City Temple Sermons* (London, 1904) and Keith Robbins, "The Spiritual Pilgrimage of the Rev. R.J. Campbell", *Journal of Ecclesiastical History*, 30, 2 (1979), 261–276.

34 R. J. Campbell, *The New Theology* (London, 1907), 173.

35 See *Rhondda Leader*, 28 March 1908.

36 For Williams see *Who's Who in Wales, 1920*, (Cardiff, 1921), 526, see also *Rhondda Leader*, 15 February 1907 and *Aberdare Leader*, 9 January 1909.

37 *Royal Commission . . . into the Church and other Religious Bodies in Wales*, xvii, 394.

38 *Rhondda Leader*, 2 May 1908.

39 Rev. J. M. Jones, *Religion and Socialism* (Merthyr Tydfil, 1910), *passim*.

40 *Rhondda Leader*, 18 May 1907. For Nicholas see also *Who's Who in Wales, 1920*, 340.

41 *Aberdare Leader*, 29 January 1910.

42 *Rhondda Leader*, 14 September 1907.

43 For the background to the establishment of the Brotherhood Church see *Aberdare Leader*, 23 January 1909 and 13 March 1909.

44 See, for example, *Aberdare Leader*, 19 December 1908 and R*hondda Leader*, 23 January 1909. Also James Griffiths, *Pages from Memory* (London, 1969), 16.

45 For Gwili see E. Cefni Jones, *Gwili:Cofiant a Phregethu* (Llandysul, 1937), 151–55 and, J. B. Smith, "John Gwili Jenkins 1872–1936", *Transactions of the honourable Society of Cymrodorion*, 1975,191–214.

46 *Merthyr Express*, 22 January 1910.

47 *Aberdare Leader*, 20 January 1906.

48 *Aberdare Leader*, 10 January 1910. Other ministerial sympathisers are noted in R. Tudur Jones, *Ffydd Ac Argyfwng Cenedl: Cristionogaeth a Diwylliant yng Nghymru, 1890–1914* (Swansea, 1982), II, 265–71.

49 *SWDN*, 22 January 1906 and quoted in K. O. Morgan, "The Gower Election of 1906", *Gower*, XII (1959), 17.

50 *Caernarvon and Denbigh Herald*, 28 August 1908.

51 See K. O. Morgan, "The New Liberalism and the Challenge of Labour: The Welsh Experience, 1885–1929", *Welsh History Review*, VI (1972), 296 and on Labour development in general 294–304.

52 Rev. R. Silyn Roberts, *Y Blaid Lafur Annibynol: Ei hanes a'i hamcan* (Blaenau Ffestiniog, 1908), 5. For a full analysis of Roberts's contribution see Cyril Parry, "The Independent Labour Party and Gwynedd Politics, 1900–20", *Welsh History Review*, IV (1968), 53–4.

53 *Carnarvon and Denbigh Herald*, 8 May 1908 quoted in R. Merfyn Jones, *The North Wales Quarrymen 1876–1922* (Cardiff, 1981), 317.

54 *Labour Leader*, 7 July 1911 and 10 July 1913.

55 J. Keir Hardie, *The Welsh Dragon and the Welsh Flag*, (Merthyr Tydfil, 1912).

56 R. W. Jones, *Y Parchedig John Puleston Jones, MA, DD* (Caernarfon, 1929), 130–31.

57 *Merthyr Express*, 1 June 1912, 15 June 1912 and Jones's article in the Baptist periodical *Seren Gomer*, March 1910.

58 *Ibid.*, 21 September 1912.

59 *SWDN*, 8 September 1911; see also K.O. Morgan, "The New Liberalism and the Challenge of Labour", 297.

60 Rev. Herbert Morgan, *The Church and the Social Problem* (Carmarthen, 1911), 11. For Morgan see *Who's Who in Wales, 1920*, 320–21.

61 National Library of Wales, Calvinistic Methodist Archives, 5924, "The Forward Movement".

62 *Rhondda Leader*, 25 April 1908.

63 *Ibid.*, 3 October 1908.

64 *Aberdare Leader*, 8 September 1906. Ordinary Chapel members also shared such views, "He (Keir Hardie) don't believe in the Bible, or God", in W. J. Edwards, *From the Valley I Came* (London, 1956), 89.

65 *Ibid.*, 3 March 1906.

66 See, for example, W. F. Phillips, *Is Socialism anti-Christian in its tendency?* (Newport, 1910); also *Y Geninen*, January 1911,17–22, and *Merthyr Express*, 26 October 1912.

67 *Y Geninen*, October 1910, 258–261.

68 Paul Davies, "The Making of A. J. Cook", *Llafur*, II (1978), 43 and *Dictionary of Welsh Biography Down to 1940* (London, 1959), 81–22.

69 F. Hodges, *My Adventures as a Labour leader* (London, 1925), 38. For a similar view see A. Horner, *Incorrigible Rebel* (London, 1960), 21.

70 James Griffiths, *Pages from Memory*, 14 and Griffiths's personal testimony to the author in an interview recorded in 1974.

71 *Glamorgan Free Press*, 22 January 1909, *ILP Conference Reports* (London, 1905–9).

72 *Rhondda Leader*, 12 December 1908.

73 *Aberdare Leader*, 23 January 1909. The background to the split is recorded in edition of 7 November 1908.

74 *Rhondda Socialist*, January 1913, 294–5.

5

Serfdom and Slavery: Women's Work in Wales, 1890–1930

Dot Jones

The search for women's past in Wales has only just begun. In England the discovery in the 1970s that half history is women's history quickly found expression in many different directions: in a surge of new research in history and the social sciences; in the setting up of feminist publishers concentrating on reprinting the work of women writers; and in the creation of Womens Studies courses in universities and colleges. In Wales the response to this shift in historical direction was more sluggish whilst, not surprisingly, the Welsh experience was almost totally ignored by those writing in the English mainstream.

Nevertheless, despite difficulties presented by the scarcity of source material, the work has begun. Angela John leads the way by including Wales in her detailed study of Victorian pit women, *By the Sweat of their Brow*, and by raising important methodological issues in her analysis of the female role in existing Welsh mining history.[1] John Williams has looked at female occupations as given in the 19th century censuses[2]; Deirdre Beddoe at Welsh women transported as convicts[3]; Neil Evans at Cardiff women active in philanthropy.[4] Oral evidence has been used as a means of investigating the more recent past in several articles: on women in the tinplate industry[5]; the migration of women from Wales to England[6]; and the lives of Rhondda women between the wars[7]. Regretfully, the list of postgraduate theses on womens' work in Wales remains a short one[8]. Indeed, much of the enthusiasm for women's history lies outside higher education in Wales, in local history societies and women's groups, and with film and video makers such as Boudicea, Red Flannel, Swansea Women's History Group. Boudicea, for example, produced a video, *We Have Been Here for All Time* showing the role of Welsh women in five periods of protest ranging from the late 18th century food riots to the womens peace movement of the 1980s. In television, HTV broke new ground with their Welsh history series *The Dragon has Two Tongues* by co-ordinating viewers groups to stimulate further interst and discussion. One of the four source packs distributed during the series contained material exclusively on women. An encouraging recent development has been the launching of *Honno* a Cardiff based womens publishing co-operative. Their first two titles, one in English, one in Welsh, told the lives of two Welsh working women — a nurse in the Crimean War and a teacher in London in the 1960s.[9]

The first objective of this paper is to add a little to these beginnings. It also aims to shift attention away from a traditional interest in labour history in terms of male-centred power struggles — the fight for trade union recognition, industrial and political conflict — and to focus instead simply on work itself and its official recognition. Finally, I hope to demonstrate that this approach is especially helpful for revealing the positive economic significance of women's labour in the past.

A recent study published by the Equal Opportunity Commission contained the allegation "that women's economic, social and occupational positions in and contributions to society are systematically belittled and obscured by simplifying conventions which give primacy to the currently 'economically active' and to 'heads of households' as reference persons for classification, the definitions in each case having an effective male bias"[10]. The occupational part of this theme is taken up here in an historical context by looking at the contribution made by female labour to the Welsh economy during the period 1890–1930. The topic is approached from two perspectives, one general and one more specific. A general view is presented through a very brief outline of the structure and changes in female occupations as portrayed by the official census figures. Part of the outcome of this review is to reveal the inadequacy of the official measures of women's work, and thus to prompt a more specific look at female labour in two very different Welsh localities: rural Cardiganshire in the west, and the Urban District of the Rhondda valleys in the S. Wales coalfield. Although most women in each of these regions were returned as 'unoccupied' by the census enumerators, this closer examination shows that their labour, quite different in each case, was indispensable to their local economies.

I. Census occupation returns

Firstly, the official version of women work in Wales as suggested by the census figures. It is perhaps worth emphasising two aspects of the general economic background which have particular relevance to women. The first is the absence of a manufacturing sector, to compare with, say, the cotton mills of Lancashire or the light engineering works of the Midlands, which in other regions of Britain provided paid employment for women as well as men. The second is the dominance in South Wales of the coal mining industry which at a peak gave direct employment to a quarter of a million men to the almost total exclusion of women.

The hint that, compared to England, there were few employment opportunities for women in Wales is substantiated by a glance at the census figures shown in Table 1. Throughout the period the participation rate (occupied as a % total in age group) is less than 25% for Wales. The comparable figure for England is about 35%. However before reading too much into the census figures, some major shortcomings should be noted[11]. Thus the tables certainly understate the extent of paid female labour[12]. We know that much of womens work was casual, temporary, seasonal, or of the type just not recorded in the census returns. For example, many Rhondda homes gave room to lodgers; but how many coalminers would consider entering their wives as "lodging-house keepers"?[13] And where, on census night, were the 4–500 women, many of them Irish, whose work unloading ships at Cardiff docks was described by several witnesses before the 1890 Royal Commission on Labour?[14] The 1891 census records just two female dock workers.

Under-recording is one problem; inconsistency another. Apart from the obvious break in classification between 1911 and 1921 there is also continuous confusion as how to classify female family labour. In Agriculture the situation is not far from chaotic. In 1881 equal weight had been given to farmers' male and female relatives returned as working on the farm. However, in 1891, instructions on the householders schedule ("Sons, or other relatives of farmers employed on the farm should be returned as 'Farmer's Son', 'Farmer's Brother', etc.") implied the exclusion of females. Even where female relatives were returned as such they were excluded from the final tables for Agriculture. Though the same instructions appear on the 1901 schedule, where female relatives assisting on the farm were "so returned" they were at least included in the final table. And from 1911 onwards the instructions indicated clearly that assisting female relatives should be included.

Not without good cause has the 1891 census been described as eccentric. To add to the confusion in Agriculture in that year, female relatives returned as assisting in household duties were included in Domestic Offices and Services[15]. The result, as table 1 shows, makes comparisons over time and between the two most important female occupation classes (Agriculture and Service) difficult. At a local level table 2 clearly shows the effect of these inconsistancies in Cardiganshire with totals for "female relatives assisting in the work of the farm" fluctuating between 0 and 1,662. In the Rhondda, confusion over keeping lodgers is the cause of the wild swings in the totals for this class — the 1891 census suggests 1174 female lodging and boarding house keepers; the 1901 census only 20, in a broader category.

With these warnings in mind, useful general points can still be extracted from the census tables. For women in Wales as a whole; a low participation rate; the dominance of the Service sector throughout; an overall move from Dress etc. to Professional, Clerical, and Sales occupations. For commercial centres, as represented by Cardiff, higher participation and a greater range of employment. For rural Wales, represented by Cardiganshire, a higher participation rate but little choice. And for mining South Wales, as represented by the Rhondda, low participation and little choice. The experience of women in the labour market was certainly very different to that of men.

II. Women in Rural Cardiganshire

So much for the census data. Now for a more detailed look at Cardiganshire, the region at the top of the official participation tables. A closer look shows restricted choices: the perennial ghettos of service and dressmaking, or else agriculture. There were comparatively few women engaged in professional occupations. Despite the growth of tourism in the later 19th century (Aberystwyth claimed the title "Queen of Welsh Watering Places"), and the mining of lead in the north of the county, the overwhelming concerns of most inhabitants were deeply rooted in agriculture.

Indeed, Cardiganshire was the heartland of traditonal rural Welsh society, a random scatter of small farms and cottages. In the early 1900s a fifth of all holdings were less than 5 acres, 70% were under 50 acres and any holding over about 150 acres was termed a "large place". As for land use, Cardiganshire farm land was mainly upland and poor; the climate too unfavourable for much besides the rearing of livestock. Cultivated crops of wheat, barley, oats were grown solely for the local needs of people and animals. Not only food but other needs too — clothes, tools, utensils — could be supplied from locally prepared materials of wool, wood, and leather. Only the ability of the larger farms to produce butter and to fatten store cattle for sale to dealers in the spring or autumn extended the agricultural industry of Cardiganshire beyond a fairly primitive closed economy. It involved a way of life which had changed little over the previous century and which remained essentially unchanged, despite emigration and some mechanisation[16], until the arrival of the Milk Marketing Board in the 1930s.

As for labour; farms and smallholdings were worked mainly by family labour. According to the census, the ratio of farm labourers to farmers was low; the ratio of females to males in agricultural occupations was high. The 1911 census seems to be the least unrealistic regarding the contribution of women to agricultural labour. A fifth of "farmers and graziers" enumerated in 1911 were female; half of the "relatives assisting in the work of the farm" were female; and if agricultural labourers and farm servants are added to these figures, one third of the total enumerated labour force in agriculture in Cardiganshire was female.

In addition, outside the conventions of census classification, larger farms were able to draw on an uncounted labour supply, through networks of interdependence which linked larger farms to particular smallholders and landless cottagers in a traditional system peculiar to Wales — a legacy of the law of Civil Obligation dating back to mediaeval and to tribal Wales.[17] Put simply, any additional labour required by larger farms (e.g. at hay and corn harvest) which could not be met by family and regular farm servants and labourers, was supplied by nearby cottagers and smallholders whose own acreage was too small for self sufficiency. In exchange for their labour, these neighbouring cottagers and smallholders received, not money wages, but a variety of goods and services throughout the year.

The most vital of these service customs for the cottager, was the use of land to grow potatoes. The setting of one potato row by the farmer on his land, with a pile of manure beside it, incurred one days' 'work' or 'potato' debt to be repaid at the corn harvest. The potatoes were used to feed the cottager's pig, two pigs if possible, one fattened as a baconer for household use, and one as a porker, sold live, to pay the rent. As David Jenkins remarks:

keeping a pig in fact functioned as a savings bank . . . pig-keeping was one of the few ways in which a cottager (and especially his wife) could convert his spare-time labour into cash.[18]

A higher network of mutual aid operated above cottager level, between neighbouring farms and smallholders involving those keeping a bull and those of less than about 60 acres keeping cows but no bull. In return for a bull's service labour was owed and repaid during the hay harvest. These examples illustrate just two of the countless ways labour, and a variety of services and produce, were exchanged without any cash transfer through the farming seasons in Cardiganshire.

These networks of exchange are especially important from the female labour point of view because, for the cottagers, women were invariably the ones sent to repay the work debt. It was women who bound the cut corn into sheaves. They also raked and turned and helped to load at the hay harvest in return for 'debt butter', or if times were hard, just for the meals provided. Their husbands often had other part time craft occupations and only helped if the women and children could not fulfill their family's obligations alone. The main burden fell upon the women.

But what of women without the support of a male head-of-household? Over 60% of women aged 20–40 were unmarried. David Jenkins found that a one out of every five holdings under 15 acres in a south Cardiganshire parish in 1901 was occupied by a widow or spinster. He continues by saying that:

they (with others who occupied cottages without land) undertook the incidental tasks of the countryside and visited farms to work in that capacity. They collected stones from the hayfield and placed them in roadside heaps to earn payment from the highways authority: some worked as quiltmakers, as dressmakers, and others specialised in the trade of making women's garters. They were casual workers at farms where they were paid for an occasional days washing or potato-sorting. Each one was connected with a particular farm in relations of interdependence.[19]

So, there was a continual mixing, at every social level, from the larger farmer who needed reserve labour to cottager whose only opportunity for employment was to supply this labour on casual demand. Unrecorded women's work was a large and essential ingredient to this mix. Moreover, the picture portrayed by the notion of mutual cooperation — a sort of social symbiosis — is superficially a very attractive one. But, if we look now at the rewards of their labour — even if we confine attention to the most basic quality-of-life measures — food, housing, health — for many women tied to agriculture in rural Cardiganshire the myth of the rural idyll soon crumbles.

Firstly, food. The diet of the cottager was notoriously monotonous, inadequate and insufficient. It was hard to believe there could be such general malnutrition in an agricultural region. In 1922 there were 20,000 pigs, 27,000 dairy cattle, over 1/4 million sheep, and almost 1/2 million poultry in Cardiganshire[20]; less than 60,000 women, men and children. Yet the cottagers were living on tea, bread, broth, and occasional salt meat.

Housing too was woefully inadequate. The one and two roomed cottages were usually of stone, some were simply whitewashed mud, with small windows either unopenable or unopened. Some were still only mud floored. Many were in bad repair and unfit for habitation. They were dark, damp, badly ventilated hovels, with no proper water supply, drainage or sanitation. Conditions were bad throughout our period. In 1920 the exasperated county Medical Officer of Health reported: "No breeder of animals could expect success if he reared his stock under conditions similar to those in which some of the children in the county are brought up".[21]

The combined effect of bad housing and poor diet was an incidence of TB one might have expected in the crowded slums of an English industrial city. In 1922 Cardiganshire had the highest death rate from pulmonary TB of any county in England and Wales. The groups at highest risk were girls and young women. Yet Cardiganshire children had a better chance at birth than most. Because of the late age of marriage in the rural areas infant mortality (a common poverty indicator) was comparatively low. However, as table 3a shows, by the age of five this advantage was lost and thereafter mortality rate do not compare as well as one might expect with the remainder of rural England and Wales as a whole. Besides a high incidence of T.B., maternal mortality was alarming enough to prompt official investigation despite the low absolute number of deaths involved. It was not just a case of poor medical services but of sheer poverty too. As the parliamentary Report on Maternal Mortality in Wales in 1936 bluntly put it " . . .in rural Wales the standard of living has always been low."[22]

With such poor rewards it was no wonder that the young women of Cardiganshire, like the young men, left in droves when the opportunity arose. Many women left Britain altogether, others went as servants to English households. Some travelled only as far as the South Wales coalfield to yet another unpaid occupation, as wives to the South Wales coalminers.

In 1911 almost 7,000 females enumerated in Glamorgan had been born in Cardiganshire (equivalent to about one quarter of the number of females born and remaining in Cardiganshire). Two and a half thousand of these women were living within the boundary of the Rhondda Urban district.

III. Women in the Rhondda

Any move from Cardiganshire to the Rhondda was in many ways a move from one extreme to another. From a traditional, rural inward looking stagnating economy to new, vigorous, urban communities where prosperity depended largely on the export of a single commodity — steam coal — supplying power around the world, in particular, fuelling the brief dominance of steam power at sea.

In 1891 the population of the Rhondda, at 88,000, had almost doubled in ten years, and it was to almost double again, to reach a peak, at 169,000 by 1924. In 1913, there were 53 large collieries, with pits and villages strung like beads, along the 30 miles of the two valleys of the Rhondda Fawr and Rhondda Fach. That same year 9,600,000 tons of coal was raised and taken by train down the valleys to be shipped mainly out of Cardiff nearly all bound for a foreign port. By 1925 the boom had collapsed and the vulnerability of a single commodity economy was exposed, but for most of our period, in economic terms, the Rhondda was a thriving and expanding region.[23]

Unlike Cardiganshire, cash was a vital part of life. Wage rates for men were high. Even at the bottom end of the scale, a labourer underground in 1913 would earn twice the 16s 4d weekly wage of a Cardiganshire farm labourer. There were shops too, in which to spend these wages. The Shops Inspector listed 2,859 shops in the Rhondda Urban District in 1913:[24]

539 sweetshops and mixed businesses
298 grocers and provision dealers
260 greengrocers
217 butchers
194 drapers, hosiers and milliners
133 retailers of intoxicating liquors
130 confectioners and bread dealers
129 tailors, clothiers and outfitters
104 fried fish and chip shops

According to the census, one out of every 18 dwelling houses was also a shop.

Besides money and shops there were other contrasts. From an aging population to a young population; from a female majority to a male majority and a correspondingly high proportion of married women. In Cardiganshire in 1911, only 37% of women aged 20–40 were married; in the Rhondda 76% of the same age group were married. These contrasts carry through to family statistics. Glamorgan and Cardiganshire consistently feature at the top of two opposing U.K. County League Tables for Large and Small family size. It is from this point on, when we look beyond the attractions of shops, a new and tidy terraced house, a husband with the possibility of high money wages; and look at the work done by women in the Rhondda, one wonders whether any move from the old to the new was a wise one. There were few paid employment opportunities for women, and domestic labour was hard labour.

Three quarters of occupied males in the Rhondda were engaged in the coalmining industry. Their demanding work was no less demanding on the women of their households. No bathrooms, no hot running water, no pithead baths. Water was heated in large iron pans or boilers on a hob or over the open fire. The men and youths of the household — husband, brother, lodger, sons — returned from their shift with bodies and clothes soaked with water, perspiration and coaldust. They expected a hot meal and a hot bath to be ready and waiting. Shift times set the daily routine in almost every house in every village along the length of the valleys. When interviewed, one Rhondda woman[25] recalled her working day at home in the interwar period when her father and seven brothers worked underground on different shifts. Baths and hot meals had to be prepared for seven in the morning after the 11–7 night shift; at three in the afternoon after the 7–3 day shift; and at eleven at night after the 3–11 afternoon shift. When for a brief time in the 1920s the men were limited by law to a 7 hr working day, one cynic wryly commented "miners work seven hours themselves and work their women seventeen"[26]. It was not the men of the Rhondda who campaigned for pithead baths in the 20s and 30s but the women. They were totally bound in a straightjacket of hard physical drudgery which was as circumscribed by convention as any rural millstone of season or tradition.

If life was hard for women in a male-headed household, it was no easier for a woman who was herself the head-of-household in mining communities where the opportunity for paid employment for women was limited. Wil Jon Edwards was born in the Cynon valley, (next valley to the east of the Rhondda Fach) in 1888 soon after his father had been killed in a mining accident. His mother found ingenious ways to keep her family from the shame of Poor Law relief. In his autobiography *From the Valley I Came* he writes of his daily chores as a boy:

Saturday, in my mother's organisation was the day I must spend washing five hundred bottles ready for her to fill with what she called small beer, a strictly non-alcoholic drink she made with balm, brown sugar and some yeast . . . Men would flock to our house on Sunday mornings to drink this small beer . . . Nearly all of them took home a few bottles to enjoy with their Sunday dinner. The profits were not great; because the beer sold at a penny a bottle, but every penny counted in my mother's economy. On Tuesdays my mother and sister would bake buns; and my job was to make them brown and attractive by brushing their tops with a specially prepared paste. Tuesday night was band of hope night at Saron Chapel; and on my way there I would deliver twenty parcels of buns to as many houses.

Wednesday was 'taffy' day, and it was my duty to change the brown mass suspended from a long nail into a more attractive light shade by working it up and down. If we finished in time, Eliza and I, rewarded with a bag full of toffee drops, would go to the Ysgol Gan, the singing school.

Friday was our great day, faggot day, when my mother made large numbers of faggots which were notably popular. . ...Friday after Friday I would deliver a dozen faggots to each of a number of households who seemed always glad to have them. We had a hundred small hot-water jugs in which the faggots were kept warm to the point of delivery.[27]

Women such as Will Edwards' mother wore themselves out in their efforts to keep their families off the outdoor relief list, but their independence must have been precarious. The extras she and others like her offered would have been the first to be dropped when times were hard.

Paid employment opportunites were limited, and work demands on Rhondda women were in excess of an ordinary domestic role by the nature of their husbands' work. The demands were also in excess on account of early marriage and large families typical of mining communities. In 1915, the Co-operative Womens' Guild published letters they had received in response to a request to members to write about their experience of Motherhood. It was a shock to many. In the preface, Sir Herbert Samuel, President of the Local Government Board, admitted it was "the first time that the facts have been stated, not by medical men or social students, but by the sufferers themselves". Letter 87 is entitled "Struggles of a Miners Wife". The writer had had seven children, one miscarriage. Only four children survived. She writes:

I dare say I could write a book on my early struggles with my seven children, and a miner's home to contend with; and many a week my husband has not had a penny of wage to bring home, besides the experience of three big strikes and many small ones.

I may say we were married nineteen years before we lost one, and then I lost my baby first, a grand little girl of two. Then, a year and a half after, I lost a fine lad of fourteen in the fever hospital, of scarlet fever and diptheria. Two years after that we lost a girl of twelve from tubercular disease of the kidneys from cow's milk. The doctor was treating her for eight years for Bright's disease of the kidneys. I brought them up breast-fed, so she must have contracted it after she was weaned. Such a clever child she was. So you will see we have had our troubles.

I may say I had very good times at confinements, except the first and the last. The youngest was born feet first, which was an awful experience, and her heart was nearly stopped beating; so I think that left her heart weak, and she cut her teeth with bronchitis. I used to get up always by the ninth day until the last. I was between forty-one and forty-two when she was born, so had to rest a bit longer, but had to see to household duties as soon as possible.[28]

The circumstances and the lack of self-concern are typical. Though mortality rates for infectious diseases fell away in the 1900s, the Rhondda continued a high infant mortality rate. Through the 1890s, pneumonia, diarrhoea, measles, whooping cough, diptheria, scarlet fever, convulsions, and other causes were annually killing one out of every twelve children under five years of age. As well as cook, washerwomen, and charlady, women of the Rhonddas could add child nurse to their list of labours. Yet, as far as official statistiscs are concerned, Rhondda women were the most 'unoccupied' of any women anywhere in England and Wales.

If we look again at the mortality tables, grouped together as table 3, we see that mining-service labour and large families were bad for womens' health. Not only was maternal and infant mortality high, but in comparison with her husband, until the age of 45, she did not fare well (see table 3a). This is confirmed by national mortality rate based on husbands occupation (see table 3c). Young wives of hewers and getters were in the highest risk category of any women with occupied husbands — "their mortality being considerably above those for all married women for almost every cause"[29].

In conclusion, what does the case of rural Cardiganshire and the mining valleys of the Rhondda tell us about female labour? Fundamentally it shows that the census occupation tables are a poor measure of womens'work and a poor measure of female participation in the formal economy of two important regions of Wales. In Cardiganshire a whole system of labour supply was left unrecorded; in the Rhondda, as in other areas of the South Wales coalfield, while the spotlight played upon the labour and the dangers of the miner's occupation, his wife's working day was longer, and at times, her life at greater risk[30]. In both regions women not only performed the usual domestic role within the confines of a household, they also formed an essential part of the labour force in their respective local economies however narrowly defined. In neither region did they receive a money wage. One definition of 'serf' is 'a slave who cannot be sold off the land but passes from one owner to another with the land' — a close enough description of the working conditions of some women in rural Wales. And slavery is the description used by Rhondda women themselves, time and again, when interviewed, sometimes bitterly, sometimes wistfully, always after speaking with pride on the standard of housework achieved, against great odds and at great personal cost. It is time we included these women in our perception of the labour process.

Notes

Acknowledgements: My thanks to John Williams for his helpful comments, and to Angela John and Paul O'Leary for several references.

1 Angela V. John, *By the Sweat of Their Brow: Women Workers at Victorian Coal Mines* (London, 1980), and "A Miner Struggle? Women's Protests in Welsh

Mining History", *Llafur* IV, 1 (1984), 72–90.

2 L. J. Williams and D. Jones, "Women at Work in Nineteenth Century Wales", *Llafur* III, 3 (1983) 20–29.

3 Deirdre Beddoe, *Welsh Convict Women*, 1979.

4 Unpublished paper given in a workshop session on 'Self-Help'at Llafur Conference, 1983, 'Working Class Women, The Welsh Experience', Polytechnic of Wales. At the same session see my paper on women's Friendly Societies, "Self-help in Nineteenth Century Wales: the Rise and Fall of the Female Friendly Society", *Llafur*, IV, 1 (1984), 14–26.

5 Sheila Owen-Jones, "Women in the Tinplate Industry: Llanelli 1930–1950", *Oral History Journal*, XV, 1 (Spring 1987), 42–9.

6 Kate Bartholomew, "On the Move" *Planet*, 57 (June/July 1986), 51–7.

7 Rosemary Crooks, " 'Tidy Women': Women in the Rhondda Between the Wars", *Oral History* vol 10 no 2, Autumn 1982,40–46.

8 Rosemary Crooks, "Women of the Rhondda Valley between the Wars", (M.A. thesis, University of Leeds, 1980). Postgraduate work in progress at the time of writing (1988) includes: Ann Jones — women in service in Cardiff; Kate Bartholomew — women's migration and emigration; Val Lloyd — womens' work in N.E. Wales coalfield.

9 Jane Williams (ed.) *An Autobiography of Elizabeth Davies* (1857; new ed. 1987); Hafina Clwyd, *Buwch ar y Lein* (1987).

10 Roger Thomas, 'Classification of Women's Occupations', 28–46, in *E.O.C. Research Bulletin* 10, (1986): *Methodological issues in gender research.*

11 For a detailed discussion see Edward Higgs, "Women, occupation and work in the Nineteenth Century Censuses", *History Workshop Journal* 23, (Spring 1987), 59–80.

12 See C.Miller, "The Hidden Workforce: female field workers in Gloucestershire, 1870–1901", *Southern History*, 6 (1984), 139–61

13 For a discussion on the classification of lodging-house keepers see Leonore Davidoff, "The Separation of Home and Work? Landladies and Lodgers in Victorian and Edwardian England" in S. Burman (ed.), *Fit Work for Women* (1979).

14 PP, 1893–94 (c 6894 XXIII) XXXVII pt 1: Royal Commission on Labour. Reports from the Lady Commissioners, Miss Eliza Orme; "Employment for Women in Wales", 233–263.

15 See comment in the 1911 Census, vol X, *Occupations and Industry, Part I*, xxv, in which the figures for 1891 are excluded from a comparison of totals for Indoor Domestic Servants 1881–1911.

16 See J. Geraint Jenkins, "Technological Improvement and Social Change in South Cardiganshire", *Agricultural History Review*, XIII, pt II (1965), 94–105.

17 J. Geraint Jenkins, *Life and Traditions in Rural Wales* (1976), 15

18 David Jenkins, *The Agricultural Community in South-West Wales at the Turn of the Twentieth Century* (Cardiff, 1971), 59.

19 *Ibid*, 44.

20 John Williams, *Digest of Welsh Historical Statistics* (2 vols: Cardiff, 1985).

21 *Annual Report of the Medical Officer of Health* (Cardiganshire County Council, 1920).

22 PP 1936–7 (cd 5423) XI, Ministry of Health, *Report on Maternal Mortality in Wales.*

23 For the history of the Rhondda to the 1950s see E.D.Lewis *The Rhondda Valleys* (Cardiff, 1959).

24 *Annual Report of the Medical Officer of Health* (Rhondda Urban District Council, 1913).

25 Mrs Jenkins, interviewed by Rosemary Crooks — see note 7.

26 Quoted by E. L. Chappell and J. A. Lovat-Fraser, *Pithead and factory Baths* (1921) and refered to in a Min. of Health Report by the S.Wales Regional Survey Committee, 1921.

27 W.J.Edwards, *From the Valley I Came* (1956).

28 Margaret Llewelyn Davies (ed) *Maternity: Letters from Working Women* (1915; reprint by Virago, 1978).

29 *Decennial Supplement of Registrar-General* (1932).

30 Elizabeth Andrews also makes this point in "Mothers and Babies", Chap.VIII of her autobiography *A Woman's Work is Never Done* (1956). Mrs Andrews was Labour Party Womens Organiser for Wales from 1919 to 1948, a vigorous campaigner for women's suffrage, maternity and child welfare, and pithead baths. She gave evidence on social conditions in S.Wales before several parliamentary investigations.

Table 1. Female occupations: Wales, Cardiff, Cardiganshire, Rhondda, 1891-1931

Number of females in occupation classes as % total occupied

WALES

Occupation class	1891 %	1901 %	1911 %
Domestic offices or service	54.9	49.3	42.0
Dress	17.1	17.8	15.5
Food, drink, lodging	9.6	9.1	13.1
Professional occupations	5.3	8.0	8.6
Agriculture	4.8	6.8	9.4
Metals, machines etc.	2.4	1.3	1.6
Commercial occupations	0.2	0.5	1.1
Total above	96.4	92.8	91.2
Total number occupied	191,908	180,424	215,681
Occupied as % fs in age group[1]	28.7	23.6	23.6

Occupation class	1911 %	1921 %	1931 %
Services, sport, recreation	49.5	44.5	47.7
Clothing workers	15.1	9.1	5.1
Agriculture	9.4	5.3	4.2
Professional, technical, etc	7.8	10.6	11.4
Sale workers	7.4	15.1	16.6
Metal manuf. and engineering	1.8	2.1	0.8
Clerical workers	1.3	5.8	6.4
Total above	92.2	92.5	92.1
Total number occupied	215,681	213,149	206,139
Occupied as % fs in age group[1]	23.6	21.2	21.0

CARDIFF

Occupation class	1891 %	1901 %	1911 %
Domestic offices or services	52.0	46.2	39.3
Dress	20.3	19.3	17.7
Food, drink, lodging	9.9	10.9	15.5
Professional occupations	7.6	9.4	9.5
Agriculture	0.2	0.1	0.1
Metals, machines etc.	0.2	0.2	0.3
Commercial occupations	0.1	2.3	3.8
Total above	90.5	88.4	86.2
Total number occupied	12,488	15,160	19,481
Occupied as % fs in age group[1]	26.6	24.2	26.9

Occupation class	1911 %	1921 %	1931 %
Service, sport, recreation		37.8	40.2
Clothing workers		10.8	8.2
Agriculture		0.2	0.1
Professional, technical etc		8.1	8.2
Sales workers		16.5	17.2
Metal manuf. and enginering		0.7	0.6
Clerical workers		12.4	12.8
Total above		86.5	87.3
Total number occupied		22,921	27,700
Occupied as % fs in age group[1]		29.2	30.9

CARDIGANSHIRE

Domestic offices or services	53.8	49.7	37.1
Dress	18.1	15.3	12.9
Food, drink, lodging	7.4	9.4	13.2
Professional occupations	2.2	4.0	4.6
Agriculture	13.9	16.2	25.9
Metals, machines etc.	2.4	1.3	1.6
Commercial occupations	0.1	0.2	0.2
Total above	95.6	94.8	94.1
Total number occupied	14,312	9,199	9,913
Occupied as % fs in age group[1]	36.6	32.5	35.6

Service, sport, recreation	45.9	48.3	52.5
Clothing workers	12.6	9.0	5.0
Agriculture	26.0	17.1	16.1
Professional, technical etc	4.4	7.8	10.1
Sales workers	5.4	9.6	9.4
Metal manuf. and engineering	0.3	0.0	0.0
Clerical workers	0.4	3.1	3.0
Total above	95.0	94.9	96.3
Total number occupied	9,913	7,518	6,299
Occupied as % fs in age group[1]	35.6	27.4	26.0

RHONDDA U.D.

Domestic offices or services	44.6	43.6	40.6
Dress	23.4	30.2	23.0
Food, drink, lodging	22.1	7.5	14.2
Professional occupations	5.8	11.4	12.4
Agriculture	0.1	0.1	0.1
Metals, machines etc	0.0	0.1	0.1
Commercial occupations	0.1	0.3	0.7
Total above	96.1	93.2	91.2
Total number occupied	6,359	5,261	7,105
Occupied as % fs in age group[1]	23.6	14.4	14.4

Service, sport, recreation	40.9	43.6
Clothing workers	12.4	4.9
Agriculture	0.1	0.1
Professional, technical etc	15.2	21.0
Sales workers	22.4	21.7
Metal manuf. and engineering	0.0	0.0
Clerical workers	4.4	5.6
Total above	95.4	96.8
Total number occupied	6,831	5,484
Occupied as % fs in age group[1]	12.5	11.4

1. 1891-1911 age 10 and over; 1921 12 yrs and over; 1931 14 yrs and over

Table 2. Agricultural labour in Cardiganshire—census returns 1891-1931

		Female	Male
1891	Farmer, Grazier	1102	4354
	.. Son, Grandson, Brother, Nephew	—	1885
	Agricultural Labourers, Farm servants	869	4261
	Others	1	199
	Total Agriculture	1972	10699
1901	Farmers, Graziers	638	2905
	.. .. Sons, Daughters or other Relatives assisting in the work of the Farm (so returned)	731	1516
	Agricultural Labourers, Farm servants	107	2531
	Others	11	286
	Total Agriculture	1487	7238
1911	Farmers, Graziers	723	3029
	.. .. Sons, Daughters or Other Relatives assisting in the work of the Farm	1662	1684
	Agricultural Labourers, Farm servants	183	2944
	Others	3	257
	Total Agriculture	2571	7914
1921	Farmers	586	3320
	Farmers' Sons, Daughters or Other Relatives assisting in the work of the Farm	413	1294
	Agricultural Labourers, Farm servants	267	2499
	Others	16	396
	Total Agriculture	1282	7509
1931	Farmers	573	3233
	Farmers' Sons, Daughters and Other Relatives assisting in the work of the Farm	223	1035
	Agricultural Labourers, Farm servants	210	2468
	Others	9	388
	Total Agriculture	1015	7124

6

"Of Men and Stones": Radicalism and Protest in North Wales, 1850–1914

R. Merfyn Jones

North Wales is a recognizable geographical area defined by the sea to the north and west and by the English border and the empty heaths of mid-Wales to the east and south. But it is an elusive notion which lacks the regional coherence and cultural and other associations of "South Wales"; moreover, definitions which might apply to one part of the area are hard to enforce elsewhere. And over it all extends the massive influence of the urban presence of the great English cities of Liverpool and Manchester; in many respects North Wales, like its coalfield which passes under the Dee to reappear in the Wirral, has to be considered, not only in a Welsh, but also in a north-west of England, context.[1] For the purposes of this study, however, the region is limited geographically to the area presently included in the counties of Clwyd and Gwynedd. During the period under discussion people would have recognised this area under the names of the historic counties of Merioneth, Caernarvonshire and Anglesey, in the west, and Denbighshire and the severed county of Flintshire, to the east.

The differences between the eastern and western poles of this northern axis are sharp, not least in linguistic characteristics and population trends. The population curve of steady growth was the same in the somewhat more urbanised east as in the west during the nineteenth century but, whereas population stagnated, or even declined, in the western counties during the twentieth century it continued to increase, except during the thirties, in the east. Culturally an opposite curve prevailed with a marked downward dip in the number of Welsh speakers along the west-east axis. The counties which now constitute Gwynedd had very high percentages of Welsh speakers and, until recent times, minimal immigration from outside; in the area now known as Clwyd, however, the proximity of English towns and cities, particularly Chester and Liverpool, and a fair degree of movement across the border, ensured lower numbers of Welsh speakers. In 1901 almost 90% of the population of Caernarvonshire was Welsh speaking, in Denbighshire the total was 62% and in Flintshire the figure fell to 49·1%.[2] This was still a substantial number of Welsh speakers, however, at almost exactly the same as the average for the whole of Wales, and parts of the eastern border area, particularly some of the coal mining communities, remained impressively resistant to anglicisation despite the fact that the main town of the area, Wrexham, situated virtually on the English border, was already significantly anglicised when visited by George Borrow in 1854, "The town is reckoned a Welsh town, but its appearance is not Welsh — its inhabitants have neither the look nor language of Welshmen", he commented then.[3]

The differences between east and west were marked, therefore, but these should not be overestimated, certainly not in the nineteenth century. Far more striking are the similarities in economic development, political response, and cultural construction which united the two corners of North Wales. "How odd", commented the American consul to Liverpool, the novelist Nathaniel Hawthorne, on a visit to Denbighshire, "that an hour or two on the railway should have brought me amongst a people who speak no English." On an excursion in 1854 to Ruthin from the seaside development at Rhyl he wrote, "It was quite unexpected to me to hear Welsh so universally and familiarly spoken; everybody spoke it.. I had an idea that Welsh was spoken rather as a freak, and in fun, than as a native language; it was so strange to think of another language being the people's actual and earnest medium of thought within so short a distance of England."[4]

In just the same was as the Welsh hills which dominated, at varying altitudes, the whole area (except for the island of Anglesey), abruptly ceased on the edge of England and the Cheshire plain, so also characteristically and intensely Welsh phenomena like the religious revival of 1904–5 stopped equally suddenly on that same border and failed to effectively travel the next fifteen or so miles to affect the city of Liverpool, or merely cross a river to infect the border town of Chester. It was the same pattern, as we shall see, which affected the political map as a Liberal Wales gazed wonderingly over to the Tory citadel on the Mersey.

From the late eighteenth century parts of North Wales were extensively developed for industrial production and mineral exploitation.[5] These developments were not bunched together in one zone but rather were they scattered throughout the region. They were as geographically separate as the Parys copper-mining complex in Anglesey and the textile and related industries in the Greenfield valley of Holywell; the pioneer iron making industry in Bersham, the slate industry of Snowdonia and the coal of Flintshire and Denbighshire; the myriad burrowings in the ground from which lead and limestone and gold (in Merionethshire there were, at the turn of the century, more than five hundred men working in the Dolgellau goldfield) were dragged; the ports along the cost which exported mineral products or led, from Holyhead, to Ireland. Because of this relatively early and impressive degree of industrialisation, which dominated the local economy, the present author has argued elsewhere that it is not useful to characterise the region as an uniformly backward one.[6] Economic and social change, characterised by large scale investment, affected North

Wales as early as elsewhere and, for some communities, with the same devastating effects as experienced by more recognisably industrial areas.

But this development does need to be put into perspective: to conceive of the matter in terms of species there were, in the 1890s, almost three times more sheep in North Wales than there were people (1,135,268 sheep in 1892 and 383,793 people in 1891); in the Southern counties of Glamorgan and Monmouthshire there were twice as many people as there were sheep (968,314 people and only 540,285 sheep). There was coal mining in both North and South Wales but the scale of the operations hardly bears comparison: in 1891 12,789 miners in North Wales were producing 3,152,000 tons.[7] By the outbreak of world war one there were 234,117 coal miners in South Wales; there were 16,257 in North Wales.

The degree of urbanisation in North Wales was also unimpressive.[8] By the late nineteenth century by far the largest town was Wrexham with its brewing and tanning industries. The town itself had a population of 15,000 but it was the centre of a substantially larger urban and mining area of perhaps 30,000 people. Four miles away there was the "largest village in Wales", the coal-mining town of Rhosllanerchrugog with a population of almost 9,000 people. It was described, in 1847, as having worse social conditions than Merthyr Tydfil with families, with an average of six children each, living in one and two roomed cottages with earth floors and peat or straw roofs. A Welsh speaking town, despite its proximity to the English border, it was to become a Liberal and later a Labour citadel with a lively political life. By the Second World War there was Labour, Communist and Welsh nationalist organisation in the village and a miners' institute of gargantuan proportions with library, billiards and choirs.

There were no other towns which could compare with the Wrexham-Rhos area. Other industrialised towns in the east such as Ruabon (mining and brick and tile manufacture), Mold (lead mining, tinplate and smelting works), Flint (paper mills and chemicals) and Brymbo (collieries and iron works) were still relatively small centres of population at the turn of the twentieth century with populations of under 5,000 each. Only Buckley (mining and brick and tile manufacture) was larger.

Further west many of the larger towns had relatively little industry and possessed very diverse economic rationales. As the nineteenth century progressed, and especially after the development of good railway links after 1850, few towns, however industrial in origin, evaded the influx of tourists and the infrastructure of that industry. From the late eighteenth century onwards North Wales (particularly, but by no means exclusively, in the mountainous west) attracted a substantial tourist trade; people flocked to the area for the physical beauty of mountain and sea. This juxtaposition of significant, if small scale, industrial development with the language of tourism and of the 'picturesque', can be disorientating. Bangor's economy was described in 1899 as: "the chief industry of the town is the export of slate, obtained from Lord Penrhyn's quarries. There is also a large influx of visitors and tourists during the summer months". Even the grim, grey, slate mining town of Blaenau Ffestiniog, with a population by the turn of the century of 11,000 (thus making it one of the largest towns in North Wales) could be perceived as both an industrial and tourist centre. As one guide commented, "During the past twenty years over 2,500,000 tons of manufactured slate were shipped from Blaenau Ffestiniog alone, and during the same period about 36,000,000 tons of rock were removed. The Vale of Ffestiniog is well worth a visit; the scenery is romantic."

From 1896 the rack-and-pinion mountain railway which took passengers to the summit of Snowdon, a hugely popular tourist attraction, started its journey from the industrial village of Llanberis. Across the lake stood one of the two largest slate quarries in the world which, employing three thousand men, had completely transformed the mountainside. This village had, in 1874, tenaciously fought to establish trade unionism in the slate industry, and had subsequently witnessed a further ferocious industrial dispute.[9] But it was also a popular tourist centre with several large hotels; it could be described by a mountain climber in 1895, before the Snowdon railway attracted even more people, as "intolerably overrun, especially during the late summer and autumn, the true lover of the mountains flees the spot, for the day-tripper is a burden and desire fails."[10]

Along the coast the new towns of Rhyl, with "sands . . .equal in solidity and smoothness to any in the kingdom", and the gracefully planned Llandudno and Colwyn Bay, favoured by invalids in winter, were all significant centres of population, and had been created specifically as fashionable Victorian watering places with their large hotels, iron piers, promenades and marine drives. On the west coast there were similar but smaller such developments in Barmouth, Cricieth and elsewhere. The proximity of the huge urban populations of Lancashire, and, slightly further away, of the Midlands, was, of course, a key factor in these developments in North Wales.

Furthermore, there were few uncomplicated capitalists in the area; the most powerful dynasty, with interests in many mineral exploitation ventures as well as massive land holdings, was that of the Williams-Wynn family of Wynnstay, near Ruabon: in 1873 it was recorded that the family owned 87,919 acres, most of them in Denbighshire, Merioneth and Montgomeryshire; in 1883 Bateman estimated the acreage as extending to 145,770 acres; on either count this was by far the largest landed estate in Wales and the Wynns expected to exercise the political power commensurate with their land holdings. In the west the largest slate mines and quarries were all owned by families who also possessed massive landed estates and lived in pseudo-baronial style. Lord Penrhyn surveyed the business possibilities offered by his extensive slate quarry from the pretensions of his enormous mock castle and the security bestowed by his 49,000 acres.[11]

The Assheton Smiths, who owned the Dinorwic quarry in Llanberis interested themselves in fox-hunting, sailing, and in their own estate menagerie. Thomas Assheton Smith and his wife had been reluctant to leave the fox-hounds on their country seat in Tedworth in order to take up his inheritance in the thin soil of Snowdonia: "Both were unwilling to leave. . . where each had so many objects of interest and enjoyment — he is favourite sport, and she her schools, her poor, and the management of the house and yards". But move they did, albeit only for relatively short stretches at a time, because of the apparently limitless wealth located in the slate mountain which he had inherited: "the mountain, " his biographer commented in 1860, "has the appearance of a colossal plum cake out of which two boys are each trying to take the largest slice he can."[12] To walk the five miles from Llanberis to the summit of Snowdon required every step to be taken on Vaenol soil. Even the indigenous fortune made by Thomas Williams and Edward Hughes from the copper deposits of Parys mountain was, by the mid-nineteenth century, expressed in the absurd folly of Kinmel castle, seat of the genealogist Hugh R. Hughes and a favourite retreat of minor royalty like H.R.H. the Duke of Sussex. Few areas in Britain were so dominated by landlordism and the social imperatives of that system.

Protest

Given all these factors — relatively small scale industrialisation, mostly in the east; little urbanisation; the prevalence of a tourist infrastructure, mainly in the west and along the coast, but not exclusively so; the overwhelming presence of landlordism and of related systems of patronage and power — then the persistence of protest and the emergence of an influential labour movement are an unexpected feature of North Wales' past which require some explanation. In the remainder of this paper we shall be concerned with the provenance, and even more so with the expression, of protest in this area and with the way in which this led North Wales to become a Liberal province out of which developed a significant, and well organised, trade union and labour movement which remained strong, if not dominant, until the 1970s. Finally the relationship between the traditions of protest and the strategies of Labour, which was not without contradictions, will be briefly considered.

During the nineteenth century at least two crucial tendencies can be discerned: first a tradition of direct protest and action which affected equally rural and industrial communities and, secondly, the growing influence and volubility of an indigenous middle-class radicalism which expressed itself most forcefully in electoral politics. Together these developments gave North Wales a reputation for both radical politics and social disorder.[13]

In the extractive industries the tradition of strike action, often associated with other forms of direct, and sometimes violent sanctions, was firmly rooted. Trade unionism was as well established in North Wales as in any other coalfield (partly the result of the influence of Lancashire radicals and organisers), but even if the union's presence came to be intermittent the level of conflict in the industry remained constant; this was most tragically displayed in the Mold riots of 1869 which led to the military shooting on a crowd of miners and their families; two colliers and two women were killed by the fusillade.[14]

In the slate industry the first recorded strike was in 1825 and, although the next half century was relatively quiescent, for the quarter of a century from 1874 the slate quarrymen of Snowdonia, who never numbered more than 14,000, were involved in a series of remarkable industrial disputes which caught the national imagination. In 1874 they defeated the main employers in the industry and established an union; in 1885 there was a strike in Llanberis, in 1892 in Blaenau Ffestiniog, and then, for eleven months in 1896–7 and for a further three years, from October 1900 to the Autumn of 1903, the three thousand quarrymen at Lord Penrhyn's quarry in Bethesda were locked out. During these disputes boycotts, picketting, and, on occasion, riot, were employed to enforce collective discipline; the military twice cantered through the streets of Bethesda.[15]

But the other extractive industries, with no history of trade union organisation, were also far from being immune to action. Disputes occurred in both the copper and the lead mines of North Wales, particularly in response to employers' attempts to lengthen hours of work, traditionally very short, or change the wages system: Halkyn miners rioted in 1822 and in 1850 miners armed with sticks won a reduction in hours in Holywell.[16] In 1853 there was a year-long strike in the Llandudno copper mines but the most dramatic conflict was that of the 500 miners at the Talgarth lead mine in 1856 which witnessed the arrival of the military to counter the increasingly violent attacks of groups of strikers: the incumbent of the parish wrote to his bishop "the first act of violence .. was the pulling down at night of a fence .. the next act of violence.. was the surrounding of Dyserth Hall the residence of the late Agent.. by some twenty or thirty persons, some of whom were dressed in women's clothes, and carried firearms, which they fired.. on the 21st October last, between 10 and 11 o'clock at night, a number of men, supposed to have been 30 or thereabout, went in a body to the Talargoch Works; and some small shot were fired into the Engine-house.. the watchman was also fired at by one of the crowd, and several small shot entered his feet and legs".[17]

In the countryside, too, squatters, cottagers and tenant farmers were involved in a variety of different struggles particularly against enclosure, the sale of Crown land or the perceived injustices of the landlord system and of the Anglican church. These reached their highest pitch in the famous "Tithe War" of the late 1880s which witnessed a cat-and-mouse campaign of defiance and ambush, conducted by farmers opposed to the payment of tithes. Redcoats in the Denbighshire hills seemed to bring the methods and passions of Irish land reformers to Wales.[18]

A lesser known example of rural discontent was the ten-year long campaign of 'outrages' conducted by cottagers and others in the parish of Caerhun, in the mountains above Conway, to prevent the stone walls of landlordism from locking out their sheep from the mountainside. The land in question had been enclosed in 1858 and two thirds of it had gone to just two landowners; the cottagers, who depended on access to the mountainside to graze their flocks of sheep, persistently knocked down during the night the high boundary walls built during the day. These massive dry stone walls which enmeshed the North Wales hills and ascended the steepest and rockiest of mountainsides in an eloquent testimony to the possessive impulse and the territorial imperative, were, along with Edward I's castles, arguably the most visible and impressive architectural features in North Wales. They required endless labour to build; they could be knocked down with ease. In 1867, nine years after the original protests, the magistrates were still debating whether to make the area into a special police district in order to "curb the lawlessness of the district".[19]

Uneasily, although at times intimately, associated with these popular protests were the campaigns of radical Liberalism developed in pulpit and newspaper column and aimed at the power of landlordism and the Anglican church. Profiting from the 1867 Reform Act, the 1870 Ballot Act and, particularly, from the 1884 Reform Act, the Liberals had wrenched control of the electoral representation from the landowners and their scions. In the general election of November 1885 the Liberals won thirty of the thirty-four Welsh parliamentary seats; in North Wales their victory was even more emphatic and they carried the day in nine out of the ten constituencies, only Denbigh Boroughs remained in Tory hands. In 1886 Tom Ellis, the son of a poor tenant farmer, won in the Merioneth constituency. A young radical lawyer called David Lloyd George was travelling the meeting halls of Caernarvonshire and Merioneth, gaining a reputation for tempestuous oratory and cool calculation and sharpening his ambitions the while. He was narrowly elected to Parliament for Caernarvon Boroughs in 1891. With the first County Council elections in 1889 the Liberal political revolution was confirmed as the Liberal army of businessmen and ministers swept to power. Following the 1885 elections the *Times* had noted that nonconformity and radicalism had become synonymous in Wales and that this had resulted in "that curious unanimity which is the characteristic feature of Welsh politics", a consensus which had rendered the Tories "so absurd a minority".[20] For a generation and more Wales was not to be a place but an idea, it did not have citizens, rather did it have adherents to the tenets of radical Liberalism and its all-embracing explanatory formulations. If there is some doubt about the scope of the democratic revolution in England during the nineteenth century, and about the survival there of aristocratic influence and patterns of allegiance, there can be no such doubt about the political process in Wales.

This period in the late nineteenth century has been described by one historian as "a surge of Welsh organizational activity which amounted to a national renaissance": Cymru Fydd, the nationalist wing of Liberalism, began on its contradictory and ultimately ineffective path in 1886, its journal was founded in 1888; the Society for the Utilization of the Welsh Language was founded in 1885; in the following year, and of particular importance in North Wales, Thomas Gee and his tenant farmer allies launched an anti-tithe organization which, in 1887, became the Welsh Land League.[21] A pack of radical Welsh language newspapers snapped at the heels of Tory landlordism and ultra radicals, like the Rev. E. Pan Jones, Mostyn, travelled the county calling for fundamental land reform.

The relationship between this nonconformist Liberalism and, in particular, the tithe reform campaign and other anti-Anglican and anti-landlord initiative, was relatively straightforward. When it came to matters of labour mobilisation and organisation the relationships with the middle-class advocates of radical Liberalism were not so uncomplicated but they could still be intimate. Electorally this can be seen in the long adhesion of the North Wales colliers to the Liberal Party. Further west the middle-class activists were even more integrated. It was a radical journalist, Ap Ffarmwr, who attempted to organise Anglesey farm workers in the 1880s. Even more dramatic was the role of middle class Liberals in the affairs of the North Wales Quarrymen's Union which was established in 1874 under direct middle-class control, a control which was to remain relatively unchallenged until the turn of the century. The two key figures in the union were the radical businessman, W. J. Parry, and W. J. Williams, who, as General Secretary of the union, also ran an accountant's firm from the union's headquarters.

The violence of some of the protests of the closing decades of the century attracted the nervous censure of Liberal leaders at times but, on the whole, they successfully recruited these struggles, whether in mine, quarry or farm into their own campaigns against the twin enemies of Anglican Church and landowners. In the slate industry the language of industrial relations — contracts, combination, bargains, wages, supervision, managerial prerogatives, the rights of workers — jostled with the vocabulary of radical Liberalism: religious discrimination, land rights, the rights of Welsh workers, universal human demands.

It was little wonder, therefore, that the besieged defenders of the old order felt that their paternalistic relationship with tenants, parishioners and workers were being disturbed by a "gang of Bethelite preachers" intent on disturbing the social peace and grabbing the political spoils. Strikes were blamed on "socialistic" plots, rural discontent on agitators inspired by the Irish example; the Welsh-language press was accused of pouring out spite and libel and was closely monitored by its opponents. For Lord Penrhyn, appearing before the Land Commission in 1893, "the Welsh Land Question was unreal in origin, and had not its source in any genuine sense of grievance on the part of the agricultural community"; for him, as for a recent historian of the land in Wales, the grievances of tenant farmers and others were a "figment of the political imagination".[22]

It was no such thing, of course; the police files of North Wales contain plenty of evidence to the contrary. The tradition of popular protest, be it in the countryside or in the mines and quarries, was securely based on an endemic sense of injustice and a sure knowledge of the means by which oppression might be resisted. What is undeniable, however, is the success with which radical Liberal propagandists harnessed so many of these protests to their own world view, even while maintaining a discrete distance between themselves and these manifestations. They created, in North Wales, an all-pervasive radical vision, an alternative 'common sense' which aspired to hegemonic proportions.

Llanddulas, 1885–86

An example of the role of this ideological construct in the context of an industrial dispute is provided by an event such as the Llanddulas limestone quarry dispute of 1885; neglected hitherto by historians it is described in detail below in order to identify the characteristics of the consciousness discussed above in the context of a labour dispute. There was no visible middle class involvement in this conflict, and neither was there any outside organisational interference, not even from a trade union. And yet the instinctual reflexes of the radical world view were manifest, particularly in the ethnic dimensions of the dispute and in the determined resistance to the military occupation of the village. (Fifty five years earlier, in 1829, a previous rebellion of the villagers, a protest against the enclosure of common land used for quarrying, had been quelled by the intervention of Fusiliers from Chester). A description and analysis of the dispute of 1885–86 should serve to illustrate the argument adumbrated above for it took place at a time when conflict in North Wales was attracting a good deal of national attention. This attention was largely focussed on the fifteen- week lock-out at the Dinorwic slate quarries which involved some three thousand men but equally dramatic was the remarkable, if small-scale, strike which broke out in November 1885 in the limestone quarries of Llanddulas, situated on the North Wales coast of Liverpool Bay near the town of Abergele.

Limestone was present near the coal seams of the Denbigh coal field and lime from the large Minera deposits was used locally in the iron industry. Limestone was also found along the coast from Abergele to the Ormes at Llandudno and was worked throughout the nineteenth century. The produce of this coastal area was taken by sea, and after mid-century by rail also, as building stone for the construction industry in Birkenhead and Liverpool, but increasingly it was processed into lime for use in the chemical industry of the upper-Mersey estuary, St. Helens and also of nearby Fflint. Llanddulas was one of the centres of production in Wales and a railroad and pier had been constructed for the transportation of the limestone as early as 1822; a further jetty was extended into the sea in the mid-1870s.[23] The companies operating in the small village were Kneeshaw, Lupton and Co.; Raynes and Co.; and the Llanddulas Quarry Co. Some five to six hundred men were employed in the quarrying of the limestone, treating it in kilns to produce lime and then transporting it to ship or train.[24]

In November 1885, Kneeshaw, Lupton and Raynes persuaded their workers to accept a reduced price, per ton, in the piece work system which operated. The men agreed to such a reduction in recognition of the depressed state of the market but they refused to sign contracts of employment which would freeze payments at the lower level for the following twelve months. They first refused to load ships already arrived at the jetty and then the men at the two quarries struck work on the Monday morning of November 23rd. When they finally produced their "manifesto" in the new year they rejected the idea of a twelve month contract as "they will not submit to be tyrannized by industrialists who neither care for their welfare nor consider their contracts in any way". If they agreed to the new contracts then they feared that "they would be abandoning themselves to a new form of slavery". The main burden of their complaint concerned wages and working conditions; particularly the fact that they often had to work at night in order to meet the demands of ships which were themselves dependent on the tides, but even these matters were expressed in the language of radicalism.[25]

The employers contradicted the strikers' figures and claimed that the men, who worked in gangs, could, on average, earn eighteen shillings to one pound a week. The men replied that they would need to be breaking rock for eighteen hours a day if they were to earn such wages. The employers responded by claiming that even though the quarries were open from six in the morning until half past five in the evening "our rockmen seldom come until 7·30 to 8·00 and leave between 4·30 to 5·00pm." When asked to work longer hours "they have invariably refused".[25] Many of the issues common in other disputes in extractive industries concerning piece-work rates and work discipline were, therefore, important issues but other matters more central to Welsh radicalism also came to the surface. These were matters which charged the dispute with all the tensions of a clash between nationalities and between people and soldiery.

The major employer, Henry Kneeshaw, lived in nearby Penmaenmawr where his company also owned the Graiglwyd 'setts' quarry (he also had other quarrying interests in North Wales including the Port Nant quarry near Llithfaen in Llyn). He was a local magistrate and a prominent supporter of the Tory party. Despite his local interests, however, he was unmistakably English and his business ventures were run from offices in Liverpool. His partners, the Luptons, were both Liverpool merchants living in Oxton, Wirral. Raynes and Co. had also ventured into the quarrying business with the Luptons but in Llanddulas they were involved independently; the three Raynes partners all described themselves as merchants and also lived in Wirral. All three companies operating in the village had their offices in Old Hall St., in the Liverpool business quarter. The limestone workers, therefore, were employed by Liverpool-based employers and almost all of the lime which they produced was sent direct to the Mersey.[27]

The limestone workers and their families, on the other hand, were overwhelmingly Welsh in origin and in speech and largely nonconformist in religion and Liberal in politics. Llanddulas was a small village of under one thousand inhabitants but it could boast of not only its Anglican Church, dedicated to St. Cymbryd, but also Baptist, Calvinistic Methodist, Independent and Wesleyan Methodist chapels.[28]

Neither Alexander Duncan, of Kneeshaw Lupton, nor John Fair of Raynes, the local managers of the two strike-bound quarries, were Welsh and this led to the quarry workers complaining not only of their competence but also of their inability to communicate with them in Welsh. In their manifesto they stated:

The manager Mr Duncan does not understand his work and consequently is not a competent person to deal with either men or stones. The same remarks apply to his sub-managers, who are men of inferior judgement and tyrannous nature. Mr. Duncan cannot speak Welsh and it is a well-known fact that a great many of the men cannot speak English.[29]

The employers respondend by pointing out that Duncan had spent twenty-five years in the management of quarries in Penmaenmawr and suggested that his residence there "entirely refutes the insinuation that he cannot make the men understand him".[30] But the clash of cultures was clearly stamped onto the character of the conflict from the start. This element was exacerbated by the arrival of the 'relief' workmen, or blacklegs, who were variously described by the villagers as "English", "foreign", "Irish" or "Rats".

The limestone quarries themselves were flanked by their limeworks where the limestone was placed in kilns for the production of lime. As the strike proceeded the employers became increasingly concerned with the state of the lime kilns and they determined to bring in men to keep them going. A week after the strike started, therefore, a dozen men from Birkenhead arrived in Llanddulas to stoke the fires. They arrived at 11·30am and immediately started packing the kilns with stone. By the time they stopped for their lunch a procession of two hundred of the strikers entered the works and, using a police constable as a go-between, informed the Birkenhead men that they had better leave. The constable explained that he could not guarantee the men's safety if they were to stay and he escorted them back to the station. As a result of this incident a dozen of the strikers were charged with intimidation and appeared before a special petty sessions in Conwy shortly afterwards. The accused marched to the court with three hundred of their colleagues and a foreman and three of the Birkenhead men gave evidence against them. They were found guilty but were leniently dealt with by the court and were only bound over to keep the peace.

By this stage the conflict had clearly developed an ethnic dimension as English blacklegs were perceived to be threatening the solidarity of a Welsh workforce. In sentencing the accused men the chairman of the Conwy bench, Rev. J. D. Jones, came as close to exculpating them as he possibly could: "as a Welshman he was sure that they would behave themselves in the future. He was proud to think that they had behaved themselves so well. It was no doubt a great provocation to see men brought from England to the works." But, he reminded them with almost a note of regret, the law had to protect everyone.[31]

The magistrate's hope that the people of Llanddulas would "behave themselves in the future" was not to be fulfilled. Within a week the Chief Constable of Caernarvonshire was urgently informing the Under-Secretary of State at the Home Office that,

the men at the quarries are on strike, they and their associates for miles around have banded themselves together to resist the employment of others in the quarries. Endeavours have been made to protect the peace, but without the least success. Rioting of a serious nature has been commenced and stones have been fairly used.[23]

The Chief Constable was referring to the employers' attempt to import more blacklegs which had been thwarted by the vigilant strikers at the village railway station. The correspondent of *The Times* commented that "again the resolute attitude of the men and the determined opposition of the women prevented the approach of the relief men". The strikers who "have picketted the neighbourhood and done their utmost to strengthen their organisation" seemed to him to control the situation: "seaward the men commanded the beaches, while the mountains at the back prevented approach from that quarter". The surrounding "varied and picturesque scenery", which was already attracting tourists to the area, was also proving to be beneficial to the strikers' manoeuvres.[33]

As the year drew to a close the police, certain magistrates and the employers collaborated with the military authorities in Chester Castle to try and import further English workers. As a result of muddle and policy disagreements, however, the plan initially failed to come off but, on January 4th, they finally succeeded in bringing in 'relief men' from

Birkenhead and Liverpool. Some one hundred soldiers of the 80th South Staffordshire Regiment were requisitioned from barracks in Manchester and joined the fifty relief men on the train in Chester. Referred to by the *Liverpool Daily Post* as "the Englishmen", they arrived on the ten o-clock train on the Monday morning when they were met by thirty-three policemen and a large crowd of strikers and their families. The soldiers leapt out of the train and "formed up on both sides of the relief men and marched out with fixed bayonets. The strikers were completely cowed."[34] The march under armed escort to the quarry was a short one but it was to reverberate through innumerable newspaper columns and radical pamphlets.[35]

The strikers comforted themselves by observing the unskilled way in which the new men, fourteen of them in Raynes' and the rest in Kneeshaw Lupton's, carried out the work and laughed "when the lime dust was being blown into their eyes". They held a mass meeting which counselled peace and foresaw the blacklegs being removed "as they are evidently unaccustomed to the task of filling and drawing the kilns". But the soldiers had brought their tents and were billeted around the neighbourhood. Fifty of them marched into the village from Abergele every day and sentries were permanently posted throughout the village; the relief men stayed in the works and were fed by the local publican.[36]

The blacklegs were sometimes referred to locally as "Irishmen", a reference to their Merseyside origins; they had been promised good wages and constant employment and "as the men out of work in the large towns are unlimited no difficulty is experienced in filling the places of the strikers".[37] But in the context of the disturbed state of North Wales in the 1880s the important thing about them was that, like the employers, they were "foreigners". Feeling ran high, and not only amongst the strikers: the chairman of the Caernarvonshire Quarter Sessions warned the Home Secretary that "it would be wrong of the proprietors to introduce English workers".[38]

Support for the strike was widespread in North Wales and the men and their families relied heavily on the financial donations of supporters throughout the region: "but for extraneous assistance, " commented the sympathetic *Daily Post*, "the strikers must have been starved into submission long since."[39] There was some support received from the North Wales Quarrymen's Union which organised slate quarrymen although its funds were being rapidly depleted by the much larger demands of the Dinorwic lock- out. The Mayor of Bangor sent sacks of flour and an anonymous "lady" personally donated £10. More significantly, local farmers who, it was reported, "deeply sympathised with them" sent flour, corn and other agricultural produce.[40] Within weeks the farmers of Denbighshire were themselves to violently encounter police and military as they themselves set out to flout the rule of church and state in the Tithe Wars.

The dispute was settled early in February, 1886, on a compromise which meant the the companies dropped the twelve-month contract and substituted and open-ended agreement which could be terminated by a fortnight's notice. The 'relief men' returned to Merseyside and unemployment. Despite the fact that the limestone workers had been in close contact with the North Wales Quarrymen's Union they did not join that union nor any of the other small unions which were attempting to cater for quarry workers. They did, however, elect their own committee which was recognised by the employers.

The strikers at Llanddulas, through their confrontation with the fixed bayonets of the soldiery and in their admixture of ethnic, political and industrial strands, demonstrated, through their actions, the way in which the ideologies of radicalism, however guarded and qualified, affected the living tissue of Welsh society. They raised no narrowly political demands but, like their co-workers in the coal mining and slate and granite quarrying communities of North Wales, they reflected and expressed a set of analyses which can only be described as political in the wider sense. They were concerned with power and its displacement. As the Chairman of the Caernarvonshire Quarter Sessions wrote to the Home Office in December 1885: "The real cause of the ill feeling among the men. . . is political. There is no doubt of it."[41]

Conclusion

The achievement of the radical ideologues of the late nineteenth century was to create a remarkable alliance, not only of social classes but also of diverse and very specific aspirations — in the case described above those of a village of limestone workers on the North Wales coast. This alliance could be distilled into manifestoes but, much more to the point, it fused into a coherent identity which could contain the contradictions and inner conflicts of a self-defined Welsh constituency. Its future was defeat, some of it self-inflicted, but its significance, and the measure of its ambition, was definitive.

This essay has been concerned with discussing the historical expression of this ideology in labour and protest actions in the second half of the nineteenth century but, in conclusion, it would seem appropriate to suggest some of the problems which the pervasive nature of this consciousness offer for the subsequent development of labourist organisation in North Wales. For out of this radical, if limited and raucously middle-class, moment emerged a class divide which led to the familiar features of labour organisation and, later, to the re-definitions which eventually led to nationalism. The conclusion about to be advanced here will suggest that this modernisation of the political terrain, whilst feeding off this tradition, and basing itself on it, need not necessarily be accepted as a step toward increased radicalism and enhanced possibilities for change but, on the contrary this process can also be interpreted as a retreat from the earlier traditions, a signalling of an acceptance of power structures, and of a tenant status for workers within power's estate.

Ironically, the first parliamentary constituency to be won by Labour in North Wales was Anglesey, in 1918, one of the least industrialised seats in Wales. No sufficient explanation for this remarkable victory has yet been advanced, although the candidate's eccentricities and military bearing were clearly factors. More understandable were Labour's 1922 victories in Arfon and in Wrexham and, following the division of Flintshire into two constituencies, in Flintshire East. Arfon was to be lost until 1945 but Wrexham was to remain North Wales' solitary Labour bastion until after the second world war when more and more constituencies fell to Labour. In 1966 all four constituencies in Gwynedd returned Labour members and in Clwyd Labour captured three of the five seats; seven constituencies out of nine went Labour, a remarkable testimony to the prevalence of Labour's influence in North Wales until recent times.[42]

And yet the achievement was not only short lived but also remarkably ineffective. Labour as an organised force emerged out of the conflicts of the nineteenth century with no alternative ideology to speak of and with an inheritance of organisational failure and weakness. The leading figures who emerged to lead the labour movement in the area were complicated but deeply reactionary figures. In the east the mining leaders were moderate and unremarkable; the astonishing figure to emerge is Arthur Deakin. In the west it was not the socialists Silyn Roberts and David Thomas who came to dominate the Labour scene but the ex-I.L.P. quarryman, and briefly, Labour M.P., Robert Thomas Jones.

R. T. Jones narrowly won the ballot for General Secretary of the North Wales Quarrymen's Union in 1908, partly because he had ILP support. He was the first quarryman to have real power in the organisation and he deliberately manoeuvred the union away from its highly political and sectarian role towards a Labour and trade union professionalism. Within months of his election he was insisting that all decision-making come through him; he deliberately prevented the union's affiliation to the Labour Party until he could ensure that he would be the Labour candidate; he established the union during the First World War, despite an almost total lack of membership, by using his contacts with local and national political figures. At times, as he showed during the bitter disagreements at the Bryneglwys mine in the 1920s, he could be a stubborn defender of the right of unions to organise and negotiate. He was a Labour functionary of some skill and success; from 1921 until 1932 he served on the General Council of the Trades Union Congress; he created a trade union out of a radical and combative movement and eschewed any challenges to the order of things. Along with many quarry employers he was a freemason; representing labour was a matter for negotiation not challenge. The radical Liberal bid for power, regional and limited as it might have been, was replaced by accommodation and the tradition of popular protest was emasculated into the rehearsed symbolism of the public demonstration. This was not achieved merely by Jones, the collapse of the economic base of the industry and the fundamental changes in the national, political scene meant that he had few choices; but his consolidation of Labour's legitimacy can hardly be interpreted as anything other than a retreat from the combative positions of the Liberal ascendancy.[43]

It was Arthur Deakin who best represented the way in which Labour in North Wales narrowed the social base of protest and cauterised all radical ambition. Born in Warwickshire in 1890 Deakin moved to Dowlais when he was ten and there started to work for Guest, Keen and Nettlefolds at the age of thirteen. Influenced, like Jones, by the ILP and his local M.P., Keir Hardie, he moved to North Wales in 1910 to work as a roll turner with a steel manufacturer in Shotton. It was here that he launched himself on a career as a trade union functionary which was eventually to lead him to being the General Secretary of the Transport and General Workers Union and, as such, the most powerful trade union leader in Britain. Briefly a member of the A.S.E. he joined the Dock, Wharf, Riverside and General Union and, despite a brief spell as General Secretary of the tiny Roll Turners Association, it was in the dockers' union, which amalgamated into the TGWU in 1922, along with R. T. Jones' NWQU, thus making the TGWU by far the most important trade union in North Wales, that he made is mark. In 1922 Deakin became Assistant District Secretary for the North Wales region of the TGWU. Ten years later he moved to London where, in 1935, he became Bevin's Assistant General Secretary. He ran the union during Bevin's period in Government and, in 1948, emerged as the most dominant, and domineering, figure in British trade unionism. Obsessively anti-communist he succeeded, in 1949, in banning Communists from office in the TGWU. A Primitive Methodist with a taste for flamboyant clothes and large cigars, he did not drink and died, of a heart attack, while addressing a May Day service in Leicester. For twenty two years his apprenticeship had been served in North Wales and he was deeply affected by the economic depression in the area during the inter war period; in 1919 he had become an alderman on Flintshire County Council, and, in 1932, was Chairman of that Local Authority.[44]

The argument being somewhat hesitantly advanced here is that Labour failed to construct, in the particular situation obtaining in North Wales, any programme for radical change; the move away from the world view of radical Liberalism and the traditions of popular protest represented many positive advances but, along with the hypocrisy and the elitism of the nineteenth century, Labour, as represented by its leaders and its organisations, jettisoned also any hegemonic ambitions. The "rise of Labour" in North Wales did not lead to any socialist challenge but rather to a narrowing of horizons and a deflection of protest.

Notes

1 In 1891 over 80,000 Welsh born people were living in Lancashire and Cheshire; this was more than there were in some Welsh counties, *Census Report* (1891).
2 *Ibid.*
3 George Borrow, *Wild Wales*, (1862), p.39.
4 Nathaniel Hawthorne, *The English Sketchbooks* (ed. R. Stewart, New York, 1941), 79,83.
5 For an account of industrialisation in North Wales see A. H. Dodd's definitive volume, *The Industrial Revolution in North Wales*, (1933, 1951).
6 R. Merfyn Jones, "Notes from the Margin: Class and Society in Ninetenth Century Gwynedd", in D. Smith, ed., *A People and a Proletariat; Essays in the History of Wales* (London, 1980).
7 *Census Report, 1891.*
8 Much of the following detail is taken from *Slaters Directory, North Wales, Cheshire and Shropshire with Liverpool* (1883); and *Bennett's Business Directory* (1899).
9 For industrial disputes in the slate industry, including the disputes in Llanberis in 1874 and 1885 see R. Merfyn Jones, *The North Wales Quarrymen, 1874–1922* (Cardiff, 1981).
10 W. P. Haskett Smith, *Climbing in the British Isles; Wales and Ireland* (1895), vi.
11 On land holding and the size of estates see J. Bateman, *Great Landowners of Great Britain* (4th ed., 1883).
12 Sir John E. Eardley-Wilmot, *Reminiscences of the late Thomas Assheton Smith Esq. or the Pursuits of an English Country Gentleman* (1860), 83.
13 This argument is developed at much greater length in R. Merfyn Jones *op. cit.*
14 A. Burge, "The Mold Riots of 1869", *Llafur*, III, 3 (1982)
15 R. Merfyn Jones, *op.cit*
16 C. J. Williams, "The Lead Miners of Flintshire and Denbighshire", *Llafur*, III, 1 (1980)
17 N.L.W., M.S. SA/MISC/364.
18 On the Tithe War see Frank Price Jones, "Rhyfel y Degwm", *Transactions of the Denbighshire Historical Society*, 2 (1953), 71–105; Robert M. Morris, "The Tithe War", *ibid.*, 32 (1983), 51–97.
19 *Caernarvon and Denbigh Herald*, 6 July 1867; Gwynedd Record Office, XQ5/1856/H/6, Quarter Sessions Records.
20 *Times*, 26 December 1885.
21 K. O. Morgan, *Rebirth of a Nation, Wales 1880–1980* (Cardiff, 1981), p.94.
22 D. W. Howell, *Land and People in nineteenth-century Wales* (London, 1977)
23 Ellis Wynne Williams, *Abergele: the Story of a Parish*, 98–9; H. Ellis Hughes, *Eminent Men of Denbighshire* (1946) p.79. See also E.P. Williams, "The Landing Places of Denbighshire", *Transactions of the Denbighshire Historical Society*, 5 (1956), 69. For a useful history of Llanddulas see B. Jones, *Llanddulas: Heritage of a Village* (1985), but although it discusses industrial relations at the quarries this book makes no mention of the dramatic events of 1885–86.
24 *Slaters Directory* (1883); *Daily Post*, 23 December 1885.
25 *Daily Post*, 22 January 1886; *Times*, 5 January 1886.
26 *Daily Post*, 30 January 1886.
27 See *Gore's Directory* (1886); *North Wales Chronicle*, 28 November 1885; *Baner ac*

Amserau Cymru, 2 December 1885; Penmaenmawr and Welsh Granite Co., *Moving Mountains* (n.d.), 17. Kneeshaw gave up control of his Penmaenmawr quarry in 1888.

28 *Baner ac Amserau Cymru*, 13 January 1886; *Slater's Directory* (1892).

29 *Daily Post* 26 January 1885. Much the same reports of the dispute were published, in different languages, in *Baner ac Amserau Cymru* and the *Liverpool Daily Post*, both Liberal newspapers; the *North Wales Chronicle* reflected the Tory view of matters.

30 *Daily Post*, 30 January 1885; *North Wales Chronicle*, 12 December 1885.

31 *Baner ac Amserau Cymru* was moderate enough in its treatment of the Llanddulas employers but described the English relief men as an "execrable rabble" whose behaviour was a disgrace and a "source of great danger to . . . morality through their drunkeness and frightful swearing."

32 Public Record Office HO144/162/A41864, Major J.M. Clayton, Chief Constable of Caernarvonshire to the Under Secretary of State at the Home Office, December 17,1885; I am indebted to John Parry, Workingmen's College, for this and other references to the Home Office papers.

33 *Times*, 5 January 1886; *Baner ac Amserau Cymru* claimed that troops had appeared briefly on that occasion. *Slaters Directory* (1892), there were several "appartments" for tourists in the village.

34 *Times*, 5 January 1886; *Daily Post* 5 January 1886.

35 See, for example, *Caernarfon and Denbigh Herald*, 2,9 and 16 January 1886.

36 *Daily Post*, 6 January 1886. To make amends the publican also provided free soup for the strikers.

37 *Ibid.* January 5,1886. See also *Baner ac Amserau Cymru*, 13 January 1886; *Times*, 12 January 1886.

38 P.R.O., H.O.144, Chairman Caernarvonshire Quarter Sessions to Home Office, December 20,1885.

39 *Daily Post*, 6 January 1886.

40 Ffestiniog slate quarrymen contributed £17, *Baner ac Amserau Cymru*, 23 December 1885; *Daily Post*, 30 December 1885; 6 January 1886.

41 P.R.O., H.O. 144, Chairman of Quarter Sessions to Home Office, December 20,1885.

42 A discussion of Labour's early development in Gwynedd will be found in Cyril Parry, *The Radical Tradition in Welsh Politics: A study of Liberal and Labour Politics in Gwynedd, 1900–20* (Hull, 1970).

43 On the career of R. T. Jones see R. Merfyn Jones, *op.cit*, Chapter X and *passim*; Owen Parry, *Undeb y Chwarelwyr, 1908–29* (1930).

44 For Arthur Deakin see V. L. Allen, *Trade Union Leadership, Based on a Study of Arthur Deakin* (1957).

7

Migration and Regional Labour Markets, 1870–1915: the Quebec Case

Bruno Ramirez

I

The relationship between migration and the development of labour markets is an aspect of industrialization that has not received from labour and social historians the attention it deserves. Partly this has resulted from a tendency to view this type of issue as falling squarely within the realm of economic history, where the basic assumption has been that a sort of overarching economic rationality has allowed to match in time and space workers willing to sell their labour power with jobs waiting to be filled.

But the economistic perspective of the labour market, with its neoclassical penchant for only wanting to see the act whereby labour power is exchanged for wages is ill equipped to account for the larger social, demographic and cultural dynamics that allowed this exchange to concentrate itself at a given time and in a given place. More often than not, that exchange was possible because labour power, whether embodied in individuals, families, or entire communities, crossed city borders, mountain ranges or oceans, in order to turn wage prospects into life projects. The massive population transfers that industrialization produced — both internationally and interregionally — are therefore as much a domain of labour history as they have been of migration studies, economic history or demography.

This paper is a modest attempt to view labour markets as tips of icebergs in deep and turbulent historical oceans. One of the challenges in this type of analytical voyage is whether one can bring together within the historical scientific imagination massive aggregate data on wage fluctuations, population movements, indexes of regional economic development etc., with — on the other hand- the story of a young Quebecois who on a given winter of the 1870s hauls lumber in a Mauricie forest, or of an Italian immigrant worker who in 1909 washes cars at the Canadian Pacific Angus Shops in Montreal, or still of a French Canadian family who in the 1890 gets off the train in a New England mill town.

The Province of Quebec lends itself quite well for this kind of historical reflection; for, throughout its major stages of industrialization the

Province's social and economic space was crossed from one end to the other by significant population movements which helped shape the final regional configuration both within and outside Quebec's borders. That these population transfers were economically motivated and that they fed emerging or consolidating labour markets is only part of our reflection; the other part has to do with the migratory phenomenon itself, with the different ways in which it articulated itself temporally and spatially, and with some of the social and cultural dynamics on which it rested.

II

Throughout the second half of the 19th century and up to the onset of the Great Depression, three major population movements dominated the Quebec social and economic landscape. Two of these movements moved into opposite geographical directions, while the third one was responsible for linking some of Europe's most depressed and marginalized areas with Quebec's major pole of industrial development, i.e., Montreal.

The first of these movements — i.e., colonization — has traditionally been viewed as falling squarely within the rural universe of the vast Quebec hinterland.[1] Of course, there is in this a basic truth that can hardly be denied. Colonization (or frontier settlement, as this is called in US historiography) was primarily the making of people leaving overcrowded rural parishes along the Lawrentian Valley and setting their compasses toward the backcountry, where vast forests still waited the civilizing axe and plough of French Canadian settlers.

There are, however, at least two types of relationships between this intrarural migratory movement and industrialization. The first is ideological and has to do with the prominent role that French Canadian clerical elites played not only in promoting and managing the settlement of the hinterland, but also in trying to make colonization a powerful antidote to the threat of urbanization, industrialization, and emigration. The other concerns the ways in which ultimately the regions of colonization became the seat of a particular industrial project marked by paternalism and marginality.

In the Mauricie region — as the works of Normand Séguin and René Hardy have recently shown — the colonization movement proceeded gradually from the ancient segneurial territories to the almost inaccessible piedmont areas, some 60 miles to the interior. It was a movement that went hand in hand with the penetration of the forest by lumber companies. The latter, having to rely on a seasonal work force willing to submit to the intensity of the extractive cycle, turned logically to the nearby settlement areas where 'colons' survived throughout the initial forest-clearing period on a mere subsistence economy. But even where forest land had been turned into arable land, 'colons' found in the lumber sites an opportunity to turn the dead season of their agricultural cycle into waged labour. Moreover, lumber *chantiers* constituted a convenient outlet for some of the colons' produces, particularly at a time when geographical isolation made access to the agricultural market all but impossible.[2]

From mid-century to the turn of the 20th century, the colonization movement in Mauricie led to the formation of twenty new parishes, bringing the total population of the region to about 50,000. It was from this reservoir of population that the forestry industry drew most of its work force, whose number fluctuated from a low of 1,800 to a high of 6,000.[3]

But the sociography of the colonization regions was also characterized by a reverse population movement. And this was true not only of Mauricie, but also of the other major colonization regions that have recently been studied, such as the Sagueney and the territories east of Rimouski.[4] Overcrowded rural parishes were in fact sending off a portion of their population southward, where smokestacks and river-propelled machinery needed the arms and backs of growing armies of men, women and children. But this reverse movement could originate not only from the old parishes, but also from the frontier parishes, among a population that had tried colonization and had found it wanting. Séguin and Hardy argue that the significant population turnover they observed in some of the frontier parishes of the Mauricie was due to the fact that colonization entailed a process of population selection in terms of age. Younger rural Quebecers, single or with small families, were the more prone to try an option — such as colonization — that translated in a protracted life of strenuous physical work and of self-subsistence. But that once these families reached a size such as to make self-subsistence impossible, they quit and left the place to younger and stronger 'colons'.[5]

Another explanation, not unrelated to the previous one, may be suggested by the high rate of desistance — i.e. prospective settlers giving up the colonization enterprise after realizing the physical and material difficulties it entailed. The testimony of a colonization agent to a commission of inquiry gives a clue concerning this type of problem; land hanger and the willingness to roll up one's sleeves were not sufficient. The settler more likely to succeed was the *colon defricheur*, as distinguished from the *colon cultivateur*,[6] and clearing forest land in the particular quebecois context required work techniques and a type of life endurance that not all prospective settlers possessed or were capable of sustaining.

By the turn of the century, the St. Jean Colonization Society, one of the largest societies of its kind which distinguished itself for its aggressive advertising and recruiting methods, experienced great difficulties in keeping prospective colons on the frontier region; clearly, a great number of them were ill prepared to undergo an arduous period of forest-clearing that foreshadowed an uncertain future.[7]

One should also add that the vision that many landless Quebecers had of becoming one day self-sufficient (if not prosperous) farmers entailed a

long-term investment in their own time and in their own physical
resources. Government regulations for the sale of forest lots were
particularly demanding. Before the settler could gain full legal possession
of his lot, he had to take up residence there during the first six months after
the sale transaction had occurred; he had to build a house not smaller than
26 by 20 feet, and he had to reside two full years; moreover he had to clear
and farm a minimum of 10 percent of the surface of his lot during the four
years following the sale transaction.[8] It was a venture that increasingly
showed its risky side as the forest frontier was pushed further to the
interior, and as the convulsions occurring in the industrial geography to
the South were making access to a wage a more appealing option.

One of the colonization regions I am presently studying, Rimouski
County, shows clearly how the interaction between colonization and
emigration is reflected in the population movements. During the 1870s and
1880s most of the movements that we have reconstituted occurred from
parish to parish within the same county or to and from neighbouring
counties. One can notice a few departures of families toward the USA or
Montreal, but they are negligible. The geography of these population
movements changes dramatically starting around the late 1880s, and
throughout the 1890s nearly all the departures reported are toward the
United States.[9]

As the 19th century moved toward a close, tens of rural counties were in
fact linked one after the other, directly or indirectly, to the great urban and
industrial poles of the American Northeast. And for a growing number of
rural Quebecers who might have been caught in the dilemma 'colonize-or-
emigrate', emigration emerged as a better and more viable alternative to
colonization because, among other things, it was an option containing a
variety of possibilities. One could resort to it as a temporary strategy; one
could move with the whole family; one could only send one or more
children, boys or girls, of working age as a way of redressing the family
economy; temporary emigration could also become a sort of testing period,
in the course of which a final strategy could be decided upon. Perhaps, one
dimension that has not yet been fully analysed and which made emigration
appear as a better alternative to colonization, was the immediacy of the
rewards one obtained for one's labour. One could almost say that the
immediate cash reward that the manufacturing system provided had the
effect of accelerating the social time during which life prospects had to be
turned into concrete individual and family economic strategies. And by the
1880s for most rural Quebecers those cash rewards were only one-day
travel away. It is not surprising then if during the two closing decades of
the century when emigration to the USA took on the character of a mass
exodus, all the possibilities that the emigration alternative foreshadowed
turned into distinct patterns.

Economic historians have long explained these economically-motivated
inter-regional population transfers in terms of the role played by both push

and pull factors. But the 'push-pull' model does not tell us much about why some rural Quebecers chose the forest while others opted for the factory beyond their country's borders. Nor can it explain why some Quebec migration streams fed some regional manufacturing labour markets, while other streams converged toward different industrial regions. Our research on Berthier and Rimouski Counties show for instance that Quebecers from the former county went overwhelmingly to Rhode Island mill towns, while those departing from Rimouski tended to go to southern Massachusetts.[10] Clearly, what linked scattered Quebec parishes to specific New England industrial centres was more than simply the making of an overarching economic rationality.

When on a late Summer day of 1899 the northern train arrived to Fall River, among the dozens, if not hundreds, Quebecers joining the local labour market there was the Boucher family. The Bouchers had waited before putting an end to a life of bare subsistence in a rural parish near Rimouski because only then their move could be based on a concrete knowledge of the conditions to be found at the other end of the trip, and on the assurance of a certain degree of assistance forthcoming from relatives already settled in Fall River. In Quebec Mr. Boucher had two cousins who had sojourned in the States "to make quick money". On the other side of the border, relatives "had been advertising" to the Boucher the advantages of moving to Fall River. The day after their arrival to the Spindle City they could already lodge on their own; and three days later the school-year started and three Boucher children could be placed in the local French Canadian parish school. Our narrator, Elmire Boucher, was only five-year old at the time. When she reached the age of fourteen, in 1908, she began working in a local textile mill, making a starting salary of $7·77 per week.[11]

The entry of the Bouchers into the Fall River labour market had been the culmination of a decision-making process that spanned over many years of rural life, and that was based on the working of solidarity mechanisms that stretched from a small and seemingly isolated Quebec parish to one of New England's most important manufacturing centres.

The point to be stressed here is that what to contemporary observes appeared as an anarchic back-and-forth movement across the Canadian/US border had increasingly become the result of carefully pondered decisions based on an expanding cognitive map of the economic and cultural universe in which one's strategy would be tried out. The current research aimed at reconstituting several migration networks linking a number of Quebec rural parishes with given industrial centres in New England should throw some much needed historical light on this dimension of labour-market development.

In his pioneering historical-geographical study, Ralph Vicero has shown how central French Canadian immigrants had become by 1900 to the labour markets of the New England textile industry.[12] And more recently, Tamara Hareven has skillfully brought to light some of the social and cultural mechanisms adopted by these immigrants to insert themselves into the labour market of a New Hampshire mill town.[13] However, neither of these authors tell us much about the historical antecedents of this population, other than referring to some standard 'push' factors such as the reproducing vitality of French Canadians and the devastating effects of agricultural crisis.

But there are at least two aspects which, if sufficiently appreciated, should help us put in a richer historical perspective the encounter between French Canadian immigrants and the New England labour markets. One is that a significant number of rural Quebecers resorted to emigration only after having tried the colonization panacea. In Quebec, colonization was more than an ideology: it was a societal project whose initial appeal rested not only on the material promises it evoked but also on the duty to fulfill the destiny of the French Canadian race. French Canadian colonization was a sort of Turner's frontier thesis in reverse: the taming of the forest would not produce a new, freer, protodemocratic *homo*; rather, it would preserve — and ultimately reinvigorate — a civilization that appeared threatened by political oppression and by social anarchy. Where this appeal managed to push the forest frontier and produce new social and cultural space, survival and conservation overruled the chances for novelty and transformation. In these cases — as Gérard Bouchard has observed- "la population s'en remet tout naturellement aux anciennes fidélités qui tissent les liens du sang, de l'entraide et de la tradition. Les élites locales trouvent là un terrain propice à l'application d'un projet de société qui met au premier rang la conservation de la foi, de la langue et des institutions, la protection de la famille, le respect des hiérarchies, l'attachement au sol, figure de la patrie, et au passé garant de l'avenir."[14]

And to a very large extent, this was the sociocultural universe that most of these regions of colonization delivered to industrial capital. As current local research is increasingly showing, in the emergence of the pulp and paper industry — whether in Mauricie or in the Sagueney region — the local clergy played a crucial role as a midwife in that process that saw the transformation of thousands of rural Quebecers into an industrial proletariat, setting ideological and organizational parameters for the nascent workers movement, and insuring that the workers' social consciousness be nurtured by submission to authority and respect for the sacrosanct doctrine of class harmony.[15] The colonization project had therefore the effect of dividing a significant portion of rural Quebecers into those who submitted to the duty of "Dieu, terre, et patrie", and those who found the will and the means to seek an alternative.

In those cases in which the colonization project was deserted, leading thousands upon thousands to take the route southward, former 'colons' had to replace a collective, national project, with one that had to be of their own making; and they had to do it with little or no industrial skills. In the American industrial wage they found the essential means for their material sustenance, but also the means that allowed them to reconstitute in a foreign land the community they had lost. Thus, the entry of Quebecers into many local labour markets in New England can hardly be divorced from the urgency to fill a communal void and to reconstitute a semblance of the social and cultural life they had known throughout their previous existence. It is not surprising then if a great deal of human investment in community building (through the creation of a rich ethnic institutional network) — much more than the search for emancipation through class activity — seems to have characterised the sociocultural dynamics of most emerging *Petits Canadas*.[16] It is in this context, I feel, that the social consciousness of a newly constituted industrial proletariat and the particular ways in which ethnicity helped shape it have to be analyzed. And this, notwithstanding the fact that by the time this desire had become a new collective project, the Quebec clergy had caught up with the new reality and had positioned itself so as to hegemonize it.

The other point revolves around the question of how the emigration project affected the traditional sexual division of labour within the French Canadian immigrant family, and in particular: what was the impact on intrafamily relationships resulting from the valorization of women's work in the textile labour market. Here again, this question can hardly be tackled without proper references to the sociocultural context that had shaped economic and family life in 19th-century rural Quebec. Even the most sophisticated study such as Hareven's tells us little on the effects resulting from the rapid transition from a context in which women's economic contribution was primarily nonmonetary, to one in which women's and children's waged work constituted a major source of family earnings.

There are reasons to believe that the psychological cost, particularly for the family head, must have been a heavy one. We know for instance that — especially in the early stage of family migration to New England labour markets — in the great majority of cases the family head was not employed in textile. Based on a sample from 18 New England textile communities, Ralph Vicero found that in 1870 only about 19% of the French Canadian family heads were employed in textile mills, whereas 67% of such families had one or more members (other than the family head) employed in textiles.[17] Coupled with data showing the relative importance of the work of wives and children as a source of family income, one is led to suggest a process of economic marginalization of the family heads within the family units. A 1874 study of 29 French Canadian families, done by the Massachusetts Bureau of Labour Statistics, found that children contributed 38% of the family income.[18] As late as 1908, the Immigration Commission found this to be still the case. Although the proportion of income coming from children's work had declined, it still constituted 33% of the total family income. Similarly although 91% of the French Canadian households surveyed the husband contributed to the family income, in only 24·3% of the cases did the husband's work represent the only source of income for the family.[19]

The marginalization of the family head may further be suspected from some data provided in 1880 by the Franco-American paper *Le Travailleur*. The inquiry found that in a Connecticut textile community about 50% of the French Canadian family heads averaged around six months work per year. In contrast, according to the author, their children in the mills were employed an average of 72 hours per week the year around.[20] It was not rare to find — as John Crowell's study pointed out — French Canadian unemployed fathers in Lowell and Lawrence attending to the housework while wives and children worked in the mills.[21]

Thus as an economic unit, the relationship that the various members of the family had with such market was one that seemed to reverse the traditional economic hierarchy that characterized family life in rural Quebec. Whereas in Quebec the father was at the centre of the family's economy, in the industrial and urban environment of New England textile communities his role was subordinate or at least complementary to that of his wife and children. The evidence is still too thin to assert conclusively the thesis of an economic marginalization of the French Canadian family head, but it seems to find some confirmation in oral history accounts. Many of these accounts stress that the major pressure to return to Quebec came from the fathers, and were often explained in terms of their difficulty in adapting to the economic recomposition which occurred within the family unit.[22]

Access to the wage and to the role of co-bread-winner did not instantaneously turn French Canadian daughters and wives into independent women; but most likely set off a process of self-valorization whose ramifications into the intertwined universe of work and community have not yet been fully investigated.

III

By the time rural Quebec had become firmly integrated into the labour market configuration of industrial New England, Montreal and its surrounding region entered a cycle of unprecedented industrial expansion and economic growth which, among other things, greatly accelerated the internal migratory flow of Quebecers toward the metropolitan region. However considerable this internal population movement proved to be, clearly it was not sufficient to meet the labour needs of the urban economy, for this is the time that witnessed the development of massive immigration of Europeans to the Quebec metropolis.

Governmental statistical reports of yearly immigrant entries to Quebec for the period that concerns us are highly unreliable (no distinction was made between immigrants destined to the Province and those who just passed through on their way to other Canadian provinces or to the USA).

This makes it impossible to have accurate estimates of the actual volume of the immigrant population which, at a given year, resided in the Province. A partial quantitative view can only be deduced from the decennial census statistics which specified the ethnic origin of the enumerated populations. Thus, the immigrant-ethnic populations whose origins were other than French or British progressed from about 26,000 in 1901, to about 158,000 in 1931. In this latter census year, more than four fifths of that population was concentrated within the Montreal region, with Jews and Italians constituting the great majority.[23]

The confluence of these two population movements — one originating in rural Quebec and the other in Europe — and its impact on labour-market developments in the Montreal region has remained largely outside the research agenda of either labour historians or economic historians. We know, for instance, very little of the social and occupational profile of those Quebecers who migrated to Montreal as compared to those who instead by- passed the metropolis and joined the labour market south of the Canadian border.

Similarly, a highly fragmented knowledge of the place of immigrant labour within the Montreal economy has emerged from the handful of studies dealing with particular industrial sectors or specific immigrant/ethnic groups.[24] But this knowledge is totally inadequate to enlighten us on the kind of inter-ethnic dynamics existing within the urban labour force, and in particular on the degree of competition that may have existed between French Canadian workers and the newly arrived European workers.

One of the most important reasons for this major historical lacuna has to do with the lack of access to what constitutes by far the most basic source for the socio-historical study of the working class. Canadian regulations, in fact, prevent access to census manuscript schedules beyond the 1891 census (unlike the US situation, where the 1900 and 1910 federal census manuscript are open to researchers); which means that the massive inflow of immigrant population that marked Quebec (and Canada) from the turn of the century to the eve of W.W.I. cannot be subjected to in-depth structural analysis (residential patterns; occupational and demographic profiles; spatial and social mobility, etc.). It is in this context, therefore, that my comments on the relationship between labour-market dynamics and immigration should be read.

Aggregate statistical data on the Montreal active workforce, as well as the existing historical literature on trade unionism in Quebec, clearly suggest the existence of a certain degree of segmentation among the urban labour force. Like most North American industrial centres, Montreal seems to have produced a labour scenario in which internal boundaries based on gender, skill, immigrant status, and race, kept workers separated into distinct labour markets.[25] And as in most other North American industrial centers (if not more), immigration and ethnicity were two crucial elements feeding the segmentation process of the Montreal labour force. We have long known, for instance, of the central place occupied by British immigrants in the early stages of the Montreal manufacturing industries; or later, of the significant concentration of Jewish workers in the local clothing industry, or of Italian immigrants in the general unskilled labour market. But studying the performance of each group in the labour market in isolation from the other groups prevents us to capture some of the larger and more complex dynamics, of which labour-market segmentation was one.

Access to the employment records of what was probably Montreal's largest single employer provides us with a rare opportunity to test the segmentation hypothesis, as well as to throw new light into this important historical issue. The employer in question — i.e., the Canadian Pacific Railway — penetrated the urban space of the Quebec metropolis through a network of a dozen or so sites, ranging from the mammoth "Angus Works" (production and maintenance of railway engines and equipment) to the various stations, railway yards, junctions and depots. Besides the mere large amount of workers the company recruited for its operations, the fact that these operations were highly diversified, give these data a strong degree of representation vis-a-vis the broader Montreal labour market.

In a recent article published in *Labour/Le Travail* I used these employment records to study the profile of Italian immigrants working at the various CPR sites during the first three decades of this century.[26] This analysis brought to light the particular occupational universe marking the CP's internal unskilled labour market. It was a market characterized by the highest degree of instability and precariousness, offering essentially dead-end jobs such as 'labourer', 'car washer', 'car cleaner', 'general helper' — jobs whose performance only required physical strength and a willingness to submit to the dictates of some foreman or departmental boss. It is not surprising that 60% of these employments lasted less than six months, and 41% less than three months; nor is it surprising to note that only one out of three Italian workers that made up our sample returned to the company for rehiring. What needs to be stressed, however, is that the segmentation mechanisms that we have observed in this particular labour market were as much a result of managerial policies as they were a function of the immigration phenomenon. In fact, for the thousands of Italian immigrants who entered and left the Montreal economy, the unskilled jobs that the CP offered served more as a way of gaining a foothold in their search for more desirable work opportunities than as employments that could be turned into stable careers. During the 1900–1915 years in particular, the period during which Italian immigration to Montreal was at its peak, more than half of the cases of separation were worker-initiated, showing that the transitory character of the CP's unskilled labour market was also the making of the Italian immigrant workers themselves. It was thus an urban labour market made possible by the constant replenishments of fresh immigrant arrivals, and by the latter's willingness to submit to its dictates for as long as they saw fit. Italian immigrants met these requirements — either out of necessity, or because nothing else was available at the moment, or still because their lack of readily marketable skills precluded better jobs; and in so doing, they kept the labour process of Montreal's largest industrial/commercial complex running.

This research is presently being enlarged to include all Montreal CPR workers regardless of their ethnic affiliations. An initial testing sample of nearly 200 randomly selected cases gives us some interesting insights into the relationship between immigration, ethnicity and occupational dynamics, as well as into the place occupied by French Canadian workers in the labour- market segmentation process.[27]

Tables I and II show the CPR workforce in terms of the major immigrant and ethnic groups that composed it, and the degree to which ethnic affiliation was reflected in the occupational hierarchy of the company. The first striking element that emerges is the under representation of native Canadians (both French and English Canadians). Taken together, they made up 45% of the entire workforce, with French Canadians being, as expected, by far the largest ethnic component. Throughout the first three decades of the century, then, the CPR's Montreal facilities drew more than half their workforce from immigrant sources, with Southern and Eastern Europeans filling the bulk of the company's internal unskilled labour market.

The underrepresentation of French Canadians relative to their numerical strength within the city's labour force cannot be easily explained, unless one takes into consideration the occupational distribution of this workforce and the ethnic stratification that existed within it. Such an analysis, in fact, suggests that French Canadian workers tended to be positioned somewhat in the middle of the occupational ladder. With few exceptions, they were conspicuously absent from the white-collar positions and from some of the top skilled positions (particularly in the metal and machine sectors, where English Canadians and British immigrants tended to prevail). At the same time, they were considerably under-represented in the unskilled sectors, where as already pointed out immigrants from Southern and Eastern Europe were predominant.

If one digs a little deeper into these data, one finds that the most common skilled position among French Canadian CP workers was 'freight carpenter', and it is highly plausible that we are dealing with a skilled occupation that, much more easily than others, could be transferred from a nonindustrial setting and adapted to an industrial context. It is premature to suggest that the top skilled jobs in the metal and machine trades may have been precluded to French Canadians because of their lack of industrial skills, just as white-collar positions were, on account of English language requirements; but it is a leading hypothesis as our research progresses.

Looking at the other side of the occupational spectrum, our sample shows clearly that the CPR attracted a significantly small proportion of French Canadian general labourers, to such an extent that the company had to resort massively to immigrant workers. Was this due to the fact that French Canadian unskilled labourers shunned the CPR and sought employment elsewhere, or was it due to the fact that the native unskilled labour force did not reproduce itself sufficiently to meet the demand of a rapidly expanding labour market? Probably both of these dynamics were operative. French Canadian unskilled labourers may have found culturally and economically more rewarding to seek a wage in sectors of the urban economy (for instance, building construction or small craft production) where work relations tended to be more personal and working conditions less regimented. At the same time, it is hard to neglect the fact that the occupational background of CP unskilled immigrant workers is so similar to that of young rural Quebecers who during that period were feeding the exodus toward New England. Clearly, then, the demand for unskilled labour coming from employers such as the CP was being unheeded by significant numbers of Quebecers who preferred to bypass the metropolitan labour market, thus choosing an American wage over an English Canadian wage.

In this paper an attempt has been made to show how the historical reconstitution of population movements can throw new light on some of the social and cultural dimensions of industrialization. Moreover, by looking at these population movements not separately but as interacting through time and space, this paper has sought to provide a more integrated understanding of the centrality of migration in the history of Quebec. Each of the three migration movements discussed in this paper had its own internal dynamics, fed particular labour markets, ad contributed in its own way to the regionalization of the north Atlantic economy. But while their history has tended to be viewed primarily as part of the history of capital and of its power to dislocate socio-economies and force people on the move, it is also the history of people interpreting life prospects, activating communal solidarities, and trying to valorize themselves not just in the market place but also in the more complex universe of civil society.

Notes

This paper grows out of two research projects presently in progress. "Histoire sociale des Italiens de Montréal, 1870–1930" (funded by the Canadian Ethnic Studies Program, Multiculturalism Sector, and by the Université de Montréal), and "French Canadian Emigration to New England, 1870–1930: A Local and Comparative Analysis" (funded by the Social Sciences and Humanities Research Council of Canada). The author expresses his gratitude to these agencies and institutions for their generous support, and thanks Jean Lamarre for his assistance in the latter project.

1 For an excellent overall assessment of the histographical production on colonization in Quebec, see Normand Séguin, "L'histoire de l'agriculture et de la colonisation au Québec depuis 1850", in Normand Séguin, ed., *Agriculture et colonisation au Quebec: aspects historiques*. (Montréal: Boréal Express, 1980), 9–37. Reference to more recent and specialized works will be made in later portions of this paper.

2 Rene Hardy and Normand Séguin, *Forête et société en Mauricie*. (Montréal: Boréal Express, 1984), especially Chapter 5.

3 *Ibid.*, 96;138.

4 For the Sagueney-Lac St. Jean region, see Gérard Bouchard, "Introduction à l'étude de la société saguenayenne aux XIXe et XXe siècles", *Revue d'histoire de l'Amerique française* XXXI, 1 (June 1977), 3–27; Christian Pouyez, et.al., *Les Saguenayens. Introduction à l'histoire des populations du Saguenay* (Québec: Presses de l'Université du Québec, 1983); Normand Séguin, *La conquête du sol au XIXe siècle*. Danielle Gauvreau, "Le peuplement de Saguenay au XIXe siècle. Mesure et caracteristiques du mouvement d'immigration jusqu'en 1911", (unpublished paper presented at the annual conference of the Canadian Historical Association, Hamilton, June 1987). For the Rimouski region, see Marie-Ange Caron et.al., *Mosaique Rimouskoise* (Rimouski, 1979); Guy Massicotte, "Rimouski et le Bas Saint-Laurent identité culturelle et développement régional", *Questions de culture*, 5 (1983), 35–60.

5 Hardy and Séguin *Forête et société*, 150–151.

6 Cited in Robert LeBlanc, "Colonisation et rapatriement au Lac-Saint-Jean. 1895–1905", *Revue d'histoire de l'Amerique française* XXXVIII, 3 (Winter 1095), 403.

7 *Ibid.*, 402, ff.

8 Séguin, *La conquête du sol*, 76–77.

9 A source permitting to follow these population movements is the 'rapport pastoral', i.e., the yearly reports that parish priests were required to send to the bishops of their diocese and which contained, among other things, the number of families departing from a given parish as well as the places of intended destination. The reports contained also information on the number of new families joining the parish and the locations these families came from. For a detailed discussion of this as well as other local archival sources and their relevance for migration research in the Quebec context see Bruno Ramirez and Jean Lamarre, "Du Québec vers les Etats-Unis: l'étude des lieux d'origine", *Revue d'histoire de l'Amerique française*, XXXVIII, 3 (Winter, 1985), 409–422.

10 Ramirez and Lamarre, *Ibid.*, 419–420.

11 Taped interview, Dept. of History, Université de Montréal, 1983. This interview is partially reproduced in Jacques Rouillard, *Ah les Etas!* (Montréal: Boréal Express, 1985), 87–99.

12 Ralph D. Vicero, "The Immigration of French Canadians to New England, 1840–1900: A Geographical Analysis", Ph.D. dissertation, University of Wisconsin, 1968.

13 Tamara Hareven, *Family Time and Industrial Time: The Relationship Between Family and Work in a New England Industrial Community* (Cambridge, Mass.: Harvard University Press, 1982).

14 Gerald Bouchard, "Ancient et nouveaux Quebecois? Mutations de la société rurale et problemes d'identité collective au XXe siècle", *Questions de Culture*, 5

(1983), 21.

15 Hardy et Séguin, *Forêt et société*, 198–201; Gérard Bouchard, "Sur l'Eglise catholique et l'industrialisation au Québec: la religion des Eudistes et les ouvriers du Bassin de Chicoutimi, 1903–1930", *Protée*, V (printemps 1976); Gilbert Vanasse, *Histoire de la Féderation des travailleurs du papier et de la forêt* (CSN), (Montréal: Editions Albert Saint-Martin, 1986).

16 Historical studies on the emergence of French Canadian communities in New England have been proliferating in the past ten years. For an excellent overview of this historiographical production see Yves Roby, "Quebec in the United States: A Historiographical Survey", *Maine Historical Society Quarterly*, XXVI, 3 (Winter 1987). 126–159.

17 Vicero, "The Immigration of French Canadians", 327.

18 *Ibid.*, 377.

19 Bruno Ramirez, "French Canadian Immigrant in the New England Cotton Industry" *Labour/Le Travailleur*, 11 (Spring 1983), 138–140.

20 *Le Travailleur*, February 6, 1880.

21 John F. Crowell, "The Employment of Children", *Andover Review*, IV (July 1985).

22 Bruno Ramirez and Jacques Rouillard, "Oral History Project on French Canadian Emigrants to New England" (SSHRCC Grant 410–81–0757), unpublished research paper, 1983.

23 The most recent attempt at measuring the ethnic composition of Montreal's population in the 19th and 20th centuries is Paul-Andre Linteau, "La monté du cosmopolitisme montréalais", *Questions de culture* 2 (1982), 23–54.

24 Ronald Rudin. *The Forgotten Quebecers: A History of English-Speaking Quebec, 1759–1980* (Québec: Institut québécois de recherche sur la culture, 1985); Bruno Ramirez, *Les premiers Italiens de Montréal: l'origine de la Petite Italie du Québec* (Montréal: Boréal Express, 1984); Denise Helly, *Les Chinois de Montréal, 1877–1951* (Québec: Institute québécois de recherche sur la culture, 1987).

25 For a useful view of this literature see Yvan Lamonde, Lucia Ferretti et Daniel Leblanc, *La culture ouvrière a Montréal, 1880–1920: bilan historiographique* (Québec: Institut québécois de recherche sur la culture).

26 Bruno Ramirez, "Brief Encounters: Italian Immigrant Workers and the CPR, 1900–1930", *Labour/Le Travail*, 17 (Spring 1986), 9–27. The following paragraphs summarize some of the conclusions contained in that article.

27 The data used in this analysis come from: Canadian Pacific Railway, "Employees Pension Plan Records", CPR Montreal Office. I am grateful to Mr. Omer Lavallee, CPR archivist, and to Mr. Walter Gregory, Head of the Pension and Actuarial Services, for graciously allowing me to consult this source.

Table 1. CPR's workforce by geographical and/or ethnic origins. Montreal, 1900-1930. N = 192.

French Canadians	37.6%
English Canadians	7.3
English	12.5
Other British	8.9
Italians	13.5
Other West Europeans	7.2
Eastern Europeans	6.7
Others	6.3
	100.0

Source: Canadian Pacific Railway, "Employees Pension Plan Records", CPR Montreal office. (Computed by the author)

Table 2. CPR's Workforce by Major Occupational Categories and Ethnic Groups. Montreal, 1900-1930.

	French-Can. %	British %	South & East Europe %
White Collar	4	20	—
Skilled	55	43	17
Semi-skilled	20	22	10
Unskilled	21	15	73
	100	100	100

Source: *Ibid* (computed by the author)

8

No Special Protection — No Sympathy: Women's Activism in the Canadian Labour Revolt of 1919

Linda Kealey

I. Introduction

No topic in Canadian labour history has elicited more debate than the Winnipeg General Strike of May-June, 1919. Viewed by most historians as a watershed in the development of labour and socialist politics, as well as in the development of state policies dealing with labour unrest and potential revolutionary threats to Canadian capital, the events of 1919 have provided the material for numerous studies of the strike itself, the rise of the One Big Union (OBU), and of repressive state policies, particularly the reaction of the Royal Canadian Mounted Police (RCMP) and its attendant security system. In recent years the historiography of the strike has taken on a decidedly revisionist tone, with the majority of writers subscribing to an analysis which stresses the national rather than local significance of these events. New studies of labour and socialist movements in the Maritimes, for example, have suggested that 1919 did not remain a western phenomenon alone. A recent study of Montreal reveals a working class offensive in 1919 which built on earlier discontents; while not strictly a 'general strike', the author demonstrates that important labour and socialist strengths existed in the city and that a militant faction of the labour movement supported the OBU despite disavowals by the moderate trade union leadership. Recent work on Toronto has also shown that Toronto's failed general strike cannot be dismissed as insignificant in the context of developing labour and socialist politics. As in other Canadian cities, the events of 1919 split the labour movement and in Toronto, the moderates were ousted from the Trades and Labor Council as a result. These studies, and others, have suggested that the events of 1919 were indicative of widespread class conflict if not potential revolution.[1]

While many of the revisionist accounts point out the importance for growing labour unrest of the trend toward organizing sectors previously unorganized, or at least weakly organized, none of these accounts adequately discuss or explain the participation of women in the events surrounding the Winnipeg General Strike and its counterparts in other Canadian centres. One recent essay on women's roles in the Winnipeg events provides a close look at that city, but no wider analysis has yet appeared. This paper will examine the general strike wave in the spring/summer of 1919 in several centres across Canada, specifically focusing on women's activism in a broad sense; some women activists were recognized as leadership figures, but most of women's active participation emerged in the various strikes which formed the building blocks of the general strike movement. The surge of organization and unrest which culminated in 1919 built upon the more general interest and momentum stemming from wartime conditions and opportunities which women also shared in. The general strike phenomenon, then, for women as for men, demonstrated class conflict and considerable unrest, heightened by the effects of a boom and bust cycle associated with war.[2]

When the Royal Commission on Industrial Relations (known as the Mathers Commission) made its tour of Canadian cities between April and June 1919, 14 women appeared to testify as to the causes of industrial unrest at the moment when conflict reached its peak. Despite their varied backgrounds, these women's testimony agreed that the high cost of living, low wages, insecurity of employment and bad housing conditions contributed to the general malaise; some spoke up directly on the subject of women's exploitation in the wage labour market, citing instances from their own experiences. Many of them traced the current turbulence to wartime conditions and the lack of business and government response to the plight of the working class, caught in a worsening situation. Such testimony gives a partial glimpse into the lives of women engaged in waged work and those who tried to maintain families on their husband's insufficient wages or meager military pensions. Labour and socialist women had been particularly active in 1917 and 1918 organizing previously unorganized women into unions, Women's Labor Leagues and soldier's wives' organizations. This activity continued in the immediate post-war period and 1919 witnessed an intensification of the trend. As the demand for women in retail, clerical and service jobs expanded, union activists, female and sometimes male, turned their attention toward women workers and unskilled workers generally. Whether the vehicle was existing American Federation of Labor 'international' unions, directly chartered federal labour unions, independent unions, or the One Big Union (OBU), the general trend was to reach out to the previously unorganized, a trend which peaked during the labour strife of 1919.[3]

This paper chronicles hitherto invisible militancy among women in the labour and socialist movements, mainly during the labour revolt of 1919, but it also addresses the aftermath later in 1919 and into 1920. The explicit intention here is not to recreate a militant 'golden past' for women activists but to suggest that the twin crises of the war period, the war itself and the state's defence of capitalism from labour militancy and socialism, mobilized labour and socialist women as never before, to defend working-class interests which included protection of the working class family, women workers and the democratic rights of organization, free speech and collective bargaining. While women activists often subsumed their interests in broad labour or socialist concerns, the suffering of the war period, the high cost of living, the enfranchisement of women, the development of a deeply-felt concern for peace and the formation of women's groups among working-class women, often based in a local community, contributed to an increased awareness of gender and a growing consciousness of working-class women's connections to the arenas of public debate and action. For some women activists the next step was electoral politics; for others, the solution emerged in revolutionary groups. By and large this new awareness remained rooted in a maternalism shared by middle-class reformers and hampered by labour and socialist acceptance of the bread-winner family model. The growth of the female waged labour force and unionization of previously unorganized women, and the public sector, 1917–20, partially challenged labour and socialist notions that women and the unskilled generally were threatening and unorganizable, more conservative and unreliable. During the crisis of 1919, however, the state certainly viewed the increased militancy coming from unskilled women and immigrant workers as a threat requiring draconian measures. The rank-and-file revolt of the last years of the war and the early reconstruction period could not be controlled as easily as the moderate Trades and Labor Congress or its international union affiliates. Censorship, internment (mostly of men but also of some women), suppression of the press, and the attack on democratic rights prompted women to utilize their resources to defend themselves and families in whatever ways they could.[4]

This paper takes a detailed look at Winnipeg women's activism and touches briefly on the activities of women in Regina, Calgary, Montreal and Toronto. In line with recent writings on women's political discourse and culture, it suggests that working-class women activists defined 'political' activity in terms of family and community needs rather than in the sense of formal political institutions; their ideal of service and caring for community and family needs arose from women's lived experiences within the realm of social reproduction as well as within the realm of production. Thus women's mobilization in the early 20th century resulted in a mixture of political expressions, some of which have not been recognized and legitimized as 'political'. Labour and socialist women participated in recognized forms of labour and socialist politics, but also in some cases created their own organizations to suit their needs. While the political agenda of women's organizations usually complemented those of their working-class male counterparts, gender- based perceptions sometimes came to the fore, creating tension between class and gender. The war years and the labour revolt of 1919 highlighted growing activism among labour and socialist women and raised occasional conflicts.[5]

II. The Winnipeg General Strike

Winnipeg was the centre of the 1919 upheaval, brought on by a confrontation between the Metal Trades Council, consisting of six unions, and recalcitrant employers who refused to recognize or deal with the industrial union style Council; also involved in the dispute was the building trades council representing various construction unions. Like the metal shop owners, the builders refused to meet with the building trades council. The result was a general strike, supported by a referendum vote taken by the Winnipeg Trades and Labor Council of its member unions. Thus, on 15 May, at 7:00 a.m., 500 women telephone operators began the general sympathetic strike, by walking out four hours before the official starting point. The official reason for the strike was the fight for collective bargaining. Beyond this, however, the strike soon became a struggle for a 'living wage', a struggle in which women had good cause to be involved. In addition, the strike provided an impetus to organize women workers in pursuit of the goal of a living wage. Later, the arrests and trials of strike leaders would add another dimension to the conflict — the defence of workers against the heavy hand of state repression.[6]

The day after the strike commenced, the Toronto *Globe* reported 2,000 women among the 30,000 strikers in Winnipeg. The precision of this estimate is unverifiable, although reports of votes for the strike indicate that those trades in which women worked voted overwhelmingly in favour of the strike. In addition to the telephone operators, sectors with large numbers of women, such as the retail clerks, garment workers, waitresses, bookbinders and confectionery workers voted strongly in favour. Women workers, both organized and unorganized, were urged to support the strike, largely through the efforts of socialist Helen Armstrong who assumed a crucial role in organizing the women for the duration of the strike. Armstrong kept the Trades and Labor Council (TLC) informed of progress in organizing women during the early days of the strike and was arrested shortly after the strike began for disorderly conduct at the Canada Bread Company property. Described in the Toronto *Star* as "business manager of the Women's Unions, " Armstrong was arrested several times in the course of the six week strike. She organized innumerable meetings for working women which aimed at organizing new unions and also served as information sessions and strategy-planning occasions. Another noteworthy accomplishment was the initiation and implementation of a dining-room to provide free meals for women strikers; men who used the facilities were expected to pay or donate what they could, thus recognizing the fact that women workers were paid less. The dining room opened on 24

May with the assistance of several men elected to help. The dining room operated on the basis of donations from individuals and organizations; Labor church services were a favourite source of funds. The Women's Labor League of Winnipeg provided the nucleus of support for the dining room; fund-raising was one of its key roles and the WLL authorized fund-raising events as well as collecting money from the Labor Church. The women on strike, however, also found it difficult to pay rent without an income and turned to the WLL and the Strike Committee for financial assistance. The Relief Committee helped to fund cash donations to women in need. Some citizens offered rooms to the women strikers and the YWCA decided to take in any woman, striker or not, who was in need. Clearly Armstrong's activities and those of the WLL were central to the well-being of women strikers.[7]

While the strike represented an opportunity to organize women workers, it also presented a chance to capitalize on existing grievances with employers. A strike of Bakery and Confectionery workers, for example, coincided with the general strike. These workers, mostly women and girls, struck because employers would not negotiate with them, thus denying the legitimacy of their union. While the strike began the day before the general walkout, more candy and confectionery workers went out on 15 May to support the demands of the strikers. Store clerks also quit work as part of the general strike, despite employer attempts to bribe them with a raise and subsequent strike-breaking efforts, all of which failed. In the latter case, the large firm of T. Eaton Company sent scab labour from Toronto, but railway workers prevented them from reaching Winnipeg. Earlier investigations of women's work in department stores had led to a Minimum Wage Board ruling on salaries and hours which had not been complied with by all employers, thus explaining in part why clerks participated in the strike. Helen Armstrong had organized clerks during the war and in May 1919 she pushed the union drive further by concentrating on women employees in the smaller stores of Winnipeg, reporting considerable success on 26 May when a large number of women clerks were added to the number of strikers.[8]

Service workers also struck in 1919, many of them waitresses employed in the numerous cafes around Winnipeg. A revitalized Cooks', Waiters' and Waitresses' union had been organized in 1914 before the outbreak of the war; the union had survived with considerable difficulty during the war and in the early days of 1919, efforts were renewed to attract new members, especially women. One day after the start of the general strike, it was reported to the TLC that the union had almost 100 percent of the restaurants organized, with full support for the general strike among its members. Despite this show of strength, a number of cafes locked out their workers, according to one report. Conditions for waitresses were akin to slave labour in many restaurants; evidence from men employed in six cafes showed that hours ranged from fourteen and a half to nine hours a day with one to three days off per month for the grand sum of fifteen dollars per month, with deductions for laundry and tips to bus boys leaving women a total of nine dollars per month to spend. Despite the Minimum Wage Board's June order covering waitresses, reports from later in 1919 and 1920 indicate that employers got away with much lower rates than the mandated $12·50 per week minimum wage, often reducing the minimum by four dollars. Employers also continued to violate the restrictions on night work for women under eighteen. The union remained out after the end of the general strike on 25 June; the *Tribune* reported 1200 members of the union still out on 27 June with demands for a ten dollar minimum for the waitresses and fifteen dollars for the men, even though the Minimum Wage Board had already ordered a higher sum for the women. By early July most of the members had returned to work, although the larger restaurants were still hostile to the union. Shaken by the strike, the union was reorganized several times in the latter part of 1919.[9]

Perhaps the most important group of women was the telephone operators whose reputation for militancy stemmed back to their successful strike in 1917 and their key role in the 1918 strike of civic workers. The telephone operators had organized in February 1917 with the help of the International Brotherhood of Electrical Workers (IBEW) and staged a three-hour walkout on 1 May 1917. The resulting investigatory board recommended wage increases and better hours and conditions. Thus in May 1918, when the civic workers of Winnipeg staged a strike, the operators played a crucial role in tying up the city; in May 1919, however, they recalled some of the errors made in the 1918 strike and forestalled their replacement by 'volunteers' by pulling all the fuses. Thus in the early days of the strike communications were curtailed within the city and with the rest of the country. The operators enthusiastically supported the strike through fund-raising events; within days, operators all over the province had joined the strike. This militancy across the province was remarkable, since in many small towns, there were only a few women employed as operators. The pressure on these women to return was intense and intimidating; some were informed that they would not be reinstated for their part in the general strike and others, from small centers, were replaced before the strike terminated. By the middle of June the Commissioner of Telephones announced that he had received 192 applications for permanent work; 43 of those hired were reinstated after signing a pledge not to participate in sympathetic strikes. Despite the operators' actions, they were not able to prevent the use of volunteers completely, nor were they able to insist on the reinstatement of former operators without loss of seniority. Doris Meakin, in IBEW representative, stated at the end of June that only half of the operators were back at work, without seniority, and that they were forced to work overtime to maintain service. She also noted that the women demanded a protest strike but no action had been taken by the union. Employer refusal to reinstate women workers in many trades plagued those who had been looking after the women strikers; Helen Armstrong reported to the TLC in early July that she was unable to cope with all the demands for help and urged the TLC to employ a woman to help these desperate women who had been arrested for vagrancy or refused relief. A committee was appointed to secure reinstatement and raise relief funds. Despite these efforts, however, many women were not rehired.[10]

Women were militant participants in street actions during the general strike as well. Several weeks into the strike, newspapers began to report incidents which demonstrated the activities of women strike supporters. The Toronto *Star* noted the predominance of women and children in the crowds that gathered at the railroad shops to prevent men from going to work; the same story reported the hostility of crowds towards automobile drivers going into Winnipeg's working-class North End to pick up domestic help. In working class area such as Weston, women were observed pulling scab firemen out of the firehall and wrecking delivery trucks owned by local department stores. Three such trucks were destroyed with wheels and merchandise smashed; in addition, the women assaulted the drivers and special police trying to protect them. A few days later several women were charged with assaulting one of the drivers and eventually fined twenty dollars and costs. Others were charged with offenses such as intimidation of shop girls and disorderly conduct; for their part in the riot of 'Bloody Saturday, ' several women were arrested for rioting and released on $1000 bail. The mayor had banned parades and warned: "Any women taking part in a parade do so at their own risk."[11]

Strike leader Helen Armstrong faced several charges of inciting to disorder and counselling to commit an indictable offence when she appeared for trial in assize court. She was accused of telling girls on strike to take newspapers away from girls selling them on the street; the two young women, Ida Krantz and Margaret Steinhauer testified that they asked Armstrong's permission to stop the selling of newspapers. The two received fines of five dollars and costs, but Helen Armstrong remained in jail for three days until bail was allowed after initially being refused by the judge. Armstrong was a feisty leader and clearly posed a threat to the authorities. George Armstrong, a prominent strike leader, was arrested along with other strike leaders a week before Helen was brought to trial; The *Star*'s special correspondent reported that when the officers came in the night to take George Armstrong away, Helen refused to let them take her husband until she ran to the North end police station to telephone the Chief of Police to check on the federal warrant for his arrest. Only then did she allow her husband to be taken away.[12]

The active and militant women of Winnipeg continued their activities after the strike finished. The repercussions of the six weeks of the general strike were felt into the summer and fall of 1919 as the trials were held. In August at the trial of some women picketers from working-class Weston, witness Fred Gouldie commented:

'He would rather face the Huns than the women of Weston.' He wanted to go to work at Eaton's, but they stopped him on the path and for nearly three weeks he did not try to pass their pickets. They were fierce — and then some. They didn't touch him but 'they were determined I shouldn't go to work.'

With the strike leaders still in jail, women helped to mount protests against their continued incarceration and the refusal to grant bail. On Labour Day in early September a giant protest parade filled the streets of Winnipeg with 7,000 protesters. The women's section, represented by the WLL, contributed two floats to the parade, one of them portraying the figures of Liberty, Equality and Fraternity, certainly a pointed comment on the long incarceration of the strike leaders. A few days later, Helen Armstrong spoke to mass meeting of women at the Winnipeg rink in which she announced WLL plans to present the visiting Prince of Wales with a petition for the release of the strike leaders. Winnipeg's chief of police threatened to prevent the WLL from parading in a body to greet the Prince of Wales, but this did not daunt Helen Armstrong who replied that the WLL would greet the Prince as private citizens, although she added that they would carry a few signs to protest the refusal to grant bail to the strike leaders. For unknown reasons the women decided not to proceed with the demonstration and a few days later the men were released on bail. When the strike trials began in late 1919 judical authorities clearly revealed their attitudes towards women's militancy during the strike. Judge Metcalfe, in answer to defence arguments about undue force being used on crowds during the police charge on 'Bloody Saturday', responded with an unambiguous statement of policy towards the presence of women on the streets:

In these days when women are taking up special obligations and assuming equal privileges with men, it may be well for me to state now that women are just as liable to ill treatment in a riot as men and can claim no special protection and are entitled to no sympathy; and if they stand and resist officers of the law they are liable to be cut down.

Implicitly the judge rendered judgment on those women who stepped outside accepted gender roles for women; those who behaved "like men" and participated in protest actions would be "cut down" by the strong arm of the law, thus losing their special "privileges" and "protections" as women. Class and gender expectations were intertwined; respectable middle class or upper class women would not participate in such unseemly behaviour.[13]

III. Labour unrest and the Mathers Commission

Clearly, the Winnipeg General Strike occupied centre stage in the spring and summer of 1919; as other writers have pointed out, however, the industrial unrest of the period extended across the country, in varying degrees and for local as well as national reasons. Activism among labour women, as workers, as union or socialist militants and as working class wives appeared to span the continent as well, although Winnipeg provides the most detailed evidence of concerted action. Working-class women testifying before the Mathers Commission detailed the conditions affecting women in their local areas; when this evidence is placed in context, it suggests the scope of women's activism in many urban centres. Outspoken women in Regina, Calgary, and Montreal appeared before the Commission to give their views; for Toronto, other evidence will be examined.[14]

One of the outspoken Saskatchewan women, Mrs. Resina Asals of Regina's WLL, outlined conditions in Regina for women, based on her experience as a working-man's wife, a mother of four and a wage earner. Asals cited examples of young inexperienced women earning $7 to $8 per week or less and noted that it was no wonder that some women turned to immoral ways on these wages. Clerks at Eaton's or Simpson's stores started out at $6 to $8. Organization of working women was difficult, she noted, referring to attempts to organize the city's waitresses and waiters during the war. The workers could thank the capitalists, however, for "awakening the worker up to the fact that he is the most important factor and that until we produce for use instead of profit this unrest will still prevail." Worsening conditions affected women directly, often forcing married women to seek employment. In her own case, as the wife of a carpenter now a disabled returned soldier, she had been forced to seek work to support the family. Her testimony also detailed Regina's poor housing and high rents which consumed one-third of the wage packet; most workers could not own their own homes because of high prices for housing, food and clothing. "Can you wonder why a woman would rather die than bring children into a world like this?" she asked. On the newly established Minimum Wage Board, her class consciousness was complimented by a strong feminist position. Not only were there no workers on the Board, there were three men and two women; if they must have men then the ratio should have been reversed. When queried further, she asserted: 'Yes, I would advocate all women and no men at all, I do not suppose the men would come and ask the women that they want would they?"[15]

Regina's labour women organized a Women's Labor League in March 1917 with Mrs. Ralph Heseltine as president. Supported by the Regina TLC, the WLL combined social events with efforts to investigate the conditions of working women and to organize them, as Asals' testimony to the Mathers Commission demonstrates. The WLL in 1919 raised money to send delegates to the June Calgary conference of the One Big Union and took a position in favour of the OBU in May; Carpenter Ralph Heseltine represented the RTLC at the Calgary convention. Regina workers supported the general sympathetic strike in a vote, but only a small number eventually turned out, suggesting the existence of considerable tension within the labour movement over these questions which resulted in a purge of the leadership in August, including Heseltine and Joseph Sambrook, both OBU supporters. The WLL, however, continued to function and cooperated with the RTLC on the minimum wage issue. The League also continued to support the Winnipeg Defense Fund by raising money.[16]

Calgary's labour women were represented before the commission by two outspoken defenders of working class women, Mary Corse and Jean McWilliam; while Corse represented the Trades and Labor Council and played a direct role on Calgary's General Strike Committee, McWilliam appeared as an individual. As a soldier's wife she had organized a Next-of-Kin Association during the war, as well a organizing laundry workers. Supporting herself and children by running a boarding house, McWilliam became increasingly radicalized during the war by her frustrations with government policies regarding soldiers' dependents, the high cost of living and wage discrimination toward women workers. She warned that revolt was imminent and stated dramatically: "If they ask us, 'Are we in favour of a bloody revolution' why any kind of revolution would be better than conditions as they are now." Like Mary Corse, McWilliam keenly felt class differences and criticized the Local Council of Women for their refusal to intervene in the firing of women laundry workers once they were unionized. McWilliam also expressed a clear sense of solidarity with working class women in commenting on Corse's testimony regarding a pregnant woman's advertisement for someone to adopt her unborn child. The mother of four children could not afford another, which led McWilliam to urge women to wake up and not sit back. "Men push us back and tell us to shut our mouths and keep quiet, " she fumed. Neither McWilliam nor Corse sat back and kept quiet. Mary Corse's testimony before the Royal Commission documented the conditions of female labour in Calgary as well as commenting on a variety of other relevant issues, such as the cost of living, the need for a living wage, the housing shortage and inflationary rents, and unequal educational opportunities for working-class children. Speaking as a working woman and mother of six children, Corse pinpointed women's working conditions as one important cause of unrest among women. "Almost every day, women are being added to the ranks of, shall I say, the socialist party or those with socialist inclinations, " she warned. The high cost of living and vast inequalities between the classes also helped to explain the unrest. As a labour representative on the Calgary School Board Corse asserted that only six percent of Calgary's children reached high school because they were needed as wage earners, thus underlining her point about class inequality. Married women also had to leave home and children in order for the family to survive; unlike many progressive women, Corse was not totally enamored of mothers' pensions, insisting that decent wages for women would help more. Corse was also more outspoken than any other woman testifying before the Commission on the need for birth control information. Class inequalities persisted here as well she noted in reference to the case of the pregnant woman with four children: "Birth control is a crime to the poor woman but the well-to-do woman who says she can only do justice to two or three children is commended for her intelligent outlook."[17]

Within a few weeks of testifying before the Commission, both women were deeply involved in a women's committee to aid the Calgary general sympathetic strike which lasted from 26 May to 25 June. Mary Corse played a particularly prominent role on the Women's Committee and the Central Strike Committee. As in Winnipeg, the labour women organized mass meetings for women, petitions, fund-raising events, and provided food for strikers. The general strike also provided the opportunity to organize a Labour Women's Council along the lines of the WLL. Corse served as president while McWilliam acted as vice-president. In addition to presenting petitions calling for the reinstatement of postal workers who had been fired by the government for taking part in sympathetic strikes, the Labour Women's Council appointed a committee to appear before the School Board to protest against teachers poisoning the minds of pupils in their comments in class that the strike was led by Bolshevists who should be shot. The School Board agreed that teachers should not force their opinions on pupils. This concern with influencces on children was a continuing feature of Calgary's LWC in the months that followed; Mary Corse's position on the School Board obviously influenced the group's activities. In November 1919 the LWC engaged in a controversy over child health and opposed a proposal that milk would be distributed to needy children by the Associated Charities; McWilliam argued for universal distribution of milk to all children and for a policy of state assistance to needy children. The controversy over child malnutrition continued to surface occasionally in 1920. In addition to these activities, the LWC, later renamed the WLL, was an active force in defending women workers and working class concerns more generally.[18]

As the Mathers Commission moved from west to east, reaching Montreal by late May, the labour situation had become critical. In Montreal itself labour unrest would peak in June, but would continue to trouble the city throughout the summer, with major strikes fought in the shipyards, in the textiles industry, in the garment industry, in the rubber industry and in the building trades, among others. While the move toward a general strike failed, recent historical work indicates a militant wave of labour and socialist activity in Montreal which drew on the discontent of the war period and a strong reaction to the anti-labour policies of the municipal government. As elsewhere, the latter part of the war witnessed waves of organization among Montreal's workers, including women in the clothing, rubber, and textile industries as well as clerical workers, salesclerks, and waitresses. Workers' clubs also grew in numbers in the immediate post-war period, providing social and political bases for Montreal workers; some affiliated with the Parti Ouvrier, Quebec's labour party. The socialist movement in Montreal drew on a multi-ethnic population with strong representation from the Jewish, Russian, Ukrainian, Italian, Polish, French, and English communities; this socialist presence was particularly striking in May, 1919 when 3,000 May Day marchers confronted the police who confiscated the red flags carried by marchers in defiance of police orders. Later in May, as the Mathers Commission gathered in Montreal, a large rally in support of the Winnipeg General Strike attracted several thousand people who listened to speeches by several representatives of various labour and socialist groups, including "socialist" Rebecca Buhay, the Social Democratic Party's Mrs. R. P. Mendelssohn, and the Parti Ouvrier's Rose Henderson. All three women were prominent in Montreal left-wing politics; Henderson was the only one of the three to testify before the Mathers Commission a few days after the rally.[19]

Henderson testified on 29 May, not as a representative of the labour party but in her official capacity as the non-Catholic probation officer for Montreal. Her work at the Juvenile Court involved her in working-class family life and she remarked on the wartime increases in the caseload of the Juvenile Court which she linked to the economic difficulties experienced by the working class; in the majority of homes fathers earned $12 to $15 per week as unskilled labourers and were only seasonally employed. The children of such families often worked for low wages as well as their mothers, especially when there were no other sources of income. The current labour unrest results, she said, from two groups: the 'underdog' class three days away from starvation whose children turned up in juvenile court and the organized mass of labour who were determined not to return to pre-war conditions. The latter group, especially the mothers, wanted a better life for their children; organized labour also greatly resented the suppression of free speech. Her solutions included getting rid of profiteers, prohibiting child labour under 16, social welfare schemes, particularly mothers' pensions and the six hour day. Women were the source of social change, according to Henderson: "I might also say that in a great many houses that I visit, it is not the father who expresses himself; I find the real revolutionist is the mother — not the man. She says openly that there is nothing but Revolution."[20]

Henderson's feminism blended with her social democratic views which combined a keen concern for women and children with a social conscience shaped by her work in the working-class areas of Montreal; for Henderson, the women of the working class offered the greatest hope for change. Her viewpoint was strongly shaped by maternal feminist convictions shared by middle and upper class women reformers of the day who also found hope for change in women as a social group generally, rather than among working class women in particular. Her class awareness, however, set her apart from these women and gave her the impetus to participate in the labour movement and later the peace movement as well. In the spring and summer of 1919 she found some common ground with more radical

Montreal women in the promise of the One Big Union.

The previously mentioned Winnipeg General Strike rally in Montreal provided Henderson and others with a platform to support both the strike and the OBU; while Henderson's speech indicated interest in the OBU, an undated letter from Henderson to R.B. Russell, Winnipeg's key figure in the general strike and the OBU campaign, indicates that Henderson was actively promoting the OBU in Northern Ontario while on an organizing tour, possibly for the ILP. She asked Russell to send her more OBU material: "I am boosting it for all its worth, the idea is catching well, " she wrote. The Montreal rally also featured a speech by Rebecca Buhay who attacked craft unionism and the capitalist press while urging working class support for the OBU. Buhay was an important figure in the radical movement in Montreal, along with her close colleague Annie Buller; both were active in the OBU, as surveillance reports indicate. An agent reported that on 13 November 1919, Buhay was elected organizer for the Montreal Local of the OBU and later, English Recording Secretary for the General Workers' Unit; Annie Buller filled the role of vice- president. Both women later played prominent roles in the Communist Party of Canada. Buller's reminiscences of Buhay, and surviving correspondence between them, indicate the close support these women gave each other in the earlier period and their shared commitment not only to socialism, but also to women's causes. Buller's first memory of Buhay was a lecture Becky gave to a group of socialist men shortly after her arrival from England; her discussion of Ibsen's *A Doll's House* stressed the need for the franchise, equal pay, and unions for exploited women workers, and established "a lasting friendship between us, " Buller noted. While both women followed socialist orthodoxy on the "woman question", they were keenly aware of the need to mobilize women as well as men.[21]

The issues brought to a head by the Winnipeg strike and the local strikes in Montreal — collective bargaining, freedom of speech, and the OBU — also brought Ms. R. P. Mendelssohn of the Social Democratic Party into the public debate. As secretary of the "socialist committee" planning the 1919 May Day parade, Mendelssohn informed the press that if violence resulted, it would be the fault of the capitalists. Municipal authorities also banned the use of public parks such as Fletcher's Field in Mount Royal Park without express permission; in early June, the police broke up a socialist gathering at the park and arrested Mendelssohn who loudly protested against the police presence and the use of mounted officers. Insisting on her right as a citizen to use the park, Mendelssohn defended the use of the park by socialists at her trial, citing previous practice and the fact that she had written the mayor for permission, but had received no answer. The charge was dismissed, despite police testimony that her actions constituted incitement to rebellion. As well as defending free speech, Mendelssohn also actively worked for the OBU and the establishment of a rival trades and labour council sympathetic to OBU goals, known as the "Industrial

Council." According to surveillance information, Mendelssohn was also a correspondent for the socialist paper, the New York *Call* and was listed by the authorities as "dangerous."[22]

Thus in Montreal, as in Winnipeg, Regina and Calgary, a nucleus of activist women existed who played public roles in the labour unrest of 1919, through the labour and socialist movement. What about the rest of the country? While other major centres did not produce women witnesses before the Mathers Commission who might provide the historian with first-hand glimpses of women's views and actions, labour unrest among women workers in specific industries was substantial in places like Toronto, Amherst, and Vancouver. Because of time limitations, only Toronto will be dealt with here.

Toronto's general sympathetic strike of 30 May to 4 June resembled Winnipeg's in so far as the metal trades were at the centre of the crisis; the eight-hour day and collective bargaining along with a 44-hour week provided the bone of contention which led to the sympathetic walkout of 44 unions and 12,000 workers. Approximately 2,000 of those who went out were garment workers, half of them women. Their support of the metal trades workers proved to be a prelude to a summer long garment workers strike which lasted from July until September. The general sympathetic strike in Toronto signified, however, more widespread activities among the previously unorganized or weakly organized, largely 'unskilled' workers, including women. The Toronto District Labor Council (TDLC) had launched an organizing drive and had within two months recruited 10,000 new members, many of them unskilled or semi-skilled workers, including candy and chocolate workers, rubber workers, and employees in the meat-packing plants. A week-long strike of packing house workers included "several hundred girls;" the conciliation board appointed to work out a settlement discussed the issue of equal pay, but failed to reach an agreement, apparently unable to reach a mutually acceptable definition of what constituted 'equal work.' The only concession aimed at the women in the final settlement was an agreement that the companies would pay one-half the cost of necessary clothing worn by the women in the plants.[23]

Waitresses and domestics in Toronto as elsewhere unionized in late 1918 and early 1919. In the case of domestic workers, the Toronto WLL assisted the women, under the guidance of Mrs. L. MacGregor, president of the WLL. The Domestic Workers Association secretary, Sarah Davies pointed out that the domestics were affiliated with the Hotel and Restaurant workers, but made their own decisions. Their goals were an eight-hour day, no apprenticeship, one day off per week, and $60 per month for 'live-outs' and $40 per month for 'live-ins'; the organization also discussed sickness and death benefits. As of 21 June, 100 women had signed up for the union which maintained its willingness to discuss matters with employers.[24]

Other groups of women workers, such as women bookbinders, textile workers, telephone operators, and waitresses, increased their union membership in the spring and summer of 1919, but the dramatic focus of the summer centered on the long garment workers's strike which began on 2 July. The general sympathetic strike had delayed the union's plan to present their demands for a new wage scale, an end to piece-work, and a 44-hour week, according to the union's representative and former member of the Central Strike Committee, S. Koldofsky. Garment workers joined strikers in the metal trades and on the street railroad in July; their demands also included limits on overtime and time and one-half for overtime, holidays, no overtime where there were unemployed garment workers, and a guarantee of a half-day's pay when called into work, whether they worked or not. While the garment workers were scattered among dozens of shops and sewed various sorts of garments, the four locals worked together under a joint board of cloak, suit, and dressmakers' locals for maximum leverage with the employers. Smaller shops came to terms with the union more quickly than the large manufacturers; the Employers' Association which included the larger firms remained unmoved, their resolve probably hardened by the simultaneous strike among the metal trades. The garment workers remained solid, however, backed by the ILGWU which sent its president to Toronto in July to bolster the strike. Striker resolve brought a number of strikers into court, arrested for interfering with scabs on the picket line. At least four young women strikers appeared in Magistrate's Court in July for heckling or striking scabs; all four were Jewish and some tensions surfaced between Jews and non-Jews in the strike. Representative Koldofsky reported to the TDLC that those who refused to honour the strike were gentiles and urged solidarity. Striker resolve, temporarily broken in mid-August, hardened after an attempt to settle with he employers by substituting a demand for week work and a minimum wage for the original demand for an end to piecework failed. The sticking point focused on recognition of the union; while the workers failed to get full recognition of the union, the strike ended in September with considerable gains and with the satisfaction that the employers had had to deal with representatives of the Cloakmakers' as a body, rather than with individual shop councils.[25]

IV. Aftermath

While local labour strife tended to occupy front stage in Toronto, the Winnipeg General Strike and the defence of the strikers was not entirely forgotten in July and August, when several of the strike leaders visited to address local audiences. A crowd of 5,000 listened to John Queen, A.A. Heaps, and T.H. Dunn when they spoke at Queen's Park in mid-July. Helen Armstrong's visit in August, sponsored by the "Women's Labor Union", probably the WLL, drew much smaller audiences, although

Armstrong herself commented favourably on the strong committees in Toronto and Hamilton when she returned to Winnipeg. When in Toronto, however, she castigated the TDLC for its "lukewarm" support of the Winnipeg strike leaders, comments which apparently hit home; a Defence Committee was appointed shortly after her remarks.[26]

Toronto labour and socialist women, however, did not emerge as strong figures in the preceding events. The local WLL was active in organizing women workers, as the example of the Domestic Workers' Association indicates. Other activities, however, seem to have preoccupied the identifiable leaders of the WLL. The summer of 1919 also witnessed a strong surge of activity centered around the Labour Educational Association (LEA), publisher of the *Industrial Banner*, and independent labour politics. At the LEA convention at the end of May, women delegates from all over the province met to set up a structure to organize women on a broad scale, not only as workers, but also as political organizers for the fall elections. Women from union auxiliaries, the Social Democratic Party, the ILP, the WLL, and women representing unions with women workers met to plan a strategy to mobilize women in the coming months. While these activities cannot be discussed here in any detail, they do suggest that a great deal of labour and socialist women's energies were focused on this campaign, which dovetailed with the surge of labour electoral success in the fall election. Toronto's WLL representatives, Mrs. Lucy McGregor and Mrs. Rose Hodgson, were active social democrats whose sympathies lay with a broad alliance of labour and socialist groups. Hodgson's political origins stemmed back to the British ILP and Christian socialism; while a strong supporter of organizing single women workers, she clearly opposed married women's work, where the husband earned an adequate wage. Hodgson introduced a resolution to that effect at the May LEA convention which passed unanimously. Lucy McGregor had been active since 1914 in the Women's Social Democratic League, affiliated to the SDP; her participation in the LEA activities suggests that she shared many of Hodgson's views. Thus, while women activists were visible in the events of 1919, their activism spread over a wide variety of labour and socialist projects, with a decided focus on a broad alliance among women.[27]

This cross-country tour of women's activism has suggested a wide variety of responses and levels of activity characterized the crisis of 1919. While the strikes themselves ended formally in the summer, the reverberations of the strike and the trials continued to be a concern of labour and socialist women. Like their male counterparts, women across the country felt a responsibility toward the strike leaders and their families as the trials were held in the fall of 1919, ultimately resulting in jail terms for most of the leaders. Winnipeg again was the centre of organization for the Defence Committee, formed shortly after the strike ended. Its main purpose was to raise funds for legal costs and for the support of strike leaders' families, but it also used fund-raising events to defend the right of collective bargaining and free speech. In Winnipeg, the Committee consisted of representatives of various labour and socialist groups, including the Winnipeg TLC, the Central Labor Council of the OBU, the Ex-Soldiers and Sailors Labor Party, the Building Trades Council, the SPC, the Labor Church, the Dominion Labor Party, and the WLL. Despite the tensions between the TLC and the OBU, the Defence Committee received support even from those unions opposed to the OBU. Financial support from union locals, individuals, and women's organizations enabled the Committee to send speakers all over the country, organize protests and publish a bulletin. In Winnipeg the WLLs raised money through dances, concerts, bazaars, and picnics, efforts which were repeated elsewhere across the country. Women speakers addressed local labour meetings and protest rallies as well; Helen Armstrong made several trips to Ontario, as noted previously; in addition to her August trip, she accompanied George Armstrong to the Hamilton Trades and Labor Congress in October, 1919, representing the WLL. "The Wild Woman of the West, " as she was dubbed by eastern newspapers, found the East too quiet for her liking. Other women also spoke to audiences in support of the Winnipeg strikers. Winona Flett, wife of the labourite strike leader Fred Dixon, spoke on the strike at a farmers' picnic in Saskatchewan in July. In the east, Sarah Johnston-Knight and Joe Knight, SPC and OBU members, gathered support in Ontario where they had moved after the purge of OBU supporters from the Edmonton TLC and the end of the general strike. Montreal's women socialists also raised money for the Defence Committee, as did the WLL in Calgary. In the latter city, Jean McWilliam was instrumental in organizing the Calgary Defence Committee, with WLL initiative playing a key role; McWilliam reported considerable interest in the outlying districts in the Defence Committee. Mary Corse also threw her energies into several protest meetings in the spring of 1920. A protest meeting held in early April passed a resolution condemning the imprisonment of the strike leaders who were "suffering in a just cause for the supposed rights of free speech." A second meeting held a few days later featured A. A. Heaps of Winnipeg; Corse also spoke and urged the working class to stand together for the welfare of their children. Scenes such as these were repeated across the country, with women in the labour and socialist movement taking important, if sometimes traditional roles, to defend controversial working-class principles.[28]

Labour and socialist women across the country responded to the post-war crisis and their newly-won enfranchisement through active involvement in election campaigns, mostly at the municipal and provincial level in 1919 and 1920. From Nova Scotia to British Columbia, women organized, supported, and sometimes ran as candidates for labour parties which included socialists, labourites, and sometimes OBU supporters. While there are many examples of this phenomenon, one case study will suffice to illustrate the extent of activity. The aftermath of the 1919 labour revolt for political activism in an electoral context was particularly noticeable in Winnipeg, where the fall municipal elections set the stage for a contest between labour and its opponents. With the Winnipeg strike trials about to begin, tensions were high and the labour movement determined to win some political power through the ballot box. The question of women's votes was a highly contentious one in Winnipeg; although women had the vote, property qualifications still limited the size of the electorate, effectively disqualifying those who did not own property, particularly women and the working class. Nevertheless, the women's vote in general was viewed as a weapon useful to labour. Helen Armstrong, at the mass protest meeting held on 7 September in the city stated: "Women's vote had given us the club. Now we wanted women to use it." In addition to the vote, three women contested the school board elections as labour candidates in December 1919. Mrs. Rose Alcin, a Jewish woman from Winnipeg's North End successfully defeated her Jewish male opponent whose views were conservative. Alcin was attacked in the press as lacking in education, to which she responded that the present educational system trained children to be "obedient slaves to the existing capitalistic order and future good members of the committee of 1,000." Running with Alcin were two other prominent labour women, Mrs. Jessie Kirk and Mrs. E. Hancox, both of whom were British-born and prominent members and speakers in various organizations, including the Labor Church, the WLL, and the Dominion Labor Party. Kirk had been fired from her job as a school teacher for her political activities, a factor which no doubt added to her decision to run. All three women candidates ran on a programme which advocated among other things, equal pay for equal work without regard to sex, free text books, open school board meetings, collective bargaining rights for teachers and the abolition of property qualifications for school trustees. Only Alcin succeeded in this election; Jessie Kirk, however, ran in 1920 for municipal council and was elected. Kirk, along with WLL and Labour Church activist, Mrs. Rowe, were elected to the executive committee of the DLP in March 1920, giving women two of the nine seats. Women were constantly urged to take public roles in he DLP by women activists and occasionally by the men; speakers urged women to use their close connections with children and even with life itself (as opposed to property) in the service of labour politics. Even before the Winnipeg General Strike, Winona Flett went so far as to urge women's participation in the DLP for the protection of men, although she pointed out that women needed relief from the drudgery of the household through cooperative schemes, for this to succeed. When the provincial election campaign of 1920 began, women in the DLP had moved in a noticeably more feminist direction, planning to run several women candidates. While both Helen Armstrong and Jessie Kirk withdrew in favour of the incarcerated strike leaders, Kirk expressed disappointment at what was clearly seen as a sacrifice for labour's cause. Winona Flett also urged women to support labour's candidates in the election, yet she also expressed regret at an election meeting of 2,000; furthermore, she urged more women to join the Labor Party to make it 50/50: ". . .she served notice there and then that they (women) would demand nothing less than a 50/50 ticket."[29]

V. Conclusion

That women were afforded "no special protection" and "no sympathy" because of their sex became only too clear during the Canadian labour revolt. Women activists faced arrest, trial, internment, and surveillance along with the men. While internment was used most often against 'enemy aliens', police and judicial activities, as well as government-sanctioned surveillance affected all. Ironically, the latter provides historians with valuable information on individuals and organizations, as well as insights into government policy on domestic surveillance and government reactions to labour unrest.

A focus on women's activism in 1919 suggests wide-ranging and variable levels of organization across the country. The patterns of strength and weakness are by no means clear-cut at this point; nevertheless, it is certainly not the case that women in the labour and socialist movement organized only in the 'radical' west. In addition, the prominence of certain groups of women workers across the country — telephone workers, garment and textile workers, waitresses and other service workers — indicates that militancy among newly organized groups of women occurred in those circumstances where support was strong from the labour and socialist movement. The existence of working class women's organizations with strong female leadership also proved vital in a number of urban centres. As with the socialist movement and the radical labour movement, lack of a national focus and viable organization tended to localize women's activism. The local nature of women's activism, however, may well have been the source of its strength as well as its weakness.

This paper has also suggested that the local context for women's activism stemmed from a redefinition of 'political' activity, based on family and community needs as well as on more formal political institutions. That this locally-based political activity usually complemented, but sometimes differed with, the aims of men, particularly in the public arena of electoral politics, serves to underline the potential for gender conflict and reminds us that sexual divisions within the working class helped to shape that experience.

Notes

1 The historiography on 1919 is too large to cite in its entirety. Standard works include: D.C. Masters, *The Winnipeg General Strike* (Toronto, 1950); David J. Bercuson, *Confrontation at Winnipeg* (Montreal, 1974); Norman Penner, ed., *Winnipeg, 1919* (Toronto, 1973) and his *The Canadian Left: A Critical Analysis* (Scarborough, 1977). See also A.R.McCormack, *Reformers, Rebels and Revolutionaries: The Western Radical Movement, 1899–1919* (Toronto, 1977) and Bercuson, *Fools and Wise Men: The Rise and Fall of the One Big Union* (Toronto, 1978). Revisionist views may be found in Gregory S. Kealey, "1919: The Canadian Labour Revolt, " *Labour/Le Travail*, 13 (Spring 1984), 11–44; Larry Peterson, "Revolutionary Socialism and Industrial Unrest in the Era of the Winnipeg General Strike: The Origins of Communist Labour Unionism in Europe and North America, " *Labour/Le Travail*, 13 (Spring 1984), 115–31; on the Maritimes, see J. Nolan Reilly, "The Emergence of Class Consciousness in Industrial Nova Scotia, 1891–1925, " unpublished PhD. thesis, Dalhousie University, 1983, chapter V; on Montreal, see Geoffrey Ewen, "La Contestation a Montreal en 1919, " *Histoire des Travailleurs Québecois* (Bulletin de R.C.H.T.Q.), 36 (Automne 1986), Vol.12, No.3, 37–62. See also a recent thesis on Vancouver's working class for a discussion of which labour groups supported the general strike in that city: James Robert Conley, "Class Conflict and Collective Action in the Working Class of Vancouver, British Columbia, 1900–1919, " PhD. thesis, Carleton University, 1986. For Toronto, see James Naylor, "Toronto, 1919, " *Historical Papers* (Canadian Historical Association, 1986), 33–55.

2 Mary Horodyski, "Women and the Winnipeg General Strike of 1919, " *Manitoba History*, No.11 (Spring 1986), 28–37, is the only published article to date on women during 1919. James E. Cronin, "Labour Insurgency and Class Formation: Comparative Perspectives on the Crisis of 1917–1920 in Europe, " *Social Science History*, Vol. 4, No.1. (Winter 1980), 125–52, argues that the crisis of these years produced similar waves of organization in many European countries, characterized by the prominent roles played by women in community-based actions, especially related to consumer issues. His book, *Labour and Society in Britain, 1918–1979* (London, 1984), 31, develops this argument further, noting also the 270 percent increase in trade union membership among women as well in Great Britain from 1914–18.

3 Royal Commission on Industrial Relations, "Evidence, " 26 April to 13 June 1919 (4 vols., mfm copy, Public Archives of Canada); the women's testimony will be discussed more directly below. For a discussion of organizing women workers during the latter part of the war, see L. Kealey, "Women and Labour During World War I: Women Workers and the Minimum Wage in Manitoba, " in Mary Kinnear, ed., *First Days, Fighting Days* (Regina, 1987); this article also looks at the Women's Labor League of Winnipeg and its activities; on soldier's wives' organizations, see L. Kealey, "Prairie Socialist Women and World War I: The Urban West, " unpublished paper, 1986. For information on the organization of women in Toronto, see Jim Naylor, "Toronto, 1919"; for Montreal, see Ewan, "La Contestation, " 45ff.; for Vancouver, see Conley, "Class Conflict, " especially chapters 9,11 and 13. On the state and immigrant

radicalism, see Gregory S. Kealey, "The State, Immigrant Radicalism, and the Canadian Labour Revolt of 1917–1920, " unpublished paper, April, 1987.

4 See Kealey, "The State, Immigrant Radicalism. . ." p.11 on the twin crises of 1914–20. A recent collection of articles edited by Ruth Milkman, *Women, Work and Protest. A Century of Women's Labour History* (Boston, 1985), usefully cautious against substituting a new myth of militancy for old myths of passivity among women workers. She carefully notes that we need to know which historical circumstances encourage or impede women's militancy; effective mobilization utilizes forms rooted in women's culture and experience. Furthermore, it is instructive to examine the sructural characteristics of unionism as well as the impact of the broader gender ideology. For the purposes of this paper, militancy denotes the participation of women in strike actions or the defence of women workers, working-class women's organizations or general working class interests by means of eonomic or political actions requiring a stand in opposition to dominant interests; while militancy may mean confrontation with the law, it does not always entail such confrontations.

5 See Angela Miles and Geraldine Finn, eds., *Feminism in Canada* (Toronto, 1983) especially Miles, "Ideological Hegemony in Political Discourse: Women's Specificty and Equality, " 213–227.; my thinking on this question has also been shaped by Jill McCalla Vickers, "Feminist Approaches to Women in Politics, " in Linda Kealey and Joan Sangster, eds., *Beyond the Vote: Canadian Women and Politics* (Toronto, 1989). It should also be noted that during the war years, tensions between working-class and middle-class women were exacerbated during labour disputes when middle-class women intervened to scab on those who were strikers, particularly in Winnipeg, 1918 and 1919 and Vancouver during 1919; these women replaced telephone operators in both cities.

6 Quote from Horodyski, "Women and the Winnipeg General Strike of 1919, " 29.

7 *Globe*, 16 May 1919, p.1; *Western Labor News (WLN)* 16 May 1919, p.8; Armstrong reported in the *WLN*, 16 May 1919, p.8 that knitting and laundry women were organized. A day long meeting was announced for the purpose of organizing all women workers in *WLN*, 19 May 1919, p.3. Organizing meetings for specific groups of women workers were reported in the WLN throughout the course of the strike. Armstrong's arrest was reported in the Toronto *Globe*, 17 May 1919 and the Toronto *Star*, 17 May 1919. The dining room was mentioned in *WLN*, 23 May 1919, p.1, under the auspices of the Women's Labor League and the administration of Helen Armstrong. Donations of food were requested in the same edition of the *WLN*, p.2. The opening of the dining room is reported in the *WLN*, 24 May 1919, p.3. Examples of Labor Church collections for the dining room appear in *WLN*, 26 May, 27 May and 2 June 1919. The *WLL* authorized fund raising events for the dining room as fragmentary evidence from the exhibits collected for the trial of the Winnipeg General Strike leaders shows. See Exhibit 175,11 June 1919, King vs. William Ivens, RG 4 A1 (Provincial Archives of Manitoba). For the Relief Committee's role, see Horodyski, "Women, " p.30 and *WLN*, 23 May 1919, p.3; for the YWCA's role, see Horodyski, *ibid.*, p.30; offers of rooms for striking women appear in *WLN*. 27 May 1919, p.2.

8 See Horodyski, "Women", p.31 and *WLN*, 16 May 1919, p.8 for confectionery workers; for store clerks, see Horodyski, "Women, " p.32 and *WLN*, 19 May

1919, p.2. Investigations of women's work in department stores occurred in 1914 under the auspices of the University Women's Club and in early 1919 by the Minimum Wage Board. See L. Kealey, "Women and Labour During World War I: Women Workers and the Minimum Wage in Manitoba, " in Mary Kinnear, ed., *First Days, Fighting Days* (Regina, 1987). On Armstrong's campaign among clerks in small stores, see the *Tribune* (Winnipeg), 26 May 1919, p.1.

9 On the organization of waitresses, see L. Kealey, "Women Workers and World War I." See *WLN*, 3 January 1919, p.1; 10 January 1919, p.1; 24 January 1919, p.1 and 31 January 1919, p.1. for the drive to increase the membership of the union. *WLN*, 16 May 1919, p.8 reported the union as nearly 100 percent organized and showed that culinary workers supported the general strike. Lockouts are listed in *WLN*, 27 May 1919, p.3. For a report on the evasions of the Minimum Wage, see *WLN*, 10 October 1919, p.8 and 17 October 1919, p.8; *Tribune*, 27 June 1919, p.5; *WLN* 28 June 1919, p.3 and 9 July 1919, p.1. Reorganization of the union is disucssed in *WLN*, 29 August 1919, p.4 and 7 November 1919, p.8. The international organizer, Mackenzie, noted that the union was "badly shaken" during the 1919 strike but was now recovering in *WLN*, 24 September 1920, p.4.

10 For a discussion of the telephone operators activities in 1917 and 1918, see L. Kealey, "Women Workers and World War I, " and Horodyski, "Women, " 32–33. *WLN*, 19 May 1919, p.4; 20 May 1919, p.2; 21 May 1919, p.3; 24 May 1919, p.3; 26 May 1919, p.4. Intimidation is reported in *WLN*, 3 June 1919, p.2. *WLN*, 14 June 1919, p.1 reported the arrival in Winnipeg of six operators from Carman who had been replaced. The statement of Telephone Commissioner George A. Watson is reprinted in the Toronto *Star*, 19 June 1919. The Winnipeg *Tribune*, 27 June 1919, p.5 reported 225 vacancies, 350 applications and the loss of seniority as well as the "no strike" pledge. Dors Meakin's statement is found in the Toronto *Star*, 30 June 1919. Helen Armstrong's report to the Winnipeg TLC is in *WLN*, 3 July 1919, p.3. The *WLN*, 10 July 1919, p.3 reported 119 operators had been refused reinstatement.

11 *Star* (Toronto), 4 June 1919, p.3; *WLN*, 5 June 1919, p.2; *Tribune* (Winnipeg), 6 June 1919, p.2; *Star*, 7 June 1919, p.1; *Tribune*, 10 June 1919; p.1; the Toronto *Star* noted that Mrs. J. McCrom was fined $20 and costs for assaulting a delivery truck driver; see *Star*, 13 June 1919, p.24; on 19 June 1919, the *Star* reported 20 women and men strikers has been fined or imprisoned on charges of intimidation. "Bloody Saturday", 21 June, followed the arrest of the strike leaders late in the evening of 16 June and in the early hours of 17 June. A silent parade to protest these arrests turned into a riot when special police and the RNWMP attacked the protesters, killing one person and injuring others. Mayor Gray's statement was quoted in the Toronto *Star*, 24 June 1919, p.9.

12 Armstrong, Krantz and Steinhauer's arrest was reported in the Winnipeg *Tribune*, 13 June 1919, p.1; Armstrong was committed for trial on 24 June and the other two were tried on the same day. See the *Tribune*, 24 June 1919, p.5; *Star*, 25 June 1919, p.4; *Tribune*, 27 June 1919, p.2 and 28 June 1919, p.5; *WLN*, 27 June 1919, p.1; *Star*, 28 June 1919; p.3; *WLN*, 28 June 1919, p.1. For the account of Helen Armstrong's actions regarding her husband's arrest, see the *Star*, 19 June 1919.

13 See *WLN*, 15 August 1919, p.8 for the quote from Gouldie; the protest parade

is described in *WLN*, 5 September 1919, p.1 and in the One Big Union (OBU) *Bulletin*, 6 September 1919, p.2. Helen Armstrong's speech at the rink and the petition campaign are covered in the Winnipeg *Tribune*, 8 September 1919, pp.1 and 4 and 9 September 1919, p.1. *WLN*, 12 September 1919, p.1 reports the release of George Armstrong on bail. Strike leaders were officially welcomed at a reception sponsored by the WLL and others; 1000 people turned out according to *WLN*, 19 September 1919, p.1. Metcalfe is quoted in *WLN*, 19 December 1919, p.6.

14 For Montreal, see Ewen, "La Contestation. . .", 40–41.

15 Royal Commission on Industrial Relations, Evidence, Saskatoon, 7 May 1919,1035–37; Regina, 8 May 1919, 1189–96.

16 The Winnipeg *Voice*, 16 March 1917, p.5 noted the creation of the Regina WLL; WLL activities reported in the Regina Trades and Labor Council Minutes of 13 August 1917,28 April 1919,8 September 1919; the OBU support appears in *WLN*, 8 May 1919, p.1; on the general outlines of the Saskatchewan labour movement, see W.J.C. Cherwinski, "Organized Labour in Saskatchewan, 1905–1945, " University of Alberta, PhD. thesis, 1972, especially Chapter 2. For tensions within the RTLC, see Minutes of 2 June 1919 and 25 August 1919; on the minimum wage issue see RTLC Minutes, 8 September 1919.

17 On McWilliam's activities during World War I and the class conscious nature of Calgary's Next-of-Kin Association, see L. Kealey, "Prairie Socialist Women and WWI: The Urban West, " unpublished paper, 1986; Royal Commission on Industrial Relations, Evidence, Calgary, 2 May 1919,782- 793 (McWilliam) and 635–650 (Corse).

18 The United Brotherhood of Carpenters and Joiners, Local 1779 (Calgary), Minutes, 29 May 1919, Glenbow-Alberta Institute, record Mary Corse's presence as a representative of the Central Strike Committee. For more information on Corse, see L. Kealey, "Prairie Socialist Women. . ." and *Woman's Century*, April 1920, p.25; Corse was born in England and married George Corse who worked in the printing trade as a machinist, linotype operator and printer at various times. The activities of the Women's Committee during the general sympathetic strike are covered in the Calgary *Strike Bulletin*, No.2,31 May 1919, No.6,7 June 1919, No.8,14 June 1919, No.9,16 June 1919, No.10,18 June 1919. The LWC was formed in direct imitation of Winnipeg's WLL after Corse met Helen Armstrong and Mrs. Logan of that city's WLL through OBU activities. The controversy over child health appears in the Calgary *Herald*, 24 November 1919, p.8, 26 November 1919, p.10 and in the *Searchlight*, 28 November 1919, p.4 and 20 February 1920, p.1. The LWC also protested working conditions for waitresses at the CPR lunch counter and lobbied for changes to Alberta's Factory Act which would benefit women workers. See *Edmonton Free Press*, 27 December 1919, p.5 and *Searchlight*, 3 September 1920, p.3. They also agitated for free treatment for tubercular patients: *Searchlight*, 23 January 1920, p.4. In 1920 they also took part in the Calgary Defense Committee, established to defend the Winnipeg General Strike leaders and the principles of collective bargaining and free speech.

19 See *Chronologie des mouvements politiques ouvriers au Québec de la fin du XIXe à 1919*, Mai 1976, 258–93, published by the Regroupement de chercheurs en histoire des travailleurs quebecois; Ewen, "La contestation. . ."; Gregory S. Kealey,

"1919. . .," 22–3; The May Day parade is described by J. Lanch, "May First in Montreal, " *Justice* (New York, publication of the ILGWU), 10 May 1919, p.3. The Winnipeg general strike rally is covered in the Montreal *Gazette*, 28 May 1919; it was sponsored by the IAM and the Amalgamated Society of Engineers. For Buhay and Mendelssohn see below.

20 Royal Commission on Industrial Relations, Evidence, Montreal, 29 May 1919,3147–3168. Henderson was born in Ireland to a family with radical views on education and politics; as a widow with a daughter to bring up, she moved from volunteer work to the juvenile court; she also had worked in factories, laundries and restaurants, living and working with the young women employed there, according to a biographical note in the *Workers Weekly* (Stellarton, N.S.), 6 August 1920. By 1920 she had joined the ILP, organizing in Ontario and the Maritimes. She also was a member of the Women's International League for Peace and Freedom; later in her life she joined the CCF and ran for a seat in Toronto in 1935 where she lived in the last years of her life. She died in Toronto on 30 January 1937.

21 The speeches are reported in the Montreal *Gazette*, 28 May 1919; Rose Henderson to R.B. Russell, no date, King vs. Ivens, Provincial Archives of Manitoba, Winnipeg (RG 4, A 1 box 3); Royal Canadian Mounted Police (RCMP), Personal History File, Rebecca Buhay, 17 November 1919 and 1 July 1920; Annie Buller, "In Memory of Becky Buhay, " *Marxist Quarterly* (December 1957- January 1958), 18–22. Buhay was born in London's East End in 1896, emigrated to Canada in 1913 and died in 1953. For more information on women in the Communist Party of Canada, see Joan Sangster, "Canadian Women in Radical Politics and Labour, 1920–1950, " McMaster University, PhD. thesis, 1984. Two CP biographies pay tribute to two prominent Montreal Communist women; Louise Watson, *She Never was Afraid: The Biography of Annie Buller* (Toronto, 1976) provides glimpses of Buhay as well; Catherine Vance, *Not by Gods But by People. . .The Story of Bella Hall Gauld* (Toronto, 1968) also provides information on the other women. Bella Hall also testifed before the Mathers Commission as a resident of the University Settlement on her work with immigrants; her brief testimony underlined the poor health of immigrant children and the miserable living conditions in general. Hall came from Winnipeg where she worked at J.S. Woodsworth's All Peoples' Mission before moving to Montreal to work at the Settlement.

22 *Daily Star* (Montreal), 1 May 1919, p.1; 2 June 1919, p.2; 10 June 1919, p.3. The Toronto *Star*, 21 July 1919, p.1. commented on the split in the Montreal labour movement and listed in Mendelssohn as actively working for the OBU; the Montreal *Daily Star*, 21 July 1919, p.3 also carried a similar story on the OBU. Public Archives of Canada, Records of the Post office, RG 13, A 2, Vol. 237, file 1537, J. N. Carter to A.J. Cawdron, 26 June 1919.

23 *Star* (Toronto), 29 May 1919, p.1; 30 May 1919, pp.1 and 9; 22 May 1919, p.2 for a report on the general organizing drive led by H. Lewis of the TDLC, also a socialist. For the meat-packing srike, see *Star*, 5 May 1919, p.1; 22 May 1919, p.2; 23 May 1919, p.2. Three days before the meat-packing strike began on 5 May, several hundred women from the Cowan Chocolate and Cocoa Co. struck for half a day for increases in wages and a reduction of hours which they negotiated, despite the fact they were not unionized; by 22 May they had been unionized with the assistance of the TDLC. See *Eastern Federationist* (New

Glasgow, Nova Scotia), 10 May 1919, p.5.

24 See reports in the *Edmonton Free Press*, 17 May 1919, p.5 and 21 June 1919, p.5; *Star*, 4 July 1919, p.9 and 21 July 1919, p.9; the *Star*, 3 July 1919, p.5, reported on a meeting of the association which discussed a nine-hour day and a $10 minimum indicating that they had perhaps been unsuccessful in pushing the shorter day and higher wage.

25 For the bookbinders, see *Industrial Banner (IB)*, 25 April 1919, p.3 and 16 May 1919, p.3; textile workers: *IB*, 6 June 1919; boot and shoeworkers: *IB*, 25 July 1919, p.3; telephone workers: *IB*, 25 April 1919, p.3. On the Garment Workers' plans to present new demands in June, see the Toronto *Star*, 4 June 1919, p.2. For events during the street car strike, especially the role of women, see *Star*, 24 June 1919, p.2 ("As usual women sympathizers were the most outspoken and vitriolic. . ."). The *Star*, 25 June 1919, p.3 covered the riot at the Lansdowne barns between strikers and scabs. The events of the garment workers' strike are covered in: *IB*, 4 July 1919, p.1; *Star*, 8 July 1919, p.20; 10 July 1919, p.4; 12 July 1919, p.4 (visit of ILGWU president Schlesinger and meeting with workers). See the Toronto *Star*, 4 July 1919, p.8 for Koldolfsky's comments on gentiles. Arrests and trials of the Jewish women strikers are covered in *Star*, 15 July 1919, p.2 (Esther Magor); 17 July 1919, p.3 (Molly Fruitman); 30 July 1919, p.3 (Ida Braman and Ada Rosenburg). The strikers had decided to abandon the strike in mid-August but renewed the struggle soon after. See the Montreal *Daily Star*, 21 August 1919, p.7. The settlement and criticisms of the strikers for almost abandoning the strike appear in *Justice*, 13 September 1919, p.1 and 20 September 1919, p.4.

26 The Toronto *Star*, 15 July 1919, p.22 reported on the address by Queen, Heaps, and Dunn. Queen and Heaps were both socialists and aldermen. Dunn represented the Great War Veterans Association. Armstrong's visit was reported in the Montreal *Daily Star*, 12 August 1919, p.11 and 19 August 1919, p.11; see also the *IB*, 15 August, p.3 and 29 August 1919, p.10. The latter carried the critical remarks made by Armstrong; Armstrong's positive remarks appeared in *WLN*, 12 September 1919, p.8.

27 The LEA announced in April 1919 that it would inaugurate a new provincial women's department of work and labour which women would control. See *IB*, 4 April 1919, p.1. The *Industrial Banner* carried a number of articles in the summer of 1919 promoting the Labor Party. See *IB*, 4 July 1919, p.1; 11 July 1919, p.1. The LEA convention in Stratford, Ontario, 24–25 May is covered in *IB*, 30 May 1919, p.4; 24 women were listed as delegates, including 11 from Toronto. In addition to Hodgson and McGregor, there were women present from the Toronto Ladies' Auxiliary of the IAM, from the Women's Social Democratic League, from the bookbinders, domestic workers and textile unions. Hodgson's Christian socialsim can be found in a letter to the *IB*, 25 April 1919, p.4, in which she described socialism as "the modern church theology" which no longer should be dreaded as revolutionary. The same issue, p.5, covered the ILP convention which identified Hodgson as a founding member of the British ILP in 1893. The convention stressed democratic control of industry and the use of evolutionary means for change, as well as passing resolutions for the release of political prisoners, the recall of Canadian troops from Siberia, a national minimum wage, shorter work days, lying-in grants for expectant mothers and a guarantee for every child of the necessities of life.

McGregor's involvement in the WSDL can be found in various issues of the *IB* beginning in September 1914.

28 David J. Bercuson, *Fools and Wise Men: The Rise and Fall of the One Big Union* (Toronto, 1978), especially chapter 6 on "Labour's Civil War." Reports of fund-raising by women appear in the OBU *Bulletin*, especially: 13 December 1919, p.1; 21 February 1920, p.1; 6 March 1920, p.4; 27 February 1920, p.4 (composition of the Defence Committee); 3 April 1920, p.4; 9 April 1920, p.5; 10 April 1920, p.4 (a bazaar and dance raised almost $2500 from 4,000 supporters); 24 April 1920, p.4 (donations from the Labour Church Women's Auxiliary and Calgary WLL); *WLN*, 7 May 1920, p.1 (May Day protest parade with 1,000 women and children, carried banner which read: "Labor's Boys of Today are the Men of Tomorrow"); OBU *Bulletin*, 22 May 1920, pp.1 and 4; 5 June 1920, p.4; 24 July 1920, p.4. Donations were received from Mrs. Mendelssohn, Montreal, Sarah Johnston-Knight, Toronto, Mr. and Mrs. A.V. Thomas, New York (Lillian Beynon Thomas, suffragist/ pacifist/ socialist/ writer, had moved to New York with her journalist husband and her sister, Frances Beynon, in 1917 in protest against pro-war sentiments in Canada; Beynon was the well-known women's page editor of the *Grain Growers Guide*). Funds also came from Winnipeg's Houseworkers Association and individuals Jewish women. On Helen Armstrong's Ontario trip, see *WLN*, 12 September 1919, p.8, and 3 October 1919, p.1. Mrs. Dixon's speech in Saskatchewan: *WLN*, 18 July 1919, p.1. Sarah Johnston-Knight's activities: OBU *Bulletin*, 25 October 1919, p.6. For Calgary, see *Searchlight*, 28 November 1919, p.4; 2 April 1920, p.3; 9 April 1920, p.4 and 28 May 1920, p.1; the Calgary *Herald*, 5 April 1920, p.8, covered the first protest meeting.

29 The Dominion Labor Party was formed in 1918; candidates for school trustee were nominated at a labour convention, 6 October 1919. See *WLN*, 10 October 1919, p.1. A Miss McBeth, school teacher, was also endorsed by labour for the West Kildonan area. The debate on abolition of property qualifications raged in early 1920. See *WLN*, 16 January 1920, p.1; 23 January 1920, p.1; 27 February 1920, p.1; 5 March 1920, p.1 and 26 March 1920, p.1. Armstrong is quoted in *WLN*, 12 September 1919, p.8. Mrs. Alcin was attacked in the *Free Press* (Winnipeg), 21 November 1919, p.13. For information on Kirk, see *FP*, 27 November 1919, p.8; her firing is noted in *WLN*, 4 October 1918, p.1. On Hancox, see *FP*, 28 November 1919, p.21. The final vote is reported in *WLN*, 5 December 1919, p.1; Alcin beat Max Steinkoff 1,728 to 1,049. Kirk's 1920 victory is reported in *WLN*, 10 December 1920, p.4. For Kirk and Rowe's election to the DLP executive, see *WLN*, 12 March 1920, p.1. For examples of appeals to women to become active in labour politics, see Ivens: *WLN*, 6 September 1918, p.8; Bland: *WLN*, 5 September 1919, p.8; Winona Flett (Mrs. Dixon): *WLN*, 7 March 1919, p.1; Rowe: *WLN*, 27 February 1920, p.1. On the provincial election fo 1920, see Armstrong and Kirk's withdrawal in *WLN*, 16 April 1920, p.1 and Winona Flett's remarks at the labour rally in *WLN*, 25 June 1920, p.1. On Winnipeg's post-strike municipal elections, see J.E. Rea, "The Politics of Conscience: Winnipeg After the Strike, " *Historical Papers*, Canadian Historical Association, 1971,276–88, and his "The Politics of Class: Winnipeg City Council, 1919–45, : in Carl Berger and Ramsay Cook, eds. *The West and the Nation* (Toronto, 1976), 232–49. Neither article notes women candidates.

9

Miners' Struggles in Western Canada: Class, Community, and the Labour Movement, 1890–1930

Allen Seager

Introduction

A study in "class, community, and the labour movement" in the context of the Canadian mining West confronts formidable obstacles, both empirical and interpretative. The canvas is as vast and geographically diverse as the territory upon which mining capital and labour were imposed, and that largely during the period under review. Unlike the highly concentrated, single-sector coal-mining communities of the East, the miners of the Far West were scattered among hundreds of mining camps, industrial villages, cities and towns in the coalfields of Alberta, and the coal and metalliferous mining areas of British Columbia. One may speak in very general terms of the expansion of a mining frontier, yet we must look also at the situation of local communities at various points on the compass of industrial growth and decline which, together with the wider transformation, structured their collective response. Economic and technological developments, as opposed to the exhaustion of resources, dictated the cycles of industrialization and deindustrialization in western mining; these were influenced, moreover, by the constraints of the 'staples' economy of the region. A shifting and often chaotic demographic picture is further complicated by the waves of migration and immigration that washed over the region from 1880s to the 1920s, leaving the western miners with a legacy of cultural fragmentation almost without parallel in Canadian industrial history.[1]

Canada's mining East produced not only a more homogeneous working class culture, but has generated a historiography that yields little or nothing in its sophistication to the Briton or the American.[2] But the 'new' labour history in Canada has largely passed by on the other side of western workers in general, and the miners in particular. Their record is rich, but a modern historiography has been slow to develop.[3] The most common theme in the 'first generation' of Canadian labour history which touch upon the subject are attempts to 'explain' largely assumed phenomena of class consciousness, militancy, and radicalism, in terms of the categories of political economy or industrial relations theory;[4] "the peculiarities of western Canadian capitalism exemplified by the naked exploitiveness of the mining camps and the transparent interlocking of capital and the state";[5] or the "sorry shibboleths" of western exceptionalism, which have paradoxically missed most of that which is important and distinctive about western labour history: labour's role in creating a new society.[6] More desultory debates over the "origins of western radicalism, " however, are not needed. In the context of mining history, there is a need to unravel the thread of working-class experience from the tapestry of myth and folklore (both popular and academic) surrounding the miner as 'archetypical proletarian', here as elsewhere, [7] and to uncover a human landscape from the overburden of untested hypotheses about life and labour on the industrial Canadian frontier.[8] This paper asserts the prior necessity of a new empirical framework for discussion, and makes a small contribution towards that end, emphasizing the context and contours of miners' struggles in the region, 1890–1930.[9] It seeks to call attention to, rather than provide answers for, the problems and questions arising from a vital and important chapter in Canadian working class history.

I

The quantitative methods of North American social history have scarcely been brought to bear upon and are in any case difficult to apply to studies of mining or other communities in the Canadian West. The resulting lack of basic information has allowed free rein for all manner of uninformed theorizing.[10] Barriers to systematic research in western mining communities often seem insuperable but one historical geographer has recently stepped into the breach with a valuable study of industrial life in the Slocan Valley of British Columbia.[11] Here, a number of small communities sprang up and within little more than a decade had been just as swiftly marginalized in the wake of the great Silver Boom of the 1890s. Save for a few localities favoured by geological conditions and investment decisions, this appears to have been a fairly typical pattern of boom-and-bust in hardrock mining communities which has done much to shape essentially negative historical impressions of all western mining communities. Even in the short life-span of industrialization in the Slocan, however, it created a complex and differentiated social structure, with a dense network of institutions of which, for the miners, the most important was the trade union. Its function was not so much collective bargaining — there was no important strike in the Slocan country after 1901 — but the administration of health and welfare, insurance and compensation matters, and other apparently benevolent activities. That was the Western Federation of Miners, "Federation of Dynamiters and Murderers" or radical vanguard of the "resource proletariat", depending on one's point of view; the author of this study, Cole Harris, was not testing hypotheses about the western working class. The nature of his sources meant that as much if not more information was forthcoming about the resident middle class in the industrial community than about the miners — a revision of received wisdom insofar as middling strata are usually assumed not to have existed at all in the "totally polarized" environment of the western mines, where miners comprised an "isolated mass" *par excellence*.[12]

The apparent lack of militancy among the miners remains to be accounted for. The presence of moderating social institutions and the population of non-miners and non-working class citizens does not, however, seem to have greatly altered the miners' 'radical' political outlook. Harris notes the millenarial ideology of the socialist movement[13] that arose like a phoenix in the mining West after 1900 (Figures, 7,8). Sandon, the Slocan Valley community where miners were concentrated, returned a strong majority for the radical Marxist Socialist Party of Canada in the Dominion elections of 1908. New Denver, its predominantly middle class neighbour, returned less than a fifth of its ballots for socialism, although here *was* situated a tiny fragment of the radical petty bourgeoisie in late nineteenth-early twentieth century British Columbia: a class whose contribution to socialism and the SPC was considerable, though usually overlooked. The New Denver contingent would certainly have been overlooked if not for the fact that the Slocan author's grandfather was its leading light! It is very difficult for an outside researcher to penetrate the external surface of these small towns. But to return to the methodological point at hand, had we not known something about the social structure of Sandon and New Denver, we would, surveying the results of the election in 1908, have been led to totally false conclusions about miners' response to socialism in two adjacent silver camps.[14]

The geographer in question was armed with little more than an intimate knowledge of his community, a large group of interviews heroically and systematically conducted, and sources of indifferent quality, such as local directories. Directories are, in fact, available for dozens of western Canadian mining towns in the late nineteenth and twentieth centuries. Attempting at first to enumerate all residents, they later evolved a strict formula that excluded all miners from enumeration: a measure of the miners' migratory ways, the growth of the mining population, and emerging class antagonism. The one thing these directories do show is the futility of theories of 'polarization' and the 'isolated mass'. The commercial, professional, and other non-mining classes leap off their pages, and if anything, there appears to be an inverse correlation between the weakness of middling strata in a given community, and radical attitudes among miners in that community. These middle class documents also negative the false assumption that non-British ethnic groups formed an undifferentiated proletarian mass in mining communities, and finally they document a certain amount of upward mobility among miners.[15]

Studies based on such sources, of course, are inevitably limited. Harris points out that information on the background of immigrants to New France is easier to obtain than the equivalent for immigrants to British Columbia. Through various expedients Harris was, however, able to piece together a collective portrait of the industrial population in the Slocan Valley which looks like a very diverse mosaic including, among other fragments, a large slice of "Old Ontario". Our geographer was unfortunately reluctant to confront the historians' catechism that British Columbia's "Inland Empire" was for all intents and purposes an American colony. This particular thesis gained prominence in the days when Canadian historical research was primarily funded by U.S. endowments, tended to emphasize the contributions of American capital, and the "mingling of the North American peoples." It gained a new dimension in labour history when scholars finally discovered movements like British Columbia's metal miners' District 6 of the Western Federation of Miners, logically assumed to be the other side of America's capitalist coin. But were they in fact? R. Parmeter Pettipiee, journalist tribune of the Western Federation in British Columbia, an electic socialist whose paper, the *Lardeau Eagle* had a wide influence in the hardrock mining community, came from Old Ontario. So did Chris Foley, then the leader of District 6, whom Pettipiece and the *Eagle* nearly elected to Parliament in 1900, on the strength of the largest single vote for any Labour or Socialist candidate in the mining West under manhood suffrage[15] [Figure 8]. These men had their own ideas about the sources of oppression in the hinterland. Pettipiece, very Canadian in this, blamed deteriorating class relations on the greed and incompetence and of British capitalists who bought out the practical entrepreneurs of the American-owned mines and replaced them with a horde of "English chappie clerks [who] assume a know-it-all attitude, adorn themselves with yellow leggings. . . and look upon the miners as so much cattle." There was a grain of truth in such critiques, which cannot, however, detain us here.[17] The point is about problems of interpretation of a labour and socialist movement in working-class milieu which remains at best unclear.

Dominion census-takers canvassed western mining areas once a decade from 1881 onwards. Miners appear as a category in the published reports in 1891 and different categories of miners ten years later (Figure 3-5). Not until 1911 is any information given about their status, immigrant or foreign-born; not until 1921 is there any information on national origins of the immigrant majority of the miners. Without the manuscript of the census, knowledge of even such a simple but vital matter as the ethnic background of the mining population is, to borrow the phrase of the once well-known but long forgotten miners' leader Frank Sherman, (founding president of District 18, UMWR, 1903–1909) impossible of achievement.

Fortunately, in 1986, the Federal government waived the customary 100-year rule of confidentiality over such documents, and released the second of the two relevant nineteenth century census manuscripts.[18] In just a few years a wealth of new information about the industrial community, at least for the nineteenth century, has become available. Herein lies some potential for a systematic approach to the social history of mining in the region, notwithstanding the immutable flaws and many imperfections in such sources and methods. Equipped with only hand techniques, we have chosen to make an initial sally into the best of two manuscripts available, that for 1891.[19]

The census of 1891 has the saving grace of having canvassed a coal-mining area on Vancouver Island which had already made the transition to industrial capitalism. The area was pulled into development by its coastal location which gave access to markets, labour, and technology which were denied other regions before the advent of the railways, but also pushed forward by state policies and entrepreneurial designs.[20]

The Island is best known for its infamous nineteenth century robber barons, the Dunsmuir clan. This family, of apparently modest origins in the Scottish coalfields, was endowed with most of the Island's natural resources by the generosity of the John A. Macdonald Tories, and a supine 'non-partisan' provincial government at Victoria, which nevertheless overrode Robert Dunsmuir's strident objections and passed, in 1877, a Coal Mines Regulation Act which was the first significant piece of legislation for Canadian workers west of Ontario.[21] A common antagonism towards the Dunsmuirs pushed farmers, coal miners, an the urban petty bourgeoisie into a series of populist alliances, which after 1900 flowered into a durable socialist tradition for which the Island is also justly famous.[22] The Dunsmuirs (colliery owners at Wellington, Ladysmith/Extension, and Cumberland in the period 1869–1910), however, are not the whole of the extraordinary story of industrial Vancouver Island. Another page or two was written by the Vancouver Island Coal Mining and Land Company (or New Vancouver Coal Company), colliery owners at Nanaimo in the period 1863–1903, and, an item of possible interest to a Welsh audience, the fictional Trencartha Tin Plate Works of Galsworthy's *Strife*.[23] As far as transparent connections between capital and the state are concerned, both firms did very well, and together, they controlled the lives of virtually every collier on Vancouver Island in the late nineteenth century (in turn, about 60 percent of the 5,038 'miners' whose heads were counted in B.C. and the North West Territories by the 1891 census). So far as exploitation goes, we have it on the authority of Samuel Gompers that the Dunsmuirs were one of the most tyrannical and villainous corporations that ever cursed the New World. But the Vancouver Coal Company falls a little short on the count of *naked* exploitation; it was described by William Lyon Mackenzie King, who built his political career by interventions in the western mines and was certainly in a position to know, as *the* model of benevolence and industrial leadership in the western mines, perhaps the Dominion.[24]

The combination of 'liberal' policies pursued in a most illiberal local environment conspired to make the Vancouver Company's domain, the City of Nanaimo, *the* centre of nineteenth century labour activism in the mining West. On February 1, 1890, a local mass meeting attended by a thousand people founded the first permanent union of mine workers in Canada west of Springhill, Nova Scotia. The Miners and Mine Labourers' Protective Association of Vancouver Island appears to have closely resembled the Provincial Workmen's Association founded in Springhill only eleven years before.[25] Both were expressions of the 'independent collier' who dominated a united front with common labour, with a vital exception that the practical prerequisite for the success of such a programme on Vancouver Island at that time was the total exclusion of one class of labour: the Chinese.[26] Nanaimo and Vancouver Island lay right on the mainline of Asiatic migration to North America; in 1889 the Chinese made up over a quarter of the Island's 3,000-strong colliery labour force (Figure 3). The formation and policies of the MMLPA, together with the Nanaimo Assembly of the Knights of Labour, with whose activities it was designed "in no way to clash",[27] were part of a remarkable campaign, whose targets were all mine owners and the provincial state, around the Oriental and other issues. Women's suffrage was raised, for example, as a rallying cry in the course of the whole community's failed strike struggle against the Dunsmuirs in 1890, which James Dunsmuir laid at the feet of "outside agitators" from Nanaimo, Rossland, Pennsylvania, Australia and elsewhere.[28] Four hundred "miners of the Nanaimo district," not thirty of whom could be induced to vote for a Knight of Labour against Robert Dunsmuir in the provincial election of 1886,[29] signed a petition for Chinese exclusion two years later, and two years after that, an MMPLA militant, Belfast-born Thomas Keith, was a member of the provincial parliament for the City of Nanaimo.[30]

The most salient of these events, however, was the signing of a collective agreement between MMLPA and the Vancouver Coal Company on July 24, 1891, evidence perhaps of manager Samuel Robins' far-sighted policies, but more immediately of effective working-class power. It was the first formal agreement at these mines, in the field, and in the region. The agreement did not have to specify Chinese exclusion, already peacefully achieved, however painful a plank on the labour platform for that group of toilers who had suffered a disproportionate share of a large number of fatalities in the collieries and for precisely that reason were successfully portrayed to the public as a menace to "our personal safety."[31] The agreement did not specify wages or conditions, which were set by the state of the trade and the customs of the workplace.[32] Nor did it specify management rights, as would all future agreements of the United Mine Workers of America.[33] It did specify an ironclad closed shop, which the

UMW would not achieve until the Second World War, together with a promise to address grievances by conciliatory means, but no "no-strike" pledge (taken by the UMW on more than one occasion). By a happy coincidence, the 1891 census in Nanaimo surveys a group of very sturdy independent trade unionists, the families that supported them, and even future leaders of the miners. Oscar Mottishaw, the pit committee-man at Cumberland whose sacking sparked the titanic "Vancouver Island strike" of 1912–1914, is listed as an infant in the City of Nanaimo in 1891.[34]

For all of the reasons listed above, any demonstrable facts about the people of Nanaimo should be welcomed by labour historians. The first fact we learned is that probably less than half of its four and half thousand inhabitants — Nanaimo was and would remain the largest of the coal-mining communities of the West — were directly dependent on the mines: 1,900 miners, miners' wives, and children, accounted for 43 percent of the city's population. The true mining population was only a little larger. Six Nanaimo miners were in jail on census day, and were excluded from the original calculation for arbitrary reasons. There were few supervisors and very few white-collar employees of the mines. A mere 21 men managed its affairs above and below; the workplace must have belonged to the 870 colliers. (Salaried employment in western Canadian mines will increase at about twice the rate of all employment from this point on.)[35] A small number of miners lived in non-mining families[36] and there is a last group among the mining population, unattached females and their dependents, who cry out for attention we have not yet been able to give. A disaster in the Nanaimo No.1 mine on May 3,1887 "cast a BLACK PALL over Nanaimo" and more than anything else, galvanized subsequent class actions.[37] The victims included fifty-one "Chinamen, names unknown, " and ninety-seven others, whose names can be found. The Chinese apparently left no dependents on this side of the water. The others left forty-six widows and 126 orphans who received no state compensation; they did, however, receive some of Robins' charity and $70,000 in miners' relief raised in a continent-wide subscription by the Knights of Labor.[38] Reports in the provincial press, condemned as sensational by the local press but undoubtedly accurate, had described their grief as "beyond portrayal": "Like Rachael of old, they refuse to be comforted." And these were not the only widows and orphans in a killer field, whose safety the nineteenth century state could not begin to secure in spite of excellent laws. The last of the big explosions in the Vancouver Island field occurred at nearby Extension in 1909, which claimed the lives of thirty craftsmen including most of the members of the Welsh Glee Club of Ladysmith, B.C.[39]

While miners' experience at the workplace was unique, it could not have comprised the whole of the working-class experience which found expression in local politics in this community; there was no other major industry apart from a thriving waterfront and hundreds of craftsworkers.

Commencing on 5 December 1891, the miners' leadership met in regular Trades Council in Nanaimo, where the list of other nineteenth century organizations includes the Coal Trimmers, Longshoremen, Teamsters, Merchants, Employees, Engineers, Tailors, Blacksmiths, and Carpenters.[40] Miners tended to live in one of three wards in the City of Nanaimo, 60 percent in the south ward, where Number 1 mine was located. This does not suggest a high degree of residential segregation among the miners.[41] Ordinary miners would have rubbed shoulders with other members of the community in the fraternal organizations in which they are known to have been involved: the Ancient Order of Foresters, whose patron, Robin Hood, was celebrated in an annual demonstration; the Oddfellows, and a number of Masonic organizations which surfaced to bury their comrades in May 1887, among whom were men respectfully described in the local press as "some of our earliest pioneers and prominent citizens". The more active would have been found in the councils of the mixed assembly of the Knights of Labor (which lost one of its leaders, Samuel H. Myers, in the 1887 disaster), the related activities of the Nanaimo Reform Club, and other aspects of community life.[42]

III

If Nanaimo in no way resembles the stereotype of the mining camp the 1891 census does support a couple of observations that have been made about workers on the industrial frontier. First, they were young. Leaving aside a dozen or so boys, whose employment was restricted (though not absolutely prohibited) by the 1877 law, [43] 55 percent of the miners were aged thirty or younger. A three-fold expansion of colliery employment in Nanaimo during the 1880s, the 1887 disaster, and the exclusion of the Chinese had produced this age structure. Can it be doubted that a union dominated by men in their twenties did not have some peculiar features? Second, and related to the first, was the presence of a large minority of men who were single and unattached (43 percent), and another large minority, more or less the same people, who lived as lodgers in local boarding houses (40 percent). Were these representative of a nomadic class, the highly mobile kind of workers who would become the object of the IWW's compelling imagery of the rebellious wage slave who truly had nothing to lose but his chains? Perhaps they were; perhaps they were not. The answer lies in a closed archive, the census manuscript for 1901.

The other part of the colliery labour force was mostly comprised of men or boys who were members of local families. Forty-six percent were heads of households, which in this community implied a high percentage of home owners. While migration was, and would long remain, the more important mechanism in the operation of the labour market, even at this early date the mining workforce was beginning to reproduce itself. Six percent of the

Nanaimo miners in 1891 were miners' sons who lived at home; 7 percent were men, mostly youths, who lived with other kin; 45 percent were married men or widowers, though 5 percent were married men with families elsewhere. Married men who lived with their spouses and a small number of miners who were single parents supported a total of 705 children, or about 2·5 per family. These children were more likely than not to have been born in British Columbia, or to have had siblings who were. The general conclusion is pretty clear. The colliery workforce falls into two broad categories, almost evenly divided: family men and their offspring, and a single, unattached men, with a marginal group falling between (Figure 1).

There is no particular reason to assume that the first group were immobile, but they were men with some sort of 'stake' in the community. The Vancouver Coal company was proud of its advocacy of working-class independence. The British-owned firm had kept itself afloat over several bad patches in the trade by selling most of its town lots and all its tied housing — a typical pattern of financial dealing among coal-mining companies, wherever they obtained freehold tenure from the Crown: which is to say that the bane, or boon, of company housing was a typically transitional stage in the evolution of most mining communities in the West.[44] Unique to the Nanaimo experience was the policy of encouraging working miners to lease agricultural smallholdings on a company lands at rates as low as 50 cents per acre: part of a wider state-inspired scheme, yielding mostly indifferent results, to settle or resettle urban-industrial workers on "Five Acre Lots" and thereby spare the new province of British Columbia from the scourges of industrial poverty, unemployment, strikes, and presumably socialism. Robins observed the "excellent moral influence of the experiments" later in the decade.[45] Such experiments, in the context of a generally low level of industrialization, where mining was never steady work and mining families (across the region) supplemented their incomes by petty agriculture, fishing, and jealously guarded hunting rights meant a basic trade-off for capital.[46] Trade cycles and wage reductions were more easily endured; on the other hand, it became difficult, if not impossible, to literally starve a community into submission. Robins' successors at Nanaimo, hard-driving scientific managers from the United States, would find this out in strikes from 108 days to fifteen months in duration in the period 1905–1914.[47]

Nanaimo on the eve of the epoch of monopoly capital was, then, a relatively benign environment for the independent collier. The ethnic character of the colliery workforce was both cause and effect of this fact. Just over 60 percent of 1891 were immigrants from the British Isles, two-thirds of them English. Another large group of skilled immigrants were from Nova Scotia, 10 percent of the Nanaimo miners. All told, the Canadian-born (at 14 percent) outnumbered the American-born (a mere 7 percent) by a margin of 2:1 (Figure 2). That Nova Scotians have hitherto been completely un-noticed by historians of western Canadian coal mining speaks, perhaps, to some pervasive colonial and regional biases. But there was also a strong tendency in western Canadian mining communities for provincial and national distinctions to be subsumed into a wider category of Anglo-Saxon or English-speaking miners — the British-born, old-stock Canadians and Americans. The Welsh (7·5 percent of the British or Irish-born in 1891) were not entirely spared the rod of ethnic condescension. A delegate of the District 18 convention of 1912 described his Welsh brothers as "not quite up to the English ways. They are good men for 'chewing the rag' and taking up grievances . . . but poor men on the Secretarial work." This sort of thing paled by comparison, however, to attitudes of the skilled towards the unskilled: Mike and John, the proverbial Slavic-Italian immigrants."I tell you just what is wrong with us, " another delegate at the 1912 convention frankly declared. "We live in a world by ourselves . . . we meet Mike and John in the street and we never even notice them."[48] By just the same token, all other ethnic distinctions diminished to the status of friendly rivalry in the face of the common front that was created in Nanaimo and elsewhere against the "indispensable enemy, " the Chinese. "I do not think we have anything to fear from the Immigration Scheme of the Coal Operators, " suggested F.H. Sherman at convention in 1907, "so long as they confine themselves to bringing in miners from Great Britain, *and other European countries* (my emphasis) Asian immigration, on the other hand, is a most serious menace (and) every effort should be made to stop this class of immigration from coming to our shores."[49] Ethnicity and cultural biases were complex phenomena that were quite adaptive to the environment.

The great migration form southern and eastern Europe that would later change the cultural face of the Western Canadian mining community had not yet commenced in earnest in the early nineties. Still, Nanaimo in 1891 had a somewhat cosmopolitan flavour, and the mining community at nearby Wellington seems to have been particularly so. The Miners and Mine Labourers' Protective Association could not and did not ignore the European, even as it agitated against the Oriental. One pit committee in 1890 included John Suggett, apparently French, a German, a Belgian, and Italian, and one "Russian Finn": a fairly representative cross-section of the smattering of non-English speaking nationalities in Nanaimo in 1891.[50] Nanaimo in the nineties had only one organized ethnic group, and a very important one, the Finns, by far the largest 'ethnic' group in the local collieries (7 percent of the miners and 70 percent of all miners born in fourteen different European countries).

The Finnish experience nicely illustrates the conjunctures between ethnic identity and the response to industrial capitalism. The Finnish community in Nanaimo-Wellington grouped itself in temperance and improvement societies that became fertile ground for the preachings of Matti Kurikka, utopian socialist intellectual, at the end of the nineties.

Kurikka persuaded a large number of miners and mining families to join his communitarian colony up the coast on Malcolm Island, another agricultural experiment initially supported by the state, in 1900. But many remained, to proselytize (in the absence of a vanguard party) for an emerging secular religion among Finnish working-class immigrants based on the trinity of radical industrial unionism, Marxian Social Democracy, and socialist feminism, in descending order of their attractiveness to, and impact upon the wider community. This was a group with little industrial and no mining experience, which explains the partial exodus from the mines. But it became the hard, militant core of the miners' movement on Vancouver Island. When shortlived coal miners' District 7 of the Western Federation of Miners began to organize on the Island, ousting the MMLPA in the process, in 1902–3, its meetings were chaired by British miners, but convened in the Finn Hall.[51]

If Nanaimo in 1891 is at all representative, the data provides some basis of comparison with later changes and continuities in the region's mining population. With the 'new' immigration of the Laurier Boom the percentage of native-born workers in the coalfields dropped below 10 percent in 1911, rising only slowly thereafter to 13–16 percent, according to the census reports for 1921 and 1931 (see Figures 3–6). Confirming our earlier impression, and for reasons that may only be speculated upon, the percentage of native-born workers in hardrock mining over the same period ranged from 19·5 to 40 percent between 1911 and 1931.[52] Oriental Exclusion would be highly successful in hardrock mining and also Alberta coal-mining, but Asian-born workers accounted for one-tenth of the colliery workforce in British Columbia as late as 1931, nearly all of them concentrated on Vancouver Island, apart from Nanaimo itself. Most twentieth century mining communities, then, would be freed from the structured racial cleavages that tortured their nineteenth century counterparts, if that may be termed a measure of working-class effectiveness and a working-class achievement. Continental Europeans would comprise up to 57·5 percent of the industrial army, in the Alberta coalfields, but the data tends to discount the relevance to western Canada of the U.S. experience, and nativist theory of 'slav invasion'. The radical restructuring of the workforce in many American mining communities made its own contribution to the historic failures of the miners' movements led by John Mitchel and John L. Lewis.[53]

British immigration continued to far outweigh the contribution of any other single group, although the presence of the British-born can be seen to have diminished in each of the three census categories of regional mining employment — B.C. collieries, hardrock mines, and Alberta collieries — from between 20 percent and 48 percent in 1921 to between 25 and 42 percent in 1931. The British presence appears to have peaked at some point prior to the First World War. Unrest in the mines between 1900 and 1914 might be laid at the feet of British miners, but was not the direct outcome of a losing battle with Slavic or Italian competition. The British Columbia Labour Commission of 1913–1915, and voluminous police reports on the Vancouver Island strike of 1912–1914, emphasize the pivotal importance of the English-speaking class: a disappointing finding for the state.[54] A payroll for the giant Crow's Nest Pass Coal Company in the B.C. interior for 1911 shows that 52 percent were English, Scots, or Welsh immigrants; another 4 percent "Canadians and Americans': 23·5 percent Italian, 16 percent "Slav"; and the remaining 4·5 percent belonging to other European nationalities, skilled immigrants from Belgium, Bohemia, Germany and France, and the Finns.[55] This area was a hotbed of labour militancy almost from the moment of the creation of a local organization in 1899 that proudly called itself, after the fashion of the independent collier, the Gladstone Miners' Union. Yet 20 years later, had the largest component of its membership been so included, the Gladstone Miners' Union (from 1919 known as the Gladstone Unit of the One Big Union, Coal Miners' District No. 1) could well have been renamed the Garibaldi Miners' Union!

The Great War, rather than capitalist developments closer to home, appears to have had the most negative impact on the British-born community in the key coal-mining sector. In 1916, for example, the whole of the English-speaking class accounted for only 29 percent of the workforce at the Crow's Nest Pass Coal Company. "Enemy aliens" (a wartime class of a somewhat arbitrary nature that did not include, in this payroll document, the Bohemians, who were Austrian citizens, together with Russians, "Finlanders, " Belgians, French and Italians) were almost as large a collectivity. Taking into consideration the industrial decline in this region after 1912, a thousand British-born miners had simply disappeared. The names of about forty of them are inscribed on the monument to the Great War dead in Fernie, B.C., which could indicate that at least half had enlisted, many never to return. *La Grand Guerre* similarly decimated the Franco-Belgian communities which at one time made up 10 percent of the whole population, and larger percentage of the coal miners, in mining communities in southwestern Alberta, where immigration had followed the flag of French mining capital after 1903. There, August 1914 was celebrated with squibs and speeches by representatives of all the *Entente* Powers, pro-war socialists (the majority, notwithstanding the dissident or divided stand of Finnish, Ukrainian, or Russian socialists, not to mention the Germans), 'loyal' nationalities from Austria Hungary, and of course the *bourgeoisie*. The wave of post-war militancy is most often connected in historians' eyes with the political activities of a handful of anti-war activists. Insofar as it was indeed connected with this most traumatic moment in the mining community's history, postwar militancy flowed instead out of complex of immigrant nationalisms and the well-founded conviction that miners had done more than their fair share in the "Great fight for Democracy."[56]

VI

Of the phenomenal transformation and capitalist expansion of the mining industry that occurred after 1891 we can but barely speak here. Hardrock mining areas produce the most dramatic reports. "During 1895", Rossland, capital of the Inland Empire built on a complex of ores, "sprang from a few shacks to a town with a population various estimated at 2,000–3,000 inhabitants, and boasts of electric light, water works, and no less than four newspapers. . . The mining plants are of the most modern (type) and include the latest and best appliances."[57] Here, on, July 16, 1895, was chartered the first of thirty-two locals of Canadian Districts 6 and 7 of the Western Federation of Miners formed between 1895 and 1905. Alberta-based District 18 of the United Mine Workers of America (District 18, with one functioning local at Nanaimo, had paper jurisdiction over Vancouver Island), comprising as many as 40 to 50 locals in Alberta and southeastern B.C. between 1903 and 1925, emerged out of the opening the Crow's Nest Pass coalfield, following the famous agreement of the same name between the Canadian Pacific Railway, and the Laurier government in 1897. Between 1898 and 1911 this region, straddling the border between British Columbia and Alberta, high in the Rocky Mountains, was flooded by at least 15,000 European settlers, over whom the native Indians are alleged to have cast a grimly prophetic curse of seven decades of "fire, flood, strife, discord, and want." (It is more likely that the superstition of the miners created this tale, but the Kootenai people obliged their descendants by lifting the spell in a 1964 ceremony.)[58]

The Crow's Nest Pass became the largest single concentration of industrial population in the mining West before the War, and its working class community continued to be the fighting edge of western Canadian mining labour even after its economic promise was betrayed by capital and the state. Employment in the local mines and coking plants peaked at 4,997 in 1913, declining to 2,808 in 1919. Crow's Nest Pass locals of the UMWA voted 2,350–73 in favour of the One Big Union and lined up for Bolshevism and workers' control in the post-war general strikes. It was one of the few mining areas in all Canada where unionism survived the open shop drive, restructuring, and 'cheap labour'immigration of the twenties, and Crow's Nest Pass provided the bulk of the miner's leadership in the West between 1900 and 1945. As the miners of Fernie developed the programme of international unionism on the lines of UMWA for the coal miners around the turn of the century, the miners of Blairemore, following the defeat of the OBU an the smashing of the impotent UMW bureaucracy by the mine owners in the twenties, developed the programme of the "Mine Workers of Union of Canada" — an idea that had first been mooted by the miners of the West, and should have been adopted by the miners of Canada, around 1908.[59] This area is well remembered in the oral tradition. " (History) is distorted and I'm wondering how the Pass story is being told for the archives," I was asked by one of several respondents to a deliberately bad-tempered article in a local newspaper in 1986:

"Willing to talk to you anytime but warning you that most of my memory is impressions . . . I was born in Frank (Alberta) November 18, 1910. My parents came from some village in Cumberland, England. Furrneau was the name I heard. By 1912 we lived at the Lime Kilns between Frank and Bellevue where George Pattinson managed the plant. In 1922 George started a hardware store in Coleman. He was on the town council and was elected Mayor over Andrew Dow the "communist" candidate by a very narrow margin. When my father started his store he knew he had to cater to the 'ethnic' element in town. The establishment had furniture and carpets (although) the newcomers needed a kitchen table and a mattress. Because of the payroll we had good teachers and doctors. I met all the women in my store . . . I remember the Chataqua in Blaimore, dances, parties Badminton in the Miners' hall Sunday afternoons, skating, good movies in Bellevue. Life was sweet for a young person like me. I look at the skeleton of Coleman [where the last mine on the Alberta side, opened in 1905, shut down in 1979] and think of the town with 2 mines working a newspaper, and trains every day. . ."

From a middle class perspective, my correspondent recalled little about industrial relations except that "strikes were a plague", but from a woman's viewpoint, urged research into the fates of the survivors of the Hillcrest, Alberto explosion of June 1914 — the largest mine disaster in Canadian history, after which Nanaimo in 1887 comes second — which killed 189 men, half of whom left widows and orphans in the Pass. There is an intriguing history of "class, community and the labour movement" here, which remains to be told.[60]

VII

We leave these impressions for a final look at some of the structural dimensions of the miners' past: first the demonstrable fact that no regional perspective can actually encompass the sectional differences that may help to explain a basic fragmentation of mining labour in the West. As even the rawest sort of data on employment and production shown in Figures 3 and 4 suggest, the historical development of coal mining in British Columbia was not similar to the historical development of coal mining in Alberta. Falling employment and output, on a secular trend, is recorded in the B.C. coal industry even before the First World War, in Alberta, during the twenties and thirties. But as the census numbers and much better data on the annual average of employment calculated by the provincial mines departments also show, coal mining was and remained a major employer. Coal mining employment in British Columbia rose from 3,974 in 1901 to 7,130 in 1912, declining thereafter to 4,654 in 1930. In Alberta, the annual average begins in 1906 at 2,800, peaks in 1921 at 10,018 declining thereafter to 8,889 in 1930. Hard rock mining (Figure 5) presents yet another picture again, and contrary to expectations raised by enthusiastic discussions of the northward expansion of the American hardrock "mining frontier", it was not that important for western Canadian miners before the thirties. Hardrock mining was *very* important for Canadian and foreign capitalism, metals production accounting for 91 percent of the declared profits of B.C. mining companies in a fifty-year period beginning in 1897. But hardrock mining employed relatively few men, unlike the coal-mining industry (that was not a 'staple', but largely dependent upon the home market). Over the first third of the twentieth century, employment in hardrock mining was essentially static, in a range of 2,330 (the annual average for 1921) to 5,488 (for 1917), figures that illustrate the wild gyrations of the international metals-market. Averaging the annual numbers over two decades for which comparable data are available, 1906–1925, we find that hardrock mining accounted for only 21·5 percent of all mining employment in the two westernmost provinces.[61]

The indices for metals-production are too complex to be summarized in a table, but the gross tonnage of ores produced in British Columbia increased form one to seven million tons a year between 1901 and 1929. This means that the productivity of the hardrock miner in British Columbia increased by 500 percent over three decades (that of the B.C. coal miner, by a slight 20 percent). Herein likes the basic difference between a traditional and a revolutionary mode of production. The first sustained a labour movement, the second destroyed one, though not without a fight, in the words of the Silverton Miners' Union in 1899: "CROMWELL AND THE GOOD PEOPLE OF ENGLAND CUT OFF THE SACRED HEAD OF CHARLES THE FIRST ... LET TYRANTS TAKE WARNING."[62] Hardrock mining either proletarianized or thrust off to the wings of history's stage a mass of free miners and petty producers in the nineteenth century. In the early twentieth century, considering the miner, in the words of a resolution of District 6, "as so much machinery or some kind of animal that lives on black bread and hog's fat, " the industry deskilled and all but eliminated hardrock mining's equivalent of the independent collier, the "self reliant miner, jack of all trades, master of several." The Western Federation of Miners often look like the Chartists of the mining West, for the very good reason that "while struggling for a co-operative Commonwealth and the establishment of justice and equality among men" they were also struggling against the tide of Political Economy itself. Their critique of the orthodoxies of the day, the alleged benefits of Trade, Investment, and Immigration, ring true to the present day. "The higher wages and fewer hours that we favour would fill this country with the most intelligent, effective, and happiest workmen of the world, a citizenship to be proud of. The dollar-a-day labourers that would most encourage the capitalists would drive every self-respecting citizen out of the country, leaving only cabins here for houses, while palaces would be built in Spokane, Butte, Salt Lake and London." Add Toronto, Montreal, Vancouver, and New York to the list and that is more or less what happened.[63]

The coal mining industry did its looting, of course, and it was also more dangerous to the worker involved in it. Coal mining was, however, the more socially and economically rational activity (according to the precepts of the miner's moral economy). And sustained legislative and industrial pressure by the coal miners eventually brought the industry's ' casualties, ' in the apt phrase of the state authorities, down to the level of the metalliferous mines, which were "comparatively light" [Figure 10].[64] Mechanization made very few inroads into its conservative practice, with the one and important exception of the very same Nanaimo collieries that produced our 1891 sample. Here, after the turn of the century, the miners paid a heavy price for Chinese exclusion (or rather, the failure of the larger programme in the competitive Island field) by the introduction of even cheaper coal-cutting machines, that weakened, then destroyed, their once-powerful union.[65] Apart from this example, it was only later and wider technological changes that eliminated the coal mines and miners with them. The Canadian railways played a particularly important role in killing off the independent collier in the West in the forties and fifties, after starving him progressively in the twenties and thirties.

The contours of miners' struggles in the region seem to reflect these cycles of industrial growth and decline, primarily in the coal mining industry, and the impact of technological change, primarily in hardrock mining. Industrial conflict was endemic in the mining industry, as the inevitably incomplete list of 250 strikes ad lockouts in Figure 6 reveals. There is no possible way of quantifying 'striker days lost' over the period 1890–1930, but we are probably in the region of twenty million, of which coal-mining disputes would have accounted for about 90 percent.[66] Except for a period of high activity around the turn of the century, however, strikes were not a plague in the hardrock mining industry (as Cole Harris local study suggests). Most of the strikers after 1905, when the Western Federation of Miners in the major copper, silver, and lead mines of the Inland Empire were forced to accept some variant of the sliding scale or worse, occurred on the margins of the industry, in remote localities, and in the smelters, which were militant during the War.[67] Not one miners' strike is recorded outside of the coal mining industry after 1921; with the failure of post-war insurgency led by the OBU, hardrock mining became a clear field for the open shop until the Second World War. The once-militant coal mines of British Columbia, where industrial decline was first in evidence, become largely quiescent after the War, with no strikes recorded after 1925. The coalfields of Alberta, the most heavily unionized sector of western Canadian mining, accounted for at least two-thirds of all strikes and lockouts involving miners in the region between 1890 and 1930.[68] Alberta coal miners alone carried the tradition of western miners' militancy forward to the end of the period under review. We can only speculate on the underlying reasons: the relative economic vigour of Alberta coal mining, and the presence of communities which had some 'frontier' characteristics, like the Drumheller Valley in the 1920s. "We owned that valley, it belonged to us, " proudly recalled a former Communist militant from the area in conversation some ten years ago. My informant was a very Welsh immigrant who insisted, however, that he came out of a "very religious Calvinistic Methodist family", suggesting some process of cultural and political syncretism at work in the western Canada of that era.[69]

VIII

Doubtless it is in the realm of politics that the miners' struggle of the era left its most indelible mark, which had to be recorded and noticed by the state and the bourgeoisie because the miners, to a remarkable degree, always played by the rules of parliamentary combat. Regardless of party or ideology, the rules of the game in the mining community were almost always the same: "appeal to the reason of our men .. appeal to their class instinct, to their class consciousness."[70] The opposition was always strong and usually clever enough to appeal to some part of the miners' class instinct — and when that strategy failed there were always others: condemnation of the miners' leadership, the appeal to religious or ethnic prejudice, drink, bribery, vote-rigging, threats and blandishments of all kinds. The miners' cause in politics was always hobbled by the salient fact that not all miners had the vote, but we have been able to find only one solid document on the thorny question of enfranchisement. There were 323 miners on the voters' list for Nanaimo District in 1885. Miners comprised 47 percent of all electors, and the 205 enfranchised miners in Nanaimo City represented 62 percent of the white males employed in local collieries in 1885.[71]

In that precise context the miners' struggle for power in the region began, a struggle that did result in the election of one miner Member of Parliament, elected from industrial Vancouver Island on a straight Labour ticket in 1900, and over a dozen provincial deputies, who were more easily elected and also more useful to the miners on the questions pertaining to state regulation of mines and protective labour legislation. B.C. coal miners had straight class representation in the provincial house for all but four of the forty years under review (1894–1898). Hardrock miners did less well, having straight class representation for less than a decade (1903–1909), and unlike the coal miners, they stopped running candidates after the War. The picture is brightened again, however, by the Alberta coal miners, who had straight class representation for 17 of the first 25 years of their provincial legislature (1909–1913,1921–30).[72]

Electoral success is *the* distinguishing characteristic of the late nineteenth and early twentieth century western Canadian mining community, occurring almost in a vacuum of successful parliamentary labour politics in the Dominion. What did it mean? The answer is unclear because, among other things, it cannot be found in miners' history, but rather in the wider history of class, politics, Labourism, Socialism, Liberalism, Conservatism and non-partisanship in the region for which there are few fixed or relevant guideposts. We do know that electoral success, a very relative thing, was only the tip of a veritable iceberg of political organization in the mining districts. The mining politicians of the Canadian West tasted the fruits of office from an orchard tilled by thousands of independent labour or socialist campaigners in at least one hundred constituency elections between 1890 and 1930 (Figures 7,8). Eight-eight percent were provincial campaigns, where the rate of success was close to one in three. But a surprising 12 percent were Dominion elections, where the rate of success was less than one in them. Most of the Dominion efforts, and large percentage of the provincial ones as well, were purely propagandistic and educational exercises which were by no means cheaply bought at $200 to $250 a time, the minimum deposit, and lost goodwill, especially with Edwardian Liberalism in the Age of Laurier and King.[73]

The mining politicians were a rogue's gallery for whom a collective biography might be useful. They ranged on the ideological scale from the tepid Tyneside liberalism of Nanaimo's Ralph Smith, who promptly joined the Grit caucus in Ottawa after his election in 1900, to the very radical Marxism of C.M. O'Brien, a full-time agitator of no fixed address, prewar provincial deputy for Rocky Mountain Alberta, the Socialist Party of Canada's favourite "Proletarian in Politics" and, incidentally, Ontario-born. The longest-serving of them, Fernie's Tom Uphill, who spent thirty six years in the British Columbia 'gas house', as he called it, was the only miner who ever ran for the Tory party, before he found a winning formula as a one-man Labour Party, who lobbied for the interests of the bankrupt municipality, of which he was the former Mayor, for coal miners, and for Communists in Victoria. Another notable was Parker Williams, a Welsh miner, elected five times on the provincial SPC slate from industrial Vancouver Island, whom the Vancouver comrades called "a decent plug, but no socialist." The most distinguished among them was James Hurst Hawthornthwaite, also of Nanaimo, son in law of Mark Bate, Sam Robins' predecessor as local mines manager: the Engels to Vancouver Island's Marx, a fishmonger named E.T. Kingsley. He spent 15 years in Victoria and nearly made it to the House of Commons, running against Smith in the federal riding of Nanaimo in 1908. None of the mining politicians was a woman, but interesting to note, the first female legislator in British Columbia was a former miners' wife whose husband and self rose to higher station, Mary Ellen Smith.[74] Most of the political losers were fairly impressive figures as well, like F.H. Sherman, who at thirty-five years of age was "fast approaching the status of a national character" and the successful leader of a successful trade union, exceedingly rare in the brutal environment of mining 'industrial relations, ' which routinely destroyed unions, the men who led them, or both: by coercion, corrosion or corruption. Sherman, born in the Forest of Dean though "predominantly Welsh", was a former chapel preacher and Gladstonian liberal who predicted in 1904 that "Organized labor in Canada will follow the example set by the 'Old Country' and will strive to be represented in the councils of the nation". In 1908 he had his last chance, but missed it, by agreeing to run on the Socialist Party ticket in a hopeless Alberta riding. He wrote Hawthornthwaite during the campaign:

Dear Comrade: I am in the thick of the fight with good prospects of a heavy vote in Calgary riding. I am sending copies of correspondence in my possession which you can use and show the people of Nanaimo how they try to fix labour leader. I had the alluring prospect of a Liberal-Labor nomination held out with a senatorship dangling at the end Jim, you know how I feel and I would rather go down and out than be a second Ralph Smith. . . that 'SKUNK'. Wishing to be able to see you in Ottawa, Yours in the Struggle, F.H. Sherman.[75]

Politics is about choices and what data from the mining community can be gleaned from Dominion elections (Figure 9) suggests that the miners themselves came to support the 'radical' option in politics, out of habit, class instinct, ideological conviction, or a combination of factors. They supported a trade union leadership that was politically engaged, or a political leadership, like the Socialist Party, that supported the miner's struggles. The Nanaimo miners elected, than rejected Ralph Smith, symbol of the more compromising attitudes of the independent collier. Although straight Labour men were probably better vote-catchers than one-plank platform socialists, the latter had a political programme, while the former did not. And there are not that many questions about the allegiance of unenfranchised miners, like the Slavs and Italians who turned up at a special mass meeting held during the Socialist Party's provincial convention at Fernie in 1908 to hear comrades Tomoshavsky and Susnar, the party's foreign-language organizers who worked, we are told, on a volunteer basis: "if one's eyes convey any information [the] meeting of two and three hundred of these nationalities in the miners' hall on Monday night fanned a fire of revolt that forbode ill for the representatives of capitalism at the next election."[76] The real question is how the prospect of "the next election" came to inspire any of the miners, even the OBU men, who were inveterate political campaigners and returned one deputy to the Alberta legislature in 1921: P.M. Christophers, the sort of Bolshevik who belonged to a Masonic lodge, claimed to yield to no man in his loyalty to King and Country, and asked for a mandate form the voters of Rocky Mountain on the basis of his need for a 'meal ticket' to feed his seven children after being blacklisted out of the coal mines, and UMWA, by the operators and American union bosses.[77]

Conclusion

This paper has intended to focus attention on, rather than offer a hypothesis about, miners' struggles in western Canada between 1890 and 1930: a period of international labour upheaval that found an echo in hundreds of miners' strikes or labour representation campaigns which were the foam on the wave of working-class, community, and labour movement protest in coal and metalliferous mining areas in the region. The social, economic, and cultural context of these struggles was quite a bit more complex than the traditional assumptions of both Marxist and liberal commentators have allowed and if it is difficult, in the late twentieth century, to generate much enthusiasm for institutional labour history, then perhaps there is hope for continuing interest in other aspects of the miners' past. New sources offer avenues of approach towards a social history of mining communities, and a recognition that there is more to mining industrial relations or mining politics than examples of Western radicalism similarly offers a wide scope for ongoing research in these areas. We have argued for a more systematic approach to the topic, while leaving issues of comparative theory and method for another time. But in the final analysis, the spirit rebels against mining historiography's "functional approaches" and "structured structures"[78] as models for the Canadian West, a region that enjoyed a particularly broad range of a lived experience in an era of colonization and settlement, as well as industrialization. Few documents, let alone conventional theories, "can generate the emotion of the time,"[79] yet those who seek to address it will find the task rewarding, if always problematic.

Notes

1 Donald Avery, *'Dangerous Foreigners': European Immigrant Workers and Labour Radicalism in Canada, 1896–1932* (Toronto, 1979), 56–58, 101–7, *passim*; Allen Seager, "Class, Ethnicity and Politics in the Alberta Coalfields, 1905–1945,"in Dirk Hoerder, ed., *'Struggle a Hard Battle': Essays on Working-Class Immigrants* (DeKalb, Ill., 1986), 304–321.

2 For an example and bibliographical guide, see Ian McKay, "The realm of Uncertainty: The Experience of Work in the Cumberland Coal Mines, 1897–1927," *Acadiensis: The Journal of the History of the Atlantic Region* (Autumn, 1986), n.7.

3 The wealth of available sources is indicated by Logan Hovis and Jeremy Mouat, "Bibliography of Mining" (typescript, 306 , University of British Columbia Library, 1986). Much of the current work is unpublished: Jeremy Mouat, "The Context of Conflict: The Western Federation of Miners in British Columbia, 1895–1903, " Paper read at the Pacific North West Labor History Association annual conference, Vancouver, 1984; Logan Hovis, "The Origins of 'Modern Mining' in the Western Cordillera, " Paper read at the BC Studies Conference,

Victoria, 1986, but see also John Douglas Belshaw, "Mining Technique and Social Division on Vancouver Island, 1848–1900, " *British Journal of Canadian Studies* (June, 1986), 45–65.

4 Daniel Drache, "The Formation and Fragmentation of the Canadian Working Class: 1820–1920, " *Studies in Political Economy*, 15 (1984), 43–90; Stuart Jamieson, *Times of Trouble: Labour Unrest and Industrial Conflict in Canada, 1900–1966* (Ottawa, 1968), 97–8, *passim*; Paul Phillips, "The National Policy and the Development of the Western Canadian Labour Movement, " in A. W. Rasporich and H. C. Klassen, eds., *Prairie Perspectives* 2 (Toronto, 1973), 41–62.

5 Ian McKay, review of A. Ross McCormack, *Reformers, Rebels, and Revolutionaries: The Western Canadian Radical Movement, 1899–1919* (Toronto, 1977), *Labour History* (Spring, 1979).

6 For a critique of western exceptionalism, as a crude dichotomy between a 'radical' West and a 'conservative' East (organically linked with the even sorrier shibboleth of North American exceptionalism), see Gregory S. Kealey, "1919: The Canadian Labour Revolt, " *Labour/Le Travail* 13 (1984), 11–44. The more genuine regional approach is suggested in Gerald Friesen, *The Canadian Prairies* (Toronto, 1984), ch.12, "Capital and Labour, 1900–1940."

7 Royden Harrison, ed., *Independent Collier: The Coal Miner as Archetypical Proletarian Reconsidered* (Hassocks, U.K., 1978), "Introduction."

8 David Jay Bercuson, "Labour Radicalism and the Western Industrial Frontier, 1897–1919, " *Canadian Historical Review* (June, 1977), 474- 499, is standard undergraduate reading fare, drawn largely from the unsatisfactory American models of Melvyn Dubofsky, "The Origins of Western Working Class Radicalism, 1895–1905, " *Labor History* (Spring, 1966), 132–154, and Vernon H. Jensen, *Heritage of Conflict: Labor Relations in the Nonferrous Metals Industry Up to 1930* (Ithaca, New York, 1950), whose extremely influential "Commons school" interpretation is largely revised in Richard E. Lingenfelter, *The Hardrock Miners: A History of the Mining Labour Movement in the American West, (1863–1895,* (Berkeley, Calif., 1974).

9 This paper is very much in the way of a progress report on research into three aspects of mining history in the Canadian West — industrial demography, strikes and lockouts, and miners' politics — that is far from complete.

10 Not to say that North American social history has been free from uninformed theorizing. See Bryan D. Palmer, "Emperor Katz' New Clothes; or with the Wizard in Oz, " *Labour/Le Travail* 13 (1984), 190–197. Yet it could be said that while the quantitative method corrupts, the lack of it corrupts absolutely. See Robert Sweeney, *Protesting History* (Montreal Business History Project, 1984).

11 Cole Harris, "Industry and the Good Life Around Idaho Peak, " *Canadian Historical Review* (September, 1985), 315–343.

12 Bercuson, "Labour Radicalism, " 166–7.

13 The historiography of the socialist movement is largely buried in unpublished theses: Ronald Grantham, "Some Aspects of the Socialist Movement in British Columbia Before 1933" (MA thesis, University of British Columbia, 1942); Thomas Robert Loosemore, "The British Columbia Labour Movement and Political Action, 1879–1906" (MA thesis, University of British Columbia, 1954); Alfred Ross Johnson, "No Compromise-No Political Trading: The Marxian Socialist Tradition in British Columbia" (Ph.D. thesis, University of British Columbia, 1975), among others.

14 Similarly, the attempt to gauge the radicalism or "the alleged radicalism" of the larger mining community by analyzing the aggregate of votes cast in mining constituencies leads to tremendous confusion. See Carlos Schwantes, *Radical Heritage: Labor, Socialism, and Reform in Washington and British Columbia 1885-1917* (Vancouver, 1979), p.182.

15 For discussion of directories, see Harris, *op.cit*, p.355; Jeremy Mouat, "The Politics of Coal: A Study of the Wellington Miners' Strike of 1890-1" (unpublished mss, courtesy of the author), 6–7; Allen Seager, "Socialists and Workers, The Western Canadian Coal Miners, 1900–1921, " *Labour/Le Travail* 16 (1985), p.52.

16 "Chris Foley Outlines the Position of the Labour Party — Plain Facts Worth Reading, " *Lardeau Eagle*, 28 November, 1900; "Foley's Address Worthy of Consideration by All Classes — Its What the People Want, " *ibid.*, 24 October, 1900, and other election material.

17 "American Mining-Mining Englishmen, " *Lardeau Eagle*, 19 April 1901. See also "Englishmen Make Dismal Failures", *Ibid.*, 27 June 1901; "Fake Companies and Stock Plunderers Killing the Industry, " *ibid.*, 9 May 1901. Another popular mining journalist of similar views and background (from London, Ontario), was R. T. Lowery, editor of *Lowery's Claim: A Journal of Truth, Humor, and Justice*, published at Nelson and New Denver, and the *Fernie Ledge*. For the British invasion of the mining industry, see Public Archives of British Columbia, Premier's Papers, Unnumbered documents, f.1895-1898.

18 The nominal census for 1881 is the subject of analysis in a forthcoming dissertation by John D. Belshaw, "British Columbians on Vancouver Island, 1848-1900: A Social History, " (Ph.D. thesis, University of London). See also, Ben Moffat, "A Community of Workingmen: The Residential Environment of Nanaimo, B.C., 1875-1891, " (MA thesis, University of British Columbia, 1982).

19 What follows are preliminary results from a research project begun in January 1987, designed to profile the whole of the mining community on Vancouver Island in 1891, data we hope to link with the far smaller 1881 population. I am greatly indebted to my assistant Marilyn Janzen, who laboured long and hard during a very sort time to generate enough information for Figures 1 and 2.

20 See Belshaw, "Mining Technique"; Daniel Thomas Gallacher, "Men, Money and Machines: Studies Comparing Factors of Production in British Columbia's Coal Industry to 1891" (Ph.D. thesis, University of British Columbia, 1979), and for one of several popular accounts, Lynn Bowen, *Boss Whistle: The Coal Miners of Vancouver Island Remember* (Lanztville, B.C. 1981).

21 *Statues of British Columba* 1877,33–63, "An Act to Make Regulations with Respect to Coal Mines, " Petition Against Coal-Mining Bill" (signed by Robert Dunsmuir and the proprietors of the Vancouver Island Coal Mining and Land Company, n.d.), B.C. *Sessional Papers*, 1877, p.504. Although 1877 was a year of labour violence in the Dunsmuir mines, it is probably true, as has been argued in the parallel Nova Scotia case five years before, that "The act was almost entirely the product of pressures exerted from within the government, not as most later amendments would be, of demands by the mining population." Certainly the issue is deserving of study along the lines of: Donald MacLeod, "Collier, Colliery Safety, and Workplace Control: The Nova Scotian Experience, 1873-1910, " *Historical Papers* (Canadian Historical Association annual, 1983),

226–253. The other basic legislation covering the mines were the B.C. Metallifeorus Mines (Inspection) Act of 1898 an the Alberta Coal Mines Regulation Act of 1908, which emerged out of a more complex dynamic among the state, capital, trade unions and politicians.

22 The best and most easily accessible survey of B.C. politics in this period remains Martin Robin, *The Rush for Spoils: The Company Province, 1871–1933* (Toronto, 1972).

23 A. W. Currie, "The Vancouver Coal Company: A Source for Galsworthy's *Strife, "Queen's Quarterly* (Spring, 1963), p.62.

24 Mouat, "Politics of Coal, " 4,19. For Makenzie King and the miners see Paul Craven, *'An Impartial Umpire': Industrial Relations and the Canadian State 1900–1911* (Toronto, 1980), ch.8: "War on the Periphery."

25 Allan Donald Orr, "The Western Federation of Miners and the Royal Commission on Industrial Disputes in 1903 with Special Reference to the Vancouver Island Miners' Strike" (MA thesis, University of British Columbia, 1958), p.63, *passim*; McKay, "By Wisdomn, Wile, or War': The Provincial Workmen's Association and the Struggle for Working-Class Independence in Nova Scotia, 1879–1897, " *Labour/Le Travail* 18 (1986), 13–62.

26 Or at least this seems to be the most logical conclusion to be drawn from what little is actually known about Chinese labour in the mines. For a particularly interesting discussion, see Jack Scott's review of Anthony B. Chan, *Gold Mountain: The Chinese in the New World* (Vancouver, 1983) in *Labour/Le Travail* 15 (1985), 195–200.

27 PABC, Vertical File, "Labour" no.1, extract from the *Nanaimo Free Press*, 1 February 1890. **28 Orr, *op.cit.*; "Strike at Wellington, " *Victoria Colonist*, 21 May 1890.

29 Robert Dunsmuir received 366 otes in Nanaimo-Wellington in 1886, Collier Sam Myers, 30 votes. There were 686 electors and 323 of them were miners. "List of Persons Entitled to Vote in the Electoral District of Nanaimo, " B.C. *Sessional Papers*, 1885,33–43.

30 For the petitioners see B.C. *Sessional Papers*, 1888,367–8. Political developments in Nanaimo and distrcit after 1886 are not easily summarized. When Robert Dunsmuir died in 1889, the double-member constituency he represented was divided into two separate constituencies (1890), then three (1894). Elections in 1894 afford the best data on labour's political strength. Of 1,658, votes cast in three ridings (each contested by nominees of the Nanaimo Reform Club, MMPLA officers Tom Keith, Tully Boyce, and Ralph Smith) 40 per cent went labour. Nanaimo city (taken by Keith by acclamation in 1890) was lost to the local Tories by only 20 votes. The voter turnout in 1894 was 85 per cent.

31 On April 26,1890, Section 4 of the 1877 Act was amended to prohibit "Chinamen" from underground work, not quite the same as total exclusion, and eventually overturned in the courts (1899). Robert Dunsmuir and Sons successfully defied this amendment, illustrating the importance of community as opposed to legislative sanctions over hiring policies.

32 Text of the 1891 agreement as an appendix to Orr's "Western Federation of Miners"in Currie, *op.cit* p.57, informs us that while the Nanaimo miners had not sympathy with the financial problems of the Vancouver Coal Company, they did accept a 10 percent reduction of wages in the years 1893–96.

33 Every agreement ever signed by the UMW contained, in the first clause, the statement that "The right to hire and discharge, the management of the mine, and the direction of the working faces are vested exclusively in the Company." The second clause of the 1911 agreement between Disrict 18 and the Western Canada Coal Operators' Association (signed after an eight months strike in the interior coalfields costing the international union $600,000) read that "It is distinctly understood and agreed between the parties, that there is to be no discrimination . . . on the part of Union men against non-union men employed." For an examination of UMW policy in the age of emerging monopoly captialsim, see Bruno Ramirez, *When Workers' Fight: The Politics of Industiral Relations in the Progressive Era* (Westport, Conn., 1978).

34 For the Vancouver Island strike, a terrible lesson in the futility of UMW policy in that context, see John Norris, "The Vancouver Island Miners, 1912–1914: A Study of an Organizational Strike, " *BC Studies* 45 (1980), 56–72.

35 The supervisory class in Nanaimo supported around 80 dependents, boosting the core mining population to 2,000 [Figure 2]. The Dominion census for 1901 still enumerated less than 500 mining officials, deputies, direbosses, etc. across B.C. and the N.W.T (Alberto), among a total workforce of about 10,000 (487 salaried to 9,787 non-salaried workers). By 1911 there were over 2,000 among 20,000 (2,005 to 17,910). The provincial Mines Department and Mines Branch (Alberta) reports contain better data on coal-mining employment than the census, but only the census provides aggregate numbers (including metalliferous mining).

36 Some 15 Nanaimo miners were the main breadwinners in households headed by their mothers, arbitrarily classed as a "non-mining family" in this discussion. Another 25 were sons of "non-mining families" (similarly classed) who lived in their father's household. These account for the bulk of the "Other kin"in Figure 1.

37 For accounts of the disaster, see *Nanaimo Free Press*, 4–7 May 1887; Victoria *Colonist*, 4–6 May 1887.

38 Eugene Forsey, *Trade Unions in Canada 1812–1902* (Toronto, 1982), p.161.

39 Viola Johnson-Cull and E. Norcross, Compilers, *Chronicle of Ladysmith and District* (Ladysmith, 1980), 82–84. Systematic research into coal-mining fatalities in B.C. has yet to be undertaken, but in the years 1887–1897 there were 358, which looks like an average of over 10 per thousand employees for the Vancouver Island field in the late nineteenth century. See note 64 below.

40 Forsey, *op.cit*, p.343.

41 Nor can a tendency towards segregation among ethnic groups in the mining population be discerned. Taking the non-British, non-American, non-native-born minority as a 'non-English speaking' class, for example, we find such individuals making up 21 percent of miners in the South Ward, 14 per cent in the North Ward, 11 percent in the Middle Ward, and 18 percent overall. The 1891 census gives few other indications of address. Nanaimo boarding houses appear to have been small; some large boarding houses containing as many as forty men, however, turn up in the Dunsmuir area — altogether a less wholesome environment.

42 Fraternal orders can be shown to have been ubiquitous in any sizeable coal-mining town in western Canada (to the leaders of the Communist Party, the colliers were "a Masonic group of Elks, etc."). Their popularity had several sources, including highly pragmatic insurance reasons. One of the great differenes between the United Mine Workers and the Western Federtion of Miners was that while both international unions flowed out of the KOL, the former renounced the benevolent function while the latter never did.

43 In theory, a boy aged 13 could work in a thin seam in British Columbia under ministerial permit, and 13 to 16 year-olds were allowable on surface jobs. But the laws and cutoms of the mining West appear to have been less tolerant of child labour than in the mining East. McKay's Cumberland mines in the 1880s employed 16 percent boys during the 1880s; the average for the Vancouver Island mines in the same decade is less than 1 percent.

44 True company towns in the mining West persisted only in more remote areas like northwestern Alberta, where mining was carried out on inalienable Crown lands and where there was no private ownership of any land prohibited by law. Robert and James Dunsmuir, however, controlled large numbers of company houses, evicting their occupants during the strikes of 1887 and 1890.

45 PABC, Premiers' Papers, vol. 13, Misc. Unnumbered documents, 1895–1898, 22-page memorandum on land settlement prepared for John Turned n.d.

46 See Resolution of the Gladstone Miners re shooting and hunting, n.d. 1906. *Ibid.* Box 27, f.15.

47 "[The miners] grow weary of discussing strike subjects . . . They seem to enjoy each day as it tolls by and maintain a cheerful air and always seem to have a little change in their pockets to but beer for one another, " PABC, Gr 68 (Attorney General's Papers), Vol.2, f. "Correspondence re Nanaimo Strike", Operative £29-S, 3 January 1914.

48 Glenbow Archives, District 18 Papers, Minutes of Convention, 1912 (Third Day), Delegate Longworth, p.34, Delegate Hyslop, p.58.

49 President's Report, District 18 convention, *Fernie Ledger*, 31 December 1907.

50 Evidence, Select Committee on the Wellington Strike, British Columbia, *Journals of the Legislature Assembly*, 1891, p.ccixxiii.

51 On the Finns see Varpu Lindstrom-Best and Allen Seager, " *Touveritar* and Finnish Canadian Women, 1900–1930, " in Christiane Harzing and Dirk Horder, eds., *The Press of Labor Migrants in Europe and North America 1880s to 1930s* (Bremen, 1985); Bowen, *Boss Whistle*, 19,25,30,56, *passim*: Ali Anderson, *History of Sointula*, (Vancouver, 1970).

52 The figure of 40 percent in 1921 seems to have been something of an anomaly caused by the low rate of employment and post-war preference of employment to English-speaking workers, later sharply reversed.

53 It cannot be shown that the Alberta coal-mining community had ever been, like its British Columbia counterpart, predominantly English-speaking. For a contemporary document, see F. J. Warne, *The Slav Invasion and the Mine Workers* (Philadelphia, 1904).

54 PABC, GR 684, Evidence, Provincial Labour Commission, vol.2, f.4, Testimony of Thomas Stockett, Western Fuel Corporation, Nanaimo: "The majority are British subjects, English and Scotch, with some Welsh, and there are a few Slavs and men of the lower sections of Europe, but not many, and those we have are a very good class of men." PAVBS, GR 68, "Correspondence re Nanaimo Strike, " *op.cit*, Operative 29-S, 28 January 1914: "It is a curious state of affairs when one can hear apparently sane men, old countrymen mostly, stand and berate their own government and prophecy all sorts of evils for the nation and in every way show the earmarks of ranting anarchists which heretofore one has associated with European peoples and anything but British born men." **55 PABC, GR 68, Vol.3, Fernie Police Letter Books, 22 August 1911 (number of miners — 2,770).

56 Glenbow Archives, Western Canada Coal Operators Association Papers, f.77, Crow's Nest Pass Coal Company, payroll list of nationalities, n.d. 1916 (number — 1,484); Allen Seager, "A Proletariat in Wild Rose Country: The Alberta Coal Miners, 1905–1945, " ch.5.

57 PABC Premiers' Paapers, f. "copies, drafts, etc., 1896", mining memorandum n.d.

58 PABC, Vertical File, "Fernie, " misc. items on "The Curse of Fernie" 1942–1964.

59 Allen Seager, "A History of the Mine Workers Union of Canada 1925–1936" (MA thesis, McGill University, 1977). An early exponent was the remarkable William Henry Jackson from Wingham, Ontario: former *aide de camp* of the rebel Riel, Knight of Labour, organizer for metal miners' District 6 WFM, and personal secretary to F.H. Sherman. At a time of souring relations between the district and international offices of the UMWA he stumped through the Crow's Nest Pass "harping on an ALL CANADIAN UNION . . . and might have been the cause of some trouble." (Glenbow Archives, District 18 Papers, Minutes of Convention, 1910, Delegate MacDonald, p.271.) "General Jaxon" appears to have been a stalking horse for Frank Sherman, who was advocating the formation of a "Canadian Miners' Federation" at the time of his death in 1909.

60 Jean Reid, correpondence with the author, 3 January 1987; a voluminuous source on local history is the 914-page *Crowsnest and its People* (Crow's Nest Pass Historical Society, Florence E. Kerr, Chairperson: Coleman, 1979).

61 Figures one employment, profits, and production from British Columbia, *Report of the minister of Mines* (1947); Alberta *Mines Branch Report* (1947).

62 PABC, Premiers' Papers, vol.25, f.5. "Resolutions Passed by the Silverton Miners' Union, 10 June 1899."

63 *Ibid.*, vol. 14 f.18, "Resolution Passed by District No.6, Western Federation of Miners" *re* 8-hr day, n.d. 1899; "jack of all trades" from *Engineering and Mining Journal*, 8 March 1913, quoted in Logan Hovis, "The Origins of 'Modern Mining'", p.24, This technological progress was not of course as even as we imply. Hovis notes, for example, the persistence of traditional hardrock mining technique in the Slocan Valley surveyed above.

64 British Columbia *Sessional Papers* Mines Reports, 1897, p.1160. There is a vast scope for research into all aspects of indutrial health and safety in the western mines. See *Transactions of the Canadian Mining Institute*, V, 1912,569–581; David Jay Bercuson, "Tragedy at Bellevue: Anatomy of a Mine Disaster, " *Labour/Le travailleur* 3 (1978), 221–231.

65 In 1916 the Western Fiel Corporation (which purchased the Nanaimo mines in 1903), was producing 82 percent of machine-mined coal in British Columbia, an output that accounted for 50 percent of local tonnage and 11 percent of provincial tonnage.

66 John Reginald Mooney, "Labour Problems in the Mining Industry of Canada" (MA thesis, University of Toronto, 1929), 199–201, *passim*, Figure 6 is drawn out of Mooney's analysis of strike data in the *Labour Gazette* (monthly); my own reading of the same document and its primary source, Department of Labour,

"Strikes and Lockouts File, " Public Archives of Canada, from 1900 and 1907, respectively; Glenbow Archives, Western Canada Coal Operators' Association Papers, f.1908, "Strikes in District 18,1919–1920": and newspaper research for British Columbia in the 1890s, courtesy of Marilyn Janzen and Douglas Cruickshank.

67 Stanley Scott, "A Profusion of Issues: Immigrant Labour the World War, and the Cominco Strike of 1917, " *Labour/le travailleur* 2 (1977), 540–78; Mike Solksi and John Smaller, *Mine-Mill: The History of the International Union of Mine, Mill and Smelter Workers in Canada Since 1895* (Ottawa, 1985). Of the strikes recorded in the metalliferous mining sector between 1902 and 1921, only about a third engaged handrock miners in the Kootenay Inland Empire, the heartland of the WFM and later Mine-Mill. The status of the WFM locals on the eve of World War One is very unclear. They were certainly present: responsible in 1913, for example, for the administration of the larger part of $112,697 in benevolent funds collected by Denver headquarters and paid out across the border to 22 Canadian locals of the union. Canada, *Report of the Deputy Minister of Labour*, 1914,114–5. But testifying at the Provincial Labour Commission, the leader of Grand Forks local 180 described industrial relations as "very far from satisfactory. . . the company fail practicaly to have anything to do with us, " and noted that the alleged Boundary (sliding) scale "isn't the same at all points in the boundary." A manager for Granby Consolidated at Phoenix (local 8) admitted that "There is a union here. You can't help recognizing the union but we don't have any dealings with the union. . . We've had no trouble with the union for a long time. We don't worry much about that." Evidence, *op.cit*, vol 5,235–6,269. On the OBU insurgency and the final demise of District 6, see Jensen, *Heritage of Conflict*, pp.459–60; Bercuson, *Fools and Wise Men: The Rise and Fall of the One Big Union* (Toronto, 197), ch.8, "Battle for the Mining Frontier: The Hardrock Miners."

68 Figure 6 includes no data on strikes in Alberta coal mines in the Territorial period (1885–1905), when the Lethbridge area was a major centre of labour activity including at least a half dozen strikes leading up to the famous 1906 confrontation. For a local study, see. A. A. den Otter, *Civilizing the West: The Galts and the Development of Western Canada* (Edmonton, 1982), 238–311. Between 1906 and 1926 60 to 80 percent of Alberta coal miners were unionized. Even in 1930 the annual directory of *Labour Organizations in Canada* counted over 30 Alberta locals of District 18, UMWA, or District 1, Mine Workers Union of Canada. B.C. coal mines were never more than 50 percent unionized prior to 1938 while in hardrock mining the figure would be in a range of virtually zero in the 1920s to roughly 75 percent at the turn of the century.

69 Interview, Art Roberts (Canadian Union of Public Employees), Calgary, 1977. Drumheller Valley mines accounted for a growing share of mining employment in Alberta, ranging from 2·5 percent in 1913 to 20 percent in 1928. They were responsible for a third of the record number of strikes in 1918 and kept the pot boiling throughout the 1920s. I am not aware of research into this field, but see, for a popular account of the 'wildest spot on the prairies', James H. Gray, *Red Lights on the Prairies* (Toronto, 1971), 171–181.

70 Glenbow Archives, District 18 Papers, Convention Minutes, 1909, Delegate Gildea, p.411. The 'rules of the game' also included a lot of electoral discrimination and irregularities. Demands for basic democratic rights and procedures "cherished by the intelligent workingmen of this province and guaranteed them by the constitution" — though certainly not the BNA Act of 1867 — are staple themes in petitions and resolutions by the miners and their unions. Quotation from PABCS, Premier's Papers, Box 25, f.809, Resolution of the Rossland Miners' Union re "rights of voters, other than assessed property holders, " n.d. 1905.

71 See above, note 29. The Vancouver Coal Company's "Colliery Returns" in the annual *Mines Report* show 327 whites, 312 Orientals, 8 native Indians, and 7 boys employed in 1885. This very excellent data for the 1880s deteriorates from the 1890s to the 1920s. Dominion electoral data, somewhat more systematic than provincial, yields some ambiguous numbers. The Federal voters in Nanaimo in 1911 represented 25 per cent of the census population of the city. The same exercise for nine other western coal-mining towns in the interior of British Columbia and Alberta produces figures in the range of 20 to 44 percent; average, 29 percent; mean, 27 percent. These are reasonably high figures but cannot account for unknown variables such as age and gender.

72 Among 15 mining deputies elected in the West between 1890 and 1926, nine were from B.C. five from Alberta; 11 were miners by trade. Three were elected on the Socialsit Party of Canada ticket, one for the schismatic Social Democratic Party. Two were straight Labour men who crossed over to the SPC caucus in Victoria between 1903 and 1909. All were born between 1860 and 1890, one in Ontario, one in Prince Edward Island, the rest in the U.K. These individuals served a collective sentence of 126 years in the legilatures.

73 Apart from socialism and community-based labour politics, the other great political project in the mining West was Liberalism, as evidenced by the defection of Ralph Smith, M.P. (1900–1911) of the MMLPA, B.C. miners' affiliation with a short-lived Liberal-Labour alliance in 1916, an the failed Liberal candidacies of at least three district officers of the UMWA in Alberta before 1914. Craven, *'An Impartial Umpire'* is the most serious consideration of Labour and Liberalism in pre-war Canada; see also Craig Heron, "Labourism and the Canadian Working Class, 1900–1914, " *Labour/Le Travail*, 13 (1984), 45–66.

74 For a biographical sketch of Mary Ellen Smith, from Framlington, Newcastle-on-Tyne, see Elizabeth Norcross, "The Right Woman at the Right Time, " in Barbara K. Latham and R. J. Pazdro, eds. *Not Just Pin Money: Selected Esays on Women's Work in British Columbia* (Victoria, B, .C. 1984).

75 Hawthornwaite Papers, Private Collection, Vancouver, F. H. Sherman to J. H. J. 11 October 1908, 'national character' from obituary and "Tribute to F. H. Sherman, " *District Ledger* (Fernie), 16 October 1909; "predominantly Welsh" from Len Richardson, "Class, Community, and Conflict: The Blackball Miners' Union, 1920–1931, " in Richardson and W. David McIntyre, eds., *Provincial Perspectives* (Christchurch, N.Z. 1981), p.107, 'old country' from Sherman, letter to *The United Mine Workers Journal*, 24 November 1904. Other Figures in the rogue's gallery may be found in McCormack, *Reformers, Rebels and Revolutionaries*: 'a decent plug' form Dorothy Gretchen Steeves, *The Compassionate Rebel: Ernest Winch and the Growth of Socialism in Western Canada* (Vancouver, 1960), p.18.

76 "Convention impressions, " *Western Clarion*, 6 June 1908.

77 Christophers' biography in *Crowsnest and its People* 465–6; Tim Buck, *Lenin and*

Canada (Toronto, 1970), 12–14.

78 Belshaw, "Mining Technique"; McKay, "Realm of Uncertainty."

79 Jean Reid, letter to the author, 16 December 1986.

Figure 1.

Household and Family
Nanaimo Coal-Mining Community 1891

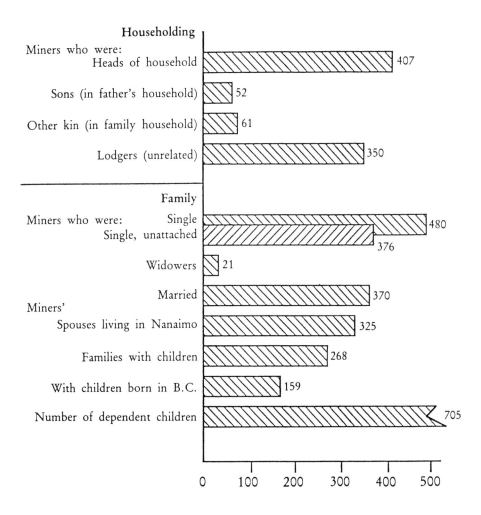

Coal-mining population: 1,900 - 2,000

Population of Nanaimo, 1891-4,595

Source: 1891 Manuscript Census

1891 Census
Population of B.C.
born in:

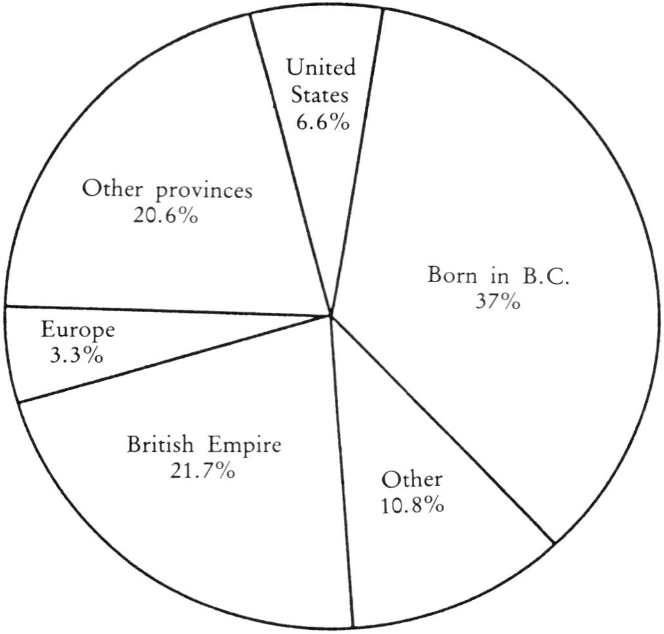

Born in B.C.
37%

United
States
6.6%

Other provinces
20.6%

Europe
3.3%

British Empire
21.7%

Other
10.8%

Figure 2.

National Origins of Nanaimo Coal Miners
1891 Census (mss)

	No. born in:	
G.B.	England	360
	Scotland & the Shetland Is.	105
	Wales	42
	Ireland	20
Canada	Nova Scotia	85
	British Columbia	19
	Other Provinces & Newfoundland	16
	United States	69
Europe	Finland	61
	Italy	22
	Germany	14
	Sweden	11
	Belgium	10
	Austria	8
	France	7
	Denmark	5
	Norway	2
	Iceland	1
	Poland	1
	Russia	1
	Spain	1
	Switzerland	1
Other	China	6
	New Zealand	2
	Australia	1
	TOTAL	**870**

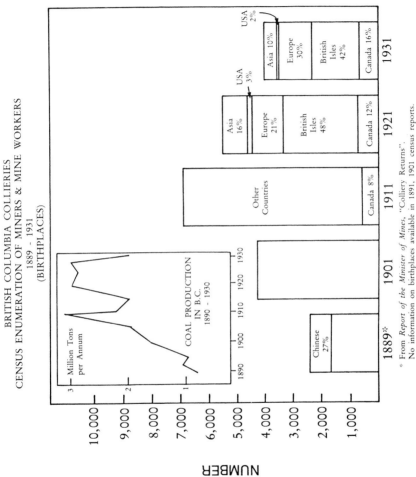

Figure 3.

BRITISH COLUMBIA COLLIERIES
CENSUS ENUMERATION OF MINERS & MINE WORKERS
1889 - 1931
(BIRTHPLACES)

COAL PRODUCTION
IN B.C.
1890 - 1930

Million Tons
per Annum

NUMBER

1889*   1901   1911   1921   1931

Chinese 27%

Other Countries

Canada 8%

Asia 16%
Europe 21%
British Isles 48%
Canada 12%
USA 3%

Asia 10%
Europe 30%
British Isles 42%
Canada 16%
USA 2%

* From *Report of the Minister of Mines*, "Colliery Returns".
No information on birthplaces available in 1891, 1901 census reports.

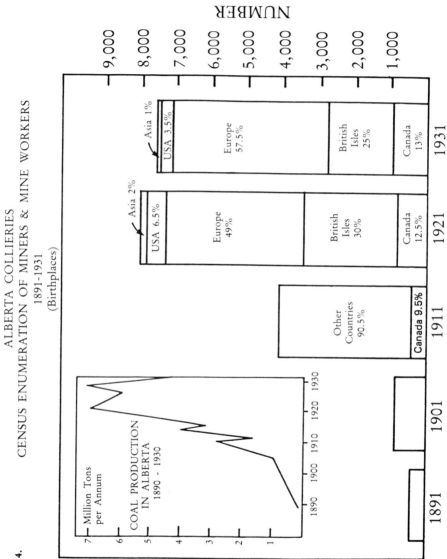

Figure 4.

ALBERTA COLLIERIES
CENSUS ENUMERATION OF MINERS & MINE WORKERS
1891-1931
(Birthplaces)

Figure 5.

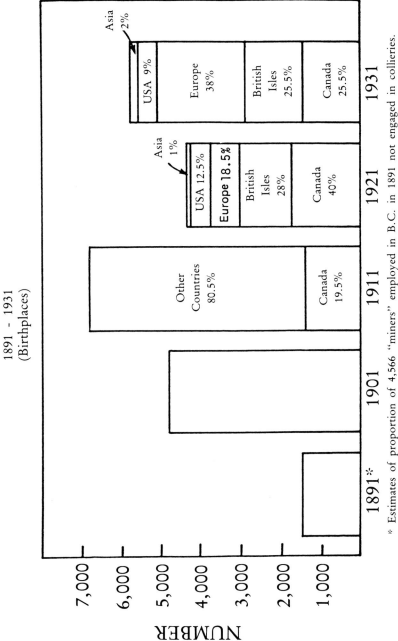

BRITISH COLUMBIA METAL MINES
CENSUS ENUMERATION OF MINERS & MINE WORKERS
1891 - 1931
(Birthplaces)

NUMBER

7,000 — 6,000 — 5,000 — 4,000 — 3,000 — 2,000 — 1,000

1891* 1901 1911 1921 1931

1891*

Other Countries 80.5%

Canada 19.5%

Asia 1%

USA 12.5%

Europe 18.5%

British Isles 28%

Canada 40%

Asia 2%

USA 9%

Europe 38%

British Isles 25.5%

Canada 25.5%

* Estimates of proportion of 4,566 "miners" employed in B.C. in 1891 not engaged in collieries.

Figure 6. Strikes and Lockouts in the Western Canadian Mines (Partial List)

1890 - 1930
NUMBER OF DISPUTES RECORDED IN:

Year	BC metal mines, smelters, quarries	BC collieries		Alta collieries	
1890		1			
1891		1			
1892					
1893	1	1			
1894		1			
1895	3				
1896					
1897					
1898	4				
1899	4				
1900	5	1			
1901	2	2			
1902		2			
1903	2	3			
1904					
1905	3	2		2	
1906	3	2		3	
1907	2	2	——district*——	2	
1908	1	2	district	2	
1909	1			3	
1910	1			1	
1911		2	——district ——	3	
1912		Vanc. Isl. ⎰ 1		1	
1913	2	strike ⎱ 1		1	
1914		1		1	
1915				2	
1916	2	2		4	
1917	1	4	——district ——	13	
1918	1	3		27	
1919	3	1	——district ——	14	
1920	4	4		15	
1921	1			5	
1922		1	——district ——	12	
1923		1		13	
1924		2	——district ——	8	
1925		1		12	
1926				4	
1927				3	
1928				5	
1929				1	
1930				2	
TOTALS	46	44		159	249

* "district" denotes a strike or lockout involving the 5,000 - 10,000 members of District 18, United Mine Workers of America, counting for one of the bold figure.

Figure 7. Provincial Elections, Western Canadian Mining Districts 1890-1930

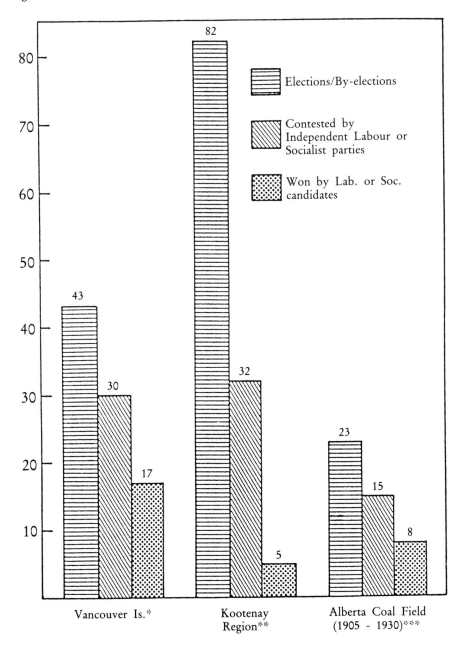

* Provincial Electoral Districts in British Columbia variously drawn as Nanaimo, Nanaimo City, Nanaimo North, Nanaimo South, Newcastle, Cowichan-Newcastle, and Comox (Industrial Vancouver Island).

** Provincial Electoral Districts in British Columbia variously drawn as Kootenay East, Kootenay West, Kootenay South, Kootenay North, Kootenay North-East, Kootenay South-East, Greenwood, Grand Forks, Nelson, Rossland, Slocan, Revelstoke, Ymir, Kaslo, Trail, Grand Forks-Greenwood, Kaslo-Slocan, Rossland-Trial, and Fernie (The Knootenays).

*** Provincial Electoral Districts variously drawn as Pincher Creek, Rocky Mountain, Lethbridge, and Edson (Alberta Coalfields).

Source: Canadian Parliamentary Guide (annual), 1890-1930.

Figure 8. Miner's Candidates for Parliament, Alberta and British Columbia 1890-1930

Name	Party	Trade-union affiliation	Federal riding	Date	Number of votes	%
Chris Foley	(Lab)	WFM	Yale-Cariboo	1900	2,562	30.5
Ralph Smith*	(Lab)	MMLPA	Vancouver Is.	1900	1,256	42.5
James Baker	(Soc)		Kootenay	1904	662	12.5
Ed Fenton	(Soc)		Nanaimo	1904	717	22.0
Wm. Davidson	(Soc)		Kootenay	1908	1,337	20.0
J.H. Hawthornthwaite	(Soc)		Nanaimo	1908	1,312	31.5
John Harrington	(Soc)		MacLeod	1908	662	6.5
F.H. Sherman	(Soc)	UMWA	Calgary	1908	743	9.0
Ed Fulcher	(Soc)		MacLeod	1911	902	12.0
W.A. Prichard	(Soc)		Nanaimo	1921	3,958	26.0
James Fairhurst	(Lab)	OBU	MacLeod	1921	1,407	14.0

Source: Reports of the Chief Returning Officer, 1905-1922
            *Elected

Figure 9.

Labour/Socialist Party Vote in British Columbia Mining Districts, National Elections, 1900-1908

Vancouver Island	1900	(Lab.)	1904	(Soc.)	1908	(Soc.)
Nanaimo (city)	542	57.7%	377	37.5%	716	54%
Ladysmith	——	——	214	42%	186	43%
Northfield	130	35.8%	53	67%	78	75%
So. Wellington	12	20%	7	22%	17	92%
Extension	48	54.5%	——	——	24	41%

Kootenay Region

"Hardrock"						
Rossland	519	51.7%	——	——	114	19%
Nelson	252	29.6%	——	——	167	21%
Sandon	178	70%	60	54%	41	58.5%
Greenwood	141	54%	116	36%	——	——
Kaslo	108	47%	——	——	19	10%
Slocan	94	64%	44	39%	26	27%
Moyie	101	85.5%	——	——	85	41%
Kimberley	61	89.7%	——	——	6	35%
Trail	34	20%	——	——	43	15%
Silverton	59	78.6%	——	——	17	39.5%
Ferguson	45	64.2%	32	60%	7	19%
Fairview	0	0%	——	——	55	35%
New Denver	45	45%	——	——	12	17.5%
Ymir Mines	51	53.6%	——	——	18	40%
Phoenix	86	57.7%	116	55%	——	——

Coal-mining:						
Fernie	74	48.7%	30	11%	123	39.5%
Michel	11	57.8%	15	46.5%	90	67%
Coal Creek	——	——	——	——	105	68%

Labour/Socialist Vote in Alberta Coal Mining Towns, National Elections, 1908-1921

	1980	(Soc)	1911	(Soc.)	1921	(Lab.)
Coleman	153	43.5%	227	57.5%	304	64%
Blairmore	13	10%	98	29%	138	36%
Frank	39	25.5%	87	44%	50	54%
Hillcrest	83	67.5%	124	70.5%	131	69%
Bellevue	64	46.5%	50	49.5%	117	61%
Lille	12	11.5%	61	67%	——	——
Canmore	54	28.5%	——	——	——	——
Bankhead	77	46%	——	——	——	——

Source: Reports of the Chief Returning Officer, Electoral Districts of Yale, Cariboo, Vancouver (Island), Kootenay, MacLeod, and Calgary 1901- 1922

Figure 10. Mining Fatalities per Thousand Employees (5-Year Averages)

	BC COAL MINES	ALTA COAL MINES	METAL MINES
1901-1905	17.5	——	3.46
1906-1910	6.41	4.78	5.00
1911-1915	4.73	7.20	5.80
1916-1920	4.79	2.75	2.74
1921-1925	3.24	2.91	2.01
NO FATALITIES, 1901-1925	901	653	409

Statistics on accidents and average annual employment in mines from the British Columbia Department of Mines, *Annual Reports*, 1900-1925, 1947; Alberta *Mines Branch Report*, 1947.

10

Canadian Mining Towns: a Photo-montage

Varpu Lindstrom-Best

The many rich mineral discoveries made in Canada during the late nineteenth and early twentieth century began an unprecedented mining boom and signaled the need for thousands of miners. Immigrants were recruited to solve the problem of labour shortage and to fill the new, dangerous and backbreaking jobs. Finns were one of the first groups of miners in Canada and hence had a significant impact in both the development of the new mining communities and the organization of the miners.

The communities reflected the sense of isolation and vulnerability that many of the newly arrived immigrants were experiencing. At the same time, the immigrants were cementing a uniformity of purpose and a sense of solidarity in the face of shared danger. Women, although disbarred from employment in the mines, were active participants in promoting the sense of community and the need for determined action.

The following photographs are selected to illustrate the primitive conditions, the dangers of mining and the human response to fight for a better life by improving both the working conditions and the social life of the mining towns.

In hope of instant riches thousands of immigrants rushed to Yukon between 1897-1904. Among the very first people to cross the treacherous mountains were many Finnish men and women who staked their claims. Few were lucky, most retreated south penniless.

Dawson City, Yukon Territory in the midst of gold fever c.1898.

Copper Cliff, Ontario, 1893.

Northern Ontario hardrock mines depended on cheap immigrant labour.

North Mine, Copper Cliff, Ontario, 1898.

Surface mining.

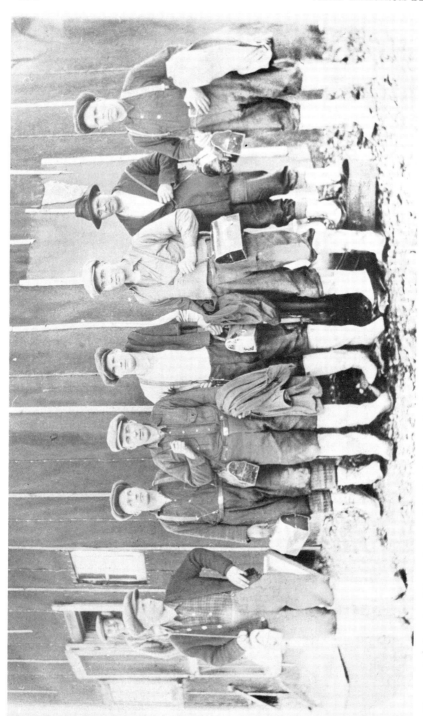

South Porcupine, Ontario, 1928.

Men spent their entire shifts underground in the deep tunnels of gold and silver mines.

The dangerous work forged a common bond between miners from many nationalities.
South Porcupine, Ontario, 1928.

Many a young man was crushed to death in the coalmines of British Columbia. Their families in the old country received only photographs of their sons' last journey. Extension, B.C. c. 1900.

Entire communities mourned the deaths of victims of large mining disasters. Mass funerals served to radicalize the miners and their families. Funeral of eight Finns and one East Ballician who died in the Hollinger Mine Disaster. Timmins, Ontario 1928.

In unorganized mining communities, leisure time was too often spent by drinking and playing cards.

Alberta, n.d.

To add meaning to their lives and strength through solidarity Finnish immigrants organized socialist political, cultural and social organizations. Finnish community in the tiny mining town of Cobalt, Ontario celebrate the Finnish Socialist Organization of Canada's summer picnic, 1916.

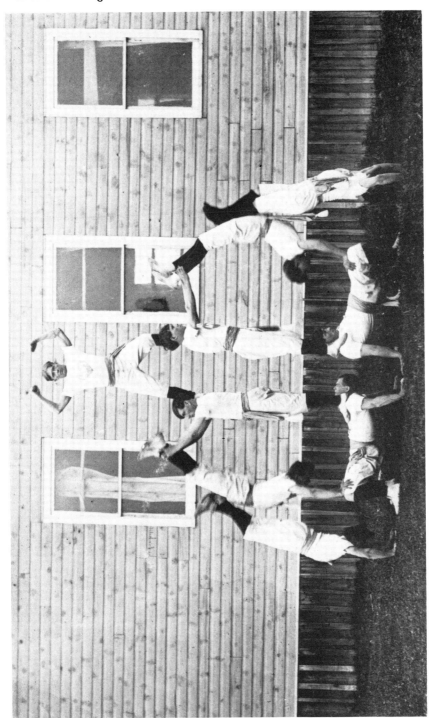

Mond Mine, Ontario Gymnastic Club, 1916.

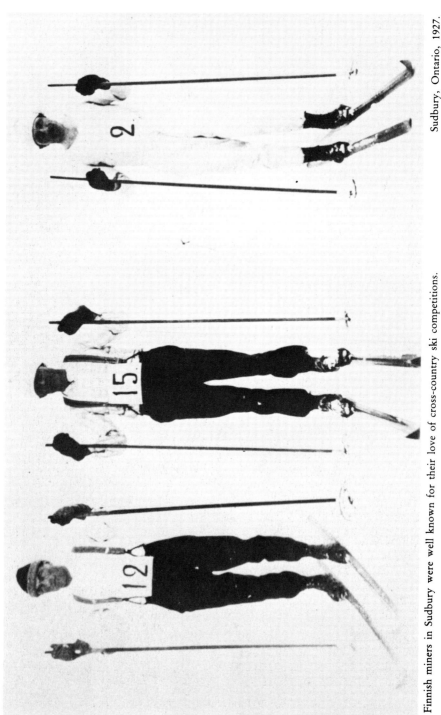

Finnish miners in Sudbury were well known for their love of cross-country ski competitions. Sudbury, Ontario, 1927.

Finnish coalminers in North Wellington, British Columbia organized a temperance society and a brass band. 1898.

Port Arthur, Ontario, c.1912.

May day parade.

11

The Parameters of Class Conflict Strikes in Canada, 1891–1930

Gregory S. Kealey

In the years 1891–1930, almost 1,100,000 Canadian workers engaged in about 5,400 strikes which lasted for just under 25,000,000 days. Not surprisingly, these strikes did not occur in any simple pattern of linear growth. Instead, like strikes elsewhere, they came in bursts or waves that initially drew on workers' sense of opportunities to be seized and subsequently fed on initial successes. Disaggregated by decade, the periods 1901–1910 and 1911–1920 emerge as the most active with 3,900 of the strikes (72 per cent) 750,000 of the strikes (69 per cent), and over 16,310,000 days of duration (66 per cent). Indeed, if we move beyond the decadal data, we can discern a series of strike waves, similar to those described by Shorter and Tilly, Cronin, and Edwards in their respective studies of France, Britain, and the United States.[1] After some introductory discussion of the general shape of our findings, this paper will look more intensively at the strike waves of this period. The paper will close with some preliminary reflections on international comparisons of strike activity in this period.

This paper presents the first major report, albeit still somewhat preliminary, of a project undertaken in the early 1980s. The project aimed to establish a new statistical time series for strikes in Canada. The final results of this work will appear in 1990 in volume three of the Historical Atlas of Canada which will contain a series of four plates specifically on Canadian labour in the years 1891–1961. In this paper, however, owing to the conference theme, I shall focus primarily on the data concerning the years 1891–1930. I will not present a full and technical report here on the reconstruction of the data set. Such a discussion appears elsewhere.[2] In addition, I want to state at the outset that the more I work on such data as I shall present here the more fully I agree with David Montgomery's argument that "any attempt to formulate a positivistic 'natural history of strikes' is doomed to failure. Strikes can only be understood in the context of the changing totality of class conflicts, of which they are a part."[3]

I

A brief look at the longer historical pattern of strikes in Canada from 1830 — 1950 provides a context for the more specific discussion of the

1890–1930 data. As can be seen in Figure 1, the Canadian nineteenth-century experience parallelled closely the country's early industrialization. Rare before the 1840s, strikes in the early years involved numerous craftsmen, but canal and railway navvies also contributed significantly.[4] The decade of the 1850s saw the first significant strike surge, when in the years 1853–1854 "an insurrection of labour" occurred. The decade in which the Canadian nation state was created was slightly quieter, but the 1870s, and especially the nine- hour struggle of 1872, presented entirely new levels of strike activity. In addition, it can be argued that by the 1870s strikes had largely replaced riots as the main expression of working-class discontent.[5] While riots did not disappear entirely, they increasingly became integrated into more formal means of protest. In the 1860s and 1870s craftsmen, especially moulders, stonecutters, and shoemakers, and miners led the way accounting for almost 75 per cent of the strikes. In the 1880s, the decade of the Great Upheaval, the unskilled increased their strike participation rate to almost 40 per cent as strikes more than doubled to 425. In regional terms Ontario dominated, accounting for 54 per cent of all strikes to 1890; Quebec followed with 28 per cent, the Maritimes with 14 per cent, and the emerging west with 4 per cent.[6] (See Table 5)

In general the nineteenth-century data with the pronounced strike waves of the early 1850s, early 1870s, and the mid-1880s lend considerable support to Tilly/Shorter's and Cronin's arguments concerning the nature of industrial conflict, which emphasizes bursts of activity.[7] If we continue simply to look at the absolute frequency of strikes in Canada, we can discern an overall pattern in the first half of the twentieth century as well. Strikes grew in absolute numbers in the 1890s, 1900s, and especially the 1910s but fell in the 1920s well below the level established in the 1900s. The number climbed above that level again in the 1930s and reached a peak in the 1940s higher even than the World War I decade. (See Figure 1.) This decadal data, of course, disguises the peaks and the troughs within the decades which can be more clearly seen on Figure 2. Here the important strike waves, as defined by Charles Tilly,[8] of 1899–1903, 1912–1913, and 1917–1920 stand out, as do the troughs of 1896–1897, 1908–1909, 1914–1915, and 1922–1930. Especially arresting is the pronounced importance of the war-time strike wave, 1917–1920. We shall return to these waves later.

In addition to frequency, of course, there are other important measures of strike activity. The number of strikers and the duration of strikes are the two other most-cited strike variables. On a national level, strikes declined in size in the 1900s, increased in the 1910s, fell slightly in the 1920s and more rapidly in the 1930s, and then exploded in the 1940s. (See Figure 4 and Table 8.) Meanwhile, duration fell constantly with the exception of the 1920s when it increased to its highest point in the decades under study. (As we shall see this is to a large extent owing to the dominance of protracted coal mining struggles in the decade.)

In this paper I must assume the general contours of the national economic picture as we currently understand them. Let me describe them briefly, however, so there is no confusion.[9] Canada burst out of the 1890s depression into a period of rapid and sustained economic growth before World War I. Massive immigration, western settlement, the construction of two new transcontinental railroad systems, metal mining booms in the west and in Northern Ontario, all figured in a major boom. In addition, massive imports of American capital in the form of branch plants brought to Canada all the advances in U.S. corporate strategies. A Canadian "second" industrial revolution took place simultaneous with the American and transformed Canadian workplaces in all the same ways. Scientific managers, multi-plant organization, assembly line production, all arrived in the two decades before World War I. The war experience simply intensified these changes. After an initial post-war depression the national economy recovered in the 1920s and received another major infusion of American capital in the late 1920s. As in the earlier wave, this set off a merger movement of significant proportions. In general, Canadian economic development closely parallelled the American in this period and the better-known generalizations of Brody, Montgomery, and Gordon, Reich and Edwards on the interaction of economic change and the working-class movement are broadly applicable.[10]

In Canadian historical writing since the 1960s, region has received considerable attention. This regional influence has been quite evident in Canadian historical writing about the working-class as well. Heavily influenced by the work of Herbert Gutman, much recent work in the field has consisted of community studies either of towns or cities or of coal-mining districts.[11] Even specific studies of strike activity have tended to be regional in focus such as McKay's work on the Maritimes from 1901–1914, Heron and Palmer's on Southern Ontario in the same period, and Jacques Rouillard and James Thwaite's studies of Quebec.[12] On occasion this regional interpretation had almost degenerated into cheerleading for the militancy of a regions' workers, often at the expense of some other regions' putative lack of radicalism. This problem is most evident in David Bercuson's attempt to retain a "western exceptionalist" argument in the face of compelling contrary evidence.[13] Indeed, to a large degree, the assertiveness of the western historian's claims has led to a distorted debate.[14]

The data we have accumulated has been disaggregated by province and we can thus consider Canadian strike activity in terms of regional variation. Table 6 shows the results of a regional tabulation. As can be seen, there has been significant variation over time, although Central Canada has always retained its dominance. Before 1900 of course, Western settlement was sparse and strikes were infrequent. Subsequently, western strike activity grew rapidly in the first two decades of the century but declined after 1920, while in the east there was a decline during the 1910s but growth through the 1920s, 1930s, and 1940s. Quebec strikes figured most prominently in the national picture in the 1920s and 1940s. Ontario, on the other hand, enjoyed its highest shares in the 1900s and 1930s.

A more intensive look at the 1890–1930 data allows further comment on provincial variation. (See Figure 4 and Table 8.) Prince Edward Island, primarily an agricultural province, trailed national statistics on all measures for each decade. New Brunswick, and Nova Scotia, however, calling into further question their image of conservatism, conformed more to the national pattern. Nova Scotia, for example, exceeded national figures for strike frequency in the 1900s and 1920s and for size in all four decades. In each case, coal and steel help to explain the higher numbers. New Brunswick, however, exceeded national frequency in the 1900s and 1910s, largely owing to the militancy of Saint John workers, but, lacking Nova Scotia's industrial concentration, was consistently beneath national size figures. In duration Nova Scotia saw longer than national average strikes in the 1900s, largely owing to the tri-partite Great Strike of 1909–1911 in the coal fields of Springhill, Inverness, and Glace Bay. The myth of Atlantic provinces' conservatism and labour quiescence takes a further beating if we consider the Newfoundland case. (See Table 7) While this material is drawn from work in progress and only concern strike frequency, it is nevertheless clear that Newfoundland workers struck often in these years. Indeed, in the Atlantic region St. John's workers were second only to those of Saint John in their propensity to strike. In St. John's longshoremen led the way, although there were also numerous craft struggles.[15]

In Central Canada, Quebec was consistently beneath the national figures for frequency but consistently above them for size, owing to large strikes in textiles and boot and shoe. On duration it was lower for the first three decades but higher in the 1920s. Ontario simply reversed that pattern. Consistently higher in frequency, due to its preponderance of small manufacturing and building trades strikes, it trailed the national figures for size in each decade. While Ontario strikes exceeded the national duration figures in the 1890s, thereafter Ontario strikes were almost identical to the national average, albeit slightly longer in the 1910s.

In the west, largely agricultural Saskatchewan behaved like Prince Edward Island in the east, falling below national figures on all measures. Manitoba, on the other hand, had more frequent strikes in the 1890s and 1900s but less frequent in the subsequent two decades. Only in the World War I decade were Manitoba strikes larger than the national average, primarily because of the general strikes of 1918 and 1919, while throughout the 40 years they were always shorter. Alberta and British Columbia, on the other hand, exceeded national figures for frequency for all decades and, with the exception of B.C. in the 1920s did the same for duration. In size Alberta in the 1900s and B.C. in the 1920s fell below national figures, but for all other decades exceeded them. (See Table 9.)

Extremely important in contributing to the provincial and regional patterns of Canadian strike activity has been the geographic distribution in the country of manufacturing and of resource extraction. The shifting regional balance of strike activity was related not only to the opening of the west but also to the nation's resource/industrial mix. The literature on strike propensity is by now huge and cannot be reviewed here. The Canadian data contain few surprises. Data problems limit these discussions to the years after 1911. (See Table 10.) The massive importance of mining in terms of frequency and size makes clear why it dominates the industrial side of Figure 4 and in the process also helps to explain the graphic dominance of British Columbia, Alberta, and Nova Scotia on the provincial side. In frequency, construction with many small local building trades strikes held second place in each decade with manufacturing in third, and transportation in fourth. In size, however, transportation, owing to a number of massive railroad strikes, switched places with construction with manufacturing maintaining the same position. Service and public administration, sectors with few organized workers, were last on both measures. In duration manufacturing struggles led with the longest average strikes followed by mining and construction in the 1910s and by transportation and service in the 1920s.

The discussion of strike issues is fraught with ambiguity. Needless to say wages almost always figure prominently, both in times of union strength and weakness. What changes, of course, is whether the strike aims to increase workers' earnings or to prevent employers' incursions against the wage packet. Thus one anticipates struggles for higher wages in periods of boom accompanied by tight labour markets and battles to maintain wage levels in periods of economic decline and high unemployment. Table 11 demonstrates this hypothesis rather well with 12 years in which strikes for wage increases exceeded 40 per cent. Of these 12, fully 7 were associated with the strike waves that we identified earlier. In the nine years in which strikes against wage cuts surpassed 20 per cent, all were in periods of economic distress. The multiplicity of issues involved in almost every strike makes generalizations about other elements in each dispute hard to sustain, but Table 11 minimally demonstrates the pervasiveness of work-related struggles and battles concerning union rights.

Similarly methods of dispute settlement throw only limited light at this gross aggregate level, especially given the high levels of indefinite responses. Yet in the years of the strike waves we can detect increases in settlements by negotiation and third-party intervention combined and, more obviously, decreases in resolutions involving the return or replacement of the striking workers. In contrast years of economic trauma for workers led to disastrous strike records. (See Table 12.) Less ambiguous are the strike results displayed in Table 13. Only in the strike wave years of 1902–1903, 1912, and 1916–1919 (with the exception of 1925) did strikers win more strikes than employers in our and the Departments of Labour's box scores. On the employers' side the depression years of 1893–1894, 1896, 1908, and 1921–1924 all saw employers' victory levels rocket above 40 per cent. If we add strikes and compromises together, workers exceeded 50 per cent overall success rates in 1900–1902, 1912, 1916–1919, and, more surprisingly, in 1925 and 1927–1930.

Table 12 shows a significant rise in 1917 and 1918 of third party intervention to settle strikes. In those late war years this state involvement reached unprecedented heights which would not be matched again until the mid-1930s. By and large it has been the state as conciliator, mediator, and manager of class conflict which has received most attention in Canada. Yet the state's coercive function was used often throughout this period as can be seen in Tables 14–16. While both the percentage of "violent" strikes and the incidents of military intervention were declining in relative terms, both measures peaked during World War I with 48 "violent" strikes and 17 incidents of military aid to the civil power. In violent strikes Ontario (48), Quebec (41), Nova Scotia (18), and British Columbia (16) led the list, while Ontario workers faced the Canadian army 16 times, Nova Scotia and Quebec workers eight times, and B.C. workers five times. By industry, street railways, general strikes (not surprisingly), fishing, water transport, railways, and mining led the way in violent encounters with a similar pattern in military interventions.[16]

II

Let us now turn to the three strike waves of the period 1890–1930 — 1899–1903, 1912–1913, and 1917–1920. (See Table 17.) In many ways the three waves are related. Certainly it can be argued that the 1917–1920 wave was simply an artificially delayed continuation of the struggles of 1912–1913 which came to an abrupt halt owing both to a depressed economy and to the outbreak of World War I. Yet, as we shall see, there were also key differences in the three waves, shifts in both geographic and industrial focus which imbued the third wave, 1917–1920, with a more menacing and insurgent character.

The 1899–1903 and 1912–1913 strike waves were heavily dominated by the combination of manufacturing, construction, and transportation strikes both in terms of number of strikes and number of strikers. (See Table 18.) Geographically the 1899–1903 wave was concentrated in Ontario, Quebec, and British Columbia, while the 1912–1913 found a more national focus. The arresting contrast, however, comes in the 1917–1920 wave in which the strikes spread themselves far more evenly through the entire working class in terms of both occupational and geographic mix. The labour revolt of 1917–1920 represents an insurgency involving almost all elements of the working class and covering the entire nation.

In the first wave of this period, 1899–1903, the 745 strikes involved just over 120,000 workers. Manufacturing figured prominently with 49 per cent of the strikes and 34 per cent of the strikers. Construction workers accounted for 23 per cent of the strikes but only 13 per cent of the strikers, while transportation workers' strikes made up 17 per cent of the total but involved 22 per cent of all strikers. The final major industrial actor, mining, accounting for 5 per cent of the strikes and 13 per cent of the strikers.

As the above figures suggest transportation and mining strikes tended to be much larger than manufacturing and especially construction strikes. Transportation and mining strikes because of their size, militancy, and often national character often seized the attention of the public and the state in this period. National strikes by Grand Trunk Railway trackmen in 1899, Canadian Pacific Railway trackmen in 1901, and non-running trades CPR workers, organized into the United Brotherhood of Railway Employees, and American Labor Union affiliate, in 1903, all gained a national audience. Equally prominent were the struggles of Western Federation of Miners metal miners in the BC interior in 1899, 1900, and 1901, and especially the Vancouver Island and Crows Nest Pass coal mining strikes of 1903. The 1903 struggles led to the appointment of a Royal Commission to investigate labour unrest in British Columbia, to the passage of the Railway Labour Disputes Act, the state's first major effort to create a role for itself in "harmonizing" class relations, and to the virulent denunciation of all unions, initially only the so-called revolutionary unions such as the UBRE and the WFM, but later broadened to include an attack on all international unions.[17]

The state's fear of the ALU unions invokes no surprise, but the state attack on the AFL, disdainfully termed the American "separation of labour, " by syndicalists, demands further explanation. The strikes in the manufacturing and construction sectors provide part of the answer, although dramatic strikes on the Quebec, Vancouver, Montreal, and Halifax waterfronts in 1901,1902, and 1903,[18] led by AFL-affiliated unions, and violence-laden strikes on the street railway systems of London, Toronto, and Montreal in 1899, 1902 and 1903 which culminated in the use of the military against the striking AFL members of the Amalgamated Street Railway Workers Union, also played a role.[19]

A closer look at the manufacturing and construction sector reveals national patterns which closely resemble the detailed city and craft studies we have of this period. In manufacturing the strikes clustered in three major areas — the metal trades and shipbuilding, boot and shoe, and clothing and textiles. Over the five-year period these three groups accounted for 55 per cent of the strikers. The metal trades and shipbuilding accounted for 32 per cent of the manufacturing strikes and almost 20 per cent of the sector strikers; clothing and textiles 16 per cent of strikes and 33 per cent of strikers; and boot and shoe 7 per cent of the strikes but 25 per cent of the strikers. Clearly the shape of strikes in these three manufacturing areas was quite different. In the metal trades strikes were small but frequent, while in clothing and textile, and in boot and shoe they tended to be less frequent but much larger.

Metal workers' strikes primarily revolved around shop floor struggles concerning control issues. Moulders and machinists fought the largest number of such battles but boiler, core, and pattern makers also participated. While active in most major Canadian cities, Ontario metal workers were the most prominent in the strikes. One particularly bitter struggle in Toronto involved almost 300 moulders against the city's major foundries. The moulders sought the nine-hour day and over eight months found themselves facing scabs, injunctions, and even *agents provocateurs*. The strike ultimately failed.[20]

Quebec workers, however, played the major role in the other strike-prone manufacturing sectors of boot and shoe and clothing and textiles. Major conflicts in boot and shoe came in Quebec City in 1900 and 1903 when industry-wide strikes occurred involving 4000 and 5000 workers respectively in lengthy struggles. Similarly, the major textile strikes occurred in Quebec. The troops were sent in to Magog to quell a strike of 900 unorganized workers against Dominion Cotton in early August 1900. Dominion Cotton defeated its workers and rid its mill of a union in Montmorency when it simply outlasted 600 Knights of Labor strikers who were forced to concede after two months on the picket line. In Valleyfield, however, 1500 workers at Montreal Cotton walked out in late January for six days but returned pending an increase. They struck again on 21 February in even larger numbers (2500), after rejecting the company's offer. They subsequently compromised and again returned, but struck again in July for four days against company employment policy. In October, when the militia was called in to break a strike by 200 construction workers building a new cotton mill, 3000 cotton workers walked out in sympathy and returned only after the troops were withdrawn.[21]

Construction strikes in this period were dominated by the building trades which constituted 81 per cent of the 174 strikes and 91 per cent of the approximately 16,000 strikers. The other construction strikes were on nine railroad, seven canal, and five highway or bridge projects. Although ubiquitous in Canadian towns and cities in these years and while generally short in duration and small in number of workers involved, there were exceptions. Some 700 Sydney, Nova Scotia bricklayers, stonemasons, and plasterers, for example, struck for seven months in 1901 before gaining a wage increase and shorter hours. That same summer almost 400 Ottawa carpenters were off the job for about six weeks to win wage increases and changes in work rules. Later that year 400 Winnipeg carpenters failed in their almost two-month long strike to gain higher wages and shorter hours. In 1903, however, Toronto was the site for a city-wide building trades strike which involved almost 1000 carpenters, over 3000 building labourers, 250 painters, and over 100 structural iron workers in a 10 week strike which the employers ultimately won.[22] The issues for Canadian building trades workers in these years were identical to those faced by their English comrades. *The Ragged Trousered Philanthropists* described the experience of North American building trades workers.

Despite defeats such as those mentioned above, strikers did well in the years 1899–1903. Strikes were largely offensive and the success rate (victories plus compromises) ranged from an 1899 low of 35 per cent to a 1902 high of 56 per cent. In 1902 and 1903 clear-cut victories outnumbered defeats. (See Table 13.)

Similarly during the second strike wave, 1912–1913, the primarily offensive strikes led to a 52 per cent success rate in 1912 and 42 per cent in

1913, although in the latter year employers' clear-cut victories rose above full workers' victories unlike 1912. As we noted earlier the dominance of manufacturing, construction, and transportation and of B.C., Ontario, and Quebec still prevailed in this pre-World War I strike wave but broadenings in geographic and industrial mix are evident compared to 1899–1903. (See Table 18.) This widening is most apparent geographically and can be explained by the much greater presence of the west. The admittedly less clear spread in industrial mix stems from a rise in strikes in the trade and service sector. Major struggles in the B.C. fishing industry and in Vancouver Island coal mining contributed to this statistical shift. In 1912 and 1913 mining accounted for 5 per cent of the strikes but 13 per cent of the strikers, while fishing constituted less than 10 per cent of the strikes but 8 per cent of the strikers. Meanwhile numerous small trade and service sector strikes composed 8 per cent of the strike total but only 1 per cent of strikers. Nevertheless, union incursions into trades and services indicates a broadening of the labour movement in this pre- war period.

A dissection of the statistics for the three largest industrial groups also shows some changes from the previous strike wave. Construction displaced manufacturing as the leader in both strikes and strikers with 36 per cent and 38 per cent compared to manufacturing's 35 and 26 per cent. Transportation trailed each with 15 per cent of strikes and 14 per cent of strikers, perhaps showing the impact of state intervention through the Conciliation Act and the Industrial Disputes Investigation Act.

The primacy of construction strikes is based not only on the 142 building trades strikes in the two years but on significant strike actions among construction workers on railroad, canal, and road projects who added 28 strikes which accounted for 45 per cent of total construction strikers. By far the most dramatic of these was the Industrial Workers of the World (IWW) strike in British Columbia on the construction sites of the Canadian Northern Railway. Some 6,000 — 7,000 railway navvies, almost all immigrants, struck for five months in the face of severe state repression and overt co-operation between the construction companies and the provincial government. At least 250 Wobblies were jailed, receiving sentences of up to 12 months for offenses such as vagrancy and infractions of the Public Health Act. Not surprisingly, in the face of such repression the strike was broken. Needless to say it lived on, commemorated in Joe Hill's "Where the Fraser River Flows."[23]

Among the urban building trade strikes of these two years one of the largest involved 2000 Winnipeg carpenters for almost six weeks in the summer of 1912. Their strike to win recognition, wages increases, and shorter hours was eventually successful.[24] Similarly, some 300 Halifax carpenters left work on 1 April 1913 and returned about a month later with a settlement largely in their favour. The historian of these carpenters notes that this strike "marked a new level of militancy and a significant broadening of perspective on the part of Local 83." He further argues, and our Winnipeg example would support his claim, that their pre-war apprenticeship in the "new rules" of monopoly capitalist society lay the groundwork for "their postwar radicalism."[25]

Interestingly, not all urban construction strikes involved skilled craftsmen and craft unions. In Ottawa in 1912 and in Hamilton in 1913 large groups of unskilled labourers, the urban equivalents of the railway navvies, struck for higher wages. In Ottawa about 1100 labourers employed on sewer projects succeeded in increasing their wages after three days of marching and demonstrating. The next year 250 Hamilton labourers, largely immigrant, working on electrical transmission lines struck for a wage increase but failed after three days which included a battle with strikebreakers.[26] Again in this case the importance lies in the suggestion that resort to strike action was spreading to workers previously uninvolved in labour activities.

In manufacturing a disaggregation of the general data suggests an intensification of the 1899–1903 pattern. In 1912 and 1913, metal trades strikes accounted for 37 per cent of all manufacturing strikes and 20 per cent of that sector's strikers; clothing and textile 25 per cent of strikes and a remarkable 50 per cent of strikers; and boot and shoe 7 and 16 per cent. The three together then represent 69 per cent of all manufacturing strikes and 86 per cent of all manufacturing strikers. One major development hidden in these statistics is the emergence of garment strikes as a major component of the textile and clothing category. Major garment strikes were fought by the United Garment Workers of America (UGWA) in Montreal in 1912 and 1913, the first involving 4,500 workers in the men's clothing industry for six weeks. The industry-wide 1912 strike succeeded in increasing wages, shortening hours, and changing pay systems and shop rules. The following year, a strike against a wage reduction at one shop involving 450 workers dragged on for five months before failing. In Hamilton in April 1913 2,000 garment workers led by the UGWA struck the city's four major clothing factories and within two weeks had won a victory. The solidarity of women workers was crucial in this victory as in the 1912 Montreal case.[27] The other major garment strike took place in Toronto in 1912 against Eaton's, the city's major department store. The strike, led by the International Ladies Garment Workers Union, quickly became a cause célèbre because of the national prominence of the firm and its Methodist owners. Originating with male sewing machine operators who refused to perform women's work (finishing) for no increase in pay, the strike was fought avowedly to save women's jobs and its Yiddish slogan translates as "We will not take morsels of bread from out sisters's mouths." Over 1,000 garment workers, about one-third women, struck in support of the 65 men. The strikers gained wide support from the labour movement and a national boycott against Eaton's enjoyed some limited success. In Montreal ILGWU workers in Eaton's shops struck in sympathy with their Toronto counterparts. Nevertheless the strike was broken after four months and the ILGWU took some years to recover in Toronto.[28] Here again the important point to note is the spread of unionism and militancy among previously unorganized sectors and specifically among immigrants and women. Also important was the concerted turn to industrial unionism by many of the craft unions, particularly in the metal trades.[29]

This process is evident as well in some of the transportation-related strikes of the period. Coal handlers on the Port Arthur docks, primarily Southern European, struck in 1912. The 250 workers won their strike but only at considerable cost because two of their Italian members received ten-year jail terms for assaulting the Chief of Police in a violent picket line altercation which left several strikers wounded and resulted in the Military being called out.[30]

Similarly street railway strikes in Port Arthur and Halifax in 1913 led to violent encounters between crowds and strikebreakers. In the Lakehead the workers lost after a month-long war with scabs and the ubiquitous Thiel detectives; the major battle in this campaign came in mid-May when a crowd overturned a street car and then attacked a police station in an attempt to free an arrested comrade. In the foray against the police station a striker was killed. In Halifax, the strike lasted only one week before a compromise settlement was reached.

Major mining struggles in Canada have played an important role in the strike waves. One example was the Vancouver Island coal strike of 1912-1914 which lasted from 16 September 1912 to 19 August 1914. Military metaphors seem inappropriate for the strike because it was actually closer to war than any other strike in this period. Violence by strikebreakers, special police, and the Canadian army was endemic and the two-year experience could only be described as an invasion of the coal towns. The miners finally returned to the mines in late summer 1914 when the outbreak of war ended the possibility of a B.C. Federation of Labor-led general strike.[31] Lest B.C. coal miners be thought to have received special treatment at the hands of the Canadian state, let us consider the parallel case of Northern Ontario gold miners who endured a seven-month struggle from mid-November 1912 to mid-June 1913 in an attempt to gain an increase in wages and shorter hours. These South Porcupine members of the Western Federation of Miners faced strikebreakers, Thiel detectives, and charges and convictions under the Industrial Disputes Investigation Act.[32]

The final, and by far the most dramatic, strike wave consisted of the labour revolt of 1917–1920. In those four years workers struck more frequently and in larger numbers than ever before in Canadian history. From 1917–1920 there were 1384 strikes involving almost 360,000 workers which expressed as percentages means those four years accounted for about 26 per cent of all Canadian strikes between 1891 and 1930 and almost 33 per cent of all strikes. As Table 18 shows this strike wave far more than its predecessors was national in scope. The previous dominance of Ontario here gives way to a more balanced nation-wide effort, although with a heavy western presence. Most evident, however, is the sectoral balance. Mining struggles played a much more significant role in the 1917–1920 strike wave, as did the impressive increase in trade and service strikes, many of them, as we shall see, involving public sector workers. Equally important is the vast increase in the other category which includes general strikes and also the spread of trade unionism and strike activity among loggers.

As in most strike waves, success fed on success. In 1917 outright workers' victories hit their highest level in the 40 year period and when combined with compromises totalled 60 per cent. The same held true for 1918, when employers' victories reached their 40 year low. In 1919 employers' victories began to climb back up, however, reaching 28 per cent, although worker gains stayed high at 54 per cent. By 1920, the wave was breaking and employers won 32 per cent outright, while workers' victories and compromises fell to 41 per cent. (See Table 13)

The literature on the events of 1917 to 1920 and especially of 1919 is huge. Moreover, I have been adding to it myself over the last few years and prefer not to repeat myself here.[33] Instead I would simply like to highlight some points that I have made previously and amplify on some others which I feel that I did not emphasize sufficiently in my previous articles.

First the 1917–1920 events in Canada were part of the same international working-class insurgency that engulfed all industrial nations in those years. The new international literature on the working-class revolt at war's end focuses on issues reflected in Canadian events. Thus James Cronin's comments about the movements' "similarity and simultaneity" applies to Canada indeed to North America, as well as to Europe.[34] In addition, as Cronin argues for Europe, the Labour revolt should be seen as continuous from the pre-war crisis. While much that was new occurred in 1917–1920, the general patterns had been amply prefigured in 1912–1913. The war contributed an intensity and a breadth to the later struggles but it did not create them.

A disaggregation of Canadian manufacturing strike data for these years demonstrates both the continuities and discontinuities. Using the same categories as before, we discover that boot and shoe almost disappeared from the strike statistics. Over the four years the industry contained only 2 per cent of the manufacturing strikes and less than 1 per cent of the strikers. Clothing and textiles, on the other hand, while nowhere near as prominent as in 1912–1913, accounted for 16 per cent of both strikes and strikers. In both industries a renewed militancy struggled for industrial unionism. Our third category, metal and shipbuilding, provides the most significant story. For here the continuities of struggle and their particular intensification owing to the war experience become clearest. The metal trades constituted 33 per cent of manufacturing strikes and 30 per cent of strikers, while its cognate industry shipbuilding added 11 per cent of strikes and 24 per cent of strikers. Workers in other manufacturing sectors who begin to show up in the data for the first time included pulp and paper (5 per cent of manufacturing strikes and strikers), rubber (2 and 3 per cent) and meat packing (2 and 4 per cent). In meat packing successful industry-wide strikes in Toronto and Montreal in 1919 set a pattern for the industry which workers in other meat packing entres fought to gain in the next two years. Here again it was new industrial unionism that won the day.[35]

In addition to the new industrial unions, which were primarily sanctioned by the AFL, trade unionism spread into other new areas. The spread of organization to increased numbers of women workers I will leave aside and the great importance of immigrant workers I have discussed elsewhere. I would note here, however, the crucial and innovative rise of public sector unionism especially at the municipal level but also among some provincial and federal workers.

Two major strikes represent two distinct manifestations of this process. The first was the month-long Winnipeg civic workers' strike of May 1918 which ended only when Borden's Minister of Labour, Senator Gideon Robertson, hurried to Winnipeg to prevent the expansion of sympathy strikes into a threatened city-wide general sympathetic strike.[36] Such discussions were led by the Winnipeg TLC but were not confined to it. The Jewish immigrant left, for example, organized a late May Help the Strikers Conference which brought together all radical elements of the Jewish community — revolutionary Marxist, Socialist-Zionist, and anarchist.[37] To end the crisis and avoid a general strike, Robertson capitulated to almost all of the civic workers' demands. In the process, he helped to cement in Winnipeg and Canadian workers' minds the efficacy of the general strike tactic. But Robertson's concession was not singular, a similar threat by the Edmonton Trades and Labour Council led to the recognition of the firemen's union in that city. In general, there was a massive expansion throughout the country of civic employees' unionism usually organized into Federal Labour Unions directly chartered by the TLC.

Federal employees also expressed massive dissatisfaction with wartime conditions. The Civil Service Federation of Canada enjoyed major growth but the story of its expansion and subsequent decline is too complicated to pursue here. Instead let us consider the second major public sector strike of 1918 namely the July 1918 national postal strike led by the Federal Association of Letter Carriers.[38] Commencing in Toronto on 22 July 1918, with at best half-hearted support from the union's national leader Alex McMordie, the strike spread across the country involving at least 20 cities and led to sympathetic walkouts by other postal workers. Supposedly settled on 15 July by McMordie, who ordered his workers back in return for a promise of a cabinet investigation, the strike continued as rank-and-file letter carriers angrily rejected the settlement. A week later Borden Cabinet Ministers Crothers and Meighen arrived in Winnipeg to negotiate a new agreement with an *ad hoc* Joint Strike Committee again in the face of a series of threatened general strikes in a number of western cities, including Winnipeg, Vancouver, and Victoria, and, significantly, by UMWA District 18. The terms of settlement included guarantees of non-discrimination against the strikers, the dismissal of all scab labour, and, amazingly, pay for the strikers for the period of the walkout.

But perhaps most alarming of all to the Canadian bourgeoisie in 1918 was the emergence of police unionism. In ten major Canadian cities TLC-affiliated police activists organized unions that year. In Ontario the provincial government set up a Royal Commission to consider the question of police unionism.[39] Only in Ottawa did civic officials quell the dissent by firing almost one-third of the force. In Toronto, Vancouver, Saint John, and Montreal, serious struggles over the question of police unionism occurred, but trade union rights won out. In Toronto, for example, despite the dire warnings of Police Magistrate Denison who remembered that during the 1886 street railway strike law and order prevailed only because "Our police force was able to keep them down." "If they had been in a union, " he concluded, "I don't suppose they would have been able to do such good work."[40] Nevertheless, Toronto Police FLU #68 gained initial recognition after a successful strike to protest the firing of 11 union leaders. Meanwhile, in Montreal a common front of some 1500 firemen and policemen struck in December. They gained victory in the aftermath of a night of rioting in which volunteer strike breakers were beaten and fire stations were occupied by crowds supporting the strikers.[41] In Vancouver the threat of a general strike after the firing of four police union leaders led to an ignominious surrender by the Chief Constable. But it was in Saint John, New Brunswick, that the degree of labour solidarity with these efforts found its most profound expression. The firing of half the force for joining a union led to a city-wide campaign organized by the labour movement to recall the police commissioners guilty of the victimization of the police unionists. The success of the recall campaign resulted in a new election in which the anti-union commissioners were defeated. These 1918 public sector successes did much to set the terms for the 1919 struggles. The extent of working-class support for the public sector workers stemmed from a combination of factors — a recognition of the generally blue-collar workers as labour, the strong World War I notions that the state was greatly indebted to the working class and should be a model employer, and finally the pervasiveness for all workers of the issues at stake in these strikes — the living wage and the recognition of the right to organize.

The brief story of the national postal strike suggests another theme which needs to be emphasized. By and large the 1917–1920, and especially 1919, insurgency was a rank-and-file revolt. In many cases, as with the letter carriers, workers simply ignored their leaders. In some cases old leaders unsympathetic to the militancy were unceremoniously dumped. For example, Arthur Puttee, a long-time Winnipeg labour leader, former lib-lab MP, and labour alderman, was removed from the editorship of *The Voice* in 1918 because of his refusal as alderman to support fully the striking civic workers. In many cities the left won control of TLCs which, of course, became the vehicle for orchestrating general and sympathetic strikes. Even where the left held control, however, leaders found themselves following rank-and-file actions in directions with which they were not always in total sympathy. This tension was especially evident among some of the Socialist Party of Canada leaders who felt the masses were not ready for actions the authorities increasingly deemed "revolutionary."

Much historical discussion of strikes, as David Montgomery has reminded us, revolves around Eric Hobsbawm's notion of workers' "learning the rules of the game" and Michelle Perrot's idea about workers' fascination "with the possibilities of the strike."[42] By 1919 Canadian workers clearly had learned the new rules that accompanied monopoly capitalism and indeed they had come to recognize that such economic organization presented them with considerable possibilities for action. They exercised those options and found themselves facing a newly united front of capital and state, both of whom, like labour, saw the outcome of the struggles of 1919–1920 as setting the pattern for the post-war world. Despite labour's new solidarities and extraordinary militancy capital triumphed. For many Canadian historians this defeat for labour has led either to liberal criticism of a state over-response or a conservative dismissal of labour's struggle as a naive and utopian "children's crusade."[43] Even the often astute Clare Pentland missed the point badly when he attributed, albeit only partially, the failure to a generation "decimated by war, exhausted by struggle, and diluted by barely literate immigrants from Europe." His argument that the "gap in capacity between bosses and workers had widened again" contains hidden assumptions almost as questionable as the ethnic chauvinism of the previous quotation.[44] But, more important, was his further and main argument that the decline of western capital in the 1920s and 1930s decimated the possibilities of working-class advance. His point about the west applies even more to the Canadian east where a process of deindustrialization evident even before the war would quicken over the next two decades. Thus, while workers had begun during World War I to act on a vision of a national labour market with national wage rates, the regional realities of Canadian capitalist development in the inter-war years would rob them of the possibility of realizing such goals. Such labour aims would reemerge during World War II. The relative quiescence of Canadian labour between the wars, of course, to some degree parallels the experience of other western nations — what Yves Lequin has termed "the great silence."[45]

But "the great silence" should not blind us to the achievements and especially the possibilities of 1919. When Sir Robert Borden, the Canadian Prime Minister of the day, composed his *Memoirs*, almost 20 years later, he noted that "In some cities there was a deliberate attempt to overthrow the existing organization of the Government and to supersede it by crude, fantastic methods founded upon absurd conceptions of what had been accomplished in Russia. It became necessary in some communities to repress revolutionary methods with a stern hand and from this I did not shrink."[46] Borden's words should be read in the same way his government's actions must be understood; they reflect the fears of a militant working class in motion and represent the harsh and rational response of the bourgeois state.[47]

III

Let us return briefly to our aggregate data simply to suggest the possibilities of a more rigourous international comparison of working-class formation. As is often the case varying methods of presenting data limits us here to two rather simplistic comparisons but from each interesting contrasts appear.

Table 19 compares the number of strikes and strikers in Britain, France, and Canada from 1891–1930. The magnitude of the struggles in Britain and France are of course far larger than in Canada but when expressed simply in percentages of strikes and strikers in the 40 year period different patterns emerge. Strikes in Britain in the 1890s played a far more prominent role than in Canada or France, while the latter countries saw higher levels than Britain in the 1901–10 decade. Canada's war and immediate post-war experience, on the other hand, resembles British experience, although Canada's statistics are the highest of the three nations. Canadian strikes in the 1920s resembled Britain in number of strikes but fell behind in strikers, probably owing to the General Strike. Both Canada and Britain trailed France in strikes. Of course, we should remember that we are only comparing patterns here not actual experiences. If we look at the actual numbers in Table 19A we should note that while France had by far the most strikes of the three countries, Britain had the largest.

Table 20 presents evidence on Canadian/American comparisons over the longer period, 1891–1950. As can be readily seen, Canada trailed in frequency in every decade except the 1920s and in size in every decade except the 1900s. Canada's low figures in the 1890s for frequency in comparison to the U.S. match the similar contrast with Britain and France and emphasize, I think, the relative immaturity of the national Canadian working-class experience of the 1890s. In subsequent decades, however, that gap was closed and Canadian strike frequency never fell below two-thirds of the American. In size Canadian strikes in the 1920s and 1930s ran about one-half of the American compared to four-fifths in the 1890s and about three-quarters in the 1910s and 1940s.

The Canadian case, then, while showing broad similarities with the American (although we should add that those similarities have been breaking down since 1960), provides further support for the notion that questions of national "exceptionalism" are largely beside the point.[48] Each national working class experience must be studied historically and understood in light of contrasting experiences, not held up against a reified model, which never existed except in the minds of Second International theorists.

Notes

I would like to acknowledge especially the research assistance of Douglas Cruikshank. In addition, my thanks for additional research aid to Jessie Chisholm and Robert Hong. For aid with graphs and figures, my thanks to Robert Hong and Susan Laskin. This project has been supported by funds from the Historical Atlas of Canada, the Social Sciences and Humanities Research Council of Canada, and the Institute for Social and Economic Research at Memorial University.

1 To cite only their major strike monographs: Edward Shorter and Charles Tilly, *Strikes in France, 1830–1968* (Cambridge 1974); James Cronin, *Industrial Conflict in Modern Britain* (London 1979); and P. K. Edwards, *Strikes in the United States, 1881–1974* (Oxford 1981). Indeed this entire project is indebted to their stimulating and innovative reconstructions of their respective national strike stories, especially to their methods and techniques.

2 Douglas Cruickshank and Gregory S. Kealey, "Strikes in Canada, 1891–1950," *Labour/Le Travail*, 20 (1987).

3 David Montgomery, "Strikes in Nineteenth-Century America," *Social Science History*, 4 (1980), 81–104.

4 On the relatively unstudied role of navvies, see Ruth Bleasdale, "Unskilled Labourers on Canadian Canals and Railways, 1840 — 1880," forthcoming.

5 This argument parallels that made by Montgomery for the U.S. and Cronin for England. See Montgomery, "Nineteenth-Century Strikes," 86- 88 and Cronin, *Industrial Conflict*, ch. 1 and 3.

6 Date on strikes and riots before 1891 are drawn from Bryan Palmer, "Labour Protest and Organization in Nineteenth-Century Canada, 1820- 1890," *Labour/Le Travail*, 20 (1987). Palmer's synthesis for the Historical Atlas of Canada, Volume 2, is in turn based on an extensive literature on Canada's nineteenth-century working-class experience. For Ontario, for example, see Bryan Palmer, *A Culture in Conflict* (Montreal 1979); Gregory S. Kealey, *Toronto Workers Respond to Industrial Capitalism* (Toronto 1980); and Palmer and Kealey, *"Dreaming of What Might Be": The Knights of Labor in Ontario* (NY 1982).

7 Cronin, *Industrial Conflict*, esp. ch. 3–5, but *passim*; Shorter and Tilly, *Strikes in France*, ch. 5.

8 For Tilly a strike wave occurs "when both the number of strikes and the number of strikers in a given year exceed the means of the previous five years by more than 50 per cent." Tilly and Shorter, *Strikes in France*, 106–7.

9 What follows draws on G.S. Kealey, "The Structure of Canadian Working-Class History" in W. J. C. Cherwinski and Kealey, eds., *Lectures in Canadian Labour and Working-Class History* (St. John's 1985) and Craig Heron and Robert Storey, "On the Job in Canada," in their *On the Job* (Montreal 1986).

10 David Montgomery, *Workers Control in America* (New York 1979); David Brody, *Workers in Industrial America* (New York 1980); and David M. Gordon, Richard Edwards, and Michael Reich, *Segmented Work, Divided Workers: The historical transformation of labor in the United States* (New York, 1982). Finally for skeptics who like their economic history undiluted, see M. C. Urquhart, "New Estimates of Gross National Product, Canada, 1870–1926: Some Implications for Canadian Development," Queen's University Institute for Economic Research, Discussion Paper, No. 586.

11 Palmer, *A Culture in Conflict*; Kealey, *Toronto Workers*; David Frank, "The Cape Breton Coal Miners, 1917–1926," Ph.D., Dalhousie, 1979; Nolan Reilly, "Emergence of Class Consciousness in Industrial Nova Scotia: Amherst, 1891–1925," Ph.D., Dalhousie, 1983; Allen Seager, "The Proletariat in Wild Rose Country: The Alberta Coal Miners, 1905–1945," Ph.D., York, 1982; Craig Heron, "Working-Class Hamilton, 1895–1930," Ph.D., Dalhousie, 1981; Wayne Roberts, "Studies in the Toronto Labour Movement," Ph.D., University of Toronto, 1978; Robert Storey, "Workers, Unions, and Steel: The Shaping of the Hamilton Working Class, 1935–1948," Ph.D., Toronto, 1982.

12 Ian McKay, "Strikes in the Maritimes, 1901–1914," *Acadiensis*, 13 (1983); Craig Heron and Bryan Palmer, "Through the Prism of the Strike: Industrial

Conflict in Southern Ontario, 1901–1914, " *Canadian Historical Review*, 57 (1977), 423–58; Jacques Rouillard, "Le militantisme des travailleurs au Québec et en Ontario niveau de syndicalisation et mouvement de grèves (1900–1980), " *Revue d'histoire de l'Amérique française*, 37 (1983), 201–25; and James Thwaites, "La grève au Québec: Une analyse quantitative exploratoire portant sur la période 1896–1915, " *Labour/Le Travail*, 14 (1984), 183–204.

13 David Jay Bercuson, "Labour Radicalism and the Western Industrial Frontier, " *Canadian Historical Review*, 58 (1977), 154–75.

14 In addition to the above, see also his *Confrontation at Winnipeg* (Montreal 1974) and *Fools and Wisemen* (Toronto 1978). Other similar claims are made in Ross McCormack, *Reformers, Rebels and Revolutionaries* (Toronto 1977) and H.C. Pentland, "The Western Canadian Labour Movement, 1847–1919, " *Canadian Journal of Political and Social Theory*, 3 (1979), 53–78.

15 Jessie Chisholm, "Strikes in St. John's, 1890–1914, " unpublished paper, Memorial University, 1987. This paper is part of Chisholm's ongoing doctoral research on the St. John's working class before World War I.

16 On military and to the civil power see Desmond Morton, "Aid to the civil power: the Canadian militia in support of social order, " *Canadian Historical Review*, 51 (1970), 407–25; Don MacGillivray, "Military aid to the civil power: the Cape Breton experience in the 1920's, " *Acadiensis*, 3 (1974), 45–64; Major J.J.B. Pariseau, *Disorders, Strikes, and Disasters: Military Aid to the Civil Power in Canada, 1867–1933* (Ottawa 1973); and his "Forces armées et maintien de l'ordre au Canada 1867–1967: un siècle d'aide au pouvoir civil, " thèse présentée pour obtenir le doctorat cycle, Université Paul Valéry III, Montpelier, 1981.

17 For more detailed accounts of these strikes see: Allen Seager, "Socialists and Workers: The Western Canadian Coal Miners, 1900–21, " *Labour/Le Travail*, 16 (1985), 23–59; Paul Phillips, *No Power Greater — A Century of Labour in BC* (Vancouver 1967); Stuart Jamieson, *Times of Trouble: Labour Unrest and Industrial Conflict in Canada, 1900–66* (Ottawa 1968); J. Hugh Tuck, "The United Brotherhood of Railway Employees in Western Canada, 1898–1905, " *Labour/Le Travail*, 11 (1983), 63–88. For the broader national response, see Robert Babcock, *Gompers in Canada* (Toronto 1974) and Paul Craven, *An Impartial Umpire: Industrial Relations and the Canadian State, 1900–1911* (Toronto 1980).

18 On the Halifax Waterfront, see Ian McKay, "Class Struggle and Merchant Capital: Labourers on the Halifax Waterfront, 1850–1902" in Bryan Palmer, ed. *The Character of Class Struggle* (Toronto 1986).

19 For a study of the London street railway strike, see Bryan Palmer, "'Give us the road and we will run it:' The Social and Cultural Matrix of an Emerging Labour Movement, " in G. S. Kealey and Peter Warrian, eds. *Essays in Canadian Working-Class History* (Toronto 1976) and Peter Lambly, "Working Conditions and Industrial Relations on Canada's Street Railways, 1900–1920, " M.A., Dalhousie University, 1983.

20 Craig Heron, "The Crisis of the Craftsman: Hamilton Metal Workers in the Early Twentieth Century" and Wayne Roberts, "Toronto Metal Workers and the Second Industrial Revolution, 1889–1914, " *Labour/Le Travail*, 6 (1980), 7–48, 49–72.

21 *Globe* (Toronto), 21 February, 1 March, 18 July, 26,27, 29, 30,31 October 1900; *Gazette* (Montreal), 25,26,27 October 1900; and *Star* (Montreal), 22,23 February, and 14,16 July 1900. See also Jacques Rouillard, *Les travailleurs du coton au Québec, 1900–1915* (Montréal 1974), 107–29.

22 For discussions of building trade workers see Wayne Roberts, "Artisans, Aristocrats and Handymen: Politics and Trade Unionism among Toronto Skilled Building Trades Workers, 1896–1914, " *Labour/Le Travail*, 1 (1976), 92–121 and Ian McKay, *The Craft Transformed: An Essay on the Carpenters of Halifax, 1885–1985* (Halifax 1985).

23 On this strike, see A. Ross McCormack, "Wobblies and Blanket- stiffs: The Constituency of the IWW in Western Canada, " in Cherwinski and Kealey, *Lectures* and his "The Industrial Workers of the World in Western Canada, 1905–1914, " *Historical Papers* (1975), 167–90.

24 *Voice* (Winnipeg), 5, 12 July 1912; NAC, RG37, vol. 300, file 3531.

25 McKay, *The Craft Transformed*, 54–63.

26 *Ottawa Citizen*, 13 July 1912; *Ottawa Journal*, 10 July 1912; *Stratford Herald*, 20 September 1913.

27 Mercedes Steedman, "Skill and Gender in the Canadian Clothing Industry, 1890–1940" in Heron and Storey, eds., *On the Job*, 152–76.

28 Ruth Frager, "Sewing Solidarity: The Eaton's Strike of 1912, " *Canadian Woman Studies*, 7 (1986), 96–8.

29 Roberts, "Toronto Metal Workers, " 71–2.

30 Jean Morrison, "Ethnicity and Violence: The Lakehead Freight Handlers Before World War I" in Kealey and Warrian, *Essays*, 143–60.

31 P.G. Silverman, "Aid of the Civil Power: The Nanaimo Coal Miners' Strike, 1912–1914, " *Canadian Defence Quarterly*, 4 (1974), 16–52; Lynn Bowen, *Boss Whistle: The Coal Miners of Vancouver Island Remember* (Lantzville, BC 1982), 131–98.

32 NAC, RG27, vol. 300, file 3618 and vol. 302, file 13 (90) A.

33 Gregory S. Kealey, "1919: The Canadian Labour Revolt, ", *Labour/Le Travail*, 13 (1984), 11–44 and the "The State, the Foreign-Language Press, and the Canadian Labour Revolt of 1917–1920, " in Christiane Harzig and Dirk Hoerder, eds. *The Press of Labour Migrants in Europe and North America, 1880s–1930s* (Bremen 1985).

34 James Cronin, "Labour Insurgency and Class Formation: Comparative Perspectives on the Crisis of 1917–1920 in Europe, " *Social Science History*, 4 (1980), 125–52. See also James Cronin and Carmen Sirianni, eds., *Work, Community and Power: The Experience of Labor in Europe and North America, 1900–1925* (Philadelphia 1983). For a third North American case, see Peter McInnis, "Newfoundland Labour and World War I: The Emergence of the Newfoundland Industrial Workers' Association, " M.A., Memorial University of Newfoundland, 1987.

35 J.T. Montague, "Trade Unionism in the Canadian Meat Packing Industry, " Ph.D., University of Toronto, 1950, 31–8 and George Sayers Bain, "The United Packinghouse, Food and Allied Workers, ", M.A., University of Manitoba, 1964, 35–67.

36 A.E. Johnson, "The Strikes in Winnipeg in May 1918. The Prelude to 1919?, " M.A., University of Manitoba, 1978.

37 R. Usiskin, "Toward a Theoretical Reformulation of the Relationship Between Political Ideology, Social Class, & Ethnicity: A Case Study of the Winnipeg Jewish Radical Community, 1905–1920, " M.A., University of Winnipeg, 1978, esp. ch.5, and her "The Winnipeg Jewish Radical Community: Its Early Formation, 1905–1918, " in *Jewish Life and Times. A Collection of Essays* (Winnipeg 1983), 155–68.

38 William Doherty, "Slaves of the Lamp: A History of the Staff Association

Movement in the Canadian Civil Service, 1860–1924, " unpublished mss., esp.
ch.9. See also NAC, Post Office Papers, RG 3, vol. 646, file 96853, "List of
Offices Affected by the 1918 Postal Strike." See also Anthony Thomson, "'The
Large and Generous View': The Debate on Labour Affiliation in the Canadian
Civil Service, 1918- 1928, " *Labour/Le Travail*, 2 (1977), 108–36.

39 Ontario, Royal Commission on Police Matters, *Report*, 1919.

40 Jim Naylor, "Toronto, 1919, " *Historical Papers* (1986), 33- 55.

41 G. Ewen, "La contestation à Montréal en 1919, " *Histoire des travailleurs
québécois. Bulletin RCHTQ*, 36 (1986), 37–62.

42 Montgomery, "Nineteenth-Century Strikes;" for Hobsbawm, see his
"Economic Fluctuations and Some Social Movements" and "Customs, Wages
and Workload" in *Labouring Men* (London 1964); for Perrot, see her magisterial
Les ouvriers en grève: France 1871–1890 (Paris 1974).

43 D.C. Masters, *The Winnipeg General Strike* (Toronto 1950); David Bercuson,
Confrontation at Winnipeg (Montreal 1974), 188.

44 H. Clare Pentland, "The Western Canadian Labour Movement, 1897–1919, "
Canadian Journal of Political and Social Theory, 3 (1979), 53–78.

45 Yves Lequin, "Social Structures and Shared Beliefs: Four Worker
Communities in the Second Industrialization, " *International Labor and Working-
Class History*, 22 (1982), 1–17.

46 Sir Robert Borden, *Memoirs* (Toronto 1938), II, 972.

47 On state repression and the creation of a new security branch see Kealey, and
S.W. Horral, "The Royal Northwest Mounted Police and Labour Unrest in
Western Canada, 1919, " *Canadian Historical Review*, 61 (1980), 169–90.

48 Ira Katznelson and Aristide R. Zolberg, eds., *Working-Class Formation:
Nineteenth-Century Patterns in Western Europe and the United States* (Princeton
1986), esp. 3–41, 397–455. See also Sean Wilenz, "Against Exceptionalism:
Class Consciousness and the American Labour Movement, " *International Labor
and Working-Class History*, 26 (1984), 1–24, and responses in 26 (1984), 25–36; 27
(1985), 35–8; and 28 (1985), 46–55.

Table 1. Strike Estimates by Province, 1891–1900

	B.C.		Man.		Ont.		Que.		N.B.		N.S.		Interprov.		Total	
	A	B	A	B	A	B	A	B	A	B	A	B	A	B	A	B
1891	7	448	2	60	15	205	4	562	1		8	172	2	2550	39	3997
1892	6	1030	1		24	995	3	175			4	1230	1	450	40	3880
1893	11	3303	2	305	20	902	7	542	4	85					44	5137
1894	6	156	4	345	11	543	8	2617	6	270	4	2300			39	6231
1895	2		1	20	19	1130	8	946	6	245	3	1000			39	3341
1896	5	2500	2	10	17	1690	2	160	3	125	1	250	1	800	31	5535
1897	4		1		16	831	8	430			3	826			34	2097
1898	5	145	2	8	26	3327	16	268			1	22	3	3000	50	3770
1899	12	5442	9	841	49	3291	23	2899	1		5	544	1	800	102	16017
1900	19	8636	1	7	65	3356	23	14397		725	32	6699	8	7600	112	27551
Total	77	21660	25	1596	262	16270	102	22996	21	725	32	6699	8	7600	530	77556

A = Number of Strikes in Progress
B = Number of Workers Involved
Note: The Northwest Territories have been deleted from the above because there was only 1 strike in 1892, and 2 in 1897 involving 10 workers for one day. Prince Edward Island apparently was strike-free in the 1890s. The Territories are included in the total.

Table 2. Strike Estimates by Province, 1901–1930

Year	B.C. A	B.C. B	Alta. A	Alta. B	Sask. A	Sask. B	Man. A	Man. B	Ont. A	Ont. B	Que. A	Que. B	N.B. A	N.B. B	P.E.I. A	P.E.I. B	N.S. A	N.S. B	Total A	Total B
1901	13	9394	1	90			7	512	62	3467	29	3273	7	124			11	2354	130	24124
1902	16	598	7	303			11	400	79	5397	30	4243	18	408	2		13	3176	170	14359
1903	30	8874	2	28			8	857	115	9587	39	14852	18	930		47	13	2717	231	38520
1904	4	899	3	400			8	151	64	3923	35	3312	12	16			17	4477	144	14006
1905	15	3266	15	1559	1	20	13	497	45	1919	23	1797	13	1414	1		18	3123	133	12936
1906	20	2039	12	2883	1	4	10	4445	78	6371	33	6146	13	601	2		18	2647	190	23812
1907	22	3747	4	554	3	98	12	1177	98	11594	46	7957	21	1653			15	5474	229	34683
1908	7	3122	11	2763	6	200	1	16	35	2567	26	9784	11	1472			6	377	97	26092
1909	12	1465	12	911	4	218	9	1572	45	2833	16	3057	7	105			13	6673	116	18686
1910	15	964			6	344	16	1231	64	6416	26	6344	6	150			9	2903	156	22363
Total	**154**	**34368**	**67**	**9491**	**21**	**884**	**95**	**10858**	**685**	**54074**	**303**	**60765**	**126**	**6873**	**5**	**47**	**133**	**33921**	**1596**	**229581**
1911	17	9304	16	6275	2	2310	10	644	71	4898	30	6515	14	188	1		7	1335	167	29459
1912	22	12173	23	3274	19	258	13	2972	100	13157	32	6996	21	903	1	26	9	243	242	43104
1913	25	13000	15	987	10	53	6	1138	114	13128	31	7810	20	1170			12	2763	234	41004
1914	14	2252	8	860	4	12	5	168	44	1957	15	4165	3	230			5	196	99	9911
1915	13	1587	8	851	3		7	121	31	1864	14	2965	3	135			5	3945	86	11480
1916	21	6381	24	6125	8	455	16	1130	75	6300	28	4415	6	325			7	1274	166	26971
1917	55	15075	53	12013	6	201	18	2264	68	8295	31	9246	5	97			18	1415	218	50327
1918	46	16371	29	7812	10	456	20	9062	112	11813	28	4782	11	3324	1	270	18	23635	305	82573
1919	73	22008	39	12534	13	2351	16	22530	158	41260	100	39530	19	4068			19	3778	427	149309
1920	124	10456	8	6323	4	100	5	392	152	20341	79	15324	15	1448	1	7	39	21133	457	76624
Total	**410**	**108607**	**223**	**57054**	**79**	**6196**	**116**	**40421**	**925**	**123013**	**388**	**101748**	**117**	**11888**	**4**	**303**	**129**	**59717**	**2401**	**520762**
1921	37	2849	11	786	11	234	10	868	79	11745	29	4993	13	1629	1	9	13	1041	208	28398
1922	15	3104	29	9669	3	73	6	464	34	3615	19	10904	3	88	1	50	9	15825	118	43792
1923	8	2947	16	4291	2	38	1	23	27	2327	25	4641	2	287			17	19998	97	34538
1924	9	4400	10	7118	1		1	60	18	1287	25	5850	1	57			9	12278	75	34316
1925	15	2918	19	6181			4	124	29	1621	24	4059					4	11574	96	29027
1926	16	1350	3	445	3	94	2	278	27	2643	17	10924					11	7379	85	23849
1927	9	815	5	765	2	115	2	75	25	3511	13	1022	4	705	1	75	16	15896	75	22303
1928	10	2671	11	2174			4	862	55	3773	12	3531	1	25	1	100	12	3866	107	17715
1929	15	691	4	324	1	56	5	144	47	5596	16	3233	1	5			13	2990	105	13120
1930	8	266	5	174	2	95	2		24	4036	13	2560	4	186			18	7050	74	14367
Total	**142**	**22011**	**113**	**31900**	**26**	**729**	**37**	**2898**	**365**	**40154**	**193**	**51717**	**29**	**2982**	**4**	**234**	**122**	**98396**	**1040**	**261425**

A = Number of Strikes in Progress
B = Number of Workers Involved
Note: Includes Interprovincial strikes in totals which are not shown here.

Table 3. Strike Estimates by Industry, 1891–1900

	Fishing & Trapping A	B	Coal A	B	Mining Other A	B	Mfrg. A	B	Const. A	B	Transp. & Pub. Util. A	B	Service A	B	Total A	B
1891	1		1	400			17	3291	15	246	5	60	2	22	39	3997
1892			1	1000			25	1122	9	1066	3	670	1	7	40	3880
1893	1	1600	5	1650			21	853	9	177	7	850	2	31	44	5137
1894	1		4	2300			23	1420	4	2100	5	380	3	112	39	6231
1895			3	1000	2		15	791	13	630	3	808			31	3341
1896	2	2500	1	250	2		13	646	7	1018	6	1121	2	32	34	5535
1897	2		1	800			11	179	14	531	4	555	3	63	50	2097
1898	1	2500			4	2730	33	2419	5	160	9	1128	2	12	54	3770
1899	2	6000	1	100	1	2000	54	4908	16	1395	24	4372	4	85	102	16017
1900			6	320			57	15276	27	1449	14	2342			112	27551
Total	10	12600	23	7880	9	4730	269	30905	119	8772	80	12286	19	364	530	77556

A = Number of Strikes in Progress
B = Number of Workers Involved
Note: The categories logging with only one strike involving 19 workers for one day, trade and other, each with no strikes have been deleted. Logging is included in the total.

Table 4. Strike Estimates by Industry, 1901–1930

Year	Logging		Mining Coal		Mining Other		Mfrg.		Const.		Trans. & Pub. Util.		Trade & Serv.		Total	
	A	B	A	B	A	B	A	B	A	B	A	B	A	B	A	B
1901	2	100	4	1760	4	1125	73	4919	20	2596	19	5576	6	48	130	24124
1902	1	30	5	2010			79	3875	43	3479	30	4816	11	119	170	14359
1903			9	5410	3	299	102	12219	68	7275	40	8893	8	324	231	38520
1904			8	2424	2	360	74	5412	32	3529	14	1295	12	116	144	14006
1905			11	5564	5	281	61	2431	33	1803	15	1843	6	164	133	12936
1906			15	4549	4	215	92	8163	46	8273	28	2554	5	58	190	23812
1907			14	8990	5	3119	98	9338	63	5876	33	6441	12	538	229	34683
1908			8	3541	3	408	43	10304	26	3269	13	8560	4	10	97	26092
1909			17	9143	2	490	41	2851	31	3241	19	1750	3	40	116	18686
1910			5	2950	4	439	64	6889	51	7473	20	4545	11	67	156	22363
Total	3	130	96	46341	32	6736	727	66401	413	46814	231	46273	78	1484	1596	229581
1911	1	33	7	9890	3	104	65	5345	52	8655	30	4974	10	491	167	29459
1912			6	2258	6	2058	78	9553	94	20875	39	7012	17	668	242	43104
1913			5	4837	6	2008	88	12427	76	10792	34	4468	22	252	234	41004
1914			3	2500	2	75	39	4887	37	2069	8	253	9	127	99	9911
1915			9	2753	3	2700	42	4307	10	241	10	1340	12	139	86	11480
1916			10	11270	3	2500	71	7539	24	1632	43	3183	14	847	166	26971
1917			22	17379	6	2310	100	17899	36	2456	39	9470	14	813	218	50327
1918			49	23623	3	1663	122	29130	30	1556	58	18248	39	8196	305	82573
1919	32	2741	22	10070	10	3498	185	58073	70	14708	40	12634	52	3175	427	149309
1920	66	3012	48	28136	14	2080	176	24291	73	10109	34	6727	43	2150	457	76624
Total	100	5786	181	112716	56	19023	966	173451	502	73093	335	68309	232	16858	2401	520762
1921	6	435	10	1456	5	189	116	19728	44	3990	11	1172	12	738	208	28398
1922	3	250	26	26475			38	10397	26	1870	12	3640	10	175	118	43792
1923	2	437	24	20844	5	1906	35	7698	15	1002	15	2572	8	79	97	34538
1924	1	1800	16	21201			30	6818	16	1049	8	133	8	2742	75	34316
1925			17	18672			48	7648	17	1499	3	131	6	86	96	29027
1926	5	1750	16	8445	1	11	40	11872	16	1208	5	515	3	24	85	23849
1927	2	770	20	16653	1	35	19	930	25	3242	4	326	4	82	75	22303
1928	5	1006	15	5033			48	5557	31	4334	4	132	4	153	107	17715
1929	3	1075	10	3049	2	70	45	2912	33	5689	3	247	5	67	105	13120
1930	2	170	15	6228			25	5497	20	1367	4	296	6	109	74	14367
Total	29	7693	169	128056	14	2211	444	79057	243	25250	69	9164	62	4255	1040	261425

A = Number of Strikes in Progress
B = Number of Workers Involved
Note: Categories Fishing, other, and interindustry have been deleted for purposes of simplification. Fishing accounted for 32 strikes, other 15, and interindustry 13. These are included in total.

Table 5. Canadian Strikes by Region, 1815-1890

Years	West	Ontario	Quebec	Matitimes	Total
1815-1859	2	64	53	13	132
1860-1879	6	134	84	52	276
1880-1890	28	253	96	48	425
Total	36	451	233	113	833

Table 6. Canadian Strikes by Region, 1815-1950

| | Percentage of Total Strikes[1] | | | |
	West	Ontario	Quebec	East
1815-1890	4.0	54.0	20.0	14.0
1891-1900	19.2	49.4	19.2	9.9
1901-1910	21.1	42.9	18.9	16.5
1911-1920	34.5	38.5	16.2	10.4
1921-1930	30.6	35.1	18.6	14.9
1931-1940	25.2	41.5	14.3	18.5
1941-1950	19.9	36.0	23.2	19.6

[1]Does not always total 100 per cent because of deletion of Yukon, Northwest Territories, and Interprovincial (except coal mining) strikes.

Table 7. Strikes in Newfoundland, 1890-1914[1]

Year	Number of Strikes	Year	Number of Strikes
1890	5	1901	4
1891	6	1902	27
1892	2	1903	19
1893	6	1904	23
1894	0	1905	11
1895	5	1906	11
1896	7	1907	23
1897	5	1908	4
1898	4	1909	5
1899	8	1910	7
1900	11	(1901-1910)	(134)
(1891-1900)	(54)	1911	10
		1912	9
		1913	7
		1914	1
		Total	220

[1]My thanks to Jessie Chisholm for the use of this data, which is drawn from her ongoing doctoral research at Memorial on the "St. John's Working Class, 1890-1914."

Table 8. Provincial Strike Shapes, 1891-1930[1]

Province and Decade	Frequency (Depth[3])	Dimensions Sizes[2] (Height[4])	Durations[2] (Width[5])
Nova Scotia			
1890[6]	32	258	25
1900s	119	369	25
1910s	99	642	19
1920s	89	834	26
Prince Edward Island			
1890s	—	—	—
1900s	41	25	15
1910s	32	75	3
1920s	30	58	15
New Brunswick			
1890s	35	56	8
1900s	186	86	21
1910s	147	154	23
1920s	32	103	24
Quebec			
1890s	36	354	12
1900s	81	223	18
1910s	77	331	20
1920s	29	281	40
Ontario			
1890s	63	88	33
1900s	124	95	23
1910s	124	165	21
1920s	40	118	30
Manitoba			
1890s	87	94	17
1900s	136	151	23
1910s	98	454	14
1920s	24	88	32
Saskatchewan			
1890s	—	—	—
1900s	55	68	13
1910s	94	113	13
1920s	23	33	19
Alberta			
1890s	—	—	—
1900s	161	176	20
1910s	244	303	14
1920s	94	298	25
British Columbia			
1890s	143	516	26
1900s	127	315	31
1910s	223	433	24
1920s	64	180	27
Canada			
1890s	55	218	25
1900s	115	180	23
1910s	123	286	20
1920s	43	270	30

[1]Average annual frequency, size, and duration of strikes in progress.
[2]Estimates of average size and duration are based only on strikes for which striker and striker days data was obtained.
[3]Total number of strikes per million non-agricultural employees.
[4]Number of strikers per strike.
[5]Average duration of strikes.
[6]1891-1900, 1901-1910, 1911-1920, 1921-1930.

Table 9. Provincial Ranking in Strike Statistics, 1891-1930

Frequency	First		Second		Third		Canada
1891-1900	BC	143	Man	87	Ont	63	55
1901-1910	NB	186	Alta	161	Man	135	115
1911-1920	Alta	243	BC	223	NB	147	123
1921-1930	Alta	94	NS	89	BC	64	43
Size							
1891-1900	BC	515	Que	353	NS	257	218
1901-1910	NS	369	BC	315	Que	222	180
1911-1920	NS	642	Man	454	BC	432	286
1921-1930	NS	834	Alta	298	Que	281	270
Duration							
1891-1900	Ont	33	BC	26	NS	25	25
1901-1910	BC	31	NS	25	Ont	23	23
1911-1920	BC	24	NB	23	Ont	21	20
1921-1930	Que	40	Man	32	Ont	30	30

Table 10. Industrial Strike Shapes, 1911-1930[1]

Industry	Frequency (Depth)		Sizes (Height)		Duration (Width)	
	1911-20	1921-30	1911-20	1921-30	1911-20	1921-30
Mining	479	301	646	749	20	15
Manufacturing	193	75	225	191	24	45
Construction	262	114	201	111	19	17
Transportation & Pub. Utilities	151	23	272	161	11	23
Service & Pub. Administration	41	10	109	78	14	22

[1]Average annual frequency, size, and duration of strikes in progress.
[2]Estimates of average size and duration are based only on strikes for which striker and striker days data was obtained.

Table 11. Strike Issues, 1891-1930[1]

Issues				Percentage of Total Issues						
	1891	1892	1893	1894	1895	1896	1897	1898	1899	1900
Earnings										
For change	26	25	24	17	27	18	36	29	42	39
Against change	3	20	22	40	18	21	15	8	9	6
Working Conditions										
Hours	16	15	—	2	9	5	13	8	3	8
Other	24	20	38	27	32	20	20	25	23	19
Unionism	18	15	8	6	7	23	8	25	18	22
Other & Indefinite	13	5	8	8	7	13	8	5	6	6

Issues				Percentage of Total Issues						
	1901	1902	1903	1904	1905	1906	1907	1908	1909	1910
Earnings										
For change	39	39	40	35	35	38	43	25	44	38
Against change	8	3	3	6	5	2	4	23	8	5
Working Conditions										
Hours	13	15	13	12	11	15	12	10	5	9
Other	24	13	16	26	26	16	16	23	18	23
Unionism	11	20	20	18	16	21	20	10	21	15
Other & Indefinite	5	10	8	3	7	8	5	9	3	10

Issues				Percentage of Total Issues						
	1911	1912	1913	1914	1915	1916	1917	1918	1919	1920
Earnings										
For change	40	41	44	23	29	50	46	44	39	45
Against change	5	3	6	24	15	6	4	3	3	3
Working Conditions										
Hours	10	16	13	4	4	9	14	12	26	15
Other	16	18	13	19	26	16	13	15	10	16
Unionism	22	16	15	23	20	17	18	16	14	16
Other & Indefinite	7	6	9	7	6	2	5	10	8	5

Issues				Percentage of Total Issues						
	1921	1922	1923	1924	1925	1926	1927	1928	1929	1930
Earnings										
For change	12	18	37	29	23	32	32	33	41	33
Against change	41	38	8	16	20	8	4	8	3	15
Working Conditions										
Hours	16	7	9	11	9	12	11	5	6	8
Other	13	12	19	23	19	21	23	23	31	17
Unionism	15	21	20	18	27	23	24	25	16	25
Other & Indefinite	3	4	7	3	2	4	6	6	3	2

[1]Issues articulated at the beginning of each strike. More than one issue for some strikes.

Table 12. Methods of Strike Settlement, 1891-1930

Methods	Percentages of Total Strikes									
	1891	1892	1893	1894	1895	1896	1897	1898	1899	1900
Negotiations	23	35	29	26	23	32	23	38	37	35
Third Party	5	7	5	3	10	3	9	2	3	10
Return of Workers	15	13	23	28	36	20	15	14	3	19
Replacement of Workers	18	13	18	10	5	19	18	18	22	11
Indefinite	39	32	25	33	26	26	35	28	30	25

Methods	Percentages of Total Strikes									
	1901	1902	1903	1904	1905	1906	1907	1908	1909	1910
Negotiations	40	38	37	40	43	46	43	28	29	38
Third Party	12	12	10	8	2	4	7	5	7	7
Return of Workers	12	9	13	17	10	14	12	27	15	15
Replacement of Workers	17	11	11	13	24	22	15	24	22	16
Indefinite	19	30	29	22	21	15	23	16	27	24

Methods	Percentages of Total Strikes									
	1911	1912	1913	1914	1915	1916	1917	1918	1919	1920
Negotiations	33	47	37	29	39	43	43	41	49	38
Third Party	7	6	6	10	13	13	18	23	13	12
Return of Workers	14	9	14	12	12	13	11	13	13	13
Replacement of Workers	16	15	15	22	20	11	7	6	8	13
Indefinite	30	23	28	27	16	20	21	17	17	24

Methods	Percentages of Total Strikes									
	1921	1922	1923	1924	1925	1926	1927	1928	1929	1930
Negotiations	37	39	40	41	57	46	50	47	41	41
Third Party	10	6	13	15	9	7	9	12	14	13
Return of Workers	14	16	20	25	6	12	20	18	17	19
Replacement of Workers	18	19	15	15	16	23	12	16	18	20
Indefinite	21	20	12	4	12	12	9	7	10	7

Table 13. Strike Results, 1891-1930

Results	Percentage of Total Strikes									
	1891	1892	1893	1894	1895	1896	1897	1898	1899	1900
Workers' Favour	18	28	16	13	8	19	6	8	23	23
Compromise	10	7	9	10	18	16	21	22	12	16
Employers' Favour	33	30	52	44	38	42	38	38	32	31
Indefinite	39	35	23	33	36	23	35	32	33	30

Results	Percentage of Total Strikes									
	1901	1902	1903	1904	1905	1906	1907	1908	1909	1910
Workers' Favour	27	35	34	28	25	24	21	20	19	19
Compromise	23	21	21	20	14	21	26	10	18	16
Employers' Favour	30	19	23	31	36	37	30	53	38	37
Indefinite	20	25	22	21	25	18	23	17	24	28

Results	Percentage of Total Strikes									
	1911	1912	1913	1914	1915	1916	1917	1918	1919	1920
Workers' Favour	15	29	21	16	21	26	40	34	30	18
Compromise	17	23	21	16	21	30	20	26	24	23
Employers' Favour	33	27	29	35	35	25	19	16	28	32
Indefinite	35	21	29	33	23	19	21	24	18	27

Results	Percentage of Total Strikes									
	1921	1922	1923	1924	1925	1926	1927	1928	1929	1930
Workers' Favour	16	15	26	16	36	26	31	28	30	27
Compromise	13	22	19	23	23	22	21	26	24	24
Employers' Favour	47	43	42	47	28	37	37	37	35	43
Indefinite	24	20	13	14	13	15	11	9	11	6

Table 14. Strikes with collective violence[1] and military intervention,[2] 1891-1930

Decade	Percentage of total strikes with collective violence	Percentage of total strikes with military intervention
1891-1900	4.5	1.0
1901-1910	2.6	.9
1911-1920	2.1	.4
1921-1930	2.9	.5
1891-1930	2.6	.6

[1]Strikes in which a group of 50 or more acted together and attempted to seize or damage persons or objects not belonging to itself.
[2]Military aid to the civil power.

Table 15. Strikes with collective violence and military intervention by industry, 1891-1930

Industry	Percentage of total strikes with collective violence	Percentage of total strikes with military intervention
Fishing & trapping	9.8	2.4
Mining	4.5	1.1
Manufacturing-Total	1.7	.4
Manuf.-Leather & textile	2.4	.4
Manuf.-Wood	2.9	1.1
Manuf.-Metal & ships	1.5	.4
Construction	1.4	.2
Transport. & Pub. Util.-Total	6.7	1.7
T.& P.U.-Steam Railway	6.3	1.0
T.& P.U.-Electric Railway	20.7	8.1
T.& P.U.-Water	7.2	1.4
Trade	1.7	—
Service	1.2	.9
General	15.4	7.7
All Industries	2.6	.6

Table 16. Strikes with collective violence, and military intervention by province and decade, 1891-1930[1]

	1890-1900		1901-1910		1911-1920		1921-1930		Total	
	CV	MI	CV	MI	CV	MI	CV	MI	CV	MI
N.S.	3	0	5	4	4	1	6	3	19	8
N.B.	0	0	1	0	2	2	2	1	5	3
P.Q.	7	2	12	2	13	3	9	1	41	8
Ont.	12	2	18	8	16	6	2	0	50	17
Man.	0	0	3	1	2	1	1	0	6	2
Sask.	0	0	1	0	0	0	0	0	1	0
Alta.	0	0	0	0	1	0	7	0	8	0
B.C.	1	1	3	0	10	4	2		18	5
Total	23	5	43	15	48	17	29	5	148	43

[1]Violence was involved in only 34 of the 43 incidents of military intervention.

Table 17. Strike Waves, 1891-1930

Year	Given Measure as a Percentage of its Mean Over the Previous Five Years[1]	
	Number of Strikes	Number of strikers
I 1899	264	382
1900	219	448
1901	198	219
1902	199	98
1903	205	224
II 1912	158	164
1913	150	147
III 1917	132	190
1918	190	296
1919	244	412
1920	190	119

[1]The above list includes years for which N *or* W is above 150 if they are contiguous to years in which both N and W exceed 150. This is a slight modification on the Tilly and Shorter useage but is in line with Edwards, *Strikes*, 258. In the stricter useage 1902, 1913, 1917, and 1920 would be deleted.

Table 18. Strike Waves by Province and Industry

	Wave I 1899-1903		Wave II 1912-1913		Wave III 1917-1920	
	% strikes	% strikers	% strikes	% strikers	% strikes	% strikers
East	12	9	13	6	10	16
Quebec	19	31	13	18	17	19
Ontario	50	21	45	31	35	23
West	18	30	28	43	38	39
Inter-Prov	1	8	1	2	1	3
Mining	5	13	5	13	12	25
Manufacturing	49	34	35	26	41	36
Construction	23	13	36	38	15	8
Transportation	17	22	15	14	12	13
Trade & Service	4	1	8	1	11	4
Other	2	17	1	8	9	14

Table 19A. Number of Strikes and Strikers in Great Britain, France, and Canada, 1891-1930

	GREAT BRITAIN[A]		FRANCE[B]		CANADA	
	STRIKES	STRIKERS (000)	STRIKES	STRIKERS (000)	STRIKES	STRIKERS (000)
1891-1900	7930	2476	4890	1020	530	78
1901-1910	4636	1484	10050	2112	1596	230
1911-1920	9187	9220	9891	3852	2401	521
1921-1930	5066	7256	9421	3130	1040	261

Table 19B. Percentage of Strikes and Strikers in Great Britain, France, and Canada, 1891-1930.

	GREAT BRITAIN[A]		FRANCE[B]		CANADA	
	STRIKES	STRIKERS	STRIKES	STRIKERS	STRIKES	STRIKERS
1891-1900	30	12	14	10	9	7
1901-1910	17	7	29	21	29	21
1911-1920	34	45	29	38	43	48
1921-1930	19	36	28	31	19	24

[A]Cronin, *Industrial Conflicts* 206-7, 209-10.
[B]Shorter and Tilly, *Strikes in Frances* 360-3.

Table 20. Frequency and Size of Strikes, Canada and the United States, 1891-1950

	Frequency[A]		Sizes[B]	
	United States[C]	Canada	United States[C]	Canada
1891-1900	113	55	274	218
1901-1910	162	115	179	180
1911-1920	143	123	397	286
1921-1930	41	43	521	270
1931-1940	80	61	432	218
1941-1950	99	70	604	452

[A]Total number of strikes per 1,000,000 non-agricultural employees.
[B]Number of strikers per strike.
[C]US data from Edwards, *Strikes*, 13.

Figure 1
Strikes in Canada, 1830–1950

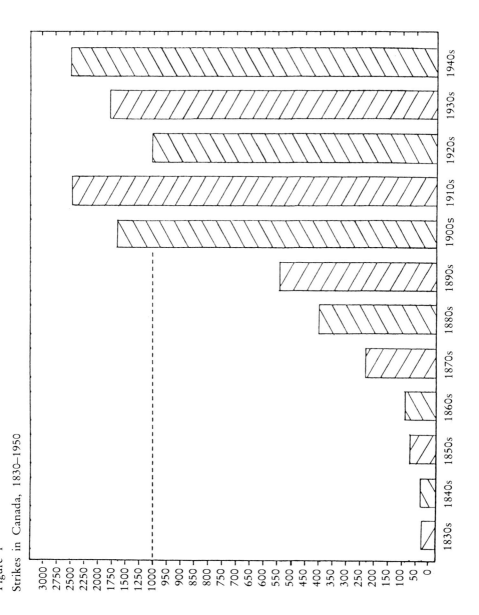

Figure 2

Number of strikes and strikers involved, 1890–1930

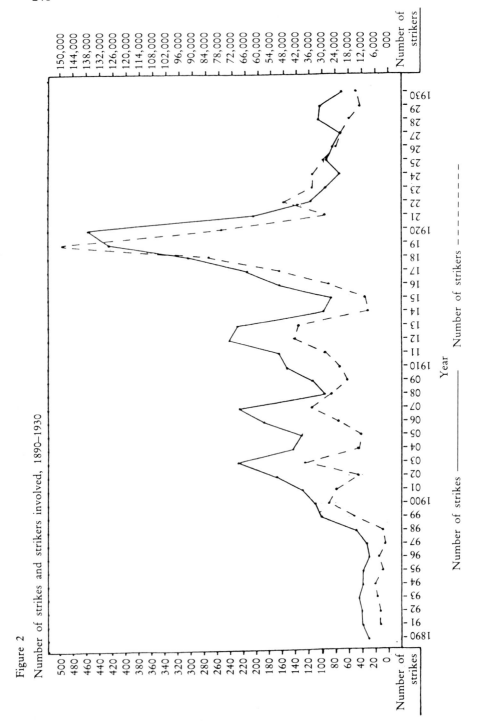

Figure 3

Trade Union Membership, 1911–1930

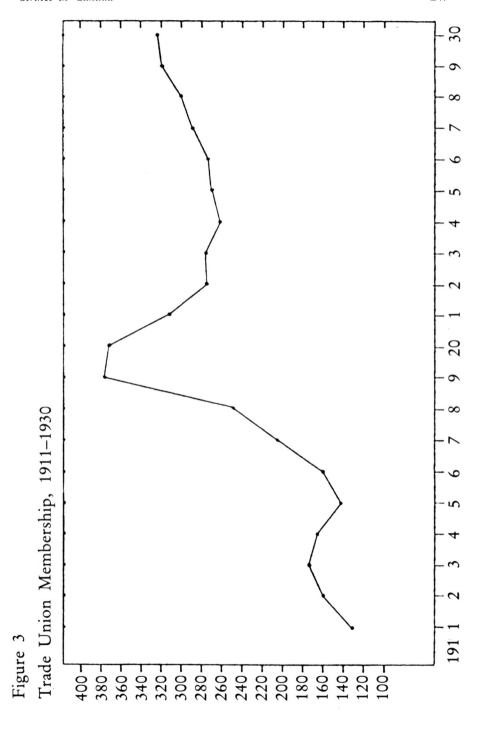

Figure 4

Strike Shapes, 1891–1950

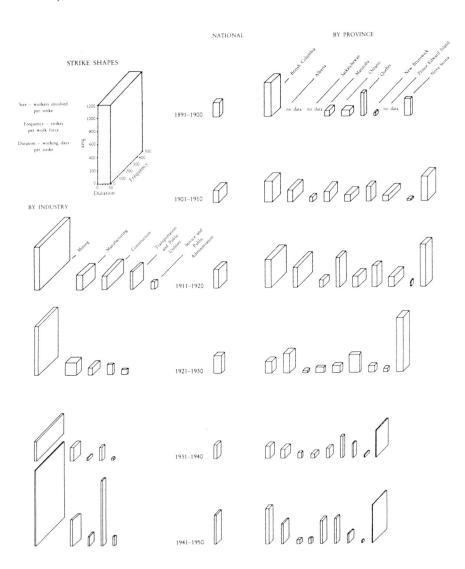

I 2

The Great Unrest in Wales 1910–1913: Questions of Evidence

Deian Hopkin

On 7 June 1911,100 Beltmen and Trolleymen in a brick factory in Swansea came out on strike, protesting at being asked to produce bricks which were thicker than previously agreed. Another 150 men were immediately laid off, but three days later all 250 returned to work when the employers agreed to meet the demand for extra pay. Four days later, several thousand dock workers and seamen in Swansea and other South Wales ports began to strike unofficially for pay, part of a strike phenomenon which quickly involved some 120,000 men around Britain, leading to episodes of violence and even some deaths. In August 145,000 railwaymen came out on strike for pay and recognition; the official strike lasted three days and was quickly settled, but not before 50,000 regular troops were deployed around Britain to keep the railways moving, and not before 6 people died in Llanelli from bullets or explosives.On 6 September, 500 fuel workers in Swansea came out on strike for a month, demanding an extra man to help push trolleys of fuel. They returned to work after a compromise agreement. [1]

These four episodes, very different in character and in outcome, and many hundreds more like them, have been aggregated in the minds of historians, and indeed contemporaries, as The Great Unrest, a phenomenon which is often said to have developed in Britain roughly between 1911 and 1914. Some historians have gone a great deal further and sought to find a wider context; workers in Germany, France, the United States and Canada, not to mention Russia, Italy and Spain, have been seen to show a similar mood of defiance and rebellion. And the context can be even wider.[2] Historians have often conflated several struggles in one historical chapter — including the militant campaign of members of the suffragette Women's Social and Political Union, and the Ulster resistance to Irish Home Rule. That was, for example, George Dangerfield's argument; that the workers' protest of 1910–13 cannot be separated from the general sense of unrest, all of it emanating from and contributing to a crisis of Liberalism which culminated in the death of that form of pre-war Liberalism through the unprincipled use of State power to quell legitimate grievance. It was, the argument continues, the end of innocence.

In Wales, an area which has contributed sustantially to the

historiography of industrial unrest, the events of the years immediately before the First World war have been seen exclusively as a working class struggle involving men and masters, epitomised most graphically in the most comprehensive piece of syndicalist literature published anywhere in Britain, *The Miners' Next Step*.[4] And yet, it may be argued , historians are selective about which episodes form part of the Great Unrest and which are just part of the normal problems of man-management relations. The seamen's strike and the railway strike of 1911, and miners' strikes of 1910 and 1912, are usually cited as the examples of the former while, by omission, the paper cutters of Cardiff or the Swansea fuel workers are not seen as significant actors. Why should this be so? Is it simply a matter of scale, perhaps, or is our view of unrest determined by some kind of preconception? If so, what are its ingredients? Questions need to be raised about the meaning of the term "Great Unrest" in the context of Wales in the pre-First World War period and which might then suggest some ways by which we might refine our ideas and seek new explanations.

The complicating factor in Wales is the degree of social violence which occurred in the South Wales coalfield and in adjoining towns during 1910–11 and which has conferred a special character on the events of the period. Time and again, it seems, strikes were the occasion for violence, picket lines became lines of conflict, policemen became militant. A good deal of work has now been done on various aspects of this phenomenon, starting with an account written by the government official chiefly responsible for keeping an eye on industrial affairs — George Askwith. His account of industrial unrest in this period is an excellent analysis as well as an important piece of first hand evidence. Numerous articles and books were written on the subject, and in recent years we have had studies of particular episodes of violence, Tonypandy, Cardiff, Llanelli and the Monmouthshire valleys. In fact, these discrete episodes of violence had very different causes and each ran a different course, ranging from the suppressed anger of Cardiff seamen against foreign sailors to the manifestly anti-Semitic outbursts in Brynmawr and Bargoed. For if Tonypandy has some coherence, Llanelli has little. Yet together these riots or social upheavals have conferred on Wales an historical reputation for rebellion which contemporaries and their descendants have tended to cherish.[5]

Of course, there have been many periods of social unrest in Britain and there has been plenty of economic dislocation over the years. But there are few periods when social and economic factors of this kind are accompanied by unusual political activity as well. The Great Unrest is also known to some historians, and to many contemporaries, as the Syndicalist Revolt.[6] The emergence and brief flourish of syndicalist ideology and practice gives the Great Unrest a potential which is intriguing and attractive. Is this perhaps the great revolution that Marx predicted? How near the brink towards political collapse was Britain? Did the First World War, in sacrificing the lives of so many thousands of young men, nevertheless save the nation from a worse fate? Or, adopting the opposing view, what on earth went wrong ?

Answering these questions is made more than a little difficult because there was no such thing as a Syndicalist party to which we can look for evidence of organisation, personnel, ideas, or even clear objectives. No syndicalist was brought before the courts of law to answer charges of organising revolution. Few avowed syndicalists can been seen among the picketing strikers and rioters of Liverpool, Hull or for that matter Tonypandy or Llanelli; and this has led one historian to coin the phrase "proto-syndicalism" in order to fill the obvious gap.[7] Certainly the ambiguities and inconsistencies in the *Miners' Next Step* reflected divisions within the ranks of those in Wales who were said to be syndicalists, although at least one prominent member of the Unofficial Reform Committee denied that they were syndicalists at all. [8] One historian has even described the syndicalists as "very much an anticlimax. . .not much more effective at reforming existing unions from within than they were at constructing new organizations". [9]

Finally, the period of the Great Unrest is also centrally placed in the chronology of the rise of Labour and in particular in Wales, where the transformation from Liberalism to Labour was both swift and thorough.[10] While the main objective of this chapter is to examine the evidence for the Great Unrest in the industrial sphere, and to see if it is rightly located in the period 1911–14, it is clear that account must be also given to the social and political unrest, if only because they were so closely linked in the eyes of contemporaries; here the question inevitably must be, is there a clear, causal relationship between all these episodes of unrest, industrial, social and political.

Whatever historians may conclude, contemporaries at least were convinced that they were witnessing what they themselves termed " the Great Unrest" or "the Labour Unrest". *The Times* gave its seal of approval to the new phenomenon by running a series of articles on the unrest and by legitimizing the term "syndicalism". Books were written, pamphlets circulated, articles produced in magazines and newspapers and endless talks and lectures given to countless audiences. [11] It is less easy for the historian to be so emphatic especially if the period is placed in a longer term context.

There is no doubt that taking the long view of the history of industrial relations introduces a number of complicating factors, not least the advent of the First World War, which appears to have introduced a range of new factors into social, political and economic history, all of which influence the pattern of industrial relations. For the purposes of this particular paper, therefore, the stopping point is 1913, the last full year before the advent of war. Clearly, it would be wrong to insist permanently on this line of demarcation but there are sound reasons for so doing at the present time, above all the nature of the evidence currently available.

There is also a problem of starting the chronology. Historians are divided over both starting and finishing dates. A number regard the arrival of Tom Mann as the symbolic inauguration of the period of "unrest" or "revolt", while others have relied more heavily on the beginning of an upward curve of strikes and days lost in the official figures in 1911. Equally, 1913 and 1914 have variously been offered as ending dates. [12] In part this depends on the emphasis placed by historians on the role of syndicalists and partly, moreover, on the interpretation of official statistics.

Indeed, the historian is confronted throughout by a problem of evidence. At present, the main source for industrial disputes in Britain is the official record In the main, the most complete evidence for industrial relations in Britain in the period 1888 to 1913 comes from the annual reports of the Chief Correspondent of the Board of Trade, published in the *Parliamentary Papers* series. The published series only runs from 1889 to 1913, but the details of individual strikes, on which this particular analysis is largely based, only begin in 1890 while the aggregate data for Wales as a whole is only provided from 1891. In order to compare individual with aggregate data, therefore, the effective starting point must be 1891 although, for historiographical reasons, it is necessary to include the strike wave of 1888–91. From 1901, however, a major change was made in the presentation of data; while the aggregate figures continued to include all reported disputes, the detailed presentation of individual strikes was confined to larger disputes.

The official data was culled from weekly reports by local labour correspondents appointed by the officials of the Board of Trade. Inevitably, questions must be asked about the reliability and comprehensiveness of such data. Clearly much depended on the efficiency and perceptiveness of such people; the total omission of agricultural workers, for example, from the reports was probably as much a reflection of the insensitivity of labour correpondents to the peculiar nature of the agricultural industry and their inability to obtain adequate information, as to low level of organisation among agricultural workers.

Other problems arise from the varied and complex nature of industrial disputes. While the compilers of the Board of Trade statistics made every effort to distinguish geographically between disputes, they were obliged to leave out of the regional calculations those disputes which were spread across the regions; so the official record consists only of those disputes which were confined to one district or region. Inevitably, as we shall see, this understates the incidence of strikes in industries which were nationally organised or where disputes tended to spread rapidly; notably the coal industry and transport. Consequently, the Welsh component of the 1911 transport strikes or the 1912 minimum wages dispute in the coal industry cannot be calculated, a serious omission from the data used in this article. In the case of the 1898 mining disputes, which largely affected Wales, no local data is available and it is impossible therefore to attribute the appropriate proportions to the counties mostly affected; this must be borne in mind in comparing sets of county or community data. A similar problem arises from disputes which extended across the annual boundary; the annual calculation of individual strikes or of days lost understated the impact of longer disputes or those which ran through the Christmas period and into the following year. Even more difficult to measure are the causes of disputes. Constrained by space and the requirements of form, causes were often concatenated and simplified ; few strikes break out over a single issue and many strikes change in character and purpose as they progress. The original cause may well be forgotten as new grievances or misunderstandings accumulate. Nevertheless, short of reconstructing the course of disputes from local newspapers, suriving company records, or from some other unexpected source, the official published statistics are the best source currently available.

Over and above this, Wales has its own problems of historical data. For centuries Wales has been treated as part of England and the task of disaggregating British official data to establish a series of Welsh statistics raises particular difficulties. It is, for example, virtually impossible to reconstruct comprehensive series of union membership statistics because so few trade unions acknowledged Wales as a distinct administrative region; the most familiar division was South Wales and the West, on the one hand, and North Wales and Cheshire, on the other. Similarly, it is difficult to reconstruct nation-wide series of Welsh wage rates to establish a comparative basis for Welsh industry

Between 1891 and 1913 a total of 972 individual strikes are recorded in the official reports, 70% occurring between 1891 and 1900. A total of 933,648 workers are included in these statistics, but 58% of these occur in the strikes after 1900. Here the full impact in the changed method of publishing individual strike statistics is seen. But there is another, more serious, difficulty which is identified in the reconciliation table, Table 5. The aggregates of individually recorded strikes fall short of the official aggregates, which means that the data set derived from the individual strikes is incomplete. The only way to solve this problem, of course, would be to undertake a re-examination of the original weekly reports, in order to compile an entirely new dataset, and it has to be acknowledged that this is a major hiatus.

There is another, potentially more serious problem. As M.J.Haynes has clearly shown, the incompleteness of the strike statistics can stem as much from the definition of a strike and the imposition of a minimum standard of measurement as from the failures of the network of correspondents.[13] Hence, the decision of an employer not to recognise a strike, despite the views of the event taken by the workers themselves, would ensure its absence from the official record. Closer examination of every episode, official and unofficial, may well reveal a high degree of underestimate.

In the absence of such precise and comprehensive data, then, any conclusions based on the official record must remain provisional. Nevertheless, despite these problems and the general crudeness of the official data, it is possible to reach certain conclusions about the course of Welsh industrial disputes between 1889 and 1913 which suggest that the experience of Wales was very different from Britain as a whole.

I

The official returns for disputes and lockouts in Britain reveals that in the years 1910 to 1913 there was a significant increase in the level and intensity of strikes in the United Kingdom generally. The Board of Trade, the Home Office and many other Departments of State were quite clearly aware of this and made frequent reference to it. Other indices, moreover, however, reinforce the impression that this is a period of unusual economic activity. A casual glance at wage levels or prices in this period, for example, reveals some sharp movements around 1910–11. First of all, after a period of relative improvement in standards of living, progress had stopped. Wages continued to rise, but prices rose faster, creating a gap which was a source of considerable discomfort to those millions of people who lived on the subsistence level or just above. Food was, after rent, the largest item of expenditure, so that any shift in the balance between wages and prices directly affected the level and quality of food consumption. The marked decline in real wages and purchasing power prompted the Liberal government to institute several inquiries into rents and prices.[14]

On the other hand, the rate of unemployment was decreasing, after reaching high levels between 1905–7. Knowles and others have shown that there is a high positive correlation between levels of employment and trade union activity — to put it another way, the greater the unemployment, the lower the level of trade union activity and here again we can see significant statistical differences between this and previous periods.[15] In a buoyant labour market, it is argued, trades unions were able to put greater pressure on employers and there is evidence that trades union activity in general was more pronounced and, indeed, effective than in other periods. The improving labour market, which is clearly observable in this period, may itself have been a stimulus to unrest.

The tendency among historians has been to accept, at face value, the aggregate figures for all industries in the whole of the United Kingdom irrespective of regional or occupational differences. Yet if there is an observable 'British' strike wave in 1910–13, the evidence is less striking for Wales as a region. Indeed, a close study of Welsh statistics raises questions about the value of aggregate British data either occupationally or chronologically for identifying and analysing strike waves.

Industrial unrest was endemic in Wales throughout the period 1889 to

1913. The level of industrial disputes, both in terms of actual numbers of strikes and the number of workers participating, was high in relation to the rest of the United Kingdom. On occasions, indeed, Welsh industrial disputes accounted for the majority of all British disputes; a remarkable fact bearing in mind that the Welsh industrial population was less than 5% of the total for the United Kingdom. Table 1 shows, indeed, that in only one year, 1911, did the Welsh strikes account for around 5% of the total number of workers on strike in the UK; even that is explained , to a large extent, by the fact that the major disputes of that year were the national strikes in transport; if it was possible to disaggregate the Welsh figures and apportion them, then it is likely that Welsh strikers accounted for more than the 5·7% displayed in the table. It is significant, however, that the level of industrial disputes in Wales in 1910- 13 was no higher and, if anything, lower than in many previous years. This raises some doubt, at least, over the appropriateness for Wales of the term "Great Unrest" as it is conventionally applied to Britain as a whole. The Great Unrest, if it can be so called, was of longer duration in Wales than anywhere, extending to all intents and purposes at least from the early 1890s.

There is a substantial change in the presentation of official data for industrial disputes after 1900. The decision to limit reporting of individual strikes to those with between 150 and 350 participants, depending on the type of industry, or to strikes which involved the loss of many thousands of working days, inevitably weighted the statistics towards large scale industries, such as mining or tinplate working. Even before this change, however, it is quite clear that judged by any criteria, the mining industry dominates the statistics. Miners, who at best represented 33% of the male labour force and 25 % of the labour force in general, accounted for half the total number of strikes before 1901 and three quarters thereafter. More significantly, 80% of all those on strike were miners and over 80% of all days lost in disputes were in the mining industry. Finally, certain mining areas were more prone to unrest than others. Disputes and strikes were largely concentrated in certain areas in the coalfield and a crucial question is the degree to which any discernible pattern of disputes can be attributed to particular communities, to groups of pits in a particular geological strata, or to pits owned by certain individuals or combines is obscure.

The industry which produced the second largest group of strike statistics was the metal industry. In 1911, metal manufacture employed some 95,000 workers in Wales of which all but 3000 were men. Proportionately, therefore, the industry was around one- third the size of the coal industry, yet the mean proportion of strikes involving tinplate and metal workers in Wales was only 8·7%. This is not to say that workers in this industry were more quiescent than their equivalents elsewhere in the United Kingdom. In some respects the scale of strike activity is similar to the miners although the pattern is different. For one thing, Welsh tinplate workers appear, from a cursory examination of the statistics, to have been far more strike prone than even the miners. Table 2 shows that Welsh miners accounted, on average, for 45% of all disputes throughout the United Kingdom, yet they accounted for only 20% of the male mining work force, which suggests that Welsh miners were twice as strike prone as the British miner as a whole. This, however, is very much a mean figure; year on year, Welsh miners often totally dominated the statistics for their occupational group, accounting for over 50% of all workers on strike in no fewer than 8 years out of 17. By contrast, tinplate workers only account for an average of 19% of metal workers on strike, but when one observes that the Welsh metal workers only account for 4% of the British metal work force, it might appear that on average, Welsh metal workers were five times more strike prone than their British equivalent. However, this is a case where the average deceives. We must recognise that there was a low level of industrial disputes in the metal industry generally in this period and even in Wales there was considerable fluctuation in the strike record of metal workers. There was a period of decline and then of recovery in the industry after the disastrous McKinley tariffs imposed during the 1890s.[16] The high point in Welsh tinplate disputes is reached at the turn of the century, roughly between 1899 and 1905; on either side of this divide, the number of Welsh workers on strike falls significantly. On only five occasions between 1897 and 1913 did the proportion exceed 10% and only twice did strikes approximate to what might be called the expected proportion given the size of the industry in Wales, around 25% of the labour force. On seven occasions, indeed, the proportion falls below 4% and during 1912–13 the average is around 3%. and this in turn is largely due to the introduction of effective conciliation machinery. In 1911, 2500 potential disputes in the tinplate industry in Wales were settled by conciliation, over 95% of all British cases that year. Whatever grievances the tinplate workers may have had, they had discovered a way of settling them.

Elsewhere, the situation was different again. From the turn of the century, the North Wales quarrymen had been engaged in bitter struggles with their employers but the decline of the industry placed the quarrymen at a mortal disadvantage which undermined their capacity for independent action.[17] The few disputes which were recorded in the quarrying industry were protracted and often ugly, but they remained few and disappeared altogether from the official statistics after 1901. Occasionally other groups of workers make a brief appearance in the statistics. In the early 1890s, for example, a number of disputes were reported in the building trade, largely over the importation of dressed stone, while the transport industry experienced brief waves of disputes in 1908 and again in 1911. None of these industries occupy more than a small fraction of the total statistics and even at the height of the 'Great Unrest' of 1910–14 they barely make any impact on the overall statistics for Wales even though the labour force in such occupations was often very substantial (see Tables 3 and 4).

No other industry, then, can be compared with the miners for the obduracy and scale of disputes. On a crude index of strike propensity, calculated as a ratio of strikers to total employed labour force and calculated within a Welsh context, miners were eight times more strike-prone than the next largest group, the tinplate workers.

But can we talk generally of miners? Throughout this analysis Wales has been taken as the central reference point. Yet it is quite clear from the evidence that the geography of industrial relations reveals some important variations in the experience of different parts of Wales. To some extent this is to be expected. Wales can be divided into clear economic zones, corresponding to the major sources of employment. While most parts of Wales contained agricultural areas to a greater or lesser degree, only one part is wholly dominated by agriculture, the middle zone extending from the Brecon Beacon mountains in the South and the Irish sea in the West, to a line from the Dovey Estuary across to Chirk in the North East. Indeed, in the North East and the North West of Wales, agriculture took second place to mining and quarrying. Elsewhere, industry and agriculture coexisted, as in the South West where metal manufacture was the second largest source of employment after agriculture, or Breconshire where there were substantial mining areas in the south. In Glamorgan and Monmouth, however, the situation was clearly quite different with agriculture occupying only a small minority of the population and mining being by far and away the dominant source of employment.

The fact that miners as a whole were more disputatious than other groups of workers is not surprising, of course. The problems of geology in South Wales was a main factor in declining productivity, acerbated by reactions to periodic wage reductions or demands for increase. [18] The industrial relations of the mining industry was dominated after 1908 by the operation of the Eight Hour Act, by the conflict over wage rates especially to take account of abnormal conditions, and by demands for a mininum wage and it was in the steam coal districts that this becomes most noticeable. The mining industry as a whole was full of potential points of conflict as seams changed direction, size and quality, and as the economics of different pits were affected by output and market price.

Within the South Wales coalfield, however, there is considerable variation from district to district, and from community to community. The absence of data from the major disputes of 1898,1911 and 1912 makes it impossible to offer more than a heuristic comparison. Variations, moroever, in the number of disputes and the number of workers involved over this particular period might well be attributable to changes in the mode of presenting the data in the official record, which eliminates the smaller strikes. Yet the increase in the number of participants suggests that the strikes that remain, so to speak, are either larger or longer, or both. This is markedly so in certain parts of the coalfield but not in others. Here, the contrast between Monmouthshire and Glamorgan is revealing. The interquartile mean rise in the number of workers on strike in Monmouth is

40%; in the Glamorgan coalfield it is ten times greater, at 400% Only three
areas in the Monmouthshire coalfield experience an increase of over 100%
in the number of workers involved in the strikes recorded between the two
periods; in Glamorgan, six areas record increases of this magnitude. There
is a strong impression given in the statistics that Glamorgan experiences a
more substantial increase in the level and magnitude of strikes than
Monmouthshire. (See Figure 1)

But it is in communities within these counties that the variation is most
striking. While accepting the limitations of this particular data set, which
certainly understates the contribution made by particular communities to
more general strikes and may also conceal the contribution made by
communities whose strikes were too small to be included in the post-1901
record, it is nevertheless clear that some communities experienced very
different levels of industrial disputes from others. Figure 2 shows the
degree of difference, for example, between registration districts within
Glamorgan, and this identifies Pontypridd and Merthyr as the locus for the
majority of strikes in the county. The level of strike activity varies
considerably even within such registration districts. Table 6 shows the very
considerable increase in the number of workers on strike over the period
under review; in particular, the Rhondda (+386%), Swansea Valley
(+531%), Aberdare (+535%) Pontypridd (+969%) and Maesteg
(+1042%). The contrast between Glamorgan and Monmouthshire is
striking with the Monmouthshire districts show a significantly lower
increase; indeed only one district in that county, Pontypool (+1384%),
comparing with Glamorgan districts. Most districts in Monmouthshire in
fact show a decrease both in the number of strikes and the number of
workers involved.

The contrast is even more marked in relation to the industrial areas on
the fringe of the coalfield. With one exception , all the urban towns along
the coast from Llanelli to Cardiff saw either a substantial decline or only a
tiny increase in the number of workers on strike. The exception was
Newport, but the figures for the town are gravely distorted by the presence
in the statistics of three miners' strikes attributed to the town which
account for over 60% of the workers on strike — indeed, one miners' strike
alone, in 1909, accounts for over half of all workers on strike over the
eleven year period. If we omit the miners, since the coalfield did not extend
to Newport (whatever the Board of Trade may have imagined), then the
town follows the same pattern of behaviour as Swansea, Cardiff, Bridgend,
Neath and Port Talbot. It is possible, of course, that the industrial
establishments in these areas were, on the whole, smaller than some of the
Glamorgan coal mines and therefore unlikely to appear in the statistics in
any case. Only a quarter of the strikes which occurred in Newport before
1901 would have found their way into the annual reports after 1902.

Elsewhere in industrial Wales, there is clearer evidence of a reduction in
industrial strikes. Llanelli is a case in point. Even allowing for the change in

data presentation, the fact remains that both the number of individual disputes and the number of workers involved fell dramatically. All but three of the 21 strikes which occurred in the tinplate industry in Llanelli before 1901 would still have been recorded under the revised method of presentation. The strikes which occurred before 1901 involved more than 300 workers. The one strike which did occur after 1901 involved less men than most of the pre-1901 strikes. By any standards, there was a marked reduction in the number of disputes in Llanelli after 1901. (See Figure 3)

Much the same applies to the coal mining industry of North Wales or the quarrying district of North West Wales, to the building and transport industries or to engineering. It is only amongst the miners of mid-Glamorgan that strikes significantly increase after 1901, but they do so in such a way as to distort the figures for the whole of Wales and moreover suggests that it is only in the aggregate, rather than in the experience of individual counties and even more so communities, that Wales is subject to anything like the strike pattern of "the Great Unrest" identified by historians.

II

Explaining the phenomenon is more difficult than describing it. A starting point may well be the communities themselves. The coalfield communities were mushrooms, whose rate of growth astonished even those contemporaries who were well used to a rapidly transforming society.[19] While the intercensal change in Wales as a whole between 1881 and 1911 was 14·5 % on average, representing a 54% increase overall over thirty years, the change in the coalfield communities was dramatically greater: Mountain Ash grew by 310%, Ogmore by 294%, Bedwellty by 760%. The Rhondda had grown from 3000 in 1861 to 152000 by 1911 — an increase of 5000%. Not every coal community grew at this prodigious rate. Many communities sprang into existence but then remained at somewhere near that level for many years. Ebbw Vale only doubled in size in the period, while Rhymney which was twice the size of Bedwellty in 1881 was half its size in 1911. On the whole, Monmouthshire grew less quickly than Glamorgan and a greater proportion of the rise of population betweeen 1891 and 1911 was due to natural increase rather than migration. Other industrial communities too only saw modest growth including communities in the Anthracite districts in the West, and in the metal processing districts of Briton Ferry. The tinplate industry fluctuated in size over the period and the population of tinplate districts was affected accordingly, while in North Wales a similar pattern occurred — there were only 600 more quarrymen in Caernarvonshire in 1911 compared with thirty years earlier and ten years later, the number had almost halved. Similarly, the proportion of miners in North East Wales dropped marginally from 22·8 to 22·4 between 1901 and 1911. Is it possible that a propensity to strike is a concomitant of growth? Such a model, however, would be difficult to validate. The community which shows the greatest absolute level of strike activity, Aberdare, has a relatively low rate of growth between 1871 and 1911, just 38%, which would appear to contradict the model.

An alternative explanation might seek to link strikes to the enterprises involved. Aberdare, the example just cited, was a town in dominated by one mining combine, the Powell Dyffryn Company, which by 1907 was paying annual dividends of 20%, a level it maintained until the outbreak of the First World War.[20] Other combines, the Ocean Coal Company, the Cory Brothers, the Crawshay Brothers and the Lewis Merthyr Consolidated Company, were important employers in areas which had a high strike record, Pontypridd, the Rhondda and Merthyr. Elsewhere in the coalfield, in Eastern Carmarthenshire and Monmouthshire, the enterprises were often very much smaller.[21]

Having established a broad pattern of disputes and participation, what about the grievances or claims which occasioned them? This is a complex issue, largely because the evidence is necessarily attenuated. Again the historiography of the Great Unrest is misleading. Any attempt to establish the root causes of industrial unrest in particular communities tends to be overshadowed by the prevalence of social violence. People went on strike for all sorts of reasons, not always what would be considered healthy reasons. Among the vast range of causes cited in the official records, strikes against wage-reducing foreigners sit side by side with strikes against wage cutting employers. There are strikes in favour of a union, but also against women. There were also strikes by youngsters protesting at their poor treatment by adult workers, and usually broken by the same. Miners went on strike over their horses' diet, and occasionally over their own; more often they objected to the introduction of safety lamps or changes in the time allowed to descend the pit, though it was the alteration in piece rates or allowances wrought by the working of new seams or changes in the size of screens which most exercised them. In other industries, there were specific grievances; objections to the longer winter hours in the building trade, or to increases in the poundage of steel which sheet millmen were expected to put in the boxes on which their piece rate was based. Youngsters were often a source of grievance because of the desire of employers to reduce labour costs by employing them, and so ironfounders objected to the arrival of more apprentices, boot and shoe workers objected to boy labour or, a variation on the theme, having to produce more children's shoes. Leisure and fringe benefits also cropped up as causes of disputes, even the amount of beer allowances which was a pressing issue in Barry. And discipline, sometimes described as victimization, was a frequent cause of strikes in most industries.

The majority of strikes were over pay, conditions and hours of work, to defend or enhance a rate. Tinplate workers were beleaguered; they tended to go on strike to protect their wages by resisting the twin demands for a reduced piece rate and increased output; their yardstick was the 1876 Wage Agreement which had been shattered by the McKinley Tariffs. Once a new equilibrium and new practices had been established, their strikes faded away. The tinplatemen eventually settled to the new wage levels under the changed conditions of the late 1890s. Equally, stonemasons fought for their skill, to prevent ready dressed stone coming in; for a time, employers sought to import stone; eventually they gave way, and the stonemasons disappear from the statistics.

Yet during the period as a whole, there is a clear and gradual increase in the proportion of strikes which can be attributed directly to trades unionism. From 1898 onwards, the proportion of such strikes increases significantly and it may be surmised that other strikes, ostensibly over wage demands, were also tied in with this general stratagem. If there is a general rise in the level of strikes in the coalfield, it is largely explained by this. The different level of activity from one pit to another may well be explained, on closer examination, by the relative zeal of different groups of miners and the resistance of mine owners. In this respect, it is interesting to note that one of the areas to show the most startling rise in strike activity, mostly over trade unionism, are those in which the coal combines were most active. All but three of the disputes which took place in Aberdare, where the Powell Dyffryn Company was best established, were concerned with issues of management or trade unionism.

Union-related disputes were indeed widespread. In 1913, for example, the year when the largest numbers of strikes related to trades unionism were recorded, there were disputes in communities as far afield as Ruabon in the North, Llanelli in the West and Pontypridd, although once again the lion's share was taken by the Rhondda Valley, Aberdare and Pontypridd. It is interesting to note that virtually all these disputes were successful — almost as though the management had decided there was no great benefit to be gained from resisting such demands. The fact that they started in the first place, however, suggests that industrial relations may have been fraught, and any attempt to examine this further again requires a detailed examination of the enterprises involved.

It is clear, then, that the militancy of Welsh miners is of far longer duration that has been suggested, most notably by Knowles who seemed to regard 1911 as the starting point.[22] In a strike prone industry, the most strike prone region for twenty five years was South Wales. If there is a moment of change, it may be argued that the turn of the century is as good as any. What does change, after 1898, is the workers' response to their predicament. The premium on Welsh coal was a product of high costs, masked by buoyant demand; the industrial relations of the South Wales coal industry is an indication of its vulnerability. Economic factors, such as the cost of production, the relative price of Welsh steam coal against other forms of coal and the impact of legislation such as the Eight Hours Act, are the determinants in that industrial relations. The South Wales Miners

Federation, for example, was formed as a response to changing economic circumstances while, as John Williams has shown recently, the Welsh coalowners were also far more litigous in pursuit of the law on contract than their English counterparts, itself a further indication of the undercurrents of uncertainty.[23]

III

In the perception of both contemporaries and historians, however, the Great Unrest is inextricably linked with social violence. The symbolic locus of the unrest is Tonypandy, with Llanelli and Cardiff close behind. The other communities merge into a vigorous, revolutionary background. Yet Tonypandy and Llanelli make little appearance in these statistics. They were not notable centres of industrial unrest — even if they once had been in the past. Recent work has shown moreover that there was only a tenuous link between industrial unrest and the politics of the workplace on the one hand, and such episodes of social unrest on the other. The occasion for the Llanelli riots was the national railway strike, yet no railwaymen appears in the list of dead, injured, arrested or convicted. In the riots in Monmouthshire in August 1911, as in those earlier in the summer in the port of Cardiff, there are obvious racial as well as economic overtones. Tonypandy, on the other hand, appears to be firmly set in the special history of mining and mining communities. Other examples of social unrest can be seen to have a unique character. The Cardiff race riots of 1919 are again qualitatively different from other disturbances in South Wales in that period.[24] The one North Wales riot, in 1919 and therefore outside the direct purview of this study, in fact involved Canadian soldiers at Kimmel Park Camp desperately anxious to return home (and who can blame them) and using the Red Flag as their passport, a unique event by any standards and one which may justly be regarded as rather untypical of Welsh riots in general; it is nonetheless intriguing that it took Canadians to unfurl the Red Flag in socialist Wales.

There is little convincing evidence that Wales had a higher propensity to social violence than other parts of the United Kingdom, whatever its historic reputation. Of course, this may be open to challenge on particular grounds, but Liverpool, Hull, the East End of London, Glasgow, Southampton, the coalfield of Yorkshire, can all proclaim their own iconographic riots. More importantly, with the exception of Cardiff and that may not be quite such an exception, there is no evidence that any one community was more prone to social violence than any others. There was no second Tonypandy riot and the citizens of Llanelli developed a collective amnesia about their riots of 1911. Equally there are no other recorded instances of further anti-Jewish violence.

Lurking underneath most of our studies of unrest, whether social or industrial, is a notion of politics. This, in a sense is the most difficult thing to quantify and the starting point must be a discussion of what politics are in the working class movement. Certainly, it would be difficult to attribute a conscious and articulated ideological motive for most of these episodes of unrest. If there was an ideology at all it was narrowly focussed within one part of the mining industry, through the work of the Unofficial Reform Committee and the rank-and-file movement. Its influence was greatest in the valleys of mid- Glamorgan. Outside the community a different perspective exists. The men shot and injured at Llanelli had nothing to do with the industry whose strike was the occasion for the riots in that town in 1911.

There is however a political unrest of a more subliminal kind in Wales in this period. Its modes of confrontation are electoral and organisational, but its dynamic stems just as much from a profound dissatisfaction and spiritual unrest, if one may put it like that, as any more dramatic forms of confrontation. These years saw the successful rise of an alternative politics, based on the emergence of working class political parties and culminating in their electoral victories in the post war years. It was however politics on an *ad hoc* and *ad hominem* basis; how else do we explain the willingness of a Trades Council in Wrexham to form a Labour Party while a Trades Council made up of members of the same trade unions refused to form one in neighbouring Rhyl? Or the reluctance of Carmarthen workers to follow the political lead of their Llanelly brethren seventeen miles away and support a Labour candidate.[16] The rise of the Labour Party owes as much to the motives and energies of individuals as to collective forces.

This subliminal form of unrest, however, had far-reaching results. If it is conceivable that there is some relation between industrial unrest and the rise of the Labour Party, it is clear that there is no direct relation between the forms and scale of that industrial unrest and the electoral breakthrough of Labour. It may be held that many of those communities which had witnessed varying degrees of industrial struggle over the time period 1890 to 1913 were in the forefront of the political change. Llanelli turned to Labour very quickly after 1918 and some at least of those who voted for the Party may have been influenced by their involvement, sometime during the previous twenty five years, in tinplate disputes [26]; the same may be true of Caernarvonshire or Wrexham, not to mention Ogmore, Aberdare, Ebbw Vale and so on. But we must also bear in mind that other areas which had been relatively active in the industrial disputes and the social unrest of the pre-war years failed to deliver political victories for Labour. The seaports of Cardiff and Newport, which did experience unrest and disorder , did not turn to Labour with the same alacrity as the coalfield.[25] It is by no means clear that there is a predictive relationship between levels of unrest and the rise of Labour. Llanelli had long since disappeared from the strike statistics by the time of the Labour victory in 1922, and much the same can be said for the Gower, Ogmore or Abertillery, not to mention Wrexham.

IV

Ultimately, far more evidence is needed to advance our understanding both of the locus and the character of unrest, such as the structure of the business enterprises involved, the pattern of ownership, the size and organisation of the pits involved in dispute, and the concept and conduct of industrial relations by the management. By the same token, more needs to be known about the communities themselves, the scale and character of in- and out-migration, the vertical and lateral dependencies with neighbouring communities, the location and distribution of housing, services, workplaces, and the role of community networks, the chapels and churches and bodies such as Trades Councils. Far more needs to be known about the recreations and leisure activities of members of different communities, to establish the degree to which they did or did not provide cohesion as well as outlet. The structure of families and the character of family life, gender relations and patriarchal culture may also need to be studied to discover whether the action of striking may not have been a reflection, in some communities, of more subliminal domestic imperatives. More widely, the study of unrest may need to be more firmly located in a world of general political and intellectual inactivity. Only by asking questions far wider than the scope of this paper, or indeed the recent political historiography of Wales, will it be possible to approach an explanation of the variegated pattern of industrial relations in Wales, the radially different behaviour of miners and other groups of workers in the various zones of Wales and the divergent response of different communities to such events.

None of this, of course, suggests that Wales was somehow immune to the Great Unrest so carefully documented by contemporaries and historians. It would be folly to suggest as much. But it is equally simplistic to argue that Wales suddenly encounters an unrest in 1910 or that it was qualitatively different from the experience in the rest of Britain. The evidence so far suggests that at the very least industrial unrest in its most obvious and easily documented form is endemic in Wales over a longer period than has hitherto been admitted. Once again it has to be stressed that the historical account is necessarily incomplete so long as the data is so imperfect. A thorough investigation of all possible sources, official and unofficial, may well reveal that the present account is flawed. Even so, there are enough signposts in the available data to suggest that in 1910, it was the rest of Britain who caught up with Wales. It may also be suggested, taking a longer time span, that a phenomenon such as the General Strike of 1926 should be placed in a larger chronological context, at the end of a long run of unrest by which time there were alternative routes for the working class to pursue than industrial confrontation. The failure of the majority of the working class to support the miners in 1926 may even be an indication that it was the miners who were out of step. At the same time, from a narrower perspective, the Great Unrest of 1910–13 in Wales does not appear quite so great after all.

Notes

I am grateful to John Williams, as always, for his valuable comments on this chapter.

1 These examples are all taken from the annual report of the Chief Labour Correspondent of the Board of Trade for 1911; *Parliamentary Papers*, 1912–13,

2 For a survey see Friedhelm Boll, "International Strike Waves: a Critical Assessment" in Wolfgang J. Mommsen and H-G. Husung (eds), *The Development of Trade Unionism in Great Britain and Germany, 1880–1914* (London, 1985), 78–99. Important earlier work includes E. Shorter and C. Tilly, *Strikes in France 1830–1968* (Cambridge, 1974) and various books and articles by James Cronin, especially "Theories of Strikes: why can't they explain the British experience", *Journal of Social History* 12 (1978–9), 194–220 and *Industrial Conflict in Modern Britain* (London, 1979). An important recent contribution is Eric Hobsbawm's essay "The 'New Unionism' in perspective" in *Worlds of Labour. Further Studies in the History of Labour* (London, 1984), also published in Mommsen and Husung, *Trade Unionism*.

3 George Dangerfield, *The Strange Death of Liberal England* (London, 1936). A somewhat similar approach is found in R. V. Sires, "Labour Unrest in England, 1910–1914", *Journal of Economic History*, XV (1955), 246–66; S. Meacham, "A Sense of an Impending Clash: English Working Class Unrest before the First World War, " *American Historical Review*, LXXVII (1972), 1343–65; E. H. Phelps Brown, *The Growth of British Industrial Relations* (London, 1965). The most notable alternative viewpoint, stressing the essentially trade union dimension of the unrest, is H. Pelling, " The Labour Unrest, 1910–14" in *Popular Politics and Society in Late Victorian Britain* (2nd ed., London 1979), 147–164. Doubt is also cast on the revolutionary nature of these struggles by John Saville who suggests a far more complex explanation of the unrest; *The Labour Movement in Britain* (London, 1988), 36–42.

4 For a discussion of the pamphlet, the Unofficial Reform Committee and, in particular, the role of Noah Ablett, see David Egan, "The Unofficial Reform Committee and the Miners' Next Step", *Llafur*, II, 3 (1978) and "Noah Ablett, 1883–1935", *Llafur*, IV, 3 (1986), 19–30. For the role of A. J. Cook see Paul Davies, *A. J. Cook* (Manchester, 1987). See also his earlier article, "The Making of A. J. Cook: His Development within the South Wales Labour Movement, 1900–1924", *Llafur*, II, 3 (1978), 43–63.

5 George Askwith, *Industrial Problems and Disputes* (London, 1920). Particular local studies are: Geoffrey Alderman, " The Anti-Jewish Riots of August 1911 in South Wales", *Welsh History Review*, 6 (1972), 190–200; K. O. Fox, "The Tonypandy Riots", *Army Quarterly and Defence Journal*, CIV (1973), 7–10; David Smith, "Tonypandy, 1910: Definitions of Community", *Past and Present*, 87 (1980), 158–184; Deian Hopkin, "The Llanelli Riots 1911", *Welsh History Review*, 11 (1982–3), 488–515; John Edwards, *Remembrance of a Riot. The Story of the Llanelli Railway Strike Riots of 1911* (Llanelli, 1988); Neil Evans, " 'The Tidal Wave of Impatience': The Cardiff General Strike of 1911" in Geraint H. Jenkins and J. Beverley Smith (eds), *Politics and Society in Wales, 1840–1922. Essays in Honour of Ieuan Gwynedd Jones* (Cardiff, 1988), 135–160.

6 Typical historiographical comment can be found in, for example, Raymond

Challinor, *The Origins of British Bolshevism* (London, 1977), esp. ch. 4; Keith Burgess, *The Challenge of Labour. Shaping British Society, 1850–1930* (London, 1980), 133–146.

7 Bob Holton, *British Syndicalism 1900–1914. Myths and Realities* (London, 1976).

8 W. H. Mainwaring quoted in J. A. Cartwright, "A Study in British Syndicalism: the Miners of South Wales, 1906–1914' (University of Wales M.Sc.thesis, 1969), 146. For Welsh syndicalism see Kenneth O. Morgan, "Socialism and Syndicalism: The Welsh Miners' Debate, 1912', Society for the Study of Labour History, *Bulletin* no.30 (Spring 1975), 22–36. See also C. A. Gwyther, "Methodism and Syndicalism in the Rhondda Valley, 1906–1926' (Sheffield University Ph.D. thesis, 1967).

9 Robert Currie, *Industrial Politics* (Oxford, 1979), 84–7ff.

10 For an excellent general account of the process see Peter Stead, " The Labour Party in Wales' in K. Brown (ed), *The First Labour Party, 1906–1914*(1985), 64–88. A detailed account of one constituency is Deian Hopkin, " The Rise of Labour: Llanelli, 1890–1922' in Geraint H. Jenkins and J. Beverley Smith (eds), *op cit*, 161–188. For a discussion of the relationship between trade unions and labour in this period, see Jon Parry, "Trade Unionism and Early Socialism in South Wales, 1890–1908", *Llafur*, IV, 3 (1986), 43–54. Valuable local studies are D. Cleaver, "Labour and Liberalism in the Gower Constituency, 1885–1910', *Welsh History Review*, XII (1985), 388–410; T. McGarry, "Labour and Society in Swansea, 1887–1918" (University of Wales Ph.D. thesis, 1986)

11 Examples azre Fred Henderson, *The Labour Unrest, What it is and what it Portends* (1912); W. Cunnungham, *The Causes of Labour Unrest* (1912); J. R. MacDonald, *Syndicalism* (1912); Philip Snowden, *Syndicalism and Socialism* (1913).

12 1910 is described by Holton as a "watershed in the development of British syndicalism" and he firmly dates the unrest from 1910; Holton, *op cit*, 52–3,73ff. Van Gore uses the term "workers' revolt" for the period 1910–14; "Rank and File Dissent" in C. Wrigley (ed), *A History of British Industrial Relations, 1875–1914* (Brighton, 1982), 66. Yet, in the same volume, Cronin emphatically places the "labour unrest" in the period 1911–13; "Strikes, 1870–1914" in Wrigley, *op.cit*, 91 ff.

13 M. J. Haynes, "Strikes" in John Benson (ed), *The Working Class in England, 1875–1914* (London, 1985), 93–4.

14 For example, *Report of an Enquiry of the Board of Trade into Working Class Rents, Housing and Retail Prices together with the Standard Rate of Wages Prevailing in certain occupations in the Principal Industrial Towns of the United Kingdom, Parliamentary Papers*, [Cd 3864., 1908].

15 K. G. J. C. Knowles, *Strikes. A Study in Industrial Conflict* (London, 1952). See also V. L. Allen, *Militant Trade Unionism* (London, 1966)

16 W. E. Michinton, *The British Tinplate Industry* (1957). A valuable study of the labour process in the tinplate industry is M. E. Daunton, "Labour and Technology in South Wales, 1870–1914" in Colin Baber and L. J. Williams, *Modern South Wales. Essays in Economic History* (Cardiff, 1986), esp 146–151. also J. H. Jones, *The Tinplate Industry. With Special Reference to its relations with the Iron and Steel Industries. A Study in economic organisation* (1914) and the same author's "Trade Unions in the Tinplate Industry", *Economic Journal*, June 1909. For the response of one company to the growing threat of competition from Germany and the United States see Edgar Jones, *A History of GKN. Volume One:*

Innovation and Enterprise, 1759–1918 (London, 1987), esp.329–78. Some structural problems of the metal industry are discussed in M. Atkinson and C. Baber, *The Growth and Decline of the South Wales Iron Industry, 1760–1880* (Cardiff, 1987)

17 R. Merfyn Jones, *The North Wales Quarrymen, 1874–1922* (Cardiff, 1981), esp. 175ff.

18 The background to this problem is outlined in J. H. Morris and L. J. Williams, *The South Wales Coal Industry, 1840–1875* (Cardiff, 1958). The problems of productivity are discussed in detail in R. H. Walters, *The Economic and Business History of the South Wales Steam Coal Industry* (New York, 1977) and the same author's "Labour Productivity in the South Wales Steam Coal Industry 1870–1914", *Economic History Review*, XXVIII (1975), 280–303. For a debate over the effects of the business cycle and of diminishing marginal returns see W. J. Hausman and B. T. Hirsch, "Wages, Leisure and Productivity in South Wales Coalmining, 1874–1914", *Llafur*, III, 3 (1982), 58–66 and Rhodri Walters' reply, *Llafur*, III, 4 (1983), 59–65. An interesting dimension is provided in T. Boyns, "Work and Death in the South Wales coalfield, 1874–1914", *Welsh History Review*, XII (1985), 514–537.

19 Recently there has been renewed interest in the process and consequence of migration into the South Wales coalfield. Dudley Baines casts doubt on the statistical basis for the earlier conclusions of Brinley Thomas that Welsh migration was qualitatively different from English migration; Dudley Baines, *Migration in a Mature Economy. Emigration and Internal Migration in England and Wales, 1861–1900*, (Cambridge 1985), esp. ch.10; Brinley Thomas, "Migration into the Glamorganshire coalfield, 1861–1911", *Economica*, 30 (1930). See Brinley Thomas' spirited reply; "A Cauldron of Rebirth: Population and the Welsh Language in the Nineteenth Century", *Welsh History Review*, XIII (1987), 418–37. An important reassessment which suggests that the bulk of in-migration was drawn from a closely-defined catchment area is Philip N. Jones, "Population Migration into Glamorgan, 1861–1911" in Prys Morgan (ed), *Glamorgan County History, Vol.VI: Glamorgan Society, 1780–1980*(Cardiff, 1988), 173–202. Some indication of the linguistic impact can be seen in W. T. Rees Pryce, "Language Areas and Changes from the late 1790s to 1981" in *op cit*, 265–314.

20 Trevor Boyns, "Growth in the Coal Industry: the Cases of Powell Duffryn and the Ocean Coal Company, 1864–1913" in Colin Baber and L. J. Williams, *Modern South Wales*, 160.

21 Some indication of the relative size of the enterprises and the pattern of ownership can be obtained from the private annual reports of the Monmouthshire and South Wales Coal Owners' Association; National Library of Wales. The scale and pace of growth by one notable combine is revealed in *The Powell Dyffryn Steam Coal Company, 1864–1914* (Aberdare, 1914)

22 Knowles, *Strikes*,

23 John Williams, "Miners and the Law of Contract, 1875–1914", *Llafur*, IV, 2,36–50. See also the same author's "Capitalists and Coalowners" in Prys Morgan (ed), *Glamorgan County History, Vol VI*, 109–128.

24 In this context, see Neil Evans , "The South Wales Race Riots of 1919", *Llafur*, III, 1 (1980), 5–29 and "The South Wales Race Riots of 1919: a documentary postcript", *Llafur*, III, 4 (1983). For a splendid discussion of the peculiar racial composition of Cardiff see his "Regulating the Reserve Army: Arabs, Blacks and the local State in Cardiff, 1919–45", *Immigrants and Minorities*, IV, 2 (1985), 68–115.

25 For an indication of the difficulties of Cardiff, see Neil Evans, "Cardiff's Labour Traditions", *Llafur*, IV, 2 (1985), 77–90.

26 For Llanelli see Deian Hopkin, *loc. cit.*

Table 1.   Welsh Disputes in Relation to U.K.

	No. of workers (000)			Working days lost (000)		
	Wales	UK	%	Wales	UK	%
1891	22.4	267.5	8.4			
1892	25.8	356.8	7.3			
1893	114.4	636.4	18.0			
1984	28.4	324.4	8.7			
1895	52.2	263.8	19.8			
1896	38.4	198.7	19.4			
1897	23.2	230.3	10.1	1216.5	10345	11.7
1898	113.8	253.9	44.8	11963.3	15289	78.2
1899	37.6	180.2	20.8	363.9	2516	14.5
1900	48.1	188.2	25.5	393.0	3152	12.5
1901	36.2	179.5	20.2	1106.4	4142	26.7
1902	73.6	256.7	28.7	701.6	3479	20.1
1903	58.0	116.9	50.0	863.3	2338	35.7
1904	20.8	87.2	23.8	325.8	1484	21.9
1905	31.5	93.5	33.8	741.6	2470	30.0
1906	70.4	217.8	32.4	663.9	3028	21.8
1907	27.7	147.5	18.8	247.5	2162	11.4
1908	39.5	295.5	13.4	549.6	10834	5.1
1919	99.6	300.8	33.2	844.5	2774	30.4
1910	108.6	515.2	20.9	2274	9894	23.0
1911	54.9	962.0	5.7	3213	10319	31.1
1912	*196.0	1463.3	13.4	* 5663	40914	13.7
1913	139.2	688.9	20.2	826.0	11630	7.1

NOTES:

The figures for Wales are for disputes which were exclusively conducted in Wales. This means that the 1908, 1911 and 1912 figures, in particular, should be taken with caution since the most substantial disputes in those years were national—railways, shipping and coal mining.

*While it is virtually impossible to attach appropriate figures in most cases, an attempt has made in these tables to include the Welsh proportion of the national mining dispute of 1912. The figures are highly notional and are included on the following basis:

150,000 miners × 35 days = 5.25 millions.

The appropriate figures have been added to the 1912 line.

Table 2. Individual Disputes Table Reconciliation

[This table seeks to reconcile the data presented in the reports of individual strikes with the aggregate published data]

	AGGREGATE DATA No. of workers (000)			TOTALS FROM INDIVIDUAL DISPUTES Wales		DISCREP-ANCY
	Wales	UK	%	Direct	Indirect	
1891	22.4	267.5	8.4	15.6	10.0	−14.2
1892	25.8	356.8	7.3	20.3	5.1	+ 1.5
1893	114.4	636.4	18.0	96.7	5.7	−10.0
1894	28.4	324.4	8.7	16.9	7.1	−15.5
1895	52.2	263.8	19.8	31.6	17.8	− 5.2
1896	38.4	198.7	19.4	30.8	9.5	+ 2.0
1897	23.2	230.3	10.1	11.5	8.8	−16.8
1898	113.8	253.9	44.8	77.8	5.8	−26.5
1899	37.6	180.2	20.8	22.1	13.3	− 5.8
1900	48.1	188.2	25.5	29.9	15.2	− 6.2
1901	36.2	179.5	20.2	16.2	6.4	−37.5
1902	73.6	256.7	28.7	40.9	21.8	−14.8
1903	58.0	116.9	50.0	41.0	2.6	−24.8
1904	20.8	87.2	23.8	8.5	3.2	−43.7
1905	31.5	93.5	33.8	18.0	4.8	−27.6
1906	70.4	217.8	32.4	51.7	10.9	−11.1
1907	27.7	147.4	18.8	15.5	3.9	−29.9
1908	39.5	295.5	13.4	18.4	6.5	−36.9
1919	99.6	300.8	33.2	87.7	11.9	0.0
1910	108.6	515.2	20.9	70.8	17.2	−17.1
1911	54.9	962.0	5.7	38.9	4.1	−21.6
1912	*196.0	1463.3	13.4	172.5	2.9	−10.5
1913	139.2	688.9	20.2	113.1	7.9	−13.1

* includes apportioned figure (see Table 1).

Table 3. Disputes in Wales by Industry: Workers Involved

COLUMN A: As proportion of UK workers in same industry
COLUMN B: As proportion of Welsh workers in general

Year	Mining		Metals		Local Authorities		Building		Transport		Misc.	
	A	B	A	B	A	B	A	B	A	B	A	B
1897	21.8	46.6	8.6	30.0	—	—	1.8	1.2	9.3	5.0	4.6	11.0
1898	61.7	96.0	14.9	2.6	—	—	7.2	1.0	—	—	0.1	0.0
1899	54.0	66.0	47.0	26.3	—	—	8.9	7.1	0.3	0.1	0.1	0.2
1900	53.3	81.0	33.0	13.5	—	—	0.8	0.3	100	3.1	0.7	0.7
1901	27.2	85.0	17.5	10.6	—	—	11.9	3.2	100	0.1	1.1	1.0
1902	32.2	91.2	42.0	8.5	—	—	0.7	0.1	100	0.1	0.4	0.1
1903	66.6	72.6	47.9	26.4	—	—	7.1	0.4	—	—	0.2	0.5
1904	40.4	89.4	15.9	9.3	—	—	1.5	0.4	7.9	0.6	0.1	0.1
1905	60.9	86.2	34.2	13.0	2.7	0.1	1.2	0.2	—	—	0.1	0.1
1906	82.7	97.5	3.8	2.1	—	—	1.4	0.3	2.6	0.1	—	—
1907	50.0	95.1	4.1	2.8	—	—	15.4	0.6	3.1	1.0	0.2	0.4
1908	42.3	93.0	2.2	3.2	100	0.1	1.4	1.0	13.9	1.7	0.4	1.6
1909	35.6	97.8	19.6	1.7	—	—	23.2	0.3	6.3	0.3	0.4	0.1
1910	33.6	91.9	10.6	5.4	21.6	0.1	40.9	0.3	9.9	1.8	0.3	0.4
1911	20.0	51.2	16.8	7.3	1.3	0.1	4.6	0.2	2.0	16.7	0.6	3.1
1912	17.7	95.6	2.5	1.4	10.3	0.2	0.5	0.0	2.9	2.9	0.7	0.4
1913	57.1	81.5	3.9	3.7	22.3	2.1	5.7	1.6	6.1	3.7	0.6	0.7
MEAN	83.8	83.3	11.4	11.7	0.5	0.2	1.1	2.8	2.6	0.6	1.3	1.6

Table 4. The Male Labour Force in Wales and the UK, 1901: Selective Data

	Wales	UK	%: Wales/UK
	(thousands)		
Agriculture	91.6	1339	6.8
Mines/Quarries	189.0	931	20.3
Metals/Engineering	68.0	1485	4.6
Transport	69.7	1409	4.9
Building	52.0	1206	4.3
Total occupied	655.7	11548	5.7

Table 5. The Male Labour Force in Wales, 1901: County Data

	Agriculture	Mines/Quarries	Metals/Engineering (thousands)	Transport	Building
Caernarfon/Merioneth	21.8	29.0	3.4	9.0	8.7
Flint/Denbigh	21.2	22.4	6.7	7.0	8.5
Montg/Cards/Radnor	46.9	3.5	3.1	5.3	10.3
Pembs/Carmarthen	27.7	11.7	13.8	8.1	6.8
Brecon	26.6	22.2	5.3	6.6	11.1
Glamorgan	3.1	37.2	12.4	13.1	6.7
Monmouth	7.5	34.7	12.2	10.6	7.4

Sources: John Williams, *Digest of Welsh Historical Statistics* (2 vols., Cardiff, 1986); B. R. Mitchell and P. Deane, *Abstract of British Historical Statistics* (Cambridge, 1962).

Table 6. Strikes by Locality

LOCALITY	1891-1900		1901-13		% CHANGE	
	A1 Disputes	B1 Total workers	A2 Disputes	B2 Total workers	A1/A2	B1/B2
WALES: TOTAL	662	385088	295	548561	−55.4	+42.4
"SOUTH WALES [generally]"	6	190450	6	132675	0.0	−30.3
GLAMORGAN	377	90468	176	301175	−53.3	+232.9
Cardiff	35	11526	14	14664	−60.0	+27.2
Swansea	99	14881	22	18027	−77.7	+27.1
Swansea Valley	15	2490	18	15733	+20.0	+531.8
Port Talbot	13	2213	1	420	−92.0	−81.0
Neath	33	4049	5	2213	−84.8	−45.4
Maesteg	13	2133	11	24363	−15.4	+1042.2
Brigend	8	1155	1	700	−87.5	−39.4
Ogmore	7	3298	5	4727	−28.6	+43.3
Rhondda	34	15284	31	74275	−8.8	+386.0
Pontypridd	23	3758	22	40189	−4.3	+969.4
Caerphilly	9	1963	2	980	−77.7	−50.0
Aberdare	34	9551	26	60658	−23.5	+535.1
Cynon Valley	4	2800	6	8681	−50.0	+210.0
Merthyr	29	8417	11	30820	−62.1	+266.2
Barry/Penarth	13	587	0	0	—	—

MONMOUTHSHIRE	139	64574	85*	120712	−38.8	+86.9
Tredegar	2	3030	8	6435	+300.0	+112.4
Blaenavon	14	3103	3	3584	−78.6	+13.4
Sirhowy Valley	5	213	0	0	—	—
Ebbw Vale	23	18195	9	14608	−60.9	−19.7
Rhymney	14	8714	12	22079	−14.3	+153.4
Abertillery	28	21770	25	30902	−10.1	+42.0
Newbridge	5	2405	3	3330	−40.0	+38.5
Risca	9	2194	1	1186	−88.9	−46.0
Newport	24	3302	7	21259	−70.8	+543.8
Pontypool	9	1167	16	17329	+78.0	+1384.9
Chepstow	6	481	0	0	—	—
CARMARTHEN-SHIRE	81	17061	10	3972	−87.6	−76.7
Llanelli	52	12513	8	2552	−84.6	−79.6
Ammanford	11	1585	0	0	—	—
Brynaman	10	2017	2	1420	−80.0	−29.6
Carmarthen	8	946	0	0	—	—
SOUTH-WEST WALES	5	287	0	0	—	—
MID-WALES	2	149	0	0	—	—
MERIONETH	5	460	0	0	—	—
CAERNARVON-SHIRE	14	8773	2**	2365	−85.7	−73.0
ANGLESEY	1	12	0	0	—	—
DENBIGHSHIRE	15	10972	10	7112	−33.3	−35.2
FLINTSHIRE	17	1784	0	0	—	—

*incl. one strike listed as "Monmouthshire [Western]", 1902.
**The Bethesda strike recorded from 1901 onwards is a continuation of the strike begun in 1900 and already recorded in the earlier table.

Figure 1: COUNTY COMPARISONS

GLAMORGAN

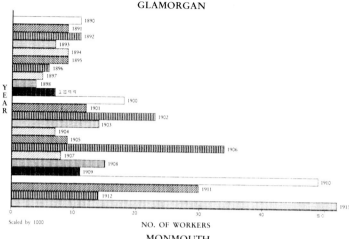

Scaled by 1000

NO. OF WORKERS

MONMOUTH

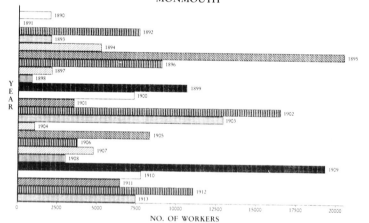

NO. OF WORKERS

CARMARTHENSHIRE

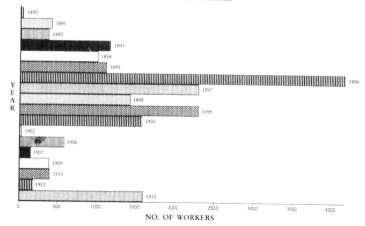

NO. OF WORKERS

Figure 2: STRIKES BY DISTRICT: GLAMORGAN

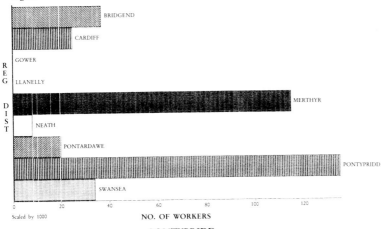

PONTYPRIDD

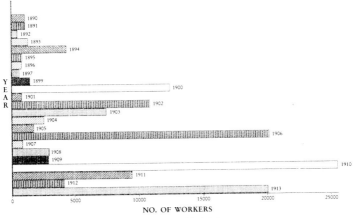

MERTHYR TYDFIL

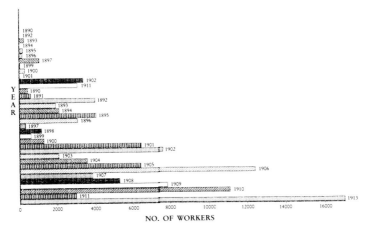

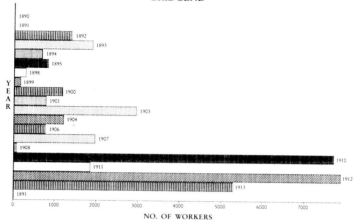

BRIDGEND

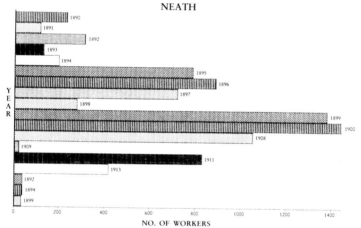

NEATH

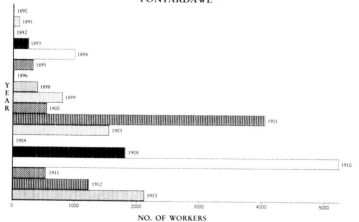

PONTARDAWE

SWANSEA

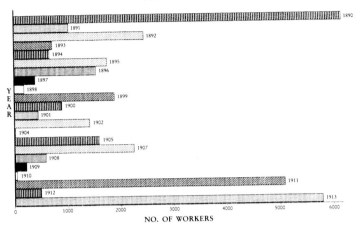

NO. OF WORKERS

CARDIFF

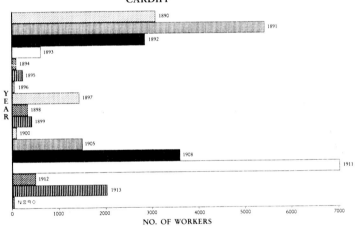

NO. OF WORKERS

Figure 3: LLANELLI STRIKES

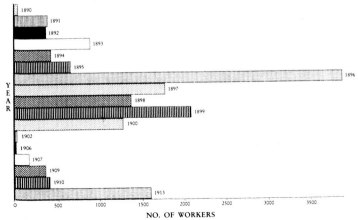

NO. OF WORKERS